*THE SPATIALITY OF EMOTION
IN EARLY MODERN CHINA*

The Spatiality of Emotion in Early Modern China

From Dreamscapes to Theatricality

Ling Hon Lam

Columbia University Press   New York

Columbia University Press wishes to express its appreciation for assistance given by the Wm. Theodore de Bary Fund in the publication of this book.

Part of chapter 2 was taken from the author's article "Cannibalizing the Heart: The Politics of Allegory and the *Journey to the West*," in *Literature, Religion, and East/West Comparison*, ed. Eric Ziolkowski (Newark: University of Delaware Press, 2005), 162–78.

A shorter version of chapter 4 was published by Brill as "A Case of the Chinese (Dis)order? The *Haoqiu zhuan* and Competing Forms of Knowledge in European and Japanese Readings," *Asian Publishing and Society* 3 (2013): 71–102.

Columbia University Press
Publishers Since 1893
New York   Chichester, West Sussex
cup.columbia.edu
Copyright © 2018 Columbia University Press
Paperback edition, 2022
All rights reserved

Library of Congress Cataloging-in-Publication Data

Names: Lam, Ling Hon, author.
Title: The spatiality of emotion in early modern China : from dreamscapes to
   theatricality / Ling Hon Lam.
Description: New York : Columbia University Press, [2018] | Includes
   bibliographical references and index. |
Identifiers: LCCN 2017052037 (print) | LCCN 2018038532 (ebook) |
   ISBN 9780231187947 (cloth) |ISBN 9780231187954 (pbk.) | ISBN 9780231547581 (electronic)
Subjects: LCSH: Chinese drama--Qing dynasty, 1644-1912--History and
   criticism. | Emotions in literature. | Space perception in literature.
Classification: LCC PL2387 (ebook) | LCC PL2387 .L36 2018 (print) | DDC
   895.12/4809--dc23
LC record available at https://lccn.loc.gov/2017052037

Cover image: Eldad Carin/Alamy Stock Photo
Cover photograph by George C. Berticevich © 2017
Moon Hill, Guangxi, China, October 1990

To my parents

Contents

Acknowledgments — ix

Prologue: Weather and Landscape — 1

CHAPTER ONE
Winds, Dreams, Theater: A Genealogy of Emotion-Realms — 19

CHAPTER TWO
The Heart Beside Itself: A Genealogy of Morals — 53

CHAPTER THREE
What Is Wrong with *The Wrong Career*?: A Genealogy of Playgrounds — 91

CHAPTER FOUR
"Not Even Close to Emotion": A Genealogy of Knowledge — 147

CHAPTER FIVE
Time-Space Is Emotion — 188

Notes — 243
Index — 323

Acknowledgments

Retrospectively, every book mirrors not the author's bio but a little scene of its own creation. In this case, the scene is set in front of the fridge's glass door in a neighborhood store. Once in a while I would pick out a carton of milk, check the "best before" date, and hear a voice: "That is the day I will put down the last sentence of the conclusion." That day did come—half a decade late. The Chinese ancients loved to say a good work outlives its mortal author, but this book survives its own countless expirations.

If the book has not turned into sour milk, it is thanks to some divine interventions. Dorothy Ko is the one who awakened me from my self-indulgence, took me down to earth, and brought this book out to the living. Wai-yee Li watched over the completion of the project with great care, so much that she spent New Year's Eve writing me feedback. Shang Wei patiently sifted through different versions of the manuscript with keen eyes and always guided me to a better route amidst the labyrinth. Patricia Sieber, my most rigorous critic and collaborator, challenged me to re-envision what the book should be like. David Der-wei Wang navigated me with his beaming advice at critical junctures and fueled me with his enthusiasm from across the fields. From Mounts Potalaka and Olympus, they are the guardians looking on my work with compassion and calling me out for its flaws.

And I have just been dancing on the Buddha's palm: Judith Zeitlin has always been there listening to my agonies, but she might still be surprised at how much of an imprint her work on various topics—from dreams to dramas to case thinking—has left on the final product. My heartfelt thanks go to her and my other great teachers who have nurtured my intellectual growth at different stages: James Chandler, Arnold Davidson, Prasenjit Duara, Wu Hung, Xiaobing Tang, and Eric Santner when I was at the University of Chicago; Chan Kwok-kow, Chen Li-fen, Lee Siu-leung, Ching-Hsien Wang, and John C.Y. Wang when I was at the HKUST; Chan Man Sing and Lee Kar Shui when I was at the University of Hong Kong; and Ho Kwai-cho, whose scholarship in Yuan arias has continued to inspire me since my high school years. I especially thank William Tay for opening my eyes; the world has never looked the same since then.

As a reconceptualization of emotion as space, my project was met with hospitality along its extended itinerary: Academia Sinica, Arizona State, Brown, Columbia, Folkwang, Fudan, Harvard, the New School, OSU, Penn State, Rutgers, UCLA, Wellesley, and Yale, in addition to various panels at the AAS and MLA conventions. I benefited a lot from exchange with Andrea Bachner, Katherine Carlitz, Chen Guanghong, Jack Chen, Kang-I Sun Chang, Eileen J. Cheng, Robert Chi, Kirk Denton, Carol Dougherty, Maram Epstein, Jane Gaines, Meow Hui Goh, Andrea Goldman, Man He, Rania Huntington, Wentao Jiang, S.E. Kile, Eugenia Lean, Haiyan Lee, Li Hui-mien, Mengjun Li, Ling Xiaoqiao, Liu Xun, Regina Llamas, Tina Lu, Keith McMahon, Anne E. McLaren, Kenny K.K. Ng, Stephen Owen, Michael A. Puett, Ying Qian, Qian Zhenmin, James Robson, Andrew Schonebaum, Shu-mei Shih, Richard So, Song Mingwei, Mark Stevenson, Wendy Swartz, Tian Yuan Tan, Giovanni Vitiello, Wang Ailing, Guojun Wang, Lingzhen Wang, Martin Woesler, Lisa Laiming Wong, Wu Guanwen, I-Hsien Wu, Shengqing Wu, Lawrence Yim, Zhao Shanlin, and Zheng Lihua. I especially thank Cynthia Brokaw, Eric Hayot, Yuming He, Ying Hu, Hua Wei, Lionel Jansen, Lydia H. Liu, David Rolston, Paul Rouzer, Catherine Swatek, Stephen H. West, and Ellen Widmer for their insightful comments and generous support. I am deeply grateful to Robert Campany, William Egginton, Eugene Wang, and Xiaofei Tian for participating in the "Space of Emotion" workshop I co-organized with Susan Lanzoni at Wellesley; and to Kwai-Cheung Lo and Laikwan Pang for their stimulating duet presentation in the "Traffic in 'Asia' " workshop I organized at Vanderbilt. I also thank the students who took my seminars on "History and Theory of Emotion" and "Time and Chinese Narrative" at UC Berkeley.

I consider myself extremely lucky being able to work with excellent colleagues, then and now, coast to coast. At Berkeley, Jinsoo An, Robert Ashmore, Mark Blum, Mark Csikszentmihalyi, Jacob Dalton, Mary Ann Doane, Hubert L. Dreyfus, H. Mack Horton, Andrew F. Jones, Dan O'Neil, Michael Nylan, Lanchih Po, Robert Sharf, Chenxi Tang, Alan Tansman, Paula Varsano, Sophie Volpp, Linda Williams, and Jonathan Zwicker never hesitate to share and help while setting a high bar for me with their outstanding scholarship. Gerald A. Figal, Yoshikuni Igarashi, Peter Lorge, Tracy Miller, Dahlia Porter, Ruth Rogaski, Allison Schachter, Samira Sheikh, Tony K. Stuart, and Ben Tran embraced me as part of the adventurous enterprise of reimagining geo-disciplinary boundaries and area studies while I was at Vanderbilt. Brief as my stay was, Ira Livingston and Iona Man-Cheong instantly treated me as family and let me bask in their research passion during that white, cold, cruel spring at Stony Brook.

But no crowd could beat the fellow alumni of Chicago, my edgy fearless wild bunch! Stimulating conversations continue over all these years. I want to thank Max Bohnenkamp, Krista Van Fleit, Anup Grewal, Kevin Huang, Fumiko Joo, Theodore Yoo Jun, Tong Lam, Sonya Lee, Li Sher-shiueh, Yuhan Li, Wei-Cheng Lin, Jason McGrath, Viren Murthy, Zhange Ni, Samuel Perry, William Schaefer, Suyoung Son, Catherine Stuer, Chun Chun Ting, Richard G. Wang, Yi Wang, Xu Peng, and Zhou Yiquan for their inspiration, patience, and friendship. I thank Daniela Licandro for bringing me back to talk about the project. Special thanks go to Dongfeng Xu, whose profound erudition and delicate cuisine have nurtured and humbled me for the past two decades, and to Paize Keulemans—the wise and even-tempered Song Jiang, a.k.a. the Timely Rain—who never gets tired of his troublemaking, zero-EQ bro.

The writing of the book has been facilitated by the Newhouse Center for the Humanities Postdoctoral Fellowship at Wellesley, the An Wang Postdoctoral Fellowship at Harvard, the Scholar Grant of the Chiang Ching-kuo Foundation for International Scholarly Exchange (USA), and the Humanities Research Fellowship at Berkeley. I sincerely thank my copyeditor Mary Severance for her brilliance in improving the manuscript under breathless pressure, as well as Do Mi Stauber for her very thoughtful work of indexing. Without Christine Dunbar's tremendous support, however, the manuscript would never have turned into a book, and the book would not be coming out at such lightning speed. Leslie R. Kriesel, Christian Winting, and Rebecca Edwards gave the production process an indispensable push toward the finish line. And it is my honor to have the book cover graced by the mesmerizing artwork of George Berticevich. My friendship with him and his wife Klaya is one of the greatest surprises, something I could have hardly expected.

The belatedness of this book has incurred overdue indebtedness and, in some cases, my unamendable regret. In memory of Zhang Hui, whose remarkable career in Ming-Qing studies was untimely cut short, I sometimes imagine a conversation and wonder how he would respond to my implicit echo of his seminal discussion of "poetic history." Siu-kit Wong supervised my BA thesis on historical narrative, but I came to better understand his pioneering studies in emotion and Chinese poetics only after he passed away. Karl S.Y. Kao showed me how erudite training in Chinese literature and theoretical insights could combine. David T. Roy, who initiated me into the world of *The Plum in the Golden Vase*, generously allowed me to use his private library. I took these for granted and gave so little back. To my late mentor Anthony C. Yu, I owe my deepest gratitude for his unreserved support for my intellectual venture. He opened the door for me in every possible sense and demonstrated what the audacity of thought against tyranny meant. Finding no way to return the favor, I can only fight to keep that door open for the generations to come.

The greatest blessing that keeps me going in the darkest hours is the loving family I have back in Hong Kong and right here in Berkeley. The distension between there and here remains a source of pain by itself, however. My parents, Chiang May Kuen and Lam Yuk Ming, sacrifice a lot for my impractical dream but never question what I have been doing all these years on the other side of the Pacific. All they ask for in return is a weekly Skype call, a mini-Truman Show: through the webcam they enjoy watching their son and daughter-in-law cook every Saturday evening. Certainly superfluous, this book is dedicated to them. For Weihong Bao, my beloved, I can find no better way to thank her than by spending the rest of my life hiking, swimming, and traveling with her (I promise!). She is more joyous than anyone about the coming of the book after having experienced firsthand every moment of my despair and frustration. Still, not for one single second did she lose faith in this project, however undeserved. She is everything I have enumerated and more: my reader and critic, my guide and peer, my classmate and colleague, my divine lady and super ego—in short, "the holy one for and with whom I cook every Saturday evening." But of course the chicken-salmon soup and all the glory go to the actual masters of this household: Popolo and Thena, the feline morphoses of Apollo and Athena. Just like their venerable predecessor Gnuni, they are the Muses behind the book (and its remaining typos). My parents seem to get the whole point by requesting only to watch me cook: there is no greater return than making a soup every weekend for the beloved ones.

THE SPATIALITY OF EMOTION IN EARLY MODERN CHINA

Prologue

Weather and Landscape

"The state of the weather soon becomes a state of mind."
—WALLACE STEVENS

"Actually, all language of landscape is just the language of emotion."
—WANG GUOWEI

1. EMOTION-REALMS

On a gloomy, rainy day in Chicago, phone calls were made as part of a psychological study. Researchers asked those who answered to describe their mood at the moment and rate their overall well-being—their sense of happiness and satisfaction with their lives. As expected, the poor weather put respondents in bad moods, which in turn induced them to give their well-being lower ratings. But if the caller, pretending to be out of town, started with a casual question—"how is the weather?"—the respondent tended to describe herself as *less* unhappy and dissatisfied. The researchers conducting the study argue that this is because we tend to explain away our bad moods by attributing them to impersonal factors such as the weather. A parallel experiment from the same research reinforces this theory: participants were put in an odd-looking room and asked to recall an unpleasant life event, and this combination would sour their mood and lower their sense of well-being. And yet, when participants were told beforehand that the room where the survey would take place was supposed to make them feel bad, their well-being ratings were more positive. Here again, bad moods were "discounted" through attribution to something impersonal—in this case, the surrounding space.¹

Tearing down the wall between feeling and thinking, recent cognitive studies emphasize the way judgment underlies emotions, and emotions in turn perpetuate themselves by shaping judgment in a closed circuit.² The weather survey, however, discloses a less cohesive picture: a momentary foul mood negatively affects my appraisal of overall well-being, but the fact that the mood colors judgment can itself be subject to another level of judgment, eventually giving my overall well-being a more positive reappraisal. This paradox arises from two conflicting premises about emotion's relationship to space, whether space is tangible (as with a room) or pervasive (as with the meteorological ambient). On one hand, the notion of attribution, insofar as it involves ascribing bad moods to the weather or the room one is in, assumes the entanglement of emotion with the "outside world." On the other hand, the "discounting" effect of attribution—the dismissal of bad moods as irrelevant once they have been tied to external factors—re-establishes the hierarchical division between inner and outer, personal and impersonal.³ The cognitive process boils down to an incongruous formulation: "I feel bad because of the weather, so I feel better about *myself*." Underneath the swing between feeling good and bad is a deeply rooted ambivalence toward space, which feels both removed from and initially proximate to our emotional life.⁴

We come across similar incongruities in traditional Chinese discourse about emotion and space, which goes back to the ancient notion of *xing* 興, or "poetic incitement." An ambiguous term closely associated since Confucius (551–479 BCE) with *the Book of Songs (Shijing* 詩經*)*, *xing* initially designated a rhetorical device of introducing a human theme through natural imagery. By extension, as Cai Yingjun 蔡英俊 notes, it refers to the "'direct arousal' of emotion . . . by stimuli from the external world." This early concern with emotional responses to outside stimuli foreshadowed fourth- and fifth-century discussions of natural scenery (*wuse* 物色) and ultimately coalesced in the discourse of "emotion-landscape mingling" (*qing jing jiao rong* 情景交融), which proliferated from the late Southern Song (mid-thirteenth century) through the end of imperial history.⁵

Some believe that this aesthetic tradition runs counter to the Cartesian divide between the human mind and the external world. According to François Jullien, the subject-object split is overridden and rendered "nominal" in China by the "interaction" between "interior emotion" (*qing* 情) and "exterior landscape" (*jing*₁ 景), which "cooperate in a single process." But Jullien reconfirms this split by using terminology that separates "interior" and "exterior" before calling out their interactions.⁶ Moreover, in his account, what happens in such interactions is less a reciprocal exchange than the indelible privileging of the interior. Insofar as landscape plays a role, it either does so internally (by "impregnating interiority") or in facilitating "both a borrowing and a detour for the interiority expressing itself." For poetic incitement to work, Jullien argues, it must go "beyond the landscape": "whereas its expression remains within the tangible, its emotion projects beyond this world." Emotion always transcends landscape.⁷

At the turn of the twentieth century, critic Wang Guowei 王國維 (1877–1927) made the subservience of landscape to emotions in traditional aesthetics crystal clear in his seminal *Treatise on Song Lyrics of the Human Realm* (*Renjian cihua* 人間詞話): "In the past, people distinguished between the language of landscape (*jing*₂*yu* 景語) and the language of emotion (*qingyu* 情語) when they discussed poetry and song lyrics. Actually, all language of landscape is no more than the language of emotion." The collapse of landscape into emotion renders landscape dispensable: "Most lyricists convey emotion through landscape. Excellent verses *exclusively put in the language of emotion* (*zhuan zuo qingyu* 專作情語) . . . have been rare and precious, then and now."⁸ No matter how balanced it may seem, the tradition of discussing emotion-landscape relationships inadvertently affirms the superiority of the emotive interior. It has been under the spell of the first-century "Great Preface" to the *Book of Songs*, the locus classicus of poetics and aesthetics: "Poetry is that to which the intent goes. Inside the heart is the intent; when expressed it becomes poetry. Affections are stirred within and take on form in words."⁹

Thus we can see the same paradox in cognitive studies and in Chinese literary thought: emotion is prioritized as "personal" and "interior" even when it is attributed to impersonal surroundings or said to mingle

Prologue 3

with landscape "out there." To say that "the state of the weather soon becomes a state of mind,"¹⁰ or that "a diffuse and overwhelming emotion like a state of mind . . . unfolds as an aura of senses, as an atmosphere,"¹¹ is to maintain interiority as the site from which emotive feedback arises. As long as we psychologize emotion as *a state of mind*, the spatiality of emotion remains elided. I propose a radical rethinking of emotion in terms of space, namely, that before any projection, association, correspondence, and causality, emotion *is* a spatial structure of which the atmospheric is just one kind among others.¹² In this book I argue that, rather than a state of mind being imprinted by, overflowing onto, or mingling with things in external space, emotion per se is spatial.

To fully explore the spatiality of emotion, one needs to go beyond the schema of "emotion-landscape mingling."¹³ Intriguingly, this may be what Wang Guowei attempted to do in the *Treatise on Song Lyrics*, which brings out the hidden agenda of that schema—apparently approvingly, only to abandon it immediately. These passages, which expose the primacy of "emotion" over "landscape" in the traditional discourse, were removed from the published versions of the treatise during Wang's lifetime.¹⁴ Such terms as "emotion" and "landscape" appear in other entries but are subsumed under the overarching term "realm" (*jing₂* 境 or *jing₂ jie* 境界):

> A realm (*jing₂*) does not only refer to landscape. Delight, anger, sadness, and joy—each is also a realm in the human heart. A work that depicts genuine feeling or genuine landscape is said to constitute a realm (*jing₂ jie*); otherwise, there is no realm.¹⁵

Yet doesn't the "realm" (now standing for either the interior or the exterior) seem to fit into the timeworn discourse of "emotion-landscape mingling"? Scholars generally believe so,¹⁶ especially since, as Xu Fuguan 徐復觀 observes, the term *jing₂ jie* itself came to signify "various levels of spiritual cultivation" in Tang-dynasty Chan Buddhism and then, by extension, "the status of a writer's spiritual (or emotive and sentimental) activities" expressed in the form of landscape in Song-dynasty poetics.¹⁷ But to Xu's dismay, Wang Guowei actually turns his back on the entire tradition by *"concentrating his discussion of realms one-sidedly on landscape per se* throughout the treatise without closely knitting landscape and emotion together."[18] In other words, against expectations, Wang's take on the "realm" reverses the primacy of emotion over landscape by going back to *jing*$_2$'s initially spatial connotations, which are preserved in its homophonic relationship to "landscape" (*jing*$_1$).[19] Instead of assuming emotion as the foundation of landscape, Wang tries to reestablish landscape as the model for emotion. More precisely, by transplanting the term "realm" from landscape to emotion, Wang demonstrates a way to approach emotion in terms of spatiality.

But Wang Guowei's spatial turn falls short of unraveling the interior when he reduces emotion to just "a realm of the human heart" and therefore risks dissolving the spatiality of emotion into an inner state of mind. To pursue Wang's approach from the point at which he turned away from it, we need to wrestle tropes and expressions from the received tradition, uncovering the spatiality of emotion that has been obscured by the conventional notion of *qing jing, jiao rong*. One such expression is *qingjing*$_2$ 情境, which I literally translate as "emotion-realm."[20] The hyphen here should not be taken as an articulation between two separate entities. Despite the disyllabic structure, the Chinese phrase *qingjing*$_2$ simply means a certain state of affairs, a "situation," which can variably be expressed as *qingxing* 情形, *qingkuang* 情況, *qingshi* 情勢, and so on.[21] In none of these compounds does *qing* ever refer to a mental state, and that is the point: emotion per se is a situation we find ourselves involved in, delivered through, and coming upon. Still used frequently in colloquial Chinese, such expressions clarify the spatiality of emotion as *external*. This does not mean that emotion is stirred by, responsive to, embodied in, or diffused across things in external reality, or that emotion is induced, suppressed, or liberated spatially, as some readings of Chinese domestic novels would suggest. Instead, in its exteriority, emotion is the structure of space as an ontological condition without which we cannot even be outside in the world getting along with one another. Esoteric as it sounds, the emotion-realm is intimately experienced in daily life when we intuitively sense the atmosphere upon stepping into a room, or when we greet a neighbor by saying, "What a sunny day!"

Prologue 5

2. FROM DREAMSCAPES TO THEATRICALITY

Often hidden by such mundane experiences is the way this spatiality of emotion undergoes and indexes significant historical changes. Instead of abstracting from the emotion-realm a universal blueprint, this study traces major historical modes of spatiality, each built on a distinctive organization of the emotion-realm. In this long and complex history, I focus on one pivotal episode that remains profoundly relevant today: the emergence of theatricality from the long-dominant regime of the dreamscape in sixteenth- to eighteenth-century China. The term "theatricality" refers to an early modern mode of spatiality in which emotion is not interior to oneself but performed by others and, conversely, it is conceivable in oneself only as enacted on behalf of others or as exhibited to an audience without oneself seeing it. In theatricality, a new sense of self-displacement informs the formation of individuals and communities by alienating subjects from their feelings, producers from products, writers from readers, and spectators from spectacles, under the combined sway of commerce, print, and theater. Theatricality, therefore, signifies not the essential origin of theater but, ironically, a historical deviation from theater, at the moment when drama became increasingly consumed through printed texts.

The maturation of theater in China dates back to the twelfth century, but at that time theatrical performance depended less on role-playing in front of spectators than on a vastly different spatial operation: conjuring a character across the threshold between this world and another. Early theater grew out of a medieval spatiality of emotion that was akin to the Buddhist-Daoist "dreamscape," through which the dreamer moved from one ephemeral mood to another, only to realize in each instance that she had "woken" to another illusion. With the rise of theatricality, the dreamer becomes an onlooker who approaches the dream from an indelible distance, feeling puzzled by and yet strongly attached to its mirage. The "spectator" comes into being when the dreamer stops moving through endless layers of the dream and pauses *in front of* the dream, trying to sympathetically identify with it. Sympathy, as will be seen throughout this book, is the most distinctive symptom of theatricality. It signals a peculiar spatial problematic: the spectator/subject is not quite in a position where she can feel, or she feels only by moving away from where she is standing.

Theatricality in early modern China emerged in fleeting interruptions of the otherwise incessant process of deliverance into one dream after another, from the interstices between the oneiric layers. For that reason, both contemporaries and modern scholars have described the phenomena of theatricality in terms borrowed from the regime of dreamscapes. This anachronistic tendency is *not* a dismissible mistake but instead a significant part of the historical dynamic through which theatricality unfolded from the dreamscape in a nonlinear fashion. The nonlinear unfolding is shaped by two kinds of interaction, together forming the full picture: on one hand, an earlier regime of spatiality shaped the context in which the new mode was ushered in, perceived, and misrecognized; on the other hand, the prior regime endured in juxtaposition with a newly emerging mode, under which its components were modified, re-contextualized, and bestowed with new meanings.

The first half of the picture is demonstrated by Goyama Kiwamu 合山究, who points out that the late Ming and early Qing (from the late sixteenth to the seventeenth century) witnessed the proliferation of the life-theater analogy. To Goyama, however, the analogy only extends such Daoist and Buddhist notions as "life resembles a dream" or "life is like an illusion."[22] In that regard, the early modern understanding of theater seems still conditioned by the medieval themes of impermanence and delusion associated with dreams. Also focusing on the problematic of illusion, Wai-yee Li's seminal work on love in traditional Chinese literature more perceptively captures the second half of the picture. She uncovers a new cultural phenomenon around the same historical periods surveyed before by Goyama: emotion took a spectacular form—a "theatrical illusion"—which both predicated itself on an "observer" and turned him into a spectacle being observed, as exemplified by Zhang Dai's 張岱 (1597–1684) fabled night "raid" of a Buddhist temple in front of which he suddenly staged a play unannounced, awakening the dazzled monks and whipping them up with light and sound before swiftly leaving them behind in the dark again.[23] This episode, which dramatizes the emergence of spectatorship in the midst of its mutual superimposition with ephemerality, raises a double question: how to understand the historical specificity of spectatorship per se and at the same time explain why it seems to be inseparable from the old regime of the dreamscape.

In her monograph on theatricality in seventeenth-century China, Sophie Volpp gives the most sophisticated account to date of related historical developments. She argues that although the notion of "the world as stage" in late Ming drama continued the Yuan legacy of using theater as a trope for "the evanescence of the affairs of this world," what it signified had shifted from the issue of ephemerality to the new problem of "social imposture" intensified by "the increasing permeability of social hierarchies and the fluidity of emblems of status" characteristic of the burgeoning mercantile economy. Stage acting, as a cunning model of "self-fashioning" in society, hurled authenticity into crisis. As Volpp notes, "If performance was the problem, discerning spectatorship was the solution. The notion of social spectatorship became a vehicle for coming to terms with the mercantile appropriation of literati cultivation."[24] Not only could an experienced viewer see through the imposture of the nouveau riche, but the grading of spectatorial sensibilities provided a new ground on which to redraw the disappearing social distinction. At the top of the ladder was the most refined spectator, who could rejoin the enchantment and "maintain illusion and disillusion in tension." A case in point is again Zhang Dai, who could at one moment play a dispassionate observer of the other five kinds of spectators at an early autumn night's West Lake and at another moment move toward and mingle with them, erasing the hierarchy he had just established.[25] It is in this more complex type of spectatorship that Volpp sees echoes of "the older phrasing of the world as stage, which concerned the vanity of human achievement."[26] In short, social spectatorship addressed the crisis of authenticity pertinent to a new socioeconomic era, which bestows a token of historicity on the nascent regime of theatricality in seventeenth-century China; but the response to the crisis remained in the coordinates of illusion and disillusion already laid out in the regime of dreamscapes. This accounts for the nonlinear superimposition from which theatricality, in an unmarked fashion, always emerged in the disguise of dreamscapes in the Chinese context.

Yet "disguise" suggests that theatricality is *not* a dreamscape, even in the Chinese context, where it has been so frequently identified as one that the mixed identification has become part of its history.

Dreamscapes would linger on into the seventeenth century and beyond, but theatricality itself is more than a redeployment of dreamscapes in a new historical context, just as spectatorship—the distinct feature of theatricality—cannot be fully exhausted in terms of illusion and disillusion, even though those terms might inform the spectator's general experience. The spatial operation underlying the oscillation between enchantment and disenchantment—that is, the delivering of a dreamer into and out of an illusion—had been modified into a spatial problematic of distance. The haunting question of every dreamer—"Having wakened up from a dream, am I in still another one?"—was rearticulated as a question typical for a spectator facing a spectacle: "Should I get closer or farther away?" What makes Zhang Dai *a spectator par excellence* is not just his return to the age-old paradox of illusion and disillusion in tension, but also his shrewd manipulation of distance as a new technique for maintaining that tension.

Historicizing spectatorship as a unique component that distinguishes theatricality from the dreamscape has further implications for understanding the history of theater. We need to understand forms of theater preceding theatricality in terms other than that of spectatorship; only in so doing can we see how theatricality emerged through restructuring the dreamscape in the Chinese context. Interest in alternative historical forms of theater has often been motivated by an aversion to the silenced, passive audience segregated from the nineteenth-century proscenium stage,[27] but archaeological attempts to redeem spectatorship by stressing its "participatory" nature in older theatrical forms miss the point that both separation and participation are parameters of the problematic of distance that defines spectatorship. To call the Song-Yuan (twelfth to fourteenth century) audience more "interactive" thanks to the absence of the "fourth wall,"[28] for instance, ultimately obscures the genuine differences between theatricality and its predecessor, the dreamscape, because by resorting to the degree of distance, we fall back on the yardstick provided by theatricality.

By contrast, to understand the Song-Yuan theater in its own terms is to see a theater *without* a spectator. This seemingly bizarre notion has only recently been hinted at in Jeehee Hong's rereading of the stage figurines on an elevated stage carved on the relief wall of excavated twelfth-century tomb chambers in Shanxi. Against the usual interpretation that they are performing for the tomb occupants, usually a deceased couple, Hong argues that both the relief figurines and the elevated stage sit on the threshold between outside and inside, underlying a process of transformation and demarcating a liminal gateway through which the deceased move from this world to the netherworld. It is in such border-crossing movements that the deceased are transported into a "fictional space" where they "impersonate themselves as if they were alive," so that "the architecture housing them is presented *as if* it were their house." Instead of having the player figurines perform for the tomb occupants, it is the tomb occupants who perform as their living selves. This discussion of the miniature theater as "a realm midway between two worlds" in the Jin tombs points toward a kind of performance that "required no spectatorship." According to Hong, the reason the player figurines require no spectator is that they "yield the actual performance to the virtual actors, i.e., the tomb occupants," who are still in need of some sort of spectators. She concludes: "By making their tombs, it is likely that some future tomb occupants imagined their descendants worshipping them in front of their images. By extension, these worshippers viewing their ancestor's image would have been assumed to be spectators of the virtual performance."[29]

To take Hong's argument further, I would argue that performance in the dreamscape is predicated not on playacting in front of the spectator but on transformation upon crossing boundaries. Even the "imagined" worshippers, therefore, are not really spectators; before they are constituted as worshippers, they have to cross the same threshold marked by the miniature theater, just as their ancestors were transformed into tomb occupants when they crossed the "realm midway between two worlds." The being who undergoes metamorphosis when delivered from one realm to another is not the spectator, but the dreamer.

"Social spectatorship" was therefore an early modern phenomenon in China not in the sense that it was modeled on theatrical spectatorship and applied what had always been essential to theater to the broader issue of social pretense in an extra-theatrical context, but in the sense that we actually witness the naissance of the "spectator" when the dreamscape was restructured into theatricality between the late sixteenth and early seventeenth centuries. In other words, theatrical spectatorship is never applied to an extra-theatrical context; rather, spectatorship per se is quintessentially extra-theatrical because, as I have already mentioned, theatricality arises from the intersection between theater and print. Theatricality is not the essence of the theatrical medium but a notion of intermediation that is beside and beyond theater. Intermediation, however, is more than a matter of technology; it comes along with the historical modifications of the emotion-realm.

Tracing the transfiguration of the subject position from dreamerhood to spectatorship, this genealogical investigation of the spatiality of emotion establishes the fundamental stratum in what Michel Foucault calls "historical ontology," an umbrella term with which he sums up his study of "how we are constituted as subjects" in "three broad areas": the knowledge of things, power relations with others, and the ethical relationship to the self. For Foucault, this "historical ontology of ourselves" aims not to justify the present way we turn into "subjects" but to expose its historical contingency and buried possibilities.[30] Though not thematized explicitly in his brief overview of the three "broad areas," "the 'schema' of time and space" as a historical variable underlies Foucault's early "archaeological" works.[31] The fundamental status of spatiality is further highlighted if we acknowledge that, almost point by point, the Foucauldian historical ontology corresponds to the late Heidegger's "history of being" in terms of periodization, style of reasoning, and critique of the present,[32] and that the late Heideggerian discussion of time-space relationships is re-centered on a revamped notion of spatiality.[33]

Furthermore, against the consensus that the early Heidegger's existential ontology—the structural dissection of human existence (Da-sein) in terms of spatiality and temporality—is "ahistorical," the Chinese theorist Li Zehou 李澤厚 proposes a culturalist version of historical ontology (*lishi benti lun* 歷史本體論) through a rereading of *Being and Time* as a theory of practice maintaining that "experience constitutes what is a priori" (*jingyan bian xianyan* 經驗變先驗). Unfortunately, Li's culturalist drive essentializes the historical practices in Chinese context as a matter of "cultural psychology" (*wenhua xinli* 文化心理) and as a result psychologizes Da-sein (*xinli cheng benti* 心理成本體) by uncritically invoking the notion of *qing*.[34] Opening up *qing* as *qingjing*$_2$ or emotion-realm, my book works toward a historical ontology explicitly and primarily as the genealogy of the spatiality of

Prologue 11

emotion, on the basis of which we can then reexamine subjectivization in histories of knowledge, power, and ethics. Separating discussions of power and ethics has unfortunately led to a misperception that the latter is depoliticized in late Foucauldian works,[35] while the constant entanglement of knowledge and power throughout Foucault's oeuvres makes it unnecessary to single out power as a separate area.[36] In place of power, therefore, I put forth the history of theater as one of the subfields of historical ontology: after all, can we talk about the contingency of subjectification without examining how a culture experiments with the way personhood is assumed onstage?

In this book, I investigate the trajectory from dreamscapes to theatricality by tracing four overlapping genealogies from the perspectives of historical ontology, moral philosophy, theater archaeology, and epistemology, respectively. Chapter 1 introduces a "genealogy of emotion-realms," dissecting the 1598 dramatic masterpiece *The Peony Pavilion* not as a celebration of the interior subject as people believe, but as a sedimentation of various historical modes of spatiality of emotion. I focus in particular on the transition from the "shared dream" where the lovers meet to "the front of the dream" as a mediating surface onto which lovers' detached images are projected.

In this light, chapter 2 reinterprets the "genealogy of morals"—a long history of philosophical discussions of emotion—less as didactics against material desire than as responses to various regimes of spatiality. We see how a new moral problematic emerged in connection to spectatorship—the subject position pertaining to theatricality—as dramatized in the sixteenth- to eighteenth-century fictional and theatrical forms of the religious allegory *The Journey to the West*.

This brings us to chapter 3, where I deal with a "genealogy of playgrounds," tracing the advent of spectatorship (or the lack thereof) through examining dramatic performance (from the early plays *Top Graduate Zhang Xie* and *The Wrong Career* to later ones *The Mad Drummer* and *The Sole Mates*) and theater architecture (from roofless stages to dancing pavilions, to passage stages, to teahouse theaters). This analysis highlights the turn of the seventeenth century as a watershed marked by the discursive explosion of sympathy.

In chapter 4, I pursue a genealogy of knowledge by examining the Japanese and European readings of the early eighteenth-century Chinese novel *The Fortunate Union* (a.k.a. *The Pleasing History*), in which we can detect two competing modes of knowledge production in the era of theatricality and sympathy—anthropology and case history—in contrast to traditional Chinese casuistry.

Chapter 5 concludes this study by advancing a critical vocabulary for a discussion of time-space *as* emotion that can transform our understanding of theatricality and sympathy in China and beyond. The Chinese genealogy of the spatiality of emotion from dreamscapes to theatricality unfolds with twists and reversals. A comparison to a different sort of dynamic in the Western context will be doubly illuminating when we see the two trajectories collide at the turn of the twentieth century on the issue of sympathy.

3. FEELING INTO/FEELING WITH

Chinese and Western paths converged earlier than is often presumed. It is just that the convergence became more obvious in the early twentieth century, as we can see in the aesthetician Zhu Guangqian's 朱光潛 (1897–1986) rereading of Wang Guowei. What draws Zhu's attention is Wang's distinction between two kinds of "realms": "the realm with me" (*you wo zhi jing*$_2$ 有我之境), within which "I observe things from my perspective (*yi wo guan wu* 以我觀物) so that things are all marked with my hues"; and "the realm without me (*wu wo zhi jing*$_2$ 無我之境)," within which "I observe things from things' perspective (*yi wu guan wu* 以物觀物) so that it is no longer known which is me and which are things."[37] Zhu Guangqian agrees on the distinction but contends that we should put it the other way around by borrowing the German notion *Einfühlung* (empathy or *yiqing zuoyong* 移情作用):

> The distinction here [between "the realm with me" and "the realm without me"] is remarkably made, but from recent aesthetics' perspective, Wang's vocabulary has to be reconsidered. What he says about "observing things from my perspective so that things are all marked with my hues" is actually "empathy," as attested by the verse he cites: "With tearing eyes I enquire the flower but the flower speaks not." Empathy results from attentively gazing at a thing to the extent that both the thing and I are forgotten, which is

what Schopenhauer calls "self-effacement." Therefore, Wang's so-called "realm with me" is actually "the realm without me" (that is, the realm of self-forgetting). As for the examples he cites to illustrate his "realm without me" . . . all actually are wonderful realms attained by poets in calm reminiscence (the so-called "attaining them in tranquility") without undergoing empathy, and therefore should have been called "the realm with me."[38]

Originally part of Zhu's *Psychology of Literature* (*Wenyi xinli xue* 文藝心理學), this bold interpretation instantly drew the attention of an early reader of the book manuscript, which remained unpublished in 1931.[39] The passage was published in Zhu's *On Poetry* (*Shilun* 詩論, 1943), and since then many have taken issue with it. Gong Pengcheng contends that the traditional Chinese ideal of self-negation (*wu wo* 無我) transcends the senses and cognition through the cultivation of the subject and is therefore incompatible with the Western idea of empathy, which still attaches to sensational intuition.[40] Avoiding such a problematic East-West opposition, Yeh Chia-ying 葉嘉瑩 more convincingly points out that Zhu Guangqian's reversal makes sense only as a distortion of Wang Guowei's Kanto-Schopenhauerian aesthetics of the sublime and beauty through the lens of Theodor Lipps's (1851–1914) theory of empathy.[41]

But Zhu Guangqian's "misapplication" of empathy to Wang Guowei turns out to be conceptually productive and—I would venture to say—historically more than "accurate." If we recast it in light of the spatiality of emotion, its pitfalls and merits can balance out. Compared to the sublime and beauty, the late nineteenth-century German discourse of *Einfühlung* was more directly grafted on the issues of space; the term was first invoked to characterize a viewer's feeling and movement provoked by the shapes and patterns of inanimate objects, typically in architecture and sculpture.[42] Susan Lanzoni has recently examined the kinesthetic dimension of *Einfühlung* when the term was translated by British psychologist Edward B. Titchener in 1909 and applied in the laboratory he directed at Cornell. There was no unified theory of empathy at this experimental stage, but most understandings orbited around the notion of *inner* feeling/motion *projected* onto an object. The anthropocentric tendency of empathy as the projection of human feelings onto things was driven home by James Ward, who translated *Einfühlung* as empathy around the same time as Titchener did but described it as "personification."[43] Ironically, the invocation of spatiality at the onset of the discussion of empathy led to a reassertion of the interior locus of emotion in opposition to the external world.

These early twentieth-century tropes of kinesthetics, inner feeling, outward projection, and anthropocentric personification of things found their way into Zhu Guangqian's *Psychology of Literature*, the original context in which Zhu rereads Wang Guowei's "realms" through the lens of empathy.[44] Besides alluding to Lipps, Zhu cites a slew of examples from European literature to show how "empathy has huge impacts on literary creation," but from here he slips into something with different historical origins and resonance:

> The French novelist Flaubert once described the process of writing *Madam Bovary* in the following passage from a letter:
>
> "It is a delicious thing to write, to be no longer yourself but to move in an entire universe of your own creating. Today, for instance, as man and woman, both lover and mistress, I rode in a forest on an autumn afternoon under the yellow leaves, and I was also the horses, the leaves, the wind, the words my people uttered, even the red sun that made them almost close their love-drowned eyes."[45]
>
> Similar confessions from other writers are numerous. Flaubert has been widely regarded as a master in realism. But even when he depicted the most objective situation, he was still *putting his body in the other's situation* (*she shen chu di* 設身處地), sharing characters' lives therein in a manner of experiencing them firsthand by himself. We can see how forced the distinction between objective and subjective is in literature.[46]

Amid the talk about the projection of inner feeling onto objects and the kinesthetic identification with their movements—two distinct takes on nineteenth-century empathy—what sticks out is the Chinese phrase *she shen chu di*, which first appeared in the sixteenth century and has become ubiquitous since then, especially in the field of drama criticism.

Prologue 15

Zhu Guangqian may have been motivated to slip in the Chinese phrase to reframe Flaubert's words by something a seventeenth-century Chinese dramatist once said about playwriting:

> Of all literary endeavors playwrighting is the most heroic, elegant, and sanitary.... If I fancy being a mandarin, I am gloriously promoted to the top at once. If I desire to leave office and live like a recluse, in a wink I am transported to a wooded hill.... If you are to construct what a character says on his behalf, you must construct the person's heart on his behalf as well first. *How can one put oneself in the other's position (she shen chu di) if not by dream travel and spirit roaming*?⁴⁷

Like Flaubert, Li Yu 李漁 (1611–1680) celebrates the magic of playwriting that turns the playwright into any personae he creates, as if he were simply projecting his desire onto whatever characters and stories he likes. But the parallels end right here: rather than projecting one's feeling onto others and reconfirming the interior locus of emotion, *she shen chu di* requires the playwright to imaginatively put himself in the situation of the other in order to feel what the other feels; hence the acknowledgment that the locus of emotion is somewhere else rather than the self. Saying what I want to say depends on imagining what the other would have to say in a different situation than mine, not the other way around.

By invoking *she shen chu di* in the context of empathy, Zhu Guangqian is not so much committing mistranslation or cultural misunderstanding as reactivating the translingual complexity of the Western term *Einfühlung* throughout its history. As Lanzoni notes, before Titchener and Ward coined "empathy" to translate *Einfühlung*, the most commonly used word for the term in the English world was "sympathy," which has a much longer history. Hence, when Titchener was constructing empathy as a new object of psychological science at the turn of the twentieth century, he could not help but compare it to "sympathy":

> We have a natural tendency to feel ourselves into what we perceive or imagine. As we read about the forest, we may, as it were, become the explorer... This tendency to feel oneself into a situation is called

16 *Prologue*

> EMPATHY;—on the analogy of sympathy, which is feeling together with another; and empathic ideas are psychologically interesting because they are the converse of perceptions; their core is imaginal, and their context is made up of sensations, the kinesthetic and organic sensations that carry the empathic meaning. Like the feeling of strangeness, they are characteristic of imagination.[48]

Titchener here establishes a pair of dichotomies that have since been reiterated by many: whereas sympathy involves "feeling together with another," keeping my feeling separate from the other's feeling, empathy obliterates that separation by "feeling into" the other. By extension, whereas the former entails judgmental attitude (pity or compassion) from an outside position, the latter nonjudgmentally eliminates the distance by taking the other's position. Ironically, the problem across the various accounts of the sympathy-empathy opposition—which boil down to "your pain"/"my pain" and judgmental/nonjudgmental dichotomies—is that empathy and sympathy are constantly trading places.[49] In fact, Titchener's definition of empathy—to feel oneself into a situation by imagination—was once the definition of sympathy. As David Marshall reminds us: "In the eighteenth century, the word [*sympathy*] suggests putting oneself in the place of someone else, taking someone else's part—a general condition or act, related to the modern word 'empathy,' of which pity, compassion, and commiseration are only specific examples."[50]

Zhu Guangqian's nearly involuntary invocation of *she shen chu di* serves as a "wormhole" traversing the artificial barrier between sympathy and empathy because it is the closest we can get in Chinese to the eighteenth-century definition of sympathy. It allows us to trace the convergence of the Chinese and Western genealogies of emotion-realms in the early modern emergence of the global regime of theatricality. On the Western side, the apparent opposition between feeling with and feeling into does not really delineate the chronological progression from sympathy to empathy that has been hailed as the watershed of the modernist era.[51] Rather, the opposition between sympathy and empathy circumscribes the whole dynamic by which theatricality in the Western context is generated and strengthened through its apparent negation—that is, through a momentary return to a pre-theatricalist dream in which one could enter another's feeling.⁵² On the Chinese side, *she shen chu di* as a symptom of theatricality has been (mis)understood in terms of the dreamscape—"How can one put oneself in the other's position if not by dream travel and spirit roaming?" This suggests the Chinese genealogy of emotion-realms follows a different trajectory determined by a different dynamic.

Between dreamscapes and theatricality, it is never a one-way street, and never just one street only. It is a complicated journey, one that we will be taking throughout the rest of this book.

CHAPTER ONE

Winds, Dreams, Theater
A Genealogy of Emotion-Realms

1. *QING* OF SOURCE UNKNOWN

"Out of *qing* forms the dream; out of the dream forms drama."[1] Thus spake the playwright Tang Xianzu 湯顯祖 (1550–1616), whose *The Peony Pavilion* (*Mudan ting* 牡丹亭, 1598) did more than any other work to define the cult of *qing* (emotion, passion, sentiment, affection, love) at the turn of the seventeenth century. Based on a short tale about Du Liniang 杜麗娘, who dies dreaming about a lover she never met and then revives thanks to her ineradicable passion, the play has gained unrivaled fame for celebrating the power of emotion to transcend life and death. According to the genesis of drama laid out by the playwright himself, however, emotion and dreams are not just themes or leitmotifs of the play, but are its origins in the most profound sense. Drama can be traced all the way to the innermost part of the human psyche where emotion resides, with the dream as the intermediate inner "stage" on which intangible emotions take visual form for the mind's eye and serve as prototypes for theatrical performance.

This genesis's implications for our understanding of Chinese literary history and of the history of emotion are intertwined. For the former, modern scholars regard drama as deriving from the grand tradition of lyricism at the core of Chinese culture—a tradition allegedly predicated on expressing the emotive interior rather than mimicking external actions.² For the latter, since emotion is understood as the interior awaiting expression, our modern account of emotion in traditional China can only be a story of suppression and emancipation. Tang Xianzu is thus often portrayed as the liberator of *qing* from a conservative ethos, and modern critics love to cite the playwright's defense of his romantic plays, in which he allegedly contrasts himself with his Neo-Confucian mentor Luo Rufang 羅汝芳 (1515–1588): "What the Master advocates is [morally sanctioned] nature (*xing* 性); what I advocate is emotion (*qing*)."³ Our understanding of emotion and its historical unfolding has affected the way we appreciate Chinese drama, and vice versa; both spring from the premise about a continual exteriorization of the interior.

But that genesis can be cast in a different light. In his foreword to *The Peony Pavilion*, Tang Xianzu writes: "*Qing*, of source unknown, runs ever deeper. The living may die of it, and the dead may come back alive."⁴ Instead of presuming that emotion is the inner origin of dreams and drama, the playwright throws into question the locus of emotion from the very beginning. Does this "unknown" simply refer to some yet-to-be-identified stimuli from material reality, so that emotional reactions still count as something within us? Or, more radically, does it refer to a certain exteriority that is irreducible to matter (since Liniang is affected by a dream without connection to any object of desire) or fantasy (otherwise, we can no longer talk about a "source unknown")? If emotion is no longer presumed to be interior, how should we make sense of the genealogy from *qing* to dreams and to drama, with the meaning of each and every term in it radically reconsidered?

2. UNDER THE WEATHER

The same complication can be found in Pan Zhiheng's 潘之恆 (1556–1622) reflection on a performance of *The Peony Pavilion*: "Only those capable of being infatuated are capable of having passion (*qing*); only those capable of having passion are capable of portraying the passion."⁵ At first glance, Pan can be understood as saying that even acting entails expressing the "true self" based on one's own emotional experience.⁶ Such a reading has to presume that *qing* quintessentially originates in the self and hence underwrites the self's truthfulness. Yet "the trajectory of passion" (*qing zhi suo zhi* 情之所之), as Pan traces it, lies less in the self than in the uncharted beyond: "It is not known where it begins, where it ends, from what it separates, with what it rejoins. Somewhere between being and nonbeing, faraway and nearby, existence and extinction, this is where it must go, but it is not known why it is so."[7] Uncanny and unbounded, this inscrutable notion of *qing* complicates the classical view that emotion is anchored in the heart, stirred up inside, and emitted from within.

These complications do not so much break with the classical view of emotion as underscore a much broader horizon of emotion within ancient sources. The unboundedness of *qing* is already suggested in the "Great Preface" by the related trope of "winds" or "airs" (*feng* 風). Before mentioning that "affections are stirred within [the heart]" (*qing dong yu zhong* 情動於中), the "Great Preface" gives us what precedes the stirred heart, namely, the encompassing atmosphere, the pervasive "winds" that stir things up (*feng yi dong zhi* 風以動之).[8] *Qing* is therefore a trembling sphere in which a continuum of motion brings things in sync with one another, with the heart being no more than one of the relay stations. This discourse of winds is traceable to "the discovery of the body in the Fourth Century B.C.," in which the body was first regarded as a composition "constituted from a series of ever more refined vital energies—*qi* 氣, *jing* 精, and *shen* 神" from the outside world, and hence the program of self-cultivation was placed "within an overarching vision of a dynamic cosmos."[9] But the flip side of this cosmological order is that the body, itself never a self-contained substance, is constantly open to being harmed by the same energies. Saturating every corner and penetrating all thresholds, the winds from the second century BCE on came to be seen as a pathological agent of either malady (in medical discourse) or melancholy (in sentimental lyrics).[10] Just as the otherwise self-enclosed body is diffused by the currents of air permeating its porous surfaces, the melancholic feeling is not an inner state of mind but an enveloping "mood" or atmosphere in which we find ourselves. Disclosing emotion as a spatial structure or sphere, the topos of winds is an emotion-realm organized around the dimension of embedment. Simply put, the human subject is embedded in the mood, not the other way around. More precisely, the subject does not exist prior to or independent of the embedment; rather, to borrow Ben Anderson's discussion of the "affective atmosphere," the embedding winds embody a "spatiality of sphere," "occurring beyond, around, and alongside the formation of

Winds, Dreams, Theater 21

subjectivity."[11] It is this "occurring beyond, around, and alongside" that constitutes the "embedment" dimension of winds.

This "embedment" dimension harbors the primordial experience of the exteriority of emotion, which is intimately felt in daily life and yet often misrecognized as external causality. We need to differentiate the exteriority of emotion from two versions of exogenous determinism. The first version draws on the traditional notion of "external things" (*waiwu* 外物) inciting emotional responses (*ying* 應) which can further be understood in terms of the ancient cosmology of "correspondence" or *gan ying* 感應 (literally, "to be affected and respond"). In Chinese poetics—some scholars thus argue—poetry is deemed spontaneous and involuntary as emotional feedback; under the sway of external stimuli, poetic composition allegedly circumvents the deliberation of the human subject.[12] And yet, in positing emotion as a response *to the external world*, this view still adopts a communication model that presupposes a subject whose interiority is initially separate from that world. Seen from this perspective, "The Great Preface" would just conform to an "established paradigm of inner and outer" by delineating the "boundaries" between human psyche and its environment. Emotional expression, in its supposedly "perfect correspondence" to the world, would remain a psychological topic only.[13]

The second and more recent version of exogenous determinism, which should be differentiated from the exteriority of emotion, stresses social and cultural processes through which emotions are experienced, articulated, categorized, and distributed. Such sociocultural interpretations have been deployed to critique the Western reduction of emotion to biological phenomena contra rationality.[14] Paradoxically, this approach, along with the breakdown of the feeling/thinking dichotomy, serves to extend rather than displace the majesty of the interior, usually in the name of cognitive psychology. Emotional experience is now regarded as an "overlearned cognitive habit," acquired through concentrated attention and motivated training with "deep goal relevance" in a social environment.[15] Cognitive studies have opened up emotion to historical investigation,[16] but it privileges *interiorization* as the essential structure of emotion. Given that emotion allows us to achieve intended purposes, it is one step away from the claim that (even without knowing it) we make *our own* decisions and judgments about how we feel;[17] emotion thus becomes the ultimate assertion of self-sovereignty.[18]

By contrast, an approach premised on the "exteriority of emotion"—by which I mean a spatial structure that allows us to be outside in the world getting along with one another, as instanced by daily references to atmospheres we have generally discussed in the prologue—sidesteps the issue of causal relationships between exterior and interior and hence avoids the reterritorization of interiority. The ancient Chinese topos of winds illustrates this in a historically specific way. The embedding winds traverse not only individuals and communities but also all categorical divisions (source and target, purpose and outcome, input and feedback, vehicle and content) required to articulate causality. In the Han exegesis, *feng* is at once (1) poetry that winds give rise to (hence a major poetic genre called *feng* or "Airs"), (2) the oral delivery (variably written as *feng* 諷) by which poetry is transported, (3) the practical functions of political admonition (*feng ci* 諷刺) and custom transformation (*feng jiao* 風教 or *feng hua* 風化) that poetry carries out, and (4) the ethos (*feng su* 風俗) that poetry edifies and transforms.[19] Short-circuiting input and feedback and permeating its own medium and effects, the cosmological force named winds therefore does not figure as an extrinsic "cause" but renders causality as such only secondary.

This topos of winds outlives antiquity and remains a prominent stratum that underlies the understanding of emotion in early modern China. In the words of the classical tale collection *History of Emotion* (*Qingshi* 情史, 1630s) compiled by Feng Menglong 馮夢龍 (1574–1646):

> Emotion is characterized by motion but is intangible; all of a sudden it moves people without having them know about it. It has the "winds" symbolism, and therefore its transformation takes the form of winds. Winds are what wanders around without going away, which belongs to the category of emotion.[20]

Writing three decades after *The Peony Pavilion*, Feng clearly has the play on his mind when he argues that emotion is an all-pervading field of cosmological forces in which humans find themselves rather than a psychological state found in humans, and that it is only in this cosmological view that a person's demise and resurrection in emotion become comprehensible: "Humans are born and perish in emotion; emotion is not born and perish in humans. People live, but emotion can make them die; people die, but emotion can make them live again."²¹

This understanding of emotion as a field of cosmological energies helps explain why, in *The Peony Pavilion*, a poem from the "Airs" section of the *Book of Songs* would affect Liniang so deeply—"for the verse, her sentimental viscera were stirred over its explication" 為詩章, 講動情腸 (43)—that her condition is compared to an "embarrassing disease" (*ganga bing* 尷尬病) contracted from the "rear garden" (*hou huayuan* 後花園), a euphemism for anal sex (93), or to possession by evil spirits, as her mother laments: "Her body, I fear, was contaminated by the Willow Spirit" 怕腰身觸污了柳精靈 (81). By the same token, Tutor Chen's tongue-in-cheek attempt to cure her with the same *Book of Songs* ("use the *Book of Songs* to cure the *Book of Songs* disease" 毛詩病用毛詩去醫 [92]) wittily reactivates this ancient view of powerful words as winds that physically impact the body, for better or worse, in an unmediated fashion. The pathology of the affecting wind continues into Liniang's afterlife. The same powerful cosmological forces that bring about her death also transform her into a ghost. In sixteenth-century medical terms, a ghost emerges from the "congestion" (*yu* 鬱) of emotion as vital energies dominated by *yin* ether, which is why the play constantly stages Liniang's apparition along with a chilly breeze (147, 149, 153, 165). And what brings her back to life, ultimately, is the cosmological energy of *yang*, hilariously preserved in "the machismo's underwear" (*zhuang nanzi de kudang* 壯男子的褲襠) donated by Tutor Chen and used in the ritual of resurrection (184).²²

In his "Inscription for the Temple of the Drama God, Master of the Pristine Fount, of Yihuang Prefecture" ("Yihuang xian xishen Qingyuanshi miao ji" 宜黃縣戲神清源師廟記) (written between 1598 and 1606), Tang Xianzu clearly has that cosmological force in mind when he mystifies the powers of theater to the extent that it is alleged to arouse "phoenixes, birds, beasts, and even barbarian spirits of Ba and Yu." Exercised on the human body, such powers can even restore lost functions and wipe out pestilence: "The blind wants to see, the deaf wants to hear, the dumb wants to sigh, the crippled wants to rise, the emotionless can be guided to have emotions, and the voiceless can be given a voice [. . .] if every household has this art, no plague and malady would break out" (*jia you ci dao, yili buzuo* 家有此道，疫癘不作).²³ The model of the way drama overwhelms its audience with penetrating affects is a pathological one. Under the sway of winds, one is constituted and treated as a patient. The subject formation in the embedding winds should therefore be called "patiency."

3. AWAKENING TO DREAMS

And yet, the embedment of winds is just one dimension of the emotion-realm found in *The Peony Pavilion*, and it hardly exhausts the nature of Chinese theater or the audience's experience in Tang Xianzu's times. By yoking together the "Great Preface" and *The Peony Pavilion*, which are separated by almost two millennia, I aim to highlight both the lasting relevance of the ancient regime of winds and the subtle modifications to the emotion-realm over time. In addition to the topos of winds, which, uneven yet diffuse, permeate all boundaries and saturate every corner,[24] making experiences present and immediate to the subject constituted therein, there is another topos that stresses layered demarcation over diffusion, alternation over immediacy, ephemerality over presence—in short, a dimension of *deliverance* over that of embedment. This is the topos of what I am calling the "dreamscape."

In the preface to the play, Tang Xianzu praised Liniang, not her lover, as the embodiment of emotion, precisely because she is infatuated unto death by an erotic dream without having met the man in reality.[25] Liniang's fatal infatuation with her own dream seems to be a thinly disguised example of auto-affection. In stressing female desire, subjectivity, and agency, however, we might assume too quickly that a dream is just an inner mental state, and that Liniang's oneiric obsession underscores her exemplary inwardness of emotion. And yet, like the heart, which is not the source of emotion but part of the motion in the air, a dream in traditional Chinese discourse does not serve as a Cartesian theater for the mind's eye; instead, it delivers us outside in the world. In his "Rhapsodies of the South" (*Chuci* 楚辭), the exiled poet Qu Yuan 屈原 (ca. 340 BCE–ca. 278 BCE) frequently takes flight in his dream, as the second-century commentator Wang Yi 王逸 explains: "The essential spirit wandering in dreams—this is a matter of homecoming" 精神夢遊，還故鄉也.[26] This journeying motif became a subgenre of dream lore under the heading of "Dream Travel" ("Mengyou" 夢遊) when the tenth-century editors compiled the Tang-dynasty tales.²⁷ Wandering out there in the world rather than trapped in their own minds, dreamers (usually a couple) in such tales could "run into each other in dreams" (*liang xiang tongmeng* 兩相通夢).²⁸ These two spatial features—dreaming as deliverance and the dreamscape as a common ground onto which dreamers get delivered—make it possible for Du Liniang and Liu Mengmei 柳夢梅 to meet in their dreams. As if to drive home the primacy of this common ground, the adaptation of *The Peony Pavilion* by Tang Xianzu's rival playwright Shen Jing 沈璟 (1553–1610) is retitled *The Story of Shared Dreams* (*Tongmeng ji* 同夢記).²⁹

For Liniang and Mengmei to enter each other's dreams, one might ask, do they not harbor a hidden desire for a mate, per the Chinese idiom that "one dreams at night of what one ponders in the daytime" (*ri you suosi, ye you suomeng* 日有所思，夜有所夢)? For the ancient, however, a dreamer does not fulfill his or her wish by retiring into the innermost phantasm called a dream; on the contrary, the dreamer, driven by what the thought is pointing to, is delivered somewhere else. The ancient interpretation of dreams is therefore not an analysis of unconscious desire but a prognostication—a deciphering of divine messages that are gathered precisely when one is spirited away. According to *A Manual of Dream Interpretation* (*Jiemeng shu* 解夢書), quoted in the late tenth century, "dreams are imagery, a matter of essential vital forces in motion, which happens when the soul leaves the body and roams around . . . The spirit wanders away while the body alone remains. It is because the heart has something to think about and forgets the body. [The wandering spirit] receives premonition from heavenly gods and comes back to inform humanity."³⁰

However, if prognostication literature is by definition forward-looking, telling one's fortune by deducing the true message of one's dream, the early Daoist philosopher Zhuangzi (ca. 369–286 BCE) looks *back* on the spatial structure of the dream as the ontological condition that undercuts the whole business of dream interpretation:

> Who banquets in a dream at dawn wails and weeps, who wails and weeps in a dream at dawn goes out to hunt. While we dream we do not know that we are dreaming, and in the middle of a dream interpret a dream within it; not until we wake do we know that we

were dreaming. Only at the ultimate awakening shall we know that it is the ultimate dream.³¹

We think we are in the position of clarifying the meaning of our dreams on the ground that we are already awakened, without knowing that one is divining one's dream within yet another dream. There is no ground or position outside the dream that can serve as an Archimedean point, because we realize we were dreaming only *in retrospect*—that is, only after we are delivered to a "waking" reality, which, with further deliverance, will again be belatedly demystified as another layer of the dream. Demarcated into layered realms of existence through which the dreamer is incessantly delivered, the topos of dreamscapes emblematizes a vastly different set of spatial structuration and problematics for emotion than the topos of winds (even though winds or "essential vital forces in motion" continued to be invoked as an explanation of dreams throughout the imperial history). Rather than a saturated field of unfiltered energies by which the human body is precariously permeated, sadness and joy are now reterritorialized as an endless layering of real and unreal, subjecting dreamers to iterative cycles of disillusionment and reenchantment. Also entailed in these diverse topoi of emotion are differences in temporal orientation: whereas the embedding winds make *present* both the patient's body and its sensations, the dreamscape is structured in such a way that the only thing the dreamer can anticipate while being incessantly delivered forth is a retrospective recognition of how deeply she has been thrown into an ever-receding background, an infinitely veiled past that is uncovered one layer at a time.

Ensnarled in the nascent dreamscape in the fourth century BCE, Zhuangzi was left with what he called "paradox in suspense" (*diaogui* 弔詭): awakening collapses into dreams and postpones forever the ultimate reality, until "we run into an ultimate sage who knows its solution tens of thousands of years later—that is just a matter of time."³² Before the ultimate awakening separates reality from illusion, the only thing Zhuangzi is certain about—as another, more famous parable from the same chapter of his book reveals—is "transformation" (*hua* 化), a notion originally associated with winds yet now appropriated to describe what happens in the dreamscape.³³ Getting around the entire question of whether I am a butterfly that dreams of being human or vice versa, all Zhuangzi can and

Winds, Dreams, Theater 27

needs to know is that the transformation of things (*wu hua* 物化) takes place during the deliverance from one dream to another.[34]

But the real solution arrived much earlier than expected, in the fourth century, when the Madhyamaka School of Mahayana Buddhism introduced to China the influential "Two Truths" or "Middle Way" doctrine, which advocates taking illusions, sensations, and dreams as the *upaya* or expedient for attaining dharma. Rather than an obstacle to awakening, the dream was now valorized as the "provisional" truth without which the truth of emptiness alone cannot be accessed.[35] The transformation (*hua*) of things, which allowed Zhuangzi to get around the unresolved dream paradox, was enhanced in eighth-century Buddhist oral performance into scenes involving "magically creative power to conjure" or "miraculous transformation" (*bian* 變) as the efficacious means of preaching to common people.[36]

It was through the cross-fertilization between Buddhism and Daoism that the dreamscape was fully developed during medieval times. One variation with an immediate concern with spatiality is the notion of "mystic vision" (*xuanlan* 玄覽), which is often correlated with and compared to dreams.[37] Its peculiar historical trajectory and practices further highlight the issue of layered exteriority. Starting from the fourth century in the texts of the Daoist Ge Hong 葛洪 (284–363) and the Buddhist monk Huiyuan 慧遠 (334–416), the "mystic vision" shifted from a Han-period topographic mapping of faraway lands toward the introspection of divinity from within. But this seemingly "inward" turn should be further explicated in terms of what Eugene Wang calls the "dual exteriority/interiority mode" of visuality in medieval Buddhist paintings. On the one hand, an "illusionistic niche" at the center of a mural, like a pictorial trope of mirrors or gateways, suggests the interior recess into the Buddha's presence within the mind; on the other, the rest of the picture, which is visually differentiated from the niche, offers a bird's-eye view of the distant vista.[38] To hold together this disjointed vision, which at once "projects both the exteriority of the cosmos out there and affirms the interiority of the mind," Wang gives an inspiring reading of Dunhuang Cave tableaux:

> As the central illusionistic niche draws the eye into it, we soon realize that the interior recess is more than a "chamber"; it in fact opens onto a distant vista. Behind the preaching Buddha is a cosmological

view: surrounded by the sea and encircled by the Iron Ring Mountains, the mushroom-shaped Mount Sumeru soars upward, flaring out at the top.... The recess is turned inside out; depth rebounds to reassert the surface; and interiority becomes exteriority. The mirroring space ruthlessly cuts into the topographic map only to transform itself into another round of topographic mapping.[39]

The apparently "inward" turn of mystic vision should therefore be thought of as being "turned inside out"; like the dreams in Zhuangzi, the Rhapsodies of the South, and *The Peony Pavilion*, this mystic vision delivers us to a "cosmos out there." But calling such a vision a "dual exteriority/interiority mode" could obfuscate the fact that exteriority is not a symmetrical alternative to interiority. Exteriority designates not the position of an object in our gaze but the spatiality of our being out there with others that grounds the entirety of the experience of mystic vision. That is precisely why, by concentrating on "mental pictures" or

FIGURE 1.1 Delivered to the exterior: Buddhist mural of Cave 217 at Mogaoku, Dunhuang, early eighth century. *Source*: Eugene Wang, *Shaping the Lotus Sutra*.

looking into the mirroring space as a gateway leading to the recessive interior, we are always thrown onto a distant vista. Strictly speaking, there is no duality in the interior/exterior mode of vision; rather, the split takes place in the layering of topographies or dreamscapes, with each "inward" turn of the gaze turning into "another round of topographical mapping." What we are accustomed to calling the "depth" of interiority is an effect of the peculiar structure of demarcation and layering in this particular mode of exteriority.

In the late sixteenth and early seventeenth centuries, Chan Buddhism came to conceive of dreams as no less real than reality and reality as no less illusory than dreams.[40] Master Zibai Zhenke 紫柏真可 (1543–1603, courtesy name Daguan 達觀) took dreams as a gradual procedure heralding sudden enlightenment, which he called "enlightenment through dreams" (*mengwu* 夢悟), an intermediate step that cannot be dispensed with or hurried through. "And hence the more one dreams, the more one becomes awake. One day when the dream karma bursts and breaks off (*mengyuan baoduan* 夢緣爆斷), the shadow of awakening is also found empty."[41] It is therefore no coincidence that Tang Xianzu, whose friendship and correspondence with Zhenke are well documented,[42] adopted a similar rhetoric in his foreword that upends Zhuangzi's paradox: "Why must emotion in the dream not be real? Is there ever a shortage of people living in their dreams?" (1) If, in 1598, this dream of emotion was celebrated in *The Peony Pavilion* as the ultimate plane that transcends everything, the nonstop operation of deliverance—thanks to which all dreams turn out to be a series of relays facilitating further enlightenment ad infinitum—inevitably led to Tang's later religious plays, *Dream of the South Branch* (*Nanke meng ji* 南柯夢記, 1600) and *Dream of Handan* (*Handan meng ji* 邯鄲夢記, 1606). The former delivers the protagonist to the "exhaustion" (*qingjin* 情盡) of emotion; the latter finishes the task by "burning up the leftover brushwood of emotion" (*shao yuqing guduo* 燒餘情榾柮).[43] The trajectory of Tang's so-called "Four Dreams" plays as a whole (including the 1590 romantic comedy *Purple Hairpin* or *Zichai ji* 紫釵記) can therefore be regarded as prescribed by Zhenke's spiritual program.

Tang Xianzu's late plays belong to the deliverance play (*dutuo ju* 度脫劇) subgenre, which had flourished since the Yuan dynasty (1271–1368).[44] The subgenre features a protagonist spirited away by a Buddhist or Daoist master into a series of nightmarish scenes called "the dreadful realms" (*e jing₂tou* 惡境頭),⁴⁵ only to wake up and realize that life at large is no more than a brief dream. Even though in some plays a strange world can be magically conjured up in front of the protagonist's eyes rather than through the topos of dreams, one can easily see that both magical invocation and the dreamscape feature delivery by a medium into and out of an illusory world.⁴⁶ The device of the dreadful realm is so powerful that it is circulated across genre boundaries into courtroom and romantic plays. In Guan Hanqin's 關漢卿 *Rescriptor-in-Waiting Bao Thrice Investigates the Butterfly Dream* (*Bao daizhi san kan hudie meng* 包待制三勘蝴蝶夢), the dream motif is less about Judge Bao's butterfly dream than about the deliverance of the condemned to his court, to jail, and finally to freedom. Despite the prophetic dream that has prompted him to be lenient, Judge Bao inexplicably decides to send the three condemned young men to death row. This has the dramatic effect of intensifying the emotions of their mother, Madame Wang, the only character who sings onstage (as prescribed by the format of Yuan *zaju* drama), channeling all the boiling feelings of the wronged. When the judge orders the release of the two elder brothers but keeps the youngest one (her only biological son) in jail, she sings: "In dreams alone will come a reunion of mother and son."⁴⁷ It is precisely this sort of dream into which Judge Bao finally delivers them at the end of the play, with an announcement that the whole family has been granted official titles by the Emperor's decree. The story's strange twists and turns cannot be fully explained on ethical and legal grounds because they represent the operation of deliverance itself, according to which the judge occupies the same position as the Daoist immortal sending his potential disciples into and out of hell.

This trope of deliverance can be romantically revamped, as in Wang Shifu's 王實甫 *The Story of the Western Wing* (*Xixiang ji* 西廂記, late thirteenth century). The scene of love at first sight at the Buddhist temple in play 1, act 1, not only depicts the beauty Cui Yingying 崔鶯鶯 as the immortal Bodhisattva Guanyin in apparition but also delivers the infatuated Student Zhang to an entirely different realm, and he has to remind himself: "This is Tushita Palace,/Don't guess it to be the heaven of Separation's Regret." But eventually, after Yingying has left, he embraces the changed realm: "What should I do with the jade maiden now gone?/The palace of Brahma I suspect to be the Wuling Spring."⁴⁸

The relationship between the goddess and the male mortal is reversed in the final act of play 1, however, where Student Zhang appropriates a Buddhist ceremony meant for the woman's deceased father so that he can see her again; symbolically, it is as if he is using the power of the ritual to summon and deliver the celestial beauty back to earth, only to sadly see the woman retreat from his sight again once the ritual is over. This motif of deliverance culminates in one of the most memorable dream scenes in Chinese literature in which the beauty is delivered to her journeying lover, who then wakes up to a bleak condition of solitude at the end of play 4 (rumored to have been the "original" ending of the whole play).

On top of these genre and thematic associations, the dreamscape figures in the early Chinese dramatic form per se. As early as the Tianbao 天寶 era (742–756), dramatic performance—characterized as provisional and suppositional—was analogous to life-as-dream. Puppet plays, for instance, were compared to evanescent dreams: "In an instant the play was over, silence befalls,/Just like a life in a dream" 須臾弄罷寂無事，還似人生一夢中.⁴⁹ The analogy continued into the eleventh and twelfth centuries, in performances that usually focused on the ephemerality of worldly success manifested by performers costumed as mock officials.⁵⁰ The clustering of mystical vision, dreams, and dramatic performance can be discerned in medieval Buddhist circumambulation and Daoist ritual pacing. With their physical movement, the circumambulators symbolically map out and enter the otherworldly realm, where they envision the myriad divine figures "like a dream."⁵¹ The particular choreography of the Daoist "Paces of Yu" (*Yu bu* 禹步) was adopted by a particular drama genre, *nuoxi* 儺戲, a kind of ritual performance that evolved from ancient shamanist dance into a dramatic form by the time of the Song dynasty (960–1279);⁵² hence the association between dramatic performance and sleepwalking. Ultimately, dreamscapes informed the spatial structure of performance venues per se in the transformations of Song-Yuan theater architecture.⁵³

While the dreamscape in the post-Han and Tang eras was propagated by the flourishing of Buddhism and Daoism—itself a symptom of the loosening of rigid social divisions and practices prescribed by Confucianism after the collapse of the Han empire—the dreamscape during the Song-Yuan, which found a new form in the early Chinese theater, was tied to economic changes in agrarian society. On one hand, the phantasmagoria of urban life in such cities as Bianliang 汴梁—the Northern Song capital and the biggest metropolis in the then-contemporary world that nurtured both commercial and religious performances and fell to the Jurchens in 1127—was remembered as a landmark of transient dreams.[54] On the other hand, as Tanaka Issei 田仲一成 reminds us, the more fundamental shift underlying the rise of the early theater occurred not in that flamboyant metropolitan center, but among villages and towns. It was during the Song period that variety performances closely associated with praying for good harvests in remote and small rural communities began to be replaced by more elaborate theatrical performances in larger villages and towns, where festive occasions and religious rituals facilitated commercial exchange.[55] Mark Elvin identifies one feature of the "medieval economic revolution in China, which may be dated between about 900 and 1200," as "the appearance of a growing number of informal markets in empty sites, towns, and cities throughout the empire. This was part cause and part effect of the collapse of the earlier system of state-controlled walled urban markets. . . . The informal, often periodic, markets increasingly became the focal points of peasants' life, and standard marketing areas seem to have been the lowest unit of sub-cultural variation."[56] Hence, the transience of dreamscapes in which the epic history of the fallen capital was memorialized turned out to be the mundane reality of myriad makeshift markets in local regions that waxed and waned along with seasonal rhythms.

4. IN FACE OF THE PAGE

A timeworn topos deployed in medieval literature under the immense influence of Buddhism and Daoism and embodied by the Song-Yuan to mid-Ming theater, the dreamscape (like winds) lingered in early modern periods. Apparently, Tang Xianzu's "Four Dreams" rearticulate the conventional life-dream-drama analogy and redeploy the terms of real/unreal and enchantment/disillusion typical of the dreamscape. *The Peony Pavilion* is more than just a "relay" play in the trajectory of interminable deliverance. It occupies a central position as a "shared dream" for romantic couples (as figured in Tang-dynasty tales) and also for the performers and the audience.

But precisely at this juncture the play frustrated the expectations of its more acute readers so much that Feng Menglong, the "Historian of Emotion," was motivated to redact Tang Xianzu's play into *The Romantic Dream* (*Fengliu meng* 風流夢) sometime after 1623. The very first thing that Feng's "General Commentary" (*zongping* 總評) complains about is that Liniang and Mengmei's dreams are temporally set apart rather than articulated as one shared dream:

> Even without prior collaboration, two dreams tally with each other—that is what makes them extraordinary. But in the original play, the male lead makes the first entry and explains his change of name on account of his dream, whereas the female lead does not enter her dream until several scenes later [in "Interrupted Dream" ("Jingmeng" 驚夢)]. The two dreams appear so disconnected that they taste awful. Now this redaction has the male lead change his name only after the female lead's dream in order to show the resonance of the love karma. The scene "[Husband and Wife] Match Dreams" ("[Fuqi] hemeng" [夫妻] 合夢) is the point of convergence.[57]

In the marginal note to the first scene of *The Romantic Dream*, Feng again criticizes Tang's arrangement: "In the original scene, [the male lead] mentions a dream right away, as if his dream and the female lead's dream are two completely separate things."[58] By situating Mengmei's dream account right after Liniang's dream scene—and by suppressing all the details in Mengmei's original account that are downright incompatible with the "Interrupted Dream" scene[59]—Feng tries to reassure us that the couple have gone through the same dream. But the most important problem is not that there are two different dreams—after all, the couple could still have *shared* all their dreams, as the Flower God apparently suggests by explaining to us that he has Mengmei delivered into Liniang's dream.[60] It is that neither Liniang nor Mengmei has any recollection of entering the other's dreams. The "point of convergence" (*jiexue* 結穴) Feng Menglong highlights in his adaptation, in which the protagonists finally realize they have met in a dream they share, is not simply absent from but fundamentally at odds with Tang's original design.

Does this ruptured dreamscape that is at once shared and jarringly disjunctive fall back on the notion of the dream as an expression of the individual interior, leading us to the familiar conclusion that Mengmei and Liniang are each obsessed with their own inner fantasies, and that their dream lovers are no more than the projected shadows of their desires? Despite his misguided attempt to squeeze *The Peony Pavilion* into the medieval model of a shared dream, Feng Menglong unwittingly shows in his *History of Emotion* how the dreamscape actually morphed into a new spatial structure of emotion at the turn of the seventeenth century:

> Dreams are the roaming of the ethereal soul (*hun* 魂). The humic soul (*po* 魄) is nothing miraculous but the ethereal soul is; by the same token, the body is nothing miraculous but a dream is. A dream can reach what has not yet happened and inspire what has not yet been thought. If it does not turn out to be accurate, we call it "dream"; if it is spot on, we call it "not-a-dream." A dream that turns out to be a dream is the unreal that looks real; a dream that turns out to be not a dream is a reality that looks more unreal! Others cannot be aware of my dream, of which only I am aware; I cannot see my ethereal soul, but others perhaps see it. I am aware of my dream but cannot understand it myself—this is because I cannot consult my own ethereal soul; others might see my ethereal soul, but my ethereal soul is not self-aware—that is just like the case of a dream. [The ethereal soul] can be detached from a living person, but can be called back even if the person has been dead. It can even possess another person's body. Is it that the ethereal soul takes the body as a tavern?[61]

Underneath the "roaming" and "real-unreal" commonplace, Feng Menglong articulates a new language of the *outsider* to make sense of dream experience. Dreaming is roaming no longer because spirit as the locus of consciousness departs from the stuporous body, as traditional prognostication literature describes, but more fundamentally because of the structure of the spirit itself, which is split into ethereal soul (*hun*, the lighter half that ascends and wanders away) and humic soul (*po*, the turbid half that sinks and stays). This relocation of the origin of dreams in the splitting of the soul in turn modifies the reason for dream skepticism: Dreams are impossible to understand not because the very ground of reality keeps collapsing into dreams, as Zhuangzi contends, but because the split soul undercuts self-consciousness per se. In place of an informative spirit that would return and communicate a divine message to humanity, Feng sees a detached and aloof "ethereal soul" that, like an undutiful child, comes home and does not feel like being asked (*hun bu ke wen* 魂不可問) where and how the night was spent. This communication breakdown with my sleep-traveling half-soul renders me an *outsider* in relation to my dream. The "outsider" position that I occupy mirrors the opposite position occupied by "other people" (*taren* 他人) vis-à-vis this dream of mine. The two positions specularly correspond: whereas I as an outsider of my dream cannot see my own ethereal soul when it sneaks out—and the ethereal soul is unable to see or be aware of itself, because it is somnambulant (*hun bu zi jue, yi you zhi hu meng ye* 魂不自覺，亦猶之乎夢也)—other people stand a chance of seeing my ethereal soul (*ren huo jian zhi* 人或見之), if they come across it. The previous problematic of being delivered through infinitely layered realms of realities and illusions is displaced by an early modern one of trying to see and understand a dream from an outside position—the position of the spectator.[62]

The shift from dreamer to spectator marks a subtle modification of the dreamscape into theatricality as the newly emergent mode of the spatiality of emotion at the turn of the seventeenth century. This historical change has often passed for continuity under the aegis of the same old drama-dream analogy, and yet it can be detected, for example, between the lines of Tang's contemporary Xie Zhaozhe 謝肇淛 (1567–1624):

> Drama and dreams are the same (*xi yu meng tong* 戲與夢同). Sorrow and joy upon separation and reunion—none of these emotions is real; affluence or poverty, high or low status—none of these situations is genuine. The transient world is just like this. Nonetheless, the unwise cheer in auspicious dreams and worry in nightmares; their countenance would be saddened over a play of torment but lit up over a play of efflorescence. Overall, people rarely avoid their vulgar view of life. Recently men of letters love picking on dramas for their deviation from historical facts. This is just as the idiom goes: "Telling a dream in front of an idiot."[63]

Apparently, Xie is reproducing the familiar structure of a dreamscape as a series of layers through which the dreamer is transported, experiencing passions and their nullification alternately; hence "the transient world" is just a dream. But within the threefold dream/drama/world analogy that is established by a couple of forthright assertions—"drama and dreams are the same" and "the transient world is just like this"— there is a significant shift in the way drama conjoins with dreams. The point of convergence no longer hinges on the protagonist undergoing ephemeral states of passion like a dreamer or a performer who crosses a threshold into the dreamlike realm of the theater. Rather, it hinges on a new analogy between dreamer and spectator: "The unwise cheer in auspicious dreams and worry in nightmares; their countenance would be saddened over a play of torment but lit up over a play of efflorescence." Instead of experiencing passions *within and through* layers of a dreamscape, the dreamer is now reconstituted as a spectator *in front of* the dream. Here we see that the old idiom, "telling a dream in front of an idiot," has acquired a brand-new meaning. The "idiot," *in front of* whom we cannot relate a dream lest he take it for the real,[64] actually marks the paradigmatic position for the dreamer-spectator. The point is no longer that the idiot has to be doubly removed as an underprivileged *outsider* (denied access to another person's dream) because he is too stupid to appreciate the unreal. On the contrary, it is the insider—the dreamer himself—who is now strangely sidelined as an onlooker to his own dream, and he does not immediately experience the dream but tries to recuperate it at a distance.

The curious rupture of shared dreams in *The Peony Pavilion* can now be understood in the context of the emergence of theatricality. To use Feng Menglong's terms, the two dreams are shared in the most disjunctive fashion precisely because Liniang and Mengmei are outsiders vis-à-vis their own dreams and each is a spectator of the other's wandering soul. Since it is their alienated half-souls—not their persons— who make love in the "Interrupted Dream" scene, one has to become a spectator to one's own ethereal soul's dream. This is more poignant for Liniang than for Mengmei, since, in Pan Zhiheng's words, "the former takes for real her dream, while the latter takes for real his life."[65] That is, the man cares about the worldly success—a beautiful spouse and an official title—that is promised in his dream rather than the dream per se. That is why only Liniang tries to retrieve what has been left once she wakes from the bygone dream by turning herself into a spectator. The play's defining moment is therefore not "Interrupted Dream"—the best-known and most frequently performed scene, which is taken from the classical tale "The Story of Du Liniang" ("Du Liniang ji" 杜麗娘記, 1594)[66]—but "Pursuing the Dream" ("Xunmeng" 尋夢), a genuinely original scene.[67]

What distinguishes "Pursuing the Dream" is the peculiar way the postdreamer tries to put things *in front of the dream*:

> Alas, I seek and seek, but nothing remains. The pavilion of the tree peonies, the peony balustrade, how can they stand so chill and lonely, no sign of human presence? How sad they make me! (*She weeps*)

[To the tune "Intertwined Jade Branches"] So desolate a place,
No other hut or kiosk near,
So hard to seek, with my amorous eyes squinted.
Clearly the white sun is put in the bright blue sky,
Momentarily not allowing one to grasp things to the front of the soul's dream.
But in a flash they seem to lively reveal themselves!
Let me walk in a circle and linger further on.
Hey, this is exactly where he crushed my gold bracelet to the ground!

    I wish to see again how that scholar

[To the tune "Yue shang"] Seduced me.
Somehow I can picture him appearing.
Slowly he is coming by,
Sluggishly he is moving away.
But gone not far—
Before clouds disperse and rain dries away,
He returns among flowers, beneath willows.
From yesterday to today
The place right under my eyes as before my mind
In the instant transforms into a terrain of love (60).[68]

38 *Winds, Dreams, Theater*

An object of desire that is before one's eyes but beyond one's reach, as suggested toward the end of this passage—this leitmotif is traceable all the way to the *Book of Songs* and remained popular throughout the medieval and late imperial periods.[69] But what makes Du Liniang the icon of late sixteenth-century theater is her strange lament earlier in the passage. She does not simply want to put things before her eyes, nor does she wish to "grasp what happened in the dream" (as Cyril Birch's authoritative translation suggests).[70] She could have tried to get back to the dream or to turn it into reality; instead, Liniang laments that the broad daylight "momentarily [does not allow her] to grasp things to the front of the soul's dream" (*meng jiao ren zhua bu dao hunmeng qian* 猛教人抓不到魂夢前). If deliverance through the ancient and medieval dreamscape turns any way out into another inside of the dream and hence repeatedly doubles up emotion in an endless interfolding of truth and falsehood, Liniang's attempt to stay with her oneiric experience of emotion *in front of* (rather than inside, outside, or through) the dream suggests a revised spatial morphology. An interstitial strand that arrests (however briefly) the otherwise incessant deliverance, this "front" (*qian* 前) is actually where the postdreamer (the spectator to the dream) stands.[71] At first glance, she is standing outside the dream but, more precisely, this "outside" has turned into a newly delineated space—the "front"—that is at once bordered on, reconnected to, and decisively split from the inside. In this deeper sense, the "front" is less an outside than an interface; the spectatorial position itself would be naught if it were separate from this mediating surface that at once flattens, articulates, and divides the inside and the outside of the dream. The spatiality of emotion is restructured and orchestrated among this being "in front of," "bordered on," "reconnected to," and "split from," altogether forming a spatial dimension that I call "faceoff," as distinct from the dimensions of embedment and deliverance.

In this "faceoff" dimension, emotion is neither a stream of motion presently synchronized with the embedding winds nor an infinitely recessed background whose unveiling is always belated and partial; rather, it is that which lies ahead and has yet to be identified with. It is this dimension that distinguishes theatricality from other modes such as winds and dreamscapes. The pertinent subject formation—namely, spectatorship, as distinct from patiency and dreamerhood—is the locus not so much of emotive interior as of the mediating surface itself, underscoring both the indelible distance from and the imaginary reconnection to emotion that lies in the yonder. Spectatorship thus foregrounds medium and mediated identification with the notion of interface.

Liniang's mediated rapport with the dream from a spectatorial position underlies—but is not reducible to—her narcissistic self-relationship, which is flaunted in the "Self-Portraiture" ("Xiezhen" 寫真) scene. After recoiling from her withered countenance in the mirror ("how could my enticing litheness of yesterday all succumb to such emaciation" 俺往日豔冶輕盈，奈何一瘦至此) (69), she transfigures it with the painting brush: "As anticipated, the picture comes to look great halfway through,/As if reborn into quite a different kind of charm" 情知畫到中間好，再有似生成別樣嬌 (70). Neither recalling her beauty from memory nor copying her mirror reflection, she is making up—with brushwork and through speech act, on silk and metaphorically on her face[72]—an ideal image she is anticipating. To say that this image is just a narcissistic projection, a fantasy insulated from the way she actually looks, would be to once again evoke the specter of interiority. Instead, what this image production empathetically relies on is an interaction of mediums—the mirror, the canvas, as well as the face—in which the spectator's body is an integral part of the media environment.[73]

In this context, spectatorship entails not passive recipients but an assemblage of mediated relationships to the self and others through the production, distribution, and exchange of assorted images. The conflicting versions of Liniang in incommensurable dreams foreshadow the symptomatic proliferation of other incongruous images of her: Mengmei fails to connect his dream lady, the portrait, and later the revenant to one another, mistaking them on every occasion for someone else. It has been noted that this dispersal of images undermines any possibility of a unitary identity,[74] but the identity crisis itself should be seen as one of the effects of the transmutation of the dreamscape into theatricality. In a sense, the wandering half-soul is a slice of resemblance peeled away from the person, and the modified dreamscape is shared not by the dreamers themselves but by their detached images. Romance commences when one image encounters another, and the so-called lovers are spectators whose interconnection is mediated by the communion of avatars and simulacra. A modern analogy would be the Facebook "friends" we make and become in a cybernetic dreamscape where nothing is meeting anything except for pictures, videos, and posts that put our "faces" on display.

Back in early modern China, this universe of simulacra already came into being on printed pages. The disjunctive yet shared dreams thematized in *The Peony Pavilion* are made manifest in the milieu in which the play was disseminated: an expanded reading public with a strong female presence, as evidenced by a slew of sentimental women readers reportedly moved to death and also by published works related to the play that incited more passionate responses. The most famous of these women, Feng Xiaoqing 馮小青 (1595–1612), might not even be a real historical figure (her name suggests "romantic charm" or *fengqing* 風情), but her imaginary status is part of the traffic in detached images propelled by the play as well as the industry of reading surrounding it.[75] Another case in point is the so-called "Three Wives' Commentary" to *The Peony Pavilion*, a work initiated by Chen Tong 陳同 (d. 1665)—Wu Ren's 吳人 (b. 1647) betrothed who died before the wedding—and completed by the second and third wives, Tan Ze 談則 (d. 1674) and Qian Yi 錢宜 (b. 1671). The three commentators never met; they were conjoined by the play they ardently invested in. Their virtual communion was opened up when their commentary was published in 1694, which symptomatically features a portrait depicting the "Du Liniang" whom Qian Yi claimed to have met in a dream—the portrait is actually just another simulacrum, a rip-off of an illustration of another drama persona Cui Yingying from the 1676 edition of *The Story of the Western Wing*.[76]

In addition to being the second most frequently reprinted Chinese play (behind *The Western Wing*), *The Peony Pavilion* is one of the most beloved plays performed on the Chinese stage. These distinctions are in conflict, however, as people have complained ever since Tang Xianzu's time that the play was written for reading rather than for performance, as reported by Zang Maoxun 臧懋循 (1560–1620): "The four plays including *The Peony Pavilion* by Tang [Xianzu] of Linchuan, some critics said, 'are books on the desktop, not operas sung in a banquet.'"[77] Attempts to redact and make *The Peony Pavilion* "performable" started with the aforementioned Shen Jing's *The Story of the Shared Dream* and Zang's 1616 *The Soul's Return* (*Huanhun ji* 還魂記). The complaints always converged on the play's disagreeableness to the ears. For Shen and Zang, Tang Xianzu's lyrics fail to conform to the prosodic rules of the Kun music that was rising to predominance at the time, though scholars today are still debating whether Tang intended to write in Kun style and whether that prosodic criticism against him was fairly made.[78] Another line of attack was more intrinsic to Tang's lyrics and harder to dismiss: his fancy compositions were too complicated to the audience's ears, as commented by the early Qing dramatist Li Yu:

> The two scenes ["Interrupted Dream" and "Pursuing the Dream"] are well written . . . but out of a hundred people who listen to *The Peony Pavilion*, do even one or two really get its intent? . . . If the author does have a deep intent here, I'm afraid it will be hard to find those who can understand it. If those who understand are so rare, why should we perform the play in a singing banquet for the delectation of both gentlemen and commoners?[79]

Ironically, Tang's original text came to be justified on prosodic grounds within the circle of Kun-style aficionados. Niu Shaoya's 鈕少雅 *Corrected Tunes from The Story of Soul's Return* (*Gezheng Huanhun ji cidiao* 格正還魂記詞調, early seventeenth century) and Ye Tang's 葉堂 *Complete Musical Notations to The Peony Pavilion* (*Mudan ting quanpu* 牡丹亭全譜, 1791) use the method of "collage of melodies" (*jiqu* 集曲) to rectify the tunes used by Tang Xianzu while retaining his words.[80] And even as the performance of scenes extracted from the play became increasingly influenced by professional actors during the Qing, Tang's idiosyncratic language continued to enchant the audience. The changes made in the extracted scenes mostly involved dialogue and stage directions, leaving the arias from the original intact.[81] Audiences were thus required to adapt their ears to the inscrutable arias. Li Yu might be right about the "inaudibility" of *The Peony Pavilion* but, as the history of its reception shows, this did not stop it from being performed and sung. As Mao Xianshu 毛先舒 (1620–1688) noted in a letter to Li Yu, "Posterity loves the fineness of Tang Xianzu's original text, so instead of using Zang Maoxun's adaptation, people insist on having the original sung."[82]

Better encountered in print than heard from the stage, the difficult text of *The Peony Pavilion* does not so much torture the audience's ears as pervert listening per se into *reading*. This synesthetic experience was first articulated by Tang Xianzu's associate Zhang Dafu 張大復 (1554–1630): "I seldom go deep in songs; what I get from them is merely sound. Yet when I listen to *The Soul's Return* [*Peony Pavilion*], I worry about whether I have got its meaning clearly."[83] Rather than dismissing the aurally incomprehensible play as inappropriate, Zhang Dafu takes it as an intriguing challenge to our ears, which are required to do the kind of close reading normally reserved for our eyes. This challenge may have been particularly appealing to Zhang, who went blind in 1593, five years before Tang Xianzu completed *The Peony Pavilion*.[84] Zhang's synesthetic experience, which he calls "ear reception" (*ershou* 耳受),[85] testifies to an important point: if *The Peony Pavilion* as a disjunctive dreamscape is embodied by the surface of printed pages on which detached images are produced, circulated, and exchanged, that surface does not dichotomize reading and performance, or eyes and ears, as critics suggest. Rather, it generates a new sensorium through the interface of print and performance. The locale of theatricality is therefore not the theater but the intersection between page and stage, and the first spectator in the nascent regime of theatricality was a blind man reading with his ears.[86]

Just as Xie Zhaozhe could not help but invoke a timeworn language of dreams to articulate the newly emergent spectatorial experience of theatricality, theatricality as intermediality tended to be described as a dreamscape, even though the shift of the dreamer's relationship to the dream appeared between the lines. As Min Guangyu 閔光瑜, who republished Tang Xianzu's *Dream of Handan* in 1621, wrote in the foreword:

> The carving of this story [on woodblocks] took place in the Precinct of Shengxi 晟溪里, and the studio is named the Long'en Hall 隆恩堂. The master Mr. Dreaming Astray (Mengmi sheng 夢迷生) said: "The plays *Dream of Handan* or *Dream of the South Branch* deploy Daoist and Buddhist allegories and liken the world to a dream.... However, [Tang Xianzu's] dream talk itself is a dream; my superfluous addition of illustrations, commentary, and annotations can be said to dream in pursuit of a dream (*meng zhong xun meng* 夢中尋夢). How far have I gone astray down this way!"[87]

Given that *Dream of Handan* was adapted from the famous eighth-century tale "The Story inside a Pillow" ("Zhen zhong ji" 枕中記), which depicts a failed examination candidate who converts to Daoism after being delivered through a dream of vanity, it is no surprise that Min Guangyu would invoke the trope of dreams at all levels, from his allegorical reading of the play to his self-reflection as a dreamer. What really intrigues us here is how he rearticulates dreamscapes in terms of woodblock printing. Unlike the character in the play who falls free through layers of the dream, Min finds himself stuck with the indelible gap between print as a dream and the playwright's vision of a dream that the printed edition with all its editorial apparatuses tried desperately to recover.[88] Min was not having a dream within a dream (*meng zhong meng* 夢中夢), from which he would be transported into a still bigger dream. His exact wording—"to dream in pursuit of a dream" (*meng zhong xun meng*)—refers to a rather different mode of spatiality, similar to the mode we traced in the scene "Pursuing the Dream" ("Xun meng") from Tang Xianzu's *The Peony Pavilion*. Du Liniang, in pursuit of a bygone dream, does not ultimately try to get back into that dream but attempts to "grasp things to the front of the soul's dream." Similarly, Min Guangyu's phrase, "to dream in pursuit of a dream" does not refer to a secondhand dream, an inferior reproduction (print) of a lost origin (theater); it bespeaks the very structure of theatricality.

Theatricality emerged at the intermediation between theater and print starting in the late sixteenth century. To take this argument one step further, theatricality is not merely an instance of what is now commonly called "multimedia" but the mode of spatiality that foregrounded the issues of media and intermediation to an unprecedented extent,[89] in contrast to older modes of spatiality in which mediation tends to be veiled or sidestepped. Permeating all boundaries, winds in effect short-circuit source and end, means and effect, vehicle and content. Distinctions among media—speech, music, dancing—are leveled by the outpouring of force that spills over from one medium to another without calling attention to the specificity of each.[90] The dreamscape, by contrast, hinges on a medium for deliverance (the shaman in the "Rhapsodies of the South," the music in temple theater, the Daoist deity in *Dream of the South Branch*, the Flower God in *The Peony Pavilion*); each dream is not substantial in and for itself but mediates still another layer of reality to which one is yet to be delivered; by deceit or through the Mahayana paradox, however, the dream substitutes itself for the real, drawing attention to its own opacity and splendor. In this threefold sense, the dreamscape could be regarded as the mode of spatiality that opens up the question of media per se. And yet the dreamscape, in its oscillation between dreams and reality, eventually obliterates their distinction and turns into a vanishing medium. Just as the Daoist and Buddhist mediums always camouflage themselves so as not to spoil the virtual reality that they conjure up in the dream, the dream itself not only initially passes for the real but is also ultimately substantiated as no less than the real in a typical move of the "two-truth" doctrine. Mediation is once again short-circuited when the medium conflates itself with what it mediates.

Theatricality persists on the question of media that was no sooner raised than prematurely foreclosed by the dreamscape. The front of the dream—the position where the spectator finds herself and tries to put things (including what is supposed to be her own emotion) in front of her—is an interface of the inside and the outside of the dream, reconnecting to the ungraspable yet accentuating the indelible abyss. If this modification of the dreamscape into the front of the dream historically arose from the intermediation between theater and print, then conversely speaking, the front of the dream as an interface structures the articulation and disjunction between different media and senses, formally enabling the issues of media and intermediation to emerge.[91]

5. GLOBALITY AND ANACHRONISM

This approach to theatricality as intermedial departs from the usual understanding of the term as the essence of theater. That understanding runs the risk of losing sight of historical specificity in associating theatricality with any and all dramatic forms, social ceremonies, cultural performances, or symbolic acts. The close association between theatricality and performativity has shifted critical attention to the perpetuation of social categories through corporeal praxis, but this proves relevant to any society.[92] History-oriented scholars in English and European studies have noted that it was in the eighteenth and nineteenth centuries that theatricality spread from the playhouse into book culture, political philosophy, gender relationships, lyrics, and novels.[93] But this too positions theater as a transhistorical essence awaiting dissemination. Only recently has the break between sixteenth-century theater and medieval drama in

Winds, Dreams, Theater 45

Europe been explored in the work of William Egginton, which historicizes theatricality as a defining spatial mode of being for modernity in contrast to the medieval Christian notion of "Real Presence." However, Egginton still regards theatricality as a matter of "the essence of theater" and theater as "a fundamental medium"—"much like print, cinema, or the digital image in their own ways"[94]—and therefore does not see theatricality as intermediation foregrounding the very issue of medium. Moreover, in broadly associating "Real Presence" with the nontheatrical nature of ancient societies across the globe, he leaves open the question how theatricality can be accounted for in a non-European context.

To answer this question, I have situated theatricality within the genealogy of emotion-realms. In early modern China, theatricality emerged as a new spatial mode of emotion following the ancient and medieval topoi of winds and dreamscapes. Theatricality arose when the dreamscape was reorganized around the "faceoff" dimension, turning the dreamer into the spectator. Comparable transformations can be investigated in the Western context, instanced by stories of the young Descartes in 1619, who dreamed of a whirlwind leaving his side in pain and, on another occasion, interpreted his own dream while still asleep.[95] If Zhuangzi deems all dream analyses impossible because there is no ground outside the dream, Descartes finds such outside ground as "a spectator,"[96] which allows him to objectify the dream and inaugurate a new science of rational knowledge.[97] Such linearity, strongly sensed in the Cartesian awakening, would be muddied on the Chinese side by the tendency of the old and the new to mingle. The anachronism of this juxtaposition often obscures the historical specificity of theatricality and leads to misrecognition.[98] In the Chinese context, this misrecognition goes in two directions: theatricality tends to be projected where it does not exist, or it is explained in terms of what it is not. In the former case, we misread other historical regimes of the spatiality of emotion as theatricality; in the latter, theatricality passes for those regimes. Sometimes both mistakes take place at once, as when theatricality is identified in the thirteenth-century play *The Injustice of Dou E* (*Gantian dongdi Dou E yuan* 感天動地竇娥冤) and is understood as the forces of human feeling whose "energy 'moves heaven and earth,' " as the Chinese title of that Yuan-dynasty play suggests.[99] When theatricality is invoked in studies of later periods (from the late Ming to the Qing), it tends to be absorbed into the question of whether one obsesses over or transcends the illusions of life as drama—a medieval motif that reverberates in sixteenth- and seventeenth-century discourse.[100] These accounts of theatricality—the former reminiscent of the spatial structure of winds, the latter of dreamscapes—are valid and insightful on their own terms. And yet, unless we sort out the distinct modes of spatiality in each historical period, we cannot capture the differences between early Chinese theater (mature in the twelfth century) and theatricality (a late sixteenth-century phenomenon), respectively. Only by tracing the historical emergence of the spectator as the distinct marker of theatricality can we understand the shift in the perception of "theater" from the Song-Yuan times to the late Ming-Qing period in terms of the spatiality of emotion.

And yet, the misrecognition of theatricality in the Chinese context should not be brushed aside; rather, it should be taken as a guide to the historical trajectory of theatricality in late imperial China. We need to explain why theatricality emerged in both China and Europe in the sixteenth century and, more important, ask whether there are divergences that have been obscured by global histories. It has been stressed that the global flow of silver from the New World to Europe and East Asia—half of which ended up in China—brought about the inception of a world system and global culture characterized by widespread trends of commodification.[101] In this context, the separation of the "spectator" as the primary entity in theatricality—which marks a rupture not only between the viewer and the display, but also between one person and others and ultimately between the feeling subject and its own feeling—underscores a general sense of estrangement introduced by the commodity form. In hindsight, it is tempting to see theatricality contribute to the global domination of capitalism and the system of nation-states toward the end of the millennium. But my account of theatricality in China, which traces a trajectory along which historical modes of spatiality of emotion interacted, highlights the ambiguities of anachronism at things' "origins" and loosens up the telos of modernity that has been firmly in place only in retrospect. We will see by the end of this study that even the seemingly decisive break from "Real Presence" that heralds the advent of theatricality in early modern Europe was plagued by similar issues of anachronism and misrecognition, which registered in the ambivalent term "theatricality" itself.[102]

Winds, Dreams, Theater 47

Refuting the teleological notion of "the sprouting of capitalism" circulated by mainland Chinese historiography, recent studies show that commodification in the late Ming (1550–1644) followed a different path than European capitalism, which led to an uneven composite of "the market economy relying on the prior operation" of the infra-economies that were self-sufficient and barter in local scale "to extract surpluses and redistribute them":

> Most villagers produced and consumed within infra-economies. Some of their product and some of what they consumed left and came in via the market economy ... but not to an extent that could enable the market economy to take over and eventually dissolve the infra-economy. The situation was different to some extent in Jiangnan, where the separation between production and consumption in weaving households pulled them away from their infra-economies. A writer in Huzhou exposes this separation when he puzzles over the popular late-Ming paradox that "Huzhou silk is all over the realm, yet there are people in Huzhou who live their lives without ever wearing a single thread of silk." ....
>
> China was not generating capitalism in the late Ming. That is not to say that China "failed" to generate capitalism. Rather, it created something else: an extensive market economy that used state communication networks to open links to local economies, organized rural and urban labor into consecutive production processes in certain regions without disrupting the rural household as the basic unit of production.[103]

In late sixteenth- to early seventeenth-century China, theatricality articulated a spatiality of emotion in which people were estranged from what they felt about others and themselves under the sway of the commodity, as some started to wonder why they hardly ever wore the silk they spun and weaved. This experience of alienation was an effect of the second commercial revolution, which featured the "routinization" of interregional commercial networking among towns and cities nationwide that had operated only on an ad hoc basis.[104] And yet, just as the general networking of the market economy emerged from the local infra-economies

48   *Winds, Dreams, Theater*

without entirely dissolving them, this new mode of spatiality coexisted with the older topoi of winds and dreamscapes.

6. SHOOTING THE INTERIOR

In this regard, *The Peony Pavilion* was pivotal not because it precipitated the triumph of the emotive interior but because it is a sedimentation of various modes of spatiality, which casts a new light on Tang Xianzu's explanation of the origin of drama that I cited at the beginning of the chapter: "Out of *qing* forms the dream; out of the dream forms drama." Too often reduced to a statement about the psychological genesis of art, Tang's remark can now be seen as a mapping schema that outlines a genealogy of emotion-realms: winds, dreamscapes, and theatricality, each of which presents a different mode of spatiality. Rather than anachronistically assuming the primacy of interiority, we need to ask how the spatiality of emotion at once fabricates and traverses this fiction of the interior. Interiority is not symmetrical to exteriority; rather, it is contingent on a specific mode of spatiality—namely, theatricality. The structure that estranges the postdreamer from her own emotion also creates an illusion that she is retiring to her inner self.[105] This interiorizing effect is attributable to the silent reading and private listening made possible by print.[106] Without grasping the whole picture of the spatiality and exteriority of emotion underlying these media practices, one could easily mistake partial phenomena of the interior for a self-sufficient interiority that is quintessential to humanity.

It is thanks to the mystifying power of the interior that the intriguing line from "Pursuing the Dream"—"Momentarily not allowing one to grasp things to the front of the soul's dream"—has been constantly misread and mis-staged. In the 2004 production (known as *The Peony Pavilion: A Youth Edition* [*Qingchun ban Mudan ting* 青春版牡丹亭]), the staging of the scene has the young actress Shen Fengying 沈豐英 appear meditative and self-absorbed: with her hands raised to her bosom, her head and eyes lowered, her gaze on her palms, she seems to be pursuing something inside her heart. Slowly turning until her back is to the audience, she glides to the back of the stage. Instead of approaching the front of the dream, this Liniang tries to sink deep inside the dream, per the English caption on the DVD: "How can I recapture what appeared *in* dream?" (see figures 1.2 and 1.3).

But in the 1986 opera film version (dir. Fang Ying 方熒), Zhang Jiqing 張繼青 (1938–), the veteran actress responsible for the art direction of the "Youth" production, takes an alternative approach to the same scene. She too raises her hands before her bosom when chanting

FIGURES 1.2 AND 1.3 The lure of the interior: 2004 stage production of the "Youth" edition of *The Peony Pavilion*.

the line, but she keeps her chin up and her eyes looking ahead, as if she is presenting something outwardly or scanning it in front of her. When she turns and glides across the garden set, she keeps her profile visible to the spectator. Not for one second does she suggest that she is engaged in soul-searching; she wanders back and forth but never slips away from what is in the front (see figures 1.4 and 1.5).

FIGURES 1.4 AND 1.5 Staying in front of the dream: Zhang Jiqing and the 1986 film *The Peony Pavilion*, courtesy of the China Film Archive.

One could contend that this contrast between the two performances is just an effect of the camerawork: in the 2004 video, the medium shot (see figure 1.2) calls attention to Liniang's downward-turned eyes and subtle facial expression, whereas the 1986 opera film includes one long shot on the actress's overall orientation to the foreground, in addition to a subtle swing of the camera that might have helped keep the actress's front view more visible. But, of course, that is exactly the point: the front of Liniang's dream takes the form of the silver screen, which has given theatricality a new lease on life in *the intermediation between theater and film.* Whether it is the fabrication of interiority or the insistence on the dream's front, it is an effect of the screen interfacing operatic acting and cinema apparatus, which are no longer separable.

How have we come to this point historically? Why does the history of theatricality tend to obscure itself, especially in the Chinese context? In what sense is this obscuration itself central to the genealogy of emotion-realms? These are the questions we will attempt to answer in the following chapters.

CHAPTER TWO

The Heart Beside Itself

A Genealogy of Morals

1. "*QING* OF SOURCE UNKNOWN" REPLAYED

In 1594, shortly before *The Peony Pavilion*, a court-crime tale appeared in *A Hundred Cases of Judge Bao* (*Bao Longtu pan baijia gong'an* 包龍圖判百家公案).[1] It depicts a widow, Madam Wang, whose chastity receives state recognition and then crumbles after she sees a public performance of *The Story of the Western Wing*:

> She was afflicted with some funny idea (*hai le niantou* 害了念頭). Her desire was stirred up, and her emotion became overwhelming (*yu dong qing sheng* 欲動情勝). She got home and nobody was around. Failing to hold back her emotion (*qing*), she happened to see her male pet monkey. . . . She instantly had her hands on its genitals so as to vent her desire (*yu* 欲). Unexpectedly, even animals share human nature (*ren xing* 人性). The monkey then had intercourse with Madam Wang. Since then they lived like husband and wife, but not one single neighbor noticed.

Then the legendary Judge Bao comes to town (though the historical figure Bao Zheng 包拯 lived almost two centuries before *The Western Wing* was written). Something about the widow incites his suspicion, but all he can find at her place is a monkey in colorful clothes, which he takes away for a few days. When the woman is summoned to collect the pet, it makes love to her right in the court. The judge announces his verdict with indignation: "You sure maintain a good code of chastity! How come you coupled with an alien kind (*yilei* 異類)?" With the archway honoring her chastity demolished and her property confiscated, Madam Wang commits suicide.

The early parts of the story are copied almost word for word from an old classical tale titled "Story of the Chaste" ("Jieyi zhuan" 節義傳, 1480s), a hagiography of a widow who committed suicide at her husband's funeral.² What distinguishes the 1594 retelling is the added scenario of theatergoing followed by bestiality, which some scholars have found distasteful.³ To me, the retold story foreshadows Tang Xianzu's account of drama and emotion in an unsettling way. According to Tang's "Inscription for the Temple of the Drama God, Master of the Pristine Fount, of Yihuang Prefecture," drama revitalizes emotions and bonds, so as to "arouse the husband-and-wife pleasure" (*dong fufu zhi huan* 動夫婦之歡). This affects not only humans but also "phoenixes, birds, beasts, and even barbarian spirits of Ba and Yu" 鳳凰鳥獸以至巴渝夷鬼,⁴ hence licensing the husband-wife relationship between the widow and her pet monkey.

Tang Xianzu's riddle about "*qing* of source unknown" becomes even more perplexing when we factor in this "alien kind." Judge Bao offers no verdict on whether the overwhelming emotion that "afflicts" the widow is exterior to her or a strange fit that has been latent within her. The only clue from the narrative is the line "unexpectedly, even animals share human nature," which suggests that the monkey acts according to its nature, which happens to be commensurate with that of humankind, and hence that emotion (*qing*) or desire (*yu*) resides within nature (*xing*), while theater is just an add-on. Ironically, this guarantee about the innermost nature of emotion hinges on a male monkey, "an alien kind." The otherness stressed in Judge Bao's verdict undercuts the commensurability between animals and humans that is presumed by the narrator and makes the case uncanny. On one hand, the male monkey's physical resemblance to man and its manlike *penetration*—the only sex act in premodern Chinese legal terms—is scandalous enough for Madam Wang to lose everything.⁵ On the other hand, the question remains whether this constitutes *adultery*, the charge usually raised against widows to deprive them of their property in late imperial China (though the story is set in the eleventh century) but applied only to humans.[6] The ambiguous nature of Madam Wang's crime is reflected in the story title: "A Verdict to Demolish the Monument of the Monkey Chaste Widow." Coupling with an alien species does not render Madam Wang unchaste; rather, it turns her into a very strange species, "Monkey Chaste Widow" (*hou jiefu* 猴節婦).

The pervasiveness of otherness problematizes the pet monkey's "nature." What is on trial is not adulterous passion,[7] but the innate status of emotion and the nature-emotion continuum. The problem is deepened by the close association between monkeys and drama, which, though archaic, became prominent in Ming-Qing drama criticism. Traceable to the Han dynasty, monkey performance became part of Tang official ritual,[8] but it was not until the late Ming that monkeys were singled out as *the* animal for performance (*xiwu* 戲物) because "they resemble humans."[9] Conversely, human actors were compared to monkeys. In Ming-Qing times, people became interested in the etymology of dramatic role types, and one theory, originating in the Yuan and cited by Zhu Quan 朱權 (1378–1448), was that two of the nine role types in *zaju* drama had names related to monkeys: *dan* 狚 (female monkey) and *nao* 猱 (a monkey subspecies).[10] In the 1580s, Zhou Qi 周祈 established the philological connection between *you* 優 (performer) and *nao* 獿 (a graphic variation of 猱), which reads as *mihou* 獼猴 (macaque) in the commentary to "The Record of Music."[11] These theories were recycled or amended throughout the Qing dynasty.[12]

Coming back to the 1594 court-crime story, if there is one thing monkeys share with humans, it is the impulse to playact. In this case, the monkey and the woman are not really husband and wife; they just live "*like* husband and wife." By the same token, Judge Bao is not really trying a case of adultery; rather, he is punishing the widow *as if* he were judging one of those cases. At issue is not the spontaneous flow of emotion out of nature but the performance of emotion through absurd role-playing—a chaste widow playing an infatuated wife of a monkey and an indignant judge trying what hardly counts as a legal case—featuring a monkey in colorful clothes.

Perhaps it is not a coincidence that the Qingyuan God of Yihuang Drama to whom Tang Xianzu paid tribute is none other than Erlang

The Heart Beside Itself 55

Shen 二郎神, worthy rival of the most famous monkey figure in China, the Monkey King Sun Wukong 孫悟空 from the sixteenth-century novel *The Journey to the West* (*Xiyou ji* 西遊記), of which the earliest extant edition was published by Shide tang 世德堂 just two years before *A Hundred Cases*. It is not surprising that Erlang Shen, as protean as Monkey in their elaborate duel—during which both transform into various animals and objects—would be worshipped as a divinity of playacting.¹³

Imposture does not pertain to the late sixteenth century, however. Its verbal marker, *qiao* 喬, appears in lost Yuan *zaju* play titles such as *The Black Whirlwind Plays the Judge* (*Heixuanfeng qiao zuoya* 黑旋風喬坐衙) and *The Black Whirlwind Plays the Teacher* (*Heixuanfeng qiao jiaoxue* 黑旋風喬教學).¹⁴ The latter was written by Gao Wenxiu 高文秀 (fl. 1251), whose play *The Black Whirlwind's Double Exploits* (*Heixuanfeng shuang xian gong* 黑旋風雙獻功) features the bandit hero "the Black Whirlwind" Li Kui's 李逵 hilarious masquerade as a country bumpkin.¹⁵ These three plays about Li's imposture found their way into the early sixteenth-century vernacular novel *Water Margin* (*Shuihu zhuan* 水滸傳).¹⁶ Focusing on the "trope of theater" in *Water Margin* and *The Journey to the West*, Mei Chun proposes to "broaden the concept of theatricality" beyond drama genres to examine how what he calls "the theatrical novel" "borrow[s] heavily from the creative usage of theater and its premises." This approach takes the novel as the reflexive extension of theatricality, which it defines in terms of two constitutive elements: first, "playacting, masquerades, metamorphoses, and other theatrical events"; second, "the perceptual dynamics of the viewer/viewed relationship."¹⁷ In this context, the sixteenth-century novels could be said to manifest, proliferate, and reflect upon the essential structure of theater already underlying early dramatic versions of both stories.

Mei goes beyond conventional source and adaptation issues by scrutinizing how the deep structure of theater informs fictional discourse. I would like to take Mei's findings one step further in order to rethink the historical formation of theatricality per se. Instead of viewing theatricality as abstracted from theater and applicable to other domains, and instead of treating the novel as a vehicle for what we have assumed about theater, we need to historicize theatricality by, first of all, taking note of varied relationships between novels and drama. The early-sixteenth-century novel *Water Margin* stands in closer kinship to—and hence is more influenced by—a larger number of drama antecedents than does *The Journey to the West*.[18] Rather than being "theatricalized" in accordance with preceding dramatic works, the latter heralded and contributed to the advent of theatricality, which was unknown in the early theater. In this sense, *The Journey to the West* in the 1592 Shide tang edition better serves our purpose to look beyond continuity and resemblance and uncover what pertains to the rise of theatricality as the new mode of the spatiality of emotion in the late sixteenth century. "Playacting, masquerades, metamorphoses, and other theatrical events" did continue to characterize theater and inform vernacular novels, but their meaning was modified in the context of the defining feature of theatricality, namely, spectatorship. What Mei calls "the perceptual dynamics of the viewer/viewed relationship" is not inherent in all forms of theater, embodied in "Water Margins" *zaju* plays, and then inherited by the novel, but is rather a new spatial configuration accompanying practices of novel reading (and the reading of play texts as if they were novels) in the flourishing print culture.

The belated birth of the spectator at the intersection between theater and print will be further explored in the next chapter. Here I propose to take the theatrical trope of the monkey as a point of entry, not only because the humanoid species emerged as the trope for playacting during the 1580s but, more important, because this trope came to intimate playacting only when, in a lesser known manner, it started signifying the spectator as the central category for theatrical performance. To go back to our 1590s court-crime story, the insertion of the monkey that plays a "husband" turns the case into a kind of performance, and it would be tempting to ascribe this heavy sense of playacting to the long-accumulated dramatic repertoire that *A Hundred Cases* draws on.[19] What makes the monkey a trope of theatricality, however, is not its ingenious enactment of emotion and desire as "human nature" but the way it constitutes *spectatorship as a position of alterity*, marked by the Monkey Chaste Widow who has watched *The Western Wing*. A powerful performance that radiates its influence to myriad beings as well is nothing new,[20] but projecting the spectator as an uncanny Other (in the form of a strange species) to the theater suggests the transfiguration from the dreamscape to theatricality. Whereas metamorphoses (status, gender, species) are at the heart of the dreamscape—or, more precisely, coterminous with the path of the dreamer through layers of dreams[21]—the Monkey Chaste Widow as the spectator traces a new liminal sphere at the border of theater.

In this chapter I aim to unpack all the issues encapsulated in the Monkey Chaste Widow case. What was the historical trajectory through which emotion was juxtaposed with, opposed to, or absorbed by terms such as "desire" and "nature"? Does this trajectory do more than tell us about social mores aiming to moderate, regulate, displace, disarm, appropriate, and expropriate emotion? Can we go underneath these moral didactics, taking their apparently hackneyed messages as telling signals about historical inflexions of the exteriority and spatiality of emotion? How is the union between emotion and nature undermined by theatricality, which posits us as spectators confronting emotion as our theatrical double? How did theatricality emerge not as the essential feature of theater but, paradoxically, appear even earlier in a vernacular novel than its drama antecedents?

I will start by examining traces of exteriority in early and medieval intellectual history and looking at how various modes of spatiality of emotion gave rise to historically specific ethico-ontological crises. The way eleventh- and twelfth-century Neo-Confucians dealt with these crises led to a complete acknowledgment of exteriority, which became an acute problem in the eyes of their sixteenth-century counterparts. As a counterreaction, philosophy and religion in the mid- and late Ming tried to exorcise exteriority in the name of the holistic "Heart" in which emotion was supposedly integrated within nature. This holistic project, however, was complicated at the meta-religious level by syncretism, which simultaneously conceals and reveals discrepancies at the "Heart" of the Three Teachings. As an allegory of syncretism, I will argue, *The Journey to the West* reveals exteriority in the indelible gap between one heart and its double and ultimately between the two hearts and the spectator. In this vein, the seventeenth-century novella *A Supplement to The Journey to the West* (*Xiyou bu* 西遊補) further highlights the figure of the spectator excluded from the stage performance of his own dream, ushering in sympathy—imagining oneself in another's position in order to feel—as a moral and aesthetic concept in China.

2. ANXIETY AND ANNOYANCE

The notion of *qing* as inborn is a timeworn one. Xunzi 荀子 (313–238 BCE) defines *qing* as "the likes, dislikes, delight, anger, sorrow, and joy of nature." According to the *Book of Rites* (*Liji* 禮記), people are capable of *qing* without learning it. An excavated text from the Guodian 郭店 tomb (late fourth century BCE) testifies to this received tradition: "*qing* is born from nature" (*qing sheng yu xing* 青[情]生於眚[性]).[22] And yet the more general usage of the word *qing* in early Chinese philosophy points to the first signs of exteriority. A. C. Graham's observation that in pre-Han literature *qing* often means reality and essence rather than subjective sentiment is highly suggestive, but he goes so far as to claim that unlike in the Neo-Confucian usage from the Song (960–1279) onward, *qing* even in Xunzi does not bear the meaning of "passions."[23] Anthony Yu retorts that *qing* is more imbued with *yu* (desire) in *Xunzi* than Graham thinks, and the two terms are even interchangeable.[24] The crux of the question remains unresolved: How can the word *qing* refer both to reality core and to emotional states? To bridge these two meanings, Chad Hansen renders *qing* as both "reality input" and "reality response."[25] This interpretation seems to vacillate deceptively—it even defeats Hansen's attempt to establish "a single, unified meaning"[26]—but it captures the ambiguity inherent in this Chinese character, namely that innateness is marked by irreducible exteriority.

Inspired by Hansen's explication of *qing* as "reality response," Xu Gang 徐鋼 puts forth "the materiality of *qing*," emphasizing that the Chinese notion of emotion focuses more on things (*wu* 物) or objects (*keti* 客體) from without that incite emotional feedbacks, whereas Western (Cartesian) philosophy tends to see emotion as originating in human subjectivity and extending to the outside world only in a secondary sense.[27] Similarly, Curie Virag discusses how classical texts like "Record of Music" ("Yueji" 樂記) emphasize the "externality of things" that set the heart in motion.[28] However, as I argued in chapter 1, stressing the stimuli from outside does not displace my response *from within*. The materiality of *qing* thus lends itself to the assertion that "man is not in fact a passive object of external stimuli but plays an active role in selecting and appraising the external world."[29] In contrast, the indeterminacy of *qing* as both input and feedback overturns the subjective locus of emotional

The Heart Beside Itself 59

response: both the input and the response itself should be searched for *outside the subject*. What is exterior is not that which incites emotion, but the spatiality of the emotion-realm per se.

The exteriority and spatiality of emotion thus cannot be reduced to the externality and materiality of things. The former, however, tends to be reified into and covered up by the latter in traditional religio-philosophical discourses, which often render emotion as an ethical issue on account of its susceptibility to things. To Zhuangzi's call for self-forgetting in following "the transformation of things," his disciples added a proviso against emotional change along with things.[30] The same dilemma later prompted Wang Bi's 王弼 (226–249) maxim that "the sage's *qing* responds to things without being implicated with them" (*shengren zhi qing, ying wu er bu lei yu wu* 聖人之情, 應物而不累於物).[31] Ji Kang 嵇康 (223–262) likewise advised that "*qing* be not tied to what is desired" (*qing bu xi yu suo yu* 情不繫於所欲).[32] Recoiling from emotion's external entanglement (which ultimately reduces *qing* to *yu* or desire, the most problematic term in Chinese moral philosophy), such didactic remarks protected the endangered interior. They should not be taken as suppressions of material desire, though. At a deeper level, they arose from the ontological ambiguity pertaining to the ancient mode of the spatiality of emotion—according to which human subjects were constituted and treated as "patients" by pervasive, pathological winds permeating bodies and souls they formed, as perceived in Warring-State self-cultivation and Han poetics and medicine. Such ontological ambiguity, which underlay and traversed the internal-external division, was only secondarily expressed as anxiety about external things. While anxiety presumes something external to be worried out, it was the source of the anxiety—the ontological ambiguity characteristic of the topos of winds—that produced and redrew the precarious boundaries in the first place.

However, we can catch a glimpse of the incipient dreamscape as early as the fourth century BCE in Zhuangzi. The ancient anxiety arising from the total immersion of winds would linger, but a way out of it through the "deliverance" dimension of the dreamscape was suggested in the early medieval era, as articulated in Ji Kang's "Treatise of Music without Emotion" ("Sheng wu ai le lun" 聲無哀樂論).[33] Before Ji, the ancients had premised that music harbored intrinsic emotional values;

more precisely, music itself was regarded as a motion of the same nature as the motion it produced in the listener's heart. Such a premise of resonance and resemblance can be found in the "On Music" ("Yue lun" 樂論) by Xunzi and the "Record of Music" in the *Book of Rites*, the two sources that deeply informed the "Great Preface" to the *Book of Songs*. By contrast, Ji Kang boldly maintains that music is neither sad nor delightful but only brings out what listeners harbor within themselves. He calls the ultimate nature of music—that is, its emotive neutrality due to its non-resemblance to any motions it causes—"Harmony" (*he* 和). Whereas ordinary listeners tend to fall into their inner commotion, a superior man (in the superior position of the performer) stays in Harmony that can nourish his life.[34] In place of the affective winds found in the "Great Preface," Ji invokes the winds called "flutes of Heaven" (*tianlai* 天籟) from Zhuangzi, the universal force that animates myriad things in the world but allows them to be themselves, just as holes, openings, and orifices of different shapes in the wilderness yield their own distinct sounds when airstreams move through them. While Zhuangzi takes this "leaving things to themselves" as the unimposing principle of the Way (*Dao* 道) that allows for diversity, Ji Kang sees it as the reason why emotion is that which individual subjects take upon themselves rather than as ascribable to music per se.[35]

By emptying out the emotionality of winds, Ji Kang seems to narrow the spatiality of emotion down to a matter of the psychological interior. But such an interior is a rhetorical construct to be overridden and dissolved under the valorized notion of Harmony. The legacy of Ji Kang does not lie in this shadowy appearance of the interior but in the claim that music, itself emotionally detached, can paradoxically deliver human subjects through various emotions. Ji's way out of the anxiety of winds, however, delivers us into an even trickier ontological ambiguity. As Ronald Egan argues, the Tang dynasty was fascinated (and also deeply annoyed) by a problematic in which a spiritually enlightened figure (usually a Buddhist reverend), in his absolute tranquility, without a trace of emotional disturbance, would play a tune that subjected the listener to an abrupt shift in mood—exemplified by Han Yu's 韓愈 (768–824) "Listening to Reverend Ying Play the Zither" ("Ting Ying Shi tan qin" 聽穎師彈琴)—while the ideal of transcending passions with music remained an alternative vein of the discourse.[36] A detached medium delivering a subject into and out of emotion or from one mood to another—whether it was a zither player in a musical performance or an immortal magician in deliverance tales—is a major characteristic of the medieval dreamscape, which was inherited by the musical troupe in Song-Yuan theater. Laid over the ancient "winds" stratum in the spatiality of emotion, the topos of dreamscape therefore does not eliminate suspicion about emotion being implicated by things; rather, anxiety about being sickened by pathological winds was duplicated by and transplanted into the new annoyance about being transported into torrents of passion only to realize that they were devoid of substance. The medieval idea of unraveling the debilitating entanglement between things and emotion should be understood in terms of this sedimentation of the topoi of emotion.

The layering of various modes of spatiality, however, complicated the whole project of disentanglement in the Song dynasty. Owing to the ontological ambiguity intrinsic to the dreamscape (in which the same medium aroused deceptive emotions and served as the means of transcendence), the apparently more intuitive tactic of disentanglement—which involved displacing emotion from things to the subject—was counterweighted by a contradictory operation in the opposite direction, which suggested that emotion be thoroughly desubjectivized in order to follow the natural way of things. These contested tactics were presented within eleventh-century Neo-Confucianism. Whereas Zhang Zai 張載 (1020–1077) was worried about the difficulty in securing one's inner nature (*ding xing* 定性) to avoid its "entanglement with external things" (*lei yu waiwu* 累於外物), Cheng Hao 程顥 (1032–1085) retorted by suggesting something close to the total relegation of *qing* to externality: "As for the constancy of heaven and earth, their mind covers myriad things so that they have no mind; as for the constancy of the sages, their emotions follow myriad affairs so that they have no emotion. . . . That is why the sages' joy and anger are *not tied to their hearts but to things.*"[37]

The twelfth century witnessed a composite articulation of these previously irreconcilable positions in the work of Zhu Xi 朱熹 (1130–1200), who assigned emotion to the side of things, as Cheng Hao had done, but subsumed emotion under the heart, as Zhang Zai did. Zhu adopted Zhang's aphorism—"the heart integrates nature and emotion" (*xin tong* xing qing 心統性情)—but shifted its focus to the hierarchical relationship between nature and emotion.[38] Employing terms from the *Doctrine of the Mean* (*Zhongyong* 中庸), Zhu dichotomized nature as the innate "immanence" (*weifa* 未發) of pure goodness and emotion as the "issuance" (*yifa* 已發) of feedback upon contact with external things.[39] The thinly disguised hierarchy of nature over emotion inevitably splits the heart that is supposed to integrate them into "the heart of the Way" (*daoxin* 道心) and "the human heart" (*renxin* 人心),[40] which correspond to the division between pure inherent nature and fallible external emotion. In short, Zhu Xi gave up the effort to untie emotion from things, not because he believed things (such as music) could transcend emotion but because marginalizing emotion by putting it in an external position allowed him to preserve a primordial state of untouchable inner nature—a conceptual fiction that Zhang Zai had stopped short of out of concern that even nature could be entangled with external things. The price Zhu Xi paid was to acknowledge the externality of emotion as the ineradicable underside of the highly distilled and abstracted notion of nature. This untouchable nature—his castle in the air—was sustainable only when emotion, conceived as external, took over all the burden of entanglement with things.

Only in this context can we understand why Zhu Xi gave a rather idiosyncratic reading of a phrase from the *Doctrine of the Mean*, *ti qunchen* 體群臣 (to incorporate the flock of officials), as "to postulate one's body in another's position in order to know his heart" (*she yi shen chu qi di yi cha qi xin* 設以身處其地以察其心).[41] The point of Zhu's reinterpretation, which obviously does not follow the original wording, lies in his technical understanding of the "heart." A courtier's heart cannot be immediately known not because it is hidden in his innermost self—nature, while deposited inside an individual, is shared by all others—but because part of his heart, his "emotion," is determined by its attachment to things, and hence has to be sought outside the person—in the circumstances with which this person is entangled. Zhu's rereading of the *Doctrine of the Mean* only makes sense with this notion of the heart, which entails the extreme exteriorization of emotion as a peculiar strategy to reconcile the anxiety pertinent to the topology of winds about being harmed by things and the ambiguous imperative to follow "the transformation of things" pertinent to the regime of dreamscapes.

Zhu Xi reduced the meaning of exteriority to an entanglement with external things instead of investigating the spatial structure that enabled the entanglement with things. Still, his daring move of leaving emotion "external" troubled thinkers during the second half of the Ming. Detractors of Zhu Xi from the early sixteenth century onward attempted to overcome this externality by incorporating emotion into the core of the moral subject. They did so by disavowing the internal/external dichotomy characteristic of Song thought, which was now deemed artificial and flawed. Wang Yangming 王陽明 (1472–1528), for instance, rejected this dichotomy by way of a chiasmic rhetoric—"immanence within issuance" (*weifa zai yifa zhi zhong* 未發在已發之中), "issuance within immanence" (*yifa zai weifa zhi zhong* 已發在未發之中)—which abolishes spatiotemporal differentiation in the name of "the holistic entity of Oneness" (*wu qianhou neiwai hunran yiti* 無前後內外渾然一體).[42] By the same token, Wang disclaimed the doubleness of the Heart in the name of "Essential Oneness" (*jingyi* 精一), arguing that the two Hearts were two sides of Oneness.[43]

Yet this Ming "progress" toward eliminating the hierarchical dyad is deceptive. More than three centuries earlier, Zhu Xi himself maintained that the Heart is the "holistic entity" (*hunlun yiwu* 渾淪一物) "integrating what is before (nature as immanence) and after (emotion as issuance)" (*tong qianhou er yan* 統前後而言),[44] and that the heart of the Way and the human heart are two states of the same heart.[45] If Zhu Xi failed to seamlessly gloss over the rupture he had introduced between nature and emotion, so did Wang Yangming. According to his admirer Liu Zongzhou 劉宗周 (1578–1645), Wang's critique of the division into two hearts repeated the defense Zhu Xi had preemptively put up,[46] and Wang's language of chiasmus, which embeds immanence and issuance in each other, was a clumsy effort that set nature and emotion farther apart. However, Liu himself reiterated chiasmic reconciliation by placing the issuance of emotion at the immanent origin of nature and vice versa and concluding that both were "of one nature" (*hun shi yixing* 渾是一性).[47]

The repetition of Zhu Xi's dilemma in Ming thinkers' supposed "solution" is symptomatic. Their invocations of holistic Oneness might seem similar to my critique of the internal-external split, but what we have here are two opposite approaches. In traversing emotion's opposition to landscape or things, I have posited exteriority as the spatiality of emotion, which underlies the production of internal-external boundaries and (as we glimpsed in chapter 1) the temporalization of past, present, and future.[48] In contrast, by ridding itself of any spatiotemporal differentiations, the holistic Oneness that Zhu and his detractors pursued was a denial of spatiality per se. Ironically, given its impulse to resolve emotion's external entanglement, the holistic entity could not help but establish itself spatially in the interior when Liu Zongzhou subsumed emotion as a property of nature and then subsumed both nature and emotion as properties of the Heart.[49]

From Zhu Xi to Wang Yangming to Liu Zongzhou, the repeated assertion of this holistic Oneness does not constitute a return to a nondualistic origin,[50] which some scholars view as the essential character of Chinese culture.[51] Nor does it present a humanistic progression toward legitimate emotion and desire, or, conversely, an increasingly cunning strategy of sanitizing and "containing" human emotion at the cost of carnal desire.[52] The history of emotion from the standpoint of exteriority invalidates the notion that natural, essential emotion and desire await containment or liberation. The problem identified in my revisionist account is not that this union between emotion and nature fails to legitimate carnal desire as the basic human instinct; rather, what is on trial is the holistic totality per se, which assimilates emotion (and sometimes desire as well) into nature by repeatedly disavowing the exteriority and spatiality of emotion, only to reconfirm it time and again.[53]

Paradoxically, Qing-dynasty fiction went in the opposite direction, bipolarizing pure emotion and carnal desire and condemning the latter in the former's name.[54] Rather than dismissing this kind of fictional work as conservative or repressive, I regard it as a site where the holistic integration of nature, emotion, and desire could potentially break down, due less to the idealistic, liberating power of literature than to the doubling and alienating effect of theatricality as the mode of the spatiality of emotion in early modern China. Later on I explore how that effect manifested itself as the oft-misunderstood phenomenon of "containment" in late seventeenth- and eighteenth-century novels.[55] But for now, let us examine how, from the late sixteenth to the first half of the seventeenth century, theatricality emerged in the centripetal figure of the "Heart," which turned out to be not one recalcitrant monkey but two or more.

3. TWO HEARTS AND THE SPECTATOR

In this regard, one can recognize the peculiar status of *The Journey to the West*; the earliest extant edition was published by the Shide tang in 1592, six years before *The Peony Pavilion*. Recent research confirms that this Shide tang edition is actually a "reprint" of an earlier version that was transcribed and printed between 1552 and 1586 or a bit later.[56] Even before this final formation of the novel, the legendary pilgrimage of the Tang-era monk Tripitaka (602–664) to India had been evolving into a syncretic allegory of the Three Religions or Teachings (*sanjiao* 三教)—Buddhism, Confucianism, and Daoism—starting in the early sixteenth century.[57] The Three Religions converge in a shared concern about cultivating the heart/mind (*xin* 心 refers to both "heart" and "mind," which are interchangeable in Chinese) and attaining the state of *yixin* 一心 or one-heartedness. Monkey's exile from and return to his master Tripitaka's pilgrimage has thus been read as a Mencian admonition to "search for your lost heart." But this reading has first to be based on the Buddhist (and later also Daoist) expression of "the Heart Monkey and the Will Horse" (*xinyuan yima* 心猿意馬), signifying wantonness in need of restraint.[58] One-heartedness is not just the didactic content but the very form for the Three-in-One syncretic teaching to hold itself together through the concentric trope, as in the thirteenth-century notion "Three Religions of One Heart" (*sanjiao yixin* 三教一心).[59] The expression takes a slightly different form, "the Oneness of the Three Religions" (*sanjiao gui yi* 三教歸一), in the Cart Slow Kingdom episode (chapter 47) when Monkey liberates the Buddhist monks from three evil Daoist masters and advises the king to "revere the monks, revere also the Daoist, and take care to nurture the talented."[60]

This Oneness of the Heart—which, as we have seen, precariously upholds the interior status of emotion within nature in the late Ming—is at once maintained and complicated in the syncretic context of the novel. The figure of the One Heart that we have seen integrate emotion with nature also brings the Three Religions together. In both cases, exteriority is nullified by a totalizing system. In the words of Lin Zhao'en 林兆恩 (1517–1598), the founder of the Three-in-One Teaching (*Sanyijiao* 三一教):

Confucius's heart is the All-Inclusive Majestic Heart (*diwang wuwai zhi xin* 帝王無外之心). You said: "I am a Confucian, and therefore keep distance from the Daoist and the Buddhist, for they are not Confucian." . . . Even if you can fulfill the name of Confucian, you make only one of a tripod's three legs. We can call this a regime that barely secures one single corner of the territories. This is definitely incomparable to the Emperor's Great Unification without exteriority, or the immensity of Confucius's Heart.[61]

Sixteenth-century syncretism is a translation practice with a dubious sense of power relations. It renders other religions in the master language of one's own persuasion, which is posited as the privileged anchorage point,[62] the "Heart" that synecdochally represents the whole.[63] Individual elements incorporated into a centripetal structure are deprived of their own value and imbued with "higher" allegorical meaning.

Ironically, throughout *The Journey to the West*, this centrifugal totalization into the Oneness of the Heart is plagued by multiplicity, as emblematized by the key reference to the Buddhist scripture *Mahāprajñā-pāramitāhr-daya Sūtra*, or in Chinese, *Mohebore boluomiduo xinjing* 摩訶般若波羅蜜多心經. The sūtra is first mentioned in chapter 19, where Tripitaka learns from the Crow's Nest Chan Master this core text for cultivating the heart (*JW* 1:389–91/220–21). Hilariously, the narrator adopts a short version of the sūtra's title: *Duoxin jing* 多心經, which literally means the "Sūtra of Many Hearts (or Mindfulness)."[64] Against the grain of the Oneness of the Heart, the novel is obsessed with the dark power of multitude, as seen in the Young Master City (*Xiaozi cheng* 小子城) episode (chapters 78–79). A heart-eating monster demands to see Tripitaka's "black heart" (*heixin* 黑心), not realizing that Tripitaka is actually Monkey in disguise. The monster is stupefied by the malevolent hearts of all varieties that emerge from Monkey's sliced-open chest:

> A red heart, a white heart, a yellow heart, an avaricious heart, a greedy heart, an envious heart, a petty heart, a competitive heart, an ambitious heart, a scornful heart, a murderous heart, a vicious heart, a fearful heart, a cautious heart, a perverse heart, a nameless obscure heart, and all kinds of wicked hearts. There was, however, not one single black heart! (*JW* 4:50/900–901)

The Heart Beside Itself

What troubles the monster most is failing to find "one single black heart" that would have served as an anchoring point under which all other innumerable and incommensurable hearts could be subsumed.⁶⁵ Overwhelmed, the monster yells in despair: "This is a monk of many hearts [*duoxin*]!" (*JW* 4:50/900).

Throughout the novel, the "Many Heart" Monkey troubles the notion of Oneness thanks to his magical ability to multiply himself and impersonate others. He himself is haunted by an uncanny double in the fake Monkey episode (chapters 56–58), which dramatizes how the Oneness of the Heart breaks down, since emotion cannot seamlessly be assimilated. In chapter 57, Tripitaka disowns Monkey after the latter brutally slays a thief, but the abrupt expulsion leads to "rough emotion" (*qing wu shun* 情無順), according to the narrator. The abandoned Monkey, with "vapors of frustration pent up" (*manhuai menqi* 滿懷悶氣), brings his complaint to the Bodhisattva and "vents anger from his heart" (*xinzhong nufa* 心中怒發) at the Boy of Goodly Wealth (*JW* 3:91-92/656, translation modified). Then on the other side, as in a cinematic montage, another "Monkey" who looks and behaves exactly the same suddenly appears in front of the Tripitaka and similarly vents his anger (*fanu shengchen* 發怒生瞋, *JW* 3:95/658). The narrative suggests that the impostor is called forth by certain erratic emotions, but does it follow that the uncanny double should simply be reduced to Monkey's inner state of mind? Should we explain away the double as an embodiment of Monkey's frustration and anger? Does the entire confrontation between the two Heart Monkeys really boil down to the selfsame Oneness of the Heart? Is it just another parable about the emotion-nature continuum, as per a maxim in the same chapter: "Feelings and nature are formally the same" (*qing xing yuanlai yi bingxing* 情性原來一裏形, *JW* 3:94/658)?

It is ultimately the Buddha who, at the end of the episode, rejects such a holistic reading. Instead of ascribing the fake Monkey to the inner commotion of one's own heart, the Buddha discloses its identity as the "sixth-eared macaque" (*liu'er mihou* 六耳獼猴, *JW* 3:116/673). As we recall, by the late sixteenth century, *nao* or *mihou* (macaque) had become associated with *you* (actor) and turned into a theatrical figure. Rather than the product of emotional vapor emitted from Monkey's heart, the sixth-eared macaque is a talented actor performing emotion on Monkey's behalf. The macaque's acting talent establishes him as the troupe leader/director when he starts training other monkeys to play Tripitaka and his other disciples. With his troupe, he aspires to perform the mission of fetching scriptures, thus turning the pilgrimage into a performance tour (*JW* 3:100–101/662). This adept impostor manages to get onstage at a perfect time and perform flawlessly not because it is generated from Monkey's emotive interior, but because it has sensitive ears that can gather information (*shan lingyin* 善聆音, *JW* 116/673). Monkey's *qi* is not the substance to which the double owes its being, but a message carried by the "informing wind" (*tongfeng* 通風) into the ears of the macaque. In contrast to a holistic cosmos in which every boundary is permeated by winds, this is a world of asymmetric communication with the Other, in the sense that the sixth-eared macaque knows all about Monkey, not vice versa. As an eavesdropper, the macaque remains forever an outsider, whose status is testified to by the Buddhist idiom "the dharma is not transmitted to the sixth ear [which means the third party]" (*fa bu chuan liu'er* 法不傳六耳) (*JW* 3:387n. 7).

Thanks to this exteriority, the monkey impostor figures as a radical Other irreducible to what is inside one's mind. As an uncanny double, the sixth-eared macaque remains the anarchic Other in proximity to Monkey's archaic origin. However proximate they are to each other, Monkey can never claim his double as his own; hence his failure to remember the macaque whose identity he actually should have "recalled." The sixth-eared macaque is reminiscent of one of Monkey's six monster brothers, who was named "the Macaque King" (*Mihou wang* 獼猴王) back in the rebellious years in Flower-Fruit Mountain (*JW* 1:139/31). The Macaque King's other agnomen—"the Great Sage of Informing Wind" (*Tongfeng dasheng* 通風大聖; *JW* 2:223/471, translation modified)—suggests that its ears are as good as the sixth-eared macaque's at information gathering.

Despite all these archaic or anachronistic traces, however, Monkey never comes to recognize the sixth-eared macaque as his sworn brother. The forgetting that accompanies proximity to the Other prevents the Other from being recuperated into the "self-possession, sovereignty, *arche*" of the Same.[66] Against the temptation of solipsism, the figure of doubling underlies the impossibility of assimilating even what is given in the vicinity. Not simply "self-splitting," doubling in its radicality testifies to the secondariness of the "self" or "ego"; put differently, the

The Heart Beside Itself 69

phenomenon of the double is not a projection from one's interior but an encroaching Other from without that is never fully encompassed and comprehended by the self. Instead of exorcizing the double as none other than oneself, we should consider the Heart Monkey himself as defined and shaped by doubling. The violent irruption of the double in the false Monkey episode is no accident; it is the dramatization of the "normative" state. Neither would the doubling really be eliminated in the wake of the sixth-eared macaque's death, because Monkey, as we already know, flaunts his power of doubling others on numerous occasions.

Hence the alleged unity of emotion and nature and the apparent denigration of "Two Hearts (or Minds)" should not be taken as a given, despite the explicit comments made by the narrator. In chapter 58, titled "Two Minds cause disorder in the great cosmos" (*JW* 3: 104/665), a "testimonial poem" seems to reinforce this sort of value judgment. It begins with the line "If one has two minds, disasters he'll breed," and for a remedy it advises people to "learn of no mind in the gate of Chan" (*JW* 3: 113/671). In the late Ming context, the Chan Buddhist language of "no mind" (*wuxin* 無心) could be translated into the Neo-Confucian teaching of singlemindedness.[67] Yet the noncoincidence between "empty" (*wu*) and "one" (*yi*) immediately impedes a smooth transition. The effect of translation is not to anchor the meaning at the One Heart but to remove the very ground the translation relies on, namely the totality of "Oneness." If a "double" is a superfluous entity relative to the authentic one, what this testimonial poem really testifies to is that the ultimate double is the "Oneness" itself. It is in the translational relation to the *zero* degree of "no mind" that the very *One*ness of the "single mind" turns into a *surplus*, a supplement rather than the originary.[68]

The testimonial poem seems to suggest that doubleness can be wiped away by asserting the Chan Buddhist teaching of negating the mind, but the verse does not end there. Its last line negates the negation by invoking the susceptibility of "Emptiness" to ceaseless translation,[69] which now drives toward another language: "Let the babe and holy embryo be formed thus quietly" (*jingyang ying'er jie shengtai* 靜養嬰兒結聖胎; *JW* 3: 113/671, translation modified). Emptiness, in its very gesture of negation, thus serves to open up a translational space for the Daoist signifiers, which not only displace the focus from the heart to the kidneys[70] but also shed new light on what follows in the narrative.

Foreseeing the two battling Pilgrims approaching, the Buddha interrupts his "Emptiness-Form" (*kong se* 空色) preaching and says to the congregation: "You are all of one mind, but take a look at two Minds in competition and strife arriving here" (*rudeng jushi yixin, qiekan erxin jingdou erlai ye* 汝等俱是一心, 且看二心競鬥而來也; *JW* 3: 113/672). Apparently, Emptiness and Oneness are privileged in opposition to doubleness. Yet, *the very pairing* of Emptiness and Oneness is neither empty nor single but blatantly redoubled. "Emptiness," insofar as it is a signifier being *preached/related* to another signifier (namely, the audience, the "one mind"), has *formally* pronounced its own doubleness. In terms of narrative and sentence structure, the "one mind" that is supposed to occupy the vantage point of seeing metonymically lapses into the "two Minds" and shifts its attention from the preaching of Emptiness.

From Emptiness through One into Two, we see a Daoist course of multiplication—not Laozi's mystical birth of beings out of the Dao, but the inevitable differentiation resulting from language lamented by Zhuangzi. The latter observes that the "One" entails both the discursive emptiness (that is, *wuyan* 無言)—as words become unnecessary in front of the "One"—*and* its own ineffaceability as a signifier that defeats this ideal state of emptiness, for the very mention of "One" already triggers the bifurcation into Two, wherefrom the Three and Multitude are irrevocably generated.[71] The immediacy of emptiness takes place only in the realm of means and mediation.[72] Can we finally dissolve the entire *Journey to the West* episode into such a Daoist allegory? Zhuangzi right away resorts to things' nature and yearns for a halt to the proliferation of language,[73] but the heavy trafficking of words in their "Journey" among the Three Teachings hurls any allegorical closure ever back into translation.[74]

Yet there is another direction in which this allegory of syncretic translation can be read. In the Buddha's preaching of emptiness to the single-minded audience that is distracted by the spectacle of the Two Hearts in combat, this allegory actually takes the form of a theater of doubling, which becomes possible only in front of the spectators who have emerged as "one" distinct spatial component facing the performance at a distance. "One-heartedness," which is often generalized as a moralistic imperative or essentialized as Chinese holism, should be understood as the hypostatization of spectatorship as a historical-ontological category around which theatricality as a new mode of the spatiality of emotion was formed in the late sixteenth century.

It was around this time that performance, a favored trope in Buddhist discourse, underwent a parallel transmutation in terms of its spatial conception. In Tang-Song times, it was already commonplace for a Buddhist master such as Mazu Daoyi 馬祖道一 (709–788) to liken himself to a performer, stressing his agency of freewheeling behind puppetry and across different venues: "A wood rod brought along, perform on any occasions come across" (*ganmu suishen feng chang zuo xi* 竿木隨身，逢場作戲).⁷⁵ At the turn of the seventeenth century, however, the analogy was reconfigured, shifting the emphasis from the performance itself to the performer-audience division (*taishang* 臺上/*taixia* 臺下), as Juelang Daosheng 覺浪道盛 (1592–1659) rephrased the commonplace: "With a wood rod brought along I go onstage, / letting those offstage make frivolous comments as they please" (*ganmu suishen shang xichang, jinjiao taixia shuo yanliang* 竿木隨身上戲場，儘教臺下說炎涼).⁷⁶ What differentiated the unenlightened from the sage also had to do with their relative positions in the theater:

> Those offstage take non-being for being, which generates joy and anger; those onstage take being as non-being, which eliminates prejudices about what is right or wrong. Taking non-being for being ties up with delusion and makes one mediocre; taking being for non-being resolves delusion and makes one a sage.⁷⁷

Such an on-/off-stage division became ontologically significant only with the historical emergence of the "spectator," in front of whom performance turned into role-playing; hence the dramatization of doubling by the monkey impostor. In other words, the "Oneness" of the audience separates itself as a distinct spatial category from the stage performance, and the split of theater into performance and spectatorship is mirrored by the split between the impostor and the role he tries to play.⁷⁸

It was in this new mode of distanced viewing that late Ming syncretism was historically constituted. Syncretism is therefore theatricalistic not in the sense of playacting, freely dressing and posing as Confucian, Daoist, or Buddhist, as a short tale from the 1640s claims.⁷⁹ Notions such as self-fashioning only invite the dubious sovereignty of the self to enter through the backdoor. Rather, the theatricality of late Ming syncretism must be comprehended through the newly emerging sense of spectatorship. The spectator facing the Two Minds in conflict prefigures the tripodal confrontation among the Three Teachings. Each of the Teachings harbors the impulse to subsume the other two in denial of this jarring distance. The One Heart's centripetal totalization, however, is undercut by its disposition to see itself slipping away into other loci, locution, and "costumes." Theatricality as the particular mode of exteriority and spatiality of emotion, wherein one is in front of, separated from, and reconnected to the dream, thus ontologically circumscribes both the syncretic hermeneutics and its discontents.

4. A DREAM NEVER MINE

This clustering of the monkey impostor, role-playing, and spectatorship might look straightforward nowadays. It actually came together as late as the turn of the seventeenth century, which is also when the fake Monkey episode belatedly entered the timeworn "Journey to the West" folklore. The episode does not exist in any thirteenth- or fourteenth-century "Journey to the West" drama. Neither is it mentioned in any early "Journey to the West" storytelling from the thirteenth century.[80] Furthermore, in contrast to the "Water Margin" plays that flaunt the Black Whirlwind as impostor, Monkey's imposture and dissimulation are hardly the focus for those early "Journey to the West" drama antecedents. In the Yuan or Ming *zaju* play *Erlang Shen Locks up the Great Sage Equal to Heaven* (*Erlang Shen suo Qitian Dasheng* 二郎神鎖齊天大聖), Monkey claims he once changed into a Daoist attendant and stole Laozi's elixir, but he never performs such tricks in the play.[81] The same applies to Yang Ne's 楊訥 *zaju* play *The Journey to the West* (*Xiyou ji*) from around the same time. Throughout this long play, which runs to twenty-four acts, Monkey only mentions that he once disguised himself as an insect, and he performs a disguise spell onstage only once.[82] Not until the late sixteenth-century novel did the "monkey impostor" motif come to the forefront. Rather than an old motif surprisingly coming late to the "Journey to the West" cycle, what we have here is a brand-new phenomenon ushered by the novel: the "One Mind" establishes itself as the spectator only when splitting away from—and therefore insinuating the condition of doubling into—the "Two Minds" in conflict. Accordingly, imposture and masquerade now play out contingent on the spectator.

In contrast, back in *The Water Margin*, even the "beholders" are not really bystanders; rather, like the impostor-performer, they are always already delivered into demarcated thresholds of the dreamscape and embedded in a field of direct communication that is reminiscent of winds. Together, embedment and deliverance form a different kind of "shared dream" than the one we saw in *The Peony Pavilion*, which is more about collective imagination and identification with the image of Du Liniang among the reading public. Probably based on the lost thirteenth-century *zaju* drama "The Black Whirlwind Plays the Judge" by Yang Xianzhi 楊顯之, chapter 74 of the novel presents a boisterous slapstick of the bandit hero Li Kui, who takes over a prefecture magistrate's residence and comes out to the courtroom at the front in the magistrate's costumes, coercing terrorized officials and officers to stage an invented lawsuit of assault for him to preside over. "Judge" Li then *convicts* the plaintiff of letting himself be beaten and sets the defendant free on the ground that beating up people is a "good fellow's" honorable deed. The courtroom farce is deliberately displayed to the crowd, whom Li Kui has "let in to watch" (*xianmen wai baixing dou fang lai kan* 縣門外百姓都放來看) inside the threshold of the front gate. More interesting, Li Kui himself joins the audience when he personally comes out to supervise the parade of the convicted before the gate (*haoling zai xianmen qian* 號令在縣門前). He takes up his hallmark axes while still wearing the magistrate's ceremony robe and shoes, and this mix of bandit and mandarin to signify his ambiguous belonging to both the "dream" and "reality" makes "the people watching at the door . . . scarcely contain their laughter" (*xianmen qian kan de baixing, nali ren de zhu xiao* 縣門前看的百姓哪裡忍得住笑). Li Kui continues pacing back and forth in front of the courthouse amid the amused townsmen (*zhengzai xianqian zou guo dong zou guo xi* 正在縣前走過東走過西), and ends up storming a classroom nearby, with the terrified children running around.[83] Wandering from one stage (the court) to another (the classroom), he brings his performance across various demarcated realms of the community.[84]

Li Kui the performer's direct interaction with his audience in the shared dream is in line with the overall ethos of *The Water Margin*, according to which a "good fellow" has to be the oral storyteller of his own heroic deed. This is most vividly exemplified by Wu Song 武松 who relates time and again his story of tiger fighting whenever an audience is available to him. The inhabitants of the "Rivers and Lakes" underworld include not only martial arts heroes but also itinerant performers who spread heroic tales onstage or through chantefables.[85] In all these details, the novel is self-reflexive about its mode of production and narrative structure, which have been much more profoundly shaped by oral culture than later vernacular novels.[86] Here, scopic sensation given by the hero and his acts is preceded and enveloped by the oral transmission of his fame. It is therefore important for the ringleader-to-be Song Jiang 宋江 to have heard of Wu Song's fame long before, so that he can later see him in a favorable light and recognize a hero in an ailing drunkard.[87] A man's character is so transparently encapsulated and communicated by his name that distortion or falsehood created by distance and relayed mediation becomes virtually insignificant. Not that there is no dissimulation and fabrication—Li Kui playing the judge or teacher has shown otherwise—but imposture for him is just another histrionic publicity event kicked off by his clamorous pronouncement of his own name.[88]

By the same token, back in the thirteenth-century *zaju* drama "The Black Whirlwind's Double Exploits," where imposture is resorted to as an expedient for a covert operation, the punch line, in Li Kui's own words, is "I can change my name to Li Kui" (even though Song Jiang presses him to come up with another name).[89] The scene continues with a long dialogue in which Li Kui answers Song Jiang's questions about how he would camouflage as a country bumpkin. Thus the viewer-viewed rapport between the "connoisseur" Song Jiang and the performer Li Kui, which Mei Chun perspicuously highlights in the "Water Margin" plays and novel,[90] is strictly speaking not a function of theatricality but that of a shared dreamscape where viewing is engulfed into the intimacy of interlocution.[91]

Following Li Kui, who throws the whole community into a tumult and engages his "connoisseur" in amusing dialogues, the sixth-eared macaque creates a standoff with the real Monkey and invites one group of audience after another to directly intervene. His impersonation is visually impenetrable; even the Jade Emperor's imp-reflecting mirror in the Heavens fails to reveal the "slightest difference between their golden fillets, their clothing, and even their hair." Only the divine animal in hell called Diting 諦聽 (Investigative Listening) could tell the impostor's true identity by perceiving sounds underground, but he is so afraid of the fiend's power that he keeps his knowledge to himself (*JW* 3:112/671). So it would take another being with superior ears to beat its rival of the same kind; and yet, just as listening in the sixth-eared macaque (an eavesdropping outsider) now implies not communal intimacy but the distance of alterity, Investigating Listening facilitates not so much a transparent transmission of the name as its cover-up. Only in the wake of such self-negation of the aural sense are the two Monkeys eventually sent over to the Buddha's Thunderclap Treasure Monastery, where the congregation of the aforementioned "holy multitude" is distinguished as "One Mind" silently looking on the Two Minds.

This new figure of the spectator marks the shift away from interlocution within a shared dreamscape to the viewing in front of the dream in theatricality. Paradoxically, this spectator cannot be found in early "Water Margin" plays or in the novel version that derives from or shares with those plays the same oral provenance, but is instead located in the late-sixteenth-century *Journey to the West*, which is less indebted to its Yuan drama antecedents. More precisely, the spectator emerges in the monkey impostor episode not found in preceding sources.[92] Only after the Shide tang edition of the novel did the monkey imposter become an important trope in eighteenth-century "Journey to the West" drama.[93] The 1740s *Precious Vessel in a Time of Efflorescence* (*Shengping baofa* 昇平寶筏), a 240-scene Qianlong court play, shows how the motif has been substantially expanded. The false Monkey incident is now elaborated in a nine-scene sequence. Usurping the throne as the Monkey King at Flower-Fruit Mountain, the sixth-eared macaque not only recruits three monkey followers to play the other pilgrims but also has another group of monkeys play the monsters that have previously been defeated. The fake pilgrims (including the false Monkey) and the fake monsters then restage the "Level-Top Mountain" story, in which Monkey tricks the monsters Golden Horn and

Silver Horn by transforming into one of their followers and then into their fox mother.[94]

This triple-layered performance—the sixth-eared macaque plays the Monkey King, who plays himself in a stage performance in which he counterfeits the others—is interrupted when the fake Pigsy, played by one of the monkeys, yells, "Don't kill me! Don't kill me! I am a fake Pigsy; I don't have good meat to serve you!"[95] A usurper staging a drama involving himself and the whole community is reminiscent of the Black Whirlwind playing the judge. But what distinguishes this eighteenth-century play is that it always sets some of its cast apart from the staged act and turns them into spectators in a "play-within-a-play" structure. At the point when the fake Monkey King announces to his "monkey juniors" (*xiaohou* 小猴, played by extras or *za* 雜) that he is going to select some of them to perform the "Level-Top Mountain" episode, a stage direction is inserted: "All the monkeys answer to his call. Half of them stand aside. Another half of the monkeys junior exits." Those who have exited reenter momentarily, costumed as Golden Horn and Silver Horn's fiendish subordinates (*xiaoyao* 小妖).[96] Those standing aside become the spectators, who burst out laughing when the monkey playing Pigsy suddenly begs for his life.

The performance comes to an end when the dramatic illusion is dispersed and the fake Monkey King tells the "fiendish subordinates" (now having restored their monkey makeup) to escort the other fake pilgrims back to the "green room" (*erfang* 耳房). Yet the other half of the monkey juniors, who have been bystanders all this time, stay behind and demand an encore. In response, the fake Monkey King turns his hair into a monkey army and a swamp of demons and has them fight each other. These monkey troops and demons in indefinite number (*buju renshu* 不拘人數) are played also by *za* extras, presumably the same crowd who played the "fiendish subordinates" moments ago and must have changed costumes after retiring to the green room. The fake Monkey King, instead of participating in this second play-within-a-play, joins the bystanders, becoming a spectator himself until he (still as a troupe leader/director) proclaims the end of the show.[97] He remains a spectator in the final part of this scene, however, when the third round of plays-within-a-play ensues as a banquet amusement, this time with all the monkey juniors performing variety plays to entertain the fake Monkey King watching behind the dinning table.⁹⁸ In short, precisely thanks to various parties changing positions, the spectatorial position is now clearly demarcated as distinct from the performance in the sense that one has to leave this position to perform, or conversely, has to stop performing upon entering it.

There is one significant fictional work that bridges the late-sixteenth-century novel *The Journey to the West* and the 1740s court drama *Shengping baofa*, foregrounding the close association between emotion, doubling, and spectatorship in the original novel. Dong Yue's 董說 (1620–1686) novella *A Supplement to the Journey to the West* (prefaced 1641) explicitly showcases oral performance of various kinds as elegy in chapter 1,⁹⁹ a "plain tale" (*pinghua* 平話) in chapter 7, a chantefable (*tanci* 彈詞) in chapter 12, and finally a *chuanqi* 傳奇 drama in chapter 13. These genres do not essentially embody the logic of theatricality—not all performances, even dramatic or theatrical ones, are "theatricalistic" in this strict sense, as the preceding discussion of "Water Margin" *zaju* plays shows. And yet, unlike the "Water Margin" novel, which is heavily influenced by its oral provenance, these oral performances are transcribed into theatricality when the voice is mediated by a novella in print. Hence performances in *Supplement* suggest the subtle reconfiguration of the spatiality of emotion, attesting the emergence of theatricality from the mode of the dreamscape.

Monkey's elegy in the opening chapter is a case in point. At the outset, he has fallen into an enormous dream conjured up by a demon, in which he finds himself impulsively slaughtering a crowd of children and women and weeping (*ti liu yanwai* 涕流眼外) over the atrocities he has committed. This remorseful moment, however, quickly yields to a show of elegiac recitation, featuring gestures of crying: "Today I'll write a eulogy for those wrongly killed. I'll put on a crying face (*kuku titi miankong* 哭哭啼啼面孔), and read it as I walk. . . . When Master hears how terrible the monsters are [and is misled into believing it is they who killed the people], his courage will fail and his heart will leap."¹⁰⁰

At first glance, this episode reproduces the timeworn distinction between "spontaneous" weeping (*qi* 泣) and ritual wailing (*ku* 哭), falling into timeless patterns of division—private and public, natural and artificial, interior and exterior.¹⁰¹ An alternative way to comprehend the juxtaposition of weeping and wailing in the novella is, first of all, to ground both modes of expression specifically in the dual composition of the dreamscape in this particular context. While Monkey's "spontaneous" weeping is induced *from within* a dream, his performance of elegiac recitation and ritual weeping takes place at the hiatus mediating *between* dreams, transporting deceased souls to another realm and delivering attendants (Tripitaka in this case) across different moods. And yet what distinguishes the novella from a typical dreamscape is its stress on spectatorship: not only is Monkey's performance of emotion put on display to deceive his audience (the Master), but the performer himself has also unwittingly situated himself in the position of the spectator being deceived, as chapter 2 continues: "From here on [Monkey] uses a thousand schemes trying to fool others, but fools himself instead" (*SJ* 33/19). Monkey, a performer from the outset, runs into trouble when he finds himself becoming an alienated spectator—this is the premise of the novella, which in this particular sense dramatizes the crux of theatricality as a new mode of the spatiality of emotion. Rather than crystallizing the " 'commonsense' wisdom of a social group or community," as other traditional oral arts do,[102] Monkey's ritual wailing presents a new problematic of spectatorship, which alienates even the performer from his own performance and redefines orality in the novella as a printed matter.

Just as in *The Journey to the West* the ancient topos of winds permeating the entire realm turns into a trope of asymmetric communication with the impostor, the medieval topos of the dreamscape prominent in *Supplement* is no longer limited to layered demarcation and deliverance but reinscribed in terms of theatricality. The novella's story proper is defined by an enveloping dream set in the so-called Green Green World (Qingqing shijie 青青世界, a pun on *qing* or emotion) ruled by the Little Moon King (Xiaoyue wang 小月王, which mosaically forms the character *qing*), and begotten by a Qing Fish spirit (Qingyu 鯖魚), where Monkey is led into other spaces and times through the Myriad Mirror Tower (Wanjing loutai 萬鏡樓台). Upon arriving in the tower for the first time in chapter 4, Monkey is so intrigued that he wants to "reflect a hundred, a thousand, ten thousand, and a hundred thousand of me," but "instead of his own image, what he saw was that every mirror contained other heavens and earths, suns and moons, mountains and forests" (*SJ* 55/60). The transparency serves as the "gateway" to myriad subdivided dreamscapes, fulfilling the function of deliverance even at the cost of specularity and foreshadowing Monkey's entry to one of the mirror worlds a chapter later.[103] And yet, the first mirror Monkey looks into in chapter 4, in which he sees the hell of the civil examination, functions less as a gateway than as a transparent screen, sidelining the dreamer in front of the dream without slipping him into it. More important than the overt social criticism of the examination system is the spectatorial mode of spatiality that enables it. In detaching specularity from the mirror, this little detail in which Monkey sees transparency instead of reflection transfers the issue of doubling from the multitude of mirrored dream worlds to the new problematic of theatricality and spectatorship, as the later parts of the novella come to illustrate.[104]

Without first seeing the dreamscape as exteriority (in that the dreamer is delivered out there into another layer of mood), we tend to read doubling and the dream world in psychological terms, finding cues in, for instance, the ending of the novella. After being rescued by the Master of the Void, Monkey learns that he had been inside a huge Qing Fish, the Demon of Passion (*Qing yao* 情妖). The Master further explains: "There were no springtime lads and lasses;/They were the root of the Qing Fish./. . . There is no Qing Fish;/It is but Monkey's passion" (*SJ* 184–86/255–61). This ending seems to literalize what an allegorical reading of the original *Journey to the West* might suggest: namely, that external phenomena are just projections from within the interior, "the plight of the dreaming mind."[105] Qiancheng Li helps clarify this reading by calling both the Qing Fish and the Master the double or "avatar" of Monkey's ego: "The challenges [Monkey] faces, however, are none other than his self, his ego—in short, his desire. . . . Only he can save himself from the spell, which comes from himself in the first place. Thus, Sun Wukong has himself to be thankful to, himself to kill, and, in Freudian terms, himself to punish."[106]

And yet, exceeding this absolute ipseity and its masochistic self-congratulation, an avatar is not really a projection of what is inside the self; quite the contrary, it is an exterior agent that feels, desires, and experiences *in place of the subject*, an augmented "prosthesis" irreducible to the self.[107] As a prosthesis, the avatar remains a body outside the body, a supplement that threatens the myth of the organic whole and an extraneous mechanism that undercuts seamless identification.[108] On top of this, however, comes a spatial paradox: as Rune Klevjer notes, in a

3D-emulated reality through a first-person camera (that is, the screen), the prosthetic avatar does not simply *extend* one's body but creates a feeling of *being there* in that gameworld:

> How can we say that the player is extending or reaching into the gameworld, while at the same time also saying that the player is "being within" and "acting from within" the gameworld? How can avatarial embodiment be both a kind of *extension* and a kind of *re-location* at the same time? The idea of the bodily prosthesis seems to contradict the idea of embodied being or presence, especially as it relates to the navigable "camera-body" that is the primary vehicle of perceptual immersion in contemporary games.[109]

To Klevjer, this paradox boils down to "the tension between the 'here' and 'there,' " between the notion of a prosthesis that tries to extend "our actual embodiment here" and the notion of "simulated or fictional embodiment" that puts "our re-located presence there." He calls that which brings together these two irreconcilable sides " 'vicarious' embodiment."[110]

Yet Klevjer ends up dissolving this tension by claiming that "our embodied self *is* actually being re-located, transported into screen space"; the act of looking into the screen/camera, which provides a first-person perspective through the avatar's eyes, reconstructs the player's whole bodily sense (following Merleau-Ponty, Klevjer calls it the "body image") as fully present over *there* in the gameworld. As the screen becomes the foundational part of the body image, it is also rendered inconspicuous to the player. As a result, "in the moment of being captured by the first-person avatar, there is no longer a bodily space *here*, in front of the screen, from which the actions extend."[111] However, this complete deliverance to a virtual reality by eliminating the "front of the screen" is less a magic effect of new media than an anachronistic fantasy that allows us to deny theatricality by returning to the dreamscape. We need to fully clarify the differences between the two modes of spatiality of emotion and ultimately to understand where anachronistic escapism comes from and whether it can actually overcome theatricality after all. In other words, instead of earnestly getting around "the tension between the 'here' and 'there' " that one has just discovered in the avatarian experience—instead of smoothing out all the incongruities in that experience in order to claim it fully as one's own—we need to recognize the hypostasized confrontation between the here and the yonder, between the two positions that the spectator is occupying at the same time, as the defining feature of theatricality. The vicarious embodiment is "fictional" not because one turns out to be in one place rather than in the other (indeed, that would be very nonfictional) but because one turns out to be in two positions that cannot be reconciled, hence simultaneously propelling the subject to identify with his avatar and making that identification impossible.[112]

What characterizes *Supplement* is therefore not a psychologization that explains things as illusions in one's own mind but the theatricality of emotion, in which Monkey as the spectator has a hard time identifying with the avatar that is supposed to feel on his behalf. *Supplement* at first presents avatars not in concrete images but as a bunch of names related to Monkey's malicious past, names that have acquired connotations unrecognizable to him—not unlike how he sees the sixth-eared macaque in the original novel. Before he arrives at the tower, Monkey keeps coming across rumors about himself: a voice behind the gates of Heaven reports that Monkey has just stolen the Palace of Magic Mists, a false charge that leaves Monkey "both amused and annoyed" (*SJ* 36/24–25); eavesdropping on the "New Tang" court, he learns he is suspected of helping his master rebel against China (*SJ* 44/36); a moment later, he runs into a group of Heaven Diggers, the actual culprits, who damaged the Palace of Magic Mists by accident but now blame Monkey for having recklessly killed people and turned the western road into a long trail of blood (*SJ* 49/47).

None of his interlocutors recognize that they are talking to Monkey; conversely, Monkey can hardly recognize the things he has allegedly done, leaving readers with the impression that the target of all this gossip is a different person. At the end of chapter 3, Heaven Diggers burst into a chorus of condemnations, using myriad names for Monkey from his dark history in the original novel: " 'Stable Boy!' 'Wine Thief!' 'Elixir Stealer!' 'Ginseng Robber!' 'Monkey Monster Tramp!' They cursed Monkey till his golden eyes blurred and his copper bones were numb" (*SJ* 51/48). For all their familiarity to both Monkey and the readers, these names are now imbued with bizarre connotations—an unreformed pilgrim, a bloodthirsty slaughterer, and an insubordinate in relation to both gods and humans—altering his profile beyond recognition. Like Monkey's wailing and other oral performances throughout the novella, these rumors serve not to rally a community through the intimacy of small talk but to problematize the aural experience of the audience in terms of theatricality and spectatorship, confronting Monkey the listener with uncanny personae that he has a hard time recognizing as his own.

This new problematic of theatricality and spectatorship is defined by a sense of alienation that makes identification at once necessary, seductive, and fallible, rerouting the apparently unmediated orality into a distancing detour of viewing. The audience might be "hailed" by the voice into a certain role, and yet this hailing underscores its insurmountable distance from the world being conjured. This happens in chapter 12 when spying on the palace of the Green Green World, Monkey overhears a *tanci* chantefable titled *Tale of the Western Journey* (*Xiyou tan* 西遊談) that the Little Moon King commissions to entertain Tripitaka. Its final lines, "Delayed days and nights at the Tower of Myriad Mirrors,/Who knows when [they]'ll see the Most Reverend of Heaven" (*SJ* 152–53/205), seem to Monkey to be referring to "him," even though the subject of the sentence is omitted. Cursing aloud, Monkey dashes out to deal the king a deadly blow, but is astonished that he has "struck only air"; nobody seems to "[have] heard and [everyone goes] on smiling and chatting." Monkey asks himself, "Am I dreaming? Or is everyone in the Green Green World eyeless, earless, and tongueless?" He cannot do anything except "jump to the opposite hill and open his eyes for a look," continuing to watch the king flirting with his master (*SJ* 155–56/208). The very moment the chantefable summons Monkey to identify with his avatar, he is pushed back from and sidelined as a spectator to the front of his dream. Monkey's back-and-forth orchestrates the modification of the dreamscape into theatricality that hinged on the reframing of sounds in the aloofness of looking.

It is at this point that a *chuanqi* drama titled *Prime Minister Sun* (*Sun Chengxiang* 孫丞相) is staged in the palace. Intriguingly, Monkey never sees the performance; he sneaks out and skips the whole show. He comes back at the end of an ensuing play, *Dream on Gaotang Terrace* (*Gaotang meng* 高唐夢). Monkey is told: "The play is almost over. Gaotang dream is already over." It is toward the end of this dream play that he hears a character mention *Prime Minister Sun*, the earlier show he has just missed:

> [Tang Xianzu's] *Dream of the South Branch* is tedious. Only *Prime Minister Sun* is ever played well. Prime Minister Sun is no other than Sun Wukong [the Monkey]. Look! His wife is so beautiful, his five sons so dashing. He started out as a monk, but came to such a good end! Such a good end! (*SJ* 166/225)[113]

The pattern of mediating orality by spectatorship once rehearsed in the *tanci* chantefable episode reappears here. Monkey overhears something about him, or more precisely, about a persona or avatar with whom he is supposed to identify, but his reception of hearsay is already marked with an ironic distance, which is in this case enhanced by the double remove of watching a play mentioning another play that one never sees.

While the chantefable *Tale of the Western Journey* causes Monkey to assume immediately that he *is* the persona being depicted but then tosses him back to the spectatorial position, the reported play *Prime Minister Sun* goes in the opposite direction by remaining remote from and uncanny to Money the spectator, even though he is given a chance to play the titular role. It is uncanny because Monkey insists he never had a wife or son, which is the case in the original novel—but not according to the dramatic tradition. Yang Ne's fourteenth-century *zaju* play, also titled *Xiyou ji*, features a monkey who marries a woman he abducted before being subdued by Bodhisattva.[114] Monkey's "son" in *Supplement* thus appears as a reminder of a dramatic representation of the "Journey to the West" story that was obscured after the success of the novel but surfaces in the novella through *Prime Minister Sun*, a play that never existed. The chance for Monkey to perform fatherhood comes when he confronts King Pāramitā in the climactic battle in chapter 15. Without realizing Monkey's identity, Pāramitā declares himself the biological son of the great Monkey King and the Iron Fan Princess. Struck by the possibility that the outlandish play may be telling the truth, Monkey still fails to assume the role of Prime Minister Sun. The series of questions he asks himself only further highlights his unbridgeable distance from his uncanny theatrical double:

Strange. . . . Is it possible that the play given the other day was real? Here's the evidence before my eyes. How could it be false? But where are my other four sons? Is my wife already dead? If she's not dead, what is she doing now? And is this one the youngest son or eldest? (*SJ* 176/247, translation modified)

As an imaginary play celebrating the desire for worldly success, *Prime Minister Sun* epitomizes the novella, which, as the author says, leads us to the "roots of passion" (*qinggen* 情根) before we can finally destroy them (*SJ* 1/191). Yet passion (*qing*) can never be claimed by the subject as his own truth; rather, it remains the "nonsubjective" knowledge of the Real.[115] It is in no way rooted in the interior subject; rather, it is exterior, out there, deposited with an unseen avatar, the ever-evasive Prime Minister Sun.

Monkey does adopt one avatar, one name of his double that again never appears in the novella. He hides himself among the military troops mustered by the Little Moon King against King Pāramitā, and his physical look changes drastically. He then introduces himself to Tripitaka—now the commander of the expedition—as the reformed "sixth-eared macaque." In this disguise, he goes on to confront his "son" King Pāramitā (*SJ* 178/243–45, translation modified). The shadow of the sixth-eared macaque hangs over the *Supplement*, in which its name is repeatedly mentioned. In chapter 10, Monkey is rescued from the trap of the Myriad Mirrors by an old man who goes under the same name—Sun Wukong—as Monkey. Monkey quickly shifts from gratitude to condemnation of his savior as the sixth-eared macaque in disguise. It turns out that the old man is Monkey's "own true spirit" and has come to save himself (*zijia jiu zijia* 自家救自家). This episode could easily pass as another example of self-salvation, implying that anything good (or bad) comes from *within* the mind itself. A closer look at the comment toward the end of the chapter (presumably from the novelist himself) not only complicates this apparent truthfulness but also reveals the ineffaceable exteriority of *two* minds:

The heart that saves the heart is the heart outside the heart (*xin wai xin* 心外心). Outside the heart there is a heart that is actually the false heart. How, then, can it save the true heart? When Monkey was enchanted by the Demon of Passion, his heart was false. His true heart understood this on its own. What saved the false heart was in fact the true heart. (*SJ* 130/169, translation modified)

What is being stressed here is the exterior relationship between the two hearts (or two bodies, as evinced by a correspondent term "the body beyond the body" or *shen wai shen* 身外身 in *JW* 1:409/235), from which the oscillation between truthfulness and falsehood is secondarily derived.[116] This exteriority underlies doubling, duplicity, and disguise in the sixth-eared macaque motif. It is no accident that when he encounters his "son" and almost comes to terms with the dramatic persona Prime Minister Sun, Monkey is disguised as the sixth-eared macaque. But, ironically, this fake impostor fails to seamlessly assume the father-husband role assigned to him in the reported play. While in the *Journey to the West* the sixth-eared macaque as Monkey's double subverts the singularity of the original by his perfect imposture, in *Supplement* he becomes the marker of imperfect enactment on the part of the spectator exhorted to identify with the avatar at a troubling distance.

Supplement expresses this indelible gap, which is inherent in emotional identification, in a curious mathematical manner. In chapter 7, Monkey, while time-traveling, hears someone call to him from another dimension. Although he is next door, the voice explains, he cannot invite Monkey in because his is "No-Man's World" (*Wuren shijie* 無人世界).

> Monkey said, "If it's No-Man's World, who's that talking about No-man?"
>
> The voice said, "Great Sage, you're so intelligent—why so dense now? I count myself out, not in 我是離身數的，卻不是連身數 (*SJ* 94/116, translation modified).[117]

To take for granted the population figure in "No-Man's World" would be to mistake an accounting that counts the counter out for one that counts the counter in. By the same token, any claim that the split between two minds is subsumable under the encompassing interiority, or that the "myriad mirrors" reflecting the phenomena of emotion are really one's own single heart, must now be understood as a misleading expression of a calculation that has deliberately left something, indeed many things, out. In *The Journey to the West*, neither Emptiness nor Oneness is sustainable, and counting oneself *out* as a way to articulate exteriority means not so much subtracting as adding more than one. Adding more than one—or adding as much as one can—is therefore a recommended way to adjust the error rate in the figure given in "No-Man's World."

5. THE ADVENT OF AGONY

A nineteenth-century commentary by a Man of the Three-in-One Way (Sanyi daoren 三一道人, pseudonym of Qian Peiming 錢培名) to *Supplement* is obviously amused by the way Monkey falls short of theatergoing:

> The one who does not see the play hears what the audience talks about it—fabulous; the one who hears the audience turns out to be the one depicted in the play—this is even more amazing![118]

Theatricality arises not from the experience of watching a play but from the performance of one's emotion at a double remove, with a "self" always already in the position of the Other and yet never fully identified as oneself. Instead of deliverance through layers of ephemeral dreams, what we have is a fleeting moment in which Monkey is facing a dream that involves him and yet can never be claimed as his own. Monkey's "facing" is even trickier than that of Du Liniang, because he only hears about the dream scene of the *Dream on Gaotang Terrace*, not to mention the entirety of *Prime Minister Sun*—and, as we have seen, the orality of what others say has been restructured by print positioning the listener as a distanced spectator who fails to see almost any plays.

What fascinates the Man of the Three-in-One Way might have bothered the moral philosopher Wang Fuzhi 王夫之 (1619–1692), who was also the foremost figure in the whole tradition of the "emotion-landscape mingling" discourse. To Wang, that poetic discourse is at the core of moral philosophy, since goodness comes from appropriate interactions between humans and Heaven, which are in turn based on the correlation between emotion and landscape.[119] What distinguishes Wang from his predecessors in that tradition is his awareness of its discursive inadequacy: while insisting that in "reality" emotion and landscape are "one," he dutifully acknowledges that the "emotion-landscape mingling" discourse always already names them as two separate entities.[120] In Wang's sophisticated handling, the discourse reaches the summit as well as its breaking point; its language is now exposed as falling short of the elusive "reality" it promises. But precisely in the ruins of the outmoded discourse, Wang comes to channel (though to his distaste) a new moral-aesthetic sensibility pertinent to the nascent era of theatricality that resonates with *Supplement* and its readers (including the Man of the Three-in-One Way). Acknowledging the indelible gap between emotion and landscape, he tries to argue not necessarily for their "fusion" but for their "wondrous match" (*miaohe* 妙合) based on the ancient cosmology of "mysterious correspondence."[121] But in practice, such correlative cosmology is no longer sufficient; any authentic emotion-landscape connection, Wang now demands, has to be empirically warranted by the poet's firsthand experience ("what one has passed through with one's own body, what one has seen with one's own eyes"); one cannot versify only "by examining some map." He then compares the inauthentic way of inciting emotion by facing a map to a distanced relationship to a drama performance in what may be called a "Prime Minister Sun" moment:

> If one listens to an opera being performed on the other side of a wall, one can hear the songs but cannot see the dances. If one is still further away, one can hear the sound of the drums, but can't even tell what play is being performed.[122]

In another note that follows in the same empirical vein and strikes even closer to *Supplement*, Wang Fuzhi takes issue with the cleverness of poetic diction that he deems disconnected from firsthand experience of the depicted scene itself. To him, the question of whether one should say "The monk" *knocks at* or *pushes open* "the gate beneath the moon" is not legitimate; it betrays that one has never set one's eyes on such scenes. To raise such questions would be, Wang says, "like talking about someone else's dream" (*ru shuo taren meng* 如說他人夢). To eliminate such distance, he advises poets to "approach the scene and meet it at one's heart" (*jijing huixin* 即景會心), and claims that word choice will be naturally made if the lines simply "follow from scene, follow from emotion."[123]

Stephen Owen detects in Wang Fuzhi's empirical turn a stance against theater and fictionality, and a fear of dramatic performance as the feigning of emotions.[124] It is worth bringing forward two complications of this interpretation. First, Wang feels suspicious not about theater in general, but about a particular kind of theater that paradoxically moves away from itself, a phenomenon we have called theatricality. Accordingly, the issue of feigned emotions is framed less by the oscillating opposition between reality and illusion, which pertains to the regime of dreamscapes, than by a sharpened sense of alienation in which the dreamer turns into a spectator looking at (or overhearing) a dream that no longer feels like his own. Wang's rhetoric of immediacy—which stresses again and again the eternal effort to "approach" (*ji* 即), to "receive" (*ying* 迎), to "meet" (*hui* 會), or to forge a "seamless wondrous match" (*miaohe wuyin* 妙合無垠) with the landscape[125]—does not simply repeat the Song-dynasty problem of the emotion-landscape *division*. Rather, it reacts to a new kind of discontent—the agony of distance and aloofness—which translates into a moral and aesthetic fear of not being able to emotionally identify with others (or even with oneself).

The second complication surfaces once theater is displaced by theatricality and the problematic of playacting is refigured into that of spectatorship or readership. The intermingling of emotion and landscape requires the poet to have point-blank, unmediated experience with the scene, but readers of the poem, most likely, are never on that spot, at least not in empirical sense. Fictionality, however undesirable to Wang's empiricism, must be admitted to the process of reproducing the poet's original experience at the site of reading, which is doubly distanced from the moment of creation and from the scene. Because reading poetry cannot help but do what "talking about someone else's dream" does, the exorcised figure of theatricality comes back to haunt Wang's poetics when he ponders the reader's experience:

"Friends and kin send no word,/Old and sick, I only have a lonely boat." Naturally this belongs to the poem "Ascending the Yueyang Tower." Try to postulate yourself as Du Fu (*she shen zuo* Duling 設身作杜陵), leaning on the railing and looking at the distant view. Then these two lines will come to your mind. This is also an example of "the landscape within emotion."[126]

Only through imagination or supposition (*she* 設) do readers manage to create an avatar in the form of Du Fu in order to get to where he once was and to meet up with the landscape he versified. Just as the issue of feigned emotion is reframed by a new issue of distance, so too is the issue of fictionality itself. Fictionality is transposed from the timeworn question of reality and illusion (*zhen-jia* 真假)—even though people love talking about it—to a new problem of how to overcome the highlighted distance by way of "imaginary" identification[127] or, in sixteenth- and seventeenth-century Chinese idioms, *she shen chu di* (putting one's body in the other's position) which Wang Fuzhi clearly has in mind. Before it became a notion in poetics, however, it entered drama criticism at the turn of the seventeenth century. Although the idiom can be traced back to a line from Zhu Xi's aforementioned commentary to the *Doctrine of the Mean*, "to postulate one's body in another's position in order to know his heart" (*she yi shen chu qi di yi cha qi xin*), Zhu's formulation, as we recall, is an amalgamation of the spatial modes of emotion preceding theatricality, a by-product of the lingering anxiety of winds in the era of the dreamscape. In contrast, despite its apparent linguistic connection, the more recently coined idiom *she shen chu di* was indicative of the emergence of a different mode of spatiality.

Thus far, we have re-scribed the genealogy of morals in terms of the genealogy of emotion-realms. In place of a monolithic picture of emotion being suppressed or contained, the ways emotion became ethically problematic and the tactics of dealing with the related problems prove prolific and manifold.[128] From the anxiety of excess and contamination, to the annoyance of being deceived and misguided, to the agony of being too far, emotion becomes an issue not because it is a transhistorical fallibility inherent to the human psyche, but because, as spatiality and exteriority, it articulates various ethico-ontological crises over time. Yet, this genealogy of morals on its own cannot fully illustrate the historical changes in which it partakes. To further clarify the context of the new imperative to *she shen chu di*, or to "put one's body in the other's position," in sixteenth- and seventeenth-century China, we need to retrace our journey, to take on another genealogy whose terms address still more directly the issues of spatiality: the genealogy of playgrounds.

CHAPTER THREE

What Is Wrong with *The Wrong Career*?

A Genealogy of Playgrounds

1. THE SPECTATOR AS LATECOMER

In the previous chapter, we looked at the different relationships to theater in two of the earliest vernacular Chinese novels: whereas *The Water Margin* derives the motifs of playacting directly from its oral provenance in Yuan drama, *The Journey to the West* departs from its early dramatic precedents and heralds new issues of spectatorship, which eventually coalesce into the elaborate play-within-a-play scene in an eighteenth-century theatrical adaptation. In this chapter I will show that the belatedness of both the spectator and the play-within-a-play is not limited to *The Journey to the West*'s story cycles. In order to pinpoint the historical transformations leading to the rise of the spectator, we need to cover a broader range of materials—textual and architectural—from the Song-Yuan to the Ming-Qing periods. I contend that the spectator and the play-within-a-play did not exist until they emerged as distinct features of theatricality. But theatricality was not fortuitously expressed through the *Journey to the West* novel and novella—it did not simply spill over from theater into adjacent literary domains. Rather, late sixteenth- and early seventeenth-century prose fiction as print matter was instrumental in instigating the transmutation of dreamscapes into theatricality. In other words, theatricality arose when theater was thrown off-center to meet print on its margins.

But one thing should be clarified before we go on: throughout this study, "spectator" is used to refer to the historically specific subject position and spatial category pertinent to theatricality; someone can be a "spectator" without actually attending a performance (since theatricality as intermediality means moving away from theater). I use "audience" as a general term for people who attend a performance. To say that the "spectator" did not exist in the regime of winds or dreamscapes therefore does not mean that there were no audiences; it only means that we need to conceptualize those audiences as "patients" or "dreamers" as defined in chapter 1. Audiences watching and reacting to plays have from early on been documented and literarily depicted,[1] as in Du Renjie's 杜仁傑 (c. 1201–1282) oft-cited aria "Zhuangjia bu shi goulan" 莊稼不識勾欄. (The country bumpkin did not know theater.)[2] But that only makes the absence of a play-within-a-play in Du's time—the absence of depictions of people watching plays within a play—more inexplicable. Though famous for its precocious self-reflexiveness, early Chinese theater curiously did not reflect upon its "spectatorship."

All these contentions—about the absence of the "spectator" in early theater, the belatedness of the "play-within-a-play," and the displacement of theater in theatricality—run counter to conventional wisdom about the history of Chinese theater, which I propose has to be radically rewritten in the context of a genealogical study of the spatiality of emotion.

2. IS THERE A PLAY IN THIS PLAY?

A Playboy from a Noble House Opts for the Wrong Career (*Huanmen zidi cuo lishen* 宦門子弟錯立身), dating from the early fourteenth century, is commonly considered to be a "truncated" relic of early southern drama. The surviving text unearthed in the *Yongle dadian* 永樂大典 in 1920 preserves the arias but minimizes the dialogues and actions. Drama historians have called the play text "elliptical, incomplete, plagued by structural flaws and plot incoherence." So when the theatrical group Beifang Kunqu juyuan 北方崑曲劇院 ("Bei Kun" hereafter) revived the play in 2003, a comprehensive revision was undertaken to "patch it up" (*xiuqi buping* 修齊補平) or, in a critic's words, "to make a vegetable patient come to life and to grow flesh out of a skeleton."[3] But the perception of "incompleteness" and the desire to make a play "complete" say more about our own assumptions about theater than about the play itself.

The major formal overhaul in the 2003 production comprises two plays-within-a-play, which seem to fit naturally into a story about a son of nobility who falls for an actress, deserts his magistrate father, and becomes an itinerant performer. The modified play starts with the actress Wang Jinbang's 王金榜 protean performance as the ghost eater Zhong Kui 鍾馗 and the moon fairy Chang E 嫦娥, which captivates the young man Wanyan Shouma 完顏壽馬. There is a long sequence in which the exiled Shouma learns the art of the variety play from street performers, and the play ends with a joint performance by Jinbang and Shouma of the Judge Bao courtroom play *Lu Zhailang* 魯齋郎, which moves Shouma's father so much that he finally reconciles with his estranged son (see figures 3.1 and 3.2). Critics have praised this metatheatrical sensibility. One writes: "Wang Jinbang and Wanyan Shouma are actors. Acting is their life in reality, and what they perform develops the whole story. The arts of performance and the narrative thus organically combine."[4]

None of these intriguing self-references to the theater, to which contemporary spectators react enthusiastically, existed in the original southern drama. Instead, a critic laments, the original contains incoherent actions, sporadic arias, and monotonous, long-winded monologues.[5] Jinbang never performs in front of her lover, and the couples stop short of performing in the presence of Shouma's father—in the original ending, the magistrate commissions a performance that happens to feature his son Shouma, but there is only an abbreviated description of what actually takes place. Let me cite the Chinese original first, followed by Wilt Idema and Stephen West's translation, with italics added to highlight the extra elements the translators have introduced to elucidate the text:

（淨叫介）（生旦上）（末上見外介）（外說關）（末裏院本）（外打認說關子配合介）[6]

The clown acts out ordering them. The young male role and the female role enter. The male role enters. *They* act out greeting the extra-male role. The extra-male role explains what has happened. The male role, <*the female role, and the young male role*> present a farce. The extra-male role acts out recognizing them, explaining what has happened, then marrying them. (Italics mine.)[7]

FIGURES 3.1 AND 3.2 Two plays-within-a-play added to the 2003 production of *The Wrong Career*.

In the Chinese original, punctuated by Qian Nanyang 錢南揚, the conversation is first between only Jinbang's father (the male role or *mo* 末) and the magistrate (the extra-male role or *wai* 外). Jinbang's father enters after Shouma (played by the young male role or *sheng* 生) and Jinbang (played by the female role or *dan* 旦) and, representing the whole troupe, he alone approaches the magistrate. We should translate the straightforward direction "mo shang jian wai jie" 末上見外介 as "the male role enters and acts out greeting the extra-male role" rather than "*they* act out greeting the extra-male role." The magistrate then recaps what has happened (*shuo guan* 說關), perhaps to explain why he summoned the troupe. It is at this point that Jinbang's father "*presents* a farce (*yuanben* 院本)"—more precisely, he reports (*bing* 稟) to his honorable client the farce they have chosen to perform. Noticeably, instead of describing the performance, the text has the magistrate recognize his son right away and authorize his marriage.

Although, as Hu Ji 胡忌 points out, judging from the thirteenth-century *The Story of the Western Wing* and the fifteenth-century *Golden Boy and Jade Girl from the Story of Mistress and Maid* (*Jintong yunü Jiao Hong ji* 金童玉女嬌紅記, hereafter *Mistress and Maid*), it is a convention of *zaju* plays to incorporate readymade *yuanben* farces into the storyline (*not* as plays-within-a-play but as actions taking place at the same diegetic level as the rest of the plot), the farces in both plays are clearly marked with the word *shang* 上, which means the farce "enters" or "goes onstage;" and the end of this interpolated *yuanben* segment is also often marked with *xia* 下, signaling that the farce "exits" or "goes offstage." Such markers are absent from the original text of *The Wrong Career*. And yet Hu believes, without textual support, that a *yuanben* play-within-a-play is staged at the end.[8] To illustrate this intriguing gap between the text and our expectations, Wilt Idema and Stephen West's refined translation introduces subtle textual changes but cautiously puts them in brackets. After "the male role" the translation adds "<*the female role, and the young male role*>," so that Jinbang's father, Jinbang, and Shouma now seem to *collectively* present—which strongly implies "perform"—a farce.[9]

And yet the absence of plays-within-a-play in *The Wrong Career* text echoes another, probably earlier, *zaju* drama attributed to Shi Junbao 石君寶 (d. 1276?), *Wind and Moon in the Courtyard of Purple Clouds*

(*Fengyue Zhiyun ting* 風月紫雲庭), whose similarities to *The Wrong Career* have been acutely captured by Idema and West.¹⁰ Shi's play depicts a similarly named playboy, Wanyan Lingchunma 完顏靈春馬, who runs away with an actress. In the only extant version, only the arias are preserved, but the play clearly shows that no theatrical performance is ever staged within the story. The last act is most telling: The actress Han Chulan 韓楚蘭 is summoned to perform, and upon her arrival she is having an internal monologue about how Lingchunma abandoned his studies for her and became an actor. Then she looks up and is surprised to find that the person who summoned her is the young man's father: "I just looked quickly into that kiosk hall,/And it scared me so that I must find some curtains to hide myself." The commissioned performance is of course canceled, and Chulan is sent to fetch Lingchunma so that he can reconcile with his father. To persuade Lingchunma to come with her, Chulan lies about an old patron who once saw him perform and now would like to reward him: "He,/Especially has some warm feelings for you,/When you first performed, in the beginning, he heard you sing."¹¹ The fact is that no one—neither the father nor the audience—has ever been given an opportunity to see how well Lingchunma actually performs.

The strongest reference to theater in *The Wrong Career* is Jinbang and Shouma's recitation of two long strings of drama titles, which they never perform within the play.¹² The forty-six titles mentioned in scenes 5 and 12 cover Yuan *zaju* dramas, Jin *yuanben* plays, and Song-Yuan southern dramas; many of these plays have been lost and little is known about their contents.¹³ These titles help historians reconstruct the early dramatic repertoire, but they hardly ring a bell for a modern audience. In the scene "Examining the Repertoire" (*"Ke yi"* 課藝), the Bei Kun adaptation devises a "remedy" for this obscurity, framing the otherwise tedious enumeration of titles that Jinbang recites from her "palm notes" (*zhangji* 掌記) with metatheatrical opening and closing remarks such as "life is like drama; drama is like life" (*xi ru rensheng, rensheng ru xi* 戲如人生，人生如戲) and "acting as if it were real" (*jiaxi zhenzuo* 假戲真做).

These interpolated metatheatrical remarks apparently repeat the oscillation between reality and illusion, a feature inherited from the dreamscape and hardly pertinent to theatricality per se.¹⁴ In that same scene, Jinbang sings to Shouma, "You are not only fond of those people in a play but even more so of this play amid people" (*ge qi ai na xi zhong ren, geng ai zhe ren zhong xi* 哥豈愛那戲中人，更愛這人中戲).[15] The interfolding of the play and people seems to confirm the mutual mirroring of the worlds inside and outside an illusion, whether it is a dream or a play. Yet the dreamscape cliché is actually reinscribed here in terms of a very different spatial structure. Beyond the apparent specularity is the spectatorial position of Shouma the theater patron watching both worlds. It is only under his amorous gaze that the people onstage turn into characters and the world offstage turns into yet another play. To Shouma, therefore, falling in love with Jinbang is an affair of spectatorship. It is via the spectatorial position that the chiasmic couplet of *xi zhong ren* and *ren zhong xi* is articulated in a compressed form of *xi zhong xi* 戲中戲, the Chinese term for a play-within-a-play, which, however, should never be confused with the more antiquated phrase *meng zhong meng* (a dream-within-a-dream). Whereas the latter denotes a dreamer being delivered across layered demarcations of the dreamscape, *xi zhong xi* is formed at the moment when a spectator is facing his or her own spectatorial position being reproduced by a character within a play. In terms of spatiality, what distinguishes a play-within-a-play from a dream-within-a-dream is less the embedded play than the spectator-within-a-play who is represented onstage by the enveloping play. Put differently, a spectator-within-a-play is conceivable, but there is no dreamer-within-a-dream in any similar sense. A dreamer-within-a-dream could only be a tautology because dreaming by default is an experience of being in a dream.

The metatheatrical moments in the Bei Kun version are therefore not just superficial ornaments; rather, they are subtly organized around the central trope of the play-within-a-play, which in turn enacts the key issue of spatiality of emotion. Since love affairs in the Bei Kun production are articulated as a matter of spectatorship, the distinct marker of theatricality, it makes perfect sense that spectatorship per se becomes thematized here in the form of a play-within-a-play, which is all about representing the spectator onstage.

The strong impulse to supplement an "incomplete" play text with plays-within-a-play and the belief that such supplements make a play *complete* are tied to our modern presumption about theater as a representational space delineated by and separated from the spectator, under whose gaze the performers turn into characters. Samuel Weber traces both this appeal and the anxiety it generates all the way back to Plato's fear of "theatrocracy" or "sovereignty of the audience." To Weber, the spectators represent "the position of the other in theater," the alterity in and through which theater becomes "beside itself," with performers entering others' bodies and roles under the audience's eyes.[16] This primary divide between the spectator and the imaginary space of theater is repeated within the imaginary space itself—"a potentially infinite *mise en abîme*," as William Egginton notes. Unlike Weber, Egginton defines theatricality as a sixteenth-century phenomenon, which he sums up with a paradoxical formulation: "the essence of theater is metatheater," not in the general sense that theater simply refers to itself and portrays life per se as already theatricalized, but in the particular sense that "metatheater is nothing other than the generalization of staging a play within a play."[17] Not just "Look at how I perform!" but more precisely, "Look at how I am being looked at"—is taken as a built-in imperative in theater. Our eternal desire to search for a play-within-a-play acts out our obsession in the era of theatricality.

Here Egginton reverses the emphasis of "metatheater" or "metaplay" in Lionel Abel's coining of those terms in 1963. What Abel saw as an unnecessary device to metatheater—namely, the play-within-a-play[18]—turns out to be the instrumental form for Egginton's conceptualization of theatricality. I would take one further step to overturn another premise in Abel's account—namely, his claim that "in the metaplay life *must* be a dream and the *world* must be a stage," and that "the spectator will either form this notion [that life is a dream] or feel its suggestiveness as a result of the play's effect."[19] In the final chapter of this book, we will examine the complex interplay between spectatorship and the dreamscape in the formation of Western theatricality. But in the rest of this chapter I will show that early modern Chinese metatheater (whose literal form is a play-within-a-play) is governed by a mode of spatiality that is precisely *not* the dreamscape. We know much less about how to describe the theater organized around the idea that "life is a dream," which explains why the description we mostly come up with is heavily dominated by the notion of metatheater. For this reason, my task here is to separate metatheater from the dreamscape.

3. A WRONG CAREER TO FIX

In its attempt to fill in the "blanks" with metatheatrical elements, the contemporary Bei Kun production of *The Wrong Career* might have conjured up the wrong ghost to the dead body. In contrast to the original early southern drama, a *chuanqi* play written three hundred years later is much more aligned with our taste for theatricality. Published in 1661, Li Yu's *Sole Mates* (*Bimuyu* 比目魚)—the title alludes to the fish symbol that signifies the union of a romantic couple—similarly depicts a scholar, Tan Chuyu 譚楚玉, who lowers himself to join a theatrical troupe where his love interest, Liu Miaogu 劉藐姑, specializes in female lead roles (*dan* 旦). In sharp contrast to *The Wrong Career*, where theater serves as an excuse for people to meet and part ways and could have been replaced by other extrinsic factors serving the same function, love between the actors in Li Yu's play is deeply rooted in the way they perform.[20] The role-type system for Chinese operas figures as their first comic obstacle. Scholar Tan, the kind of character routinely played by an actor specializing as a male lead (*sheng*), is assigned to play "painted face" (*jing* 淨) roles—typically stalwarts or villains—while the male lead goes to the clown (*chou* 丑), a hilarious mismatch with Miaogu, the female lead.[21]

It has recently been argued that this kind of outlandish confusion makes fun of the role-type system and "demonstrates Li Yu's desire to manipulate the magic of theatricality in portraying and transforming characters and to suggest the theatricality of social identities."[22] In my reading, this categorical confusion between a scholar and a clown highlights less a playful self-reference to the role-type system per se than a more specific kind of comment on spatiality, hinting at the rupture between the performance of the *sheng* actor playing Scholar Tan onstage and the potential performance of Scholar Tan in the capacity of the *jing* on the second-degree stage within the play.[23] Such a spatial split turns out to be less an obstacle to romantic love than its very condition. As Tan discovers after he snatches back the male lead role from the clown in scene 10, it is not enough simply to restore the alignment between role-type and actor. Due to restrictions against romantic relationships among troupe members, the only time the male and female leads are allowed to get physically intimate is when they play lovers onstage. It is only when the spatial split if foregrounded in the form of a play-within-a-play that the romance becomes possible.

What is peculiar about a play-within-a-play, therefore, is less its content than the spatial split that produces "interior spectator" (*spectateurs intéreurs*) within the principal play, marking the "change of level" (*changement de niveau*) between actions in the exterior performance and those in the interior one.[24] Before a play-within-a-play is staged in scene 15,[25] Miaogu ponders the meaning of its spatial structure:

> Whereas other actors and actresses prefer being offstage, because onstage they have to exert themselves and offstage they can relax, we prefer the stage, because offstage we have to hold ourselves above suspicion, while onstage we can play husband and wife. Onstage, he takes me as his real wife, and I take him as my real husband. Not one single line ever fails to go deep into our hearts and the marrow of our bones. The audience looks on it as a play, but what we perform is the truth. If a play is performed as the truth with incessant pleasure, of course the performance will turn out most magnificent.[26]

It is with respect to the audience that the truthfulness of their love can be established and displayed to themselves. The inability of the spectators to fully understand their love turns out to be a positive factor: it delineates the distinction between the stage and audience space and cocoons the two lovers in an intimate world—in other words, this world is made possible by the outsiders' unknowing eyes.

By investing actors (Miaogu and Scholar Tan) with sincere emotion, Li Yu suggests that he is redeeming the virtue of performance, which others have blamed for emptying out human emotions and relationships. The goal of redemption is pronounced in scene 1 of *Sole Mates*, where a persona, Li Yu's mouthpiece, comes out and sings: "This play is different from the others./The male lead is a man of emotion./The female lead behaves as a chaste wife./On our behalves the author makes theater honorable./So grateful that we pay him back with singing and acting."[27] Along the same lines, in her preface to *Sole Mates*, the seventeenth-century poet and anthologist Wang Duanshu 王端淑 describes Li Yu's project in the following way: "[Li Yu] assigns the thoughts of scrupulous men and chaste women to those actors and variety show performers."[28] By assigning sincere feelings to theater, Li Yu both implicitly acknowledges the charge against performance and sets out to defend this "wrong career."

Such a reading is reversed, however, once the underlying structure of emotion is characterized as theatricalistic in nature. This happens later in the same scene when, in a refutation of her mother Liu Jiangxian 劉絳仙 (the troupe owner and an actress herself), who wants her to play a concubine of the villainous merchant Qian Wanguan 錢萬貫, Miaogu claims that by making Scholar Tan the male lead, her parents have virtually married her to him. To support this unlikely claim, she explains how this virtual marriage has been underwritten by spectators:

> Onstage we crossed our arms and drank from each other's cup. We threw the flower bunch to the audience. . . .
>
> [Mother:] If your marriage is disputed in front of the magistrate, who would be your witness?
> [Miaogu:] Those audiences, with their ten thousands of eyes open, they all say we are a heavenly couple. Would we ever run out of witnesses for our marriage?[29]

In this context, Wang Duanshu's statement needs to be reversed. It is not that emotion has to be evoked to support the legitimacy of theater; quite the contrary, it is only through being staged in front of the audience and performed for the eyes of others that emotion becomes possible. In the words of the commentator Qinhuai Zuihou 秦淮醉侯 (Du Jun 杜濬 1611–1687), "Being a couple onstage in the eyes of thousands of people—that is romance par excellence, which is much more interesting than bedchamber affairs."[30] Precisely when they are playing their "genuine" selves, the theatricalistic structure has always already subjected them to self-othering, where even the most immediate auto-affection goes by way of the other, forcing them to perceive themselves from the spectatorial perspective.[31] In the commentator's words: "When the male and female leads perform this play, they are not playing characters from ancient times; rather, it is an 'I' dealing with an 'I.' How can this be done perfunctorily?"[32]

This point becomes still clearer in the first staging of a play-within-a-play (scene 15). Apparently submitting to her mother's pressure, Miaogu consents to the arranged marriage on one condition: she must be allowed to perform a scene of her choosing on the birthday of the water deity Marquis Pacifier-of-Waves at Lord Yan's Temple (Yan gong miao 晏公廟). Miaogu picks a scene from an early southern drama *The Thorn Hairpin* (*Jingchai ji* 荊釵記), "Plunging into the River with a Rock" ("Baoshi toujiang" 抱石投江), in which the female protagonist drowns herself after an evil suitor forces her husband to send her a divorce letter. Miaogu changes the script into an expression of indignation against Qian Wanguan, who is in the audience.[33] Even the villain is gratified by her performance until she ends it abruptly by throwing herself into the stream. Like the lovers' intimacy, her martyrdom hinges on the gaze of others.

Li Yu's attempt to redeem the "wrong career" of performance by assigning emotion to theater proves only that emotion is structured through and through by theatricality. It is precisely this acute sense of role-playing for the spectator that separates *Sole Mates* from *The Wrong Career*. Modern scholars have celebrated Li Yu's metatheatrical sensibility, and we have become so accustomed to theatricality that we tend to look for it in the wrong place—or in our case, in *The Wrong Career*, which strangely falls short of staging a play-within-a-play. We should not dismiss this "lack" as evidence of a primitive theater in which theatricality had not yet come of age.[34] In the rest of this chapter, I will draw on both the history of performance and the history of theater architecture to show no play is staged within *The Wrong Career* because early Chinese theater represents a different mode of spatiality predicated not on the spectator. Once we stop treating theatricality as a transcendent essence and spectatorship as a universal category found in all forms of theater, we can at long last historicize the birth of the spectator as a phenomenon pertinent to late Ming and Qing China.

4. RITUAL, THEATER, PRINT

A ritual manual called *Notebook for Transmitting the Ritual* (*Lijie chuanbu* 禮節傳簿) provides us with information about the context in which a lost version of *The Wrong Career* was staged in the Song-Yuan period. The *Notebook*, discovered in a Shanxi village in 1985, records the format and repertoire of dramatic performance for *yingshen saishe* 迎神賽社 processions (hereafter *sai*), the liturgical ritual of receiving and paying back to the gods. The ritual took place over three days at the temple or on a stage facing it; five other ad hoc stages scattered across the village would also be used. In the checklist of plays staged in accordance with the twenty-eight mansions dating system, a lost *yuanben* version of *The Wrong Career* is mentioned on nine out of the twenty-eight occasions, which is pretty impressive—second only to what we call the Lord Guan dramas (*Guan gong xi* 關公戲), which include four different titles and score twenty-one counts in total.[35] Though this *yuanben* version has been lost and virtually no details about it have survived, Liao Ben has argued that since the *Notebook* preserves quite a number of musical tunes, dramatic titles, and performance forms pertaining to the Song-Yuan periods, the *yuanben* version of *The Wrong Career* is probably the earliest antecedent to two *zaju* versions, from which the extant southern drama was in turn derived.[36]

In short, the *Notebook for Transmitting the Ritual*, dated 1574, preserves the remnants of much earlier formats and contexts in which Chinese plays were staged in the eleventh to early fourteenth centuries. Theater historians have found records of the earliest theatrical stages in temples dating from 1080 and 1101, a few decades before urban commercial theaters developed in the Xuanhe 宣和 era (1119–1126).[37] Whereas commercial theaters died out in the Ming and were revived only after the late seventeenth century, temple theaters carrying ritual functions continued to thrive and constituted much of the dramatic performance experienced by the whole society throughout Ming-Qing times. It is tempting to argue that the depletion of metatheatrical moments (by which we mean specifically the lack of the play-within-a-play) in the southern drama text can be explained by its "ritual" connection, which is indirectly revealed by the deep involvement of its *yuanben* antecedent in the *sai* ceremony.[38]

The elimination of distance between performers and audience has been noted by David Johnson and others in ritual dramas such as the Mulian plays and the Lord Guan plays traceable back to Song-Yuan times, in which actors would go offstage to wander and combat across the village and play hide and seek among the crowd, which participated in the action, so as to exorcise symbolically or deliver stray spirits.[39] Similarly, two other plays listed in the *Notebook* are still performed locally today: *Whipping the Malady Ghost* (*Bianda Huanglao gui* 鞭打黃癆鬼) and *Beheading the Drought Demon* (*Zhan Hanba* 斬旱魃). Both of the malicious spirits are invoked onstage but run into the audience, and villagers join the pursuit. Deities also descend to oversee or conduct the execution.[40] According to the *Notebook*, on three out of nine occasions involving the *yuanben* version of *The Wrong Career*, the play would be staged back to back with the *Breaching Five Passes* (*Guo wu guan* 過五關), a.k.a. *Slaying Generals at Five Passes* (*Wu guan zhan jiang* 五關斬將), one of the Lord Guan plays that have been well documented by fieldworks. In this kind of performance, with clear exorcistic implications, Lord Guan is constantly on the move from one stage to another, slaying his enemies.[41] Followed by villagers in the costume of other characters, he chats freely with the audience and gets snacks from street peddlers, spatially encompassing the entire community.[42]

On another occasion, *The Wrong Career* would be performed after the dancing play *Dances of the Tang Monk Fetching Sūtras from Western Heavens* (*Tang Seng xitian qu jing wu* 唐僧西天取經舞), which involves more than a hundred characters.[43] Also, on the occasion corresponding to the last, twenty-eighth, mansion, *The Wrong Career* would be followed by a *zaju* drama *The Twenty-eight Mansions Pay Homage to the Three Purities* (*Ershiba xiu chao Sanqing* 二十八宿朝三清), underscoring the completion of a full cycle. The common feature across these performances closely associated with *The Wrong Career* is the multitude of roles that demand collective participation. In this light, it becomes clear how *The Wrong Career*, depicting a family of itinerant actors and a dandy leaving home and then returning, fits in with these ritual performances.

Johnson, in his recent monograph on ritual opera, establishes a typology that distinguishes exorcistic plays from plays purported to be "offerings" to deities.[44] Both types of ritual opera, however, are characterized by a lack of differentiation between performer and audience, as testified by the two different groups of plays performed along with *The Wrong Career*: *Whipping the Malady Ghost*, *Beheading the Drought Demon*, and *Slaying Generals at Five Passes* on the one hand, *Dances of the Tang Monk Fetching Sutures from Western Heavens* and

The Twenty-eight Mansions Pay Homage to the Three Purities on the other hand. Either by the freewheeling mobility of performers across the village, or by involving the community at large onstage, these two groups of plays bespeak a more general characteristic of ritual opera, namely, a sense of congregation that renders the performer/audience distinction irrelevant. According to Victor Turner, that is precisely what makes ritual different from theater:

> Ritual, unlike theatre, does not distinguish between audience and performers. Instead, there is a congregation whose leaders may be priests, party officials, or other religious or secular ritual specialists, but all share formally and substantially the same set of beliefs and accept the same system of practices. . . . Theatre—from the Greek *theasthai*, "to see, to view"—is rather different. [Richard] Schechner . . . has recently argued that: "Theater comes into existence when a separation occurs between audience and performers. The paradigmatic theatrical situation is a group of performers soliciting an audience who may or may not respond by attending. The audience is free to attend or stay away—and if they stay away it is the theater that suffers, not its would-be audience. In ritual, stay-away means rejecting the congregation—or being rejected by it, as in excommunication, ostracism, or exile."[45]

Theatricality, in Weber's words, presupposes an audience occupying "the position of the other in theater," a locus of alterity that signifies the separation between performers and audience. Such a "position of the other in theater" is not available to the attendants of ritual drama, since everyone in the community is by default inside and inseparable from the event.

Now we can see that the theatricality of *Sole Mates* hinges on Miaogu's comic misrecognition when the actress regards a stage performance as her wedding ceremony. It is "misrecognition," not because theater has no performative efficacy over reality as ritual does, nor because she has mistaken theater for ritual. Rather, it is because, precisely when she is trying to turn theater into ritual, Miaogu actually treats those attendants as onlookers, eyewitnesses—that is, as spectators—in effect turning ritual into theater. This reversal is dramatized in scene 15 when a play-within-a-play is staged in front of Lord Yan's Temple to celebrate the birthday of the water deity Marquis Pacifier-of-Waves.[46] Miaogu appropriates this ritual performance of *The Thorn Hairpin* to stage her highly publicized suicide in the role of the female martyr in front of the audience. Even though she is directly addressing—repeatedly pointing at—the villainous merchant Qian Wanguan 錢萬貫, Qian applauds Miaogu's innovation—"Good scold! Good scold! There has never been such a section before"—without realizing that he is the one being scolded.[47] In other words, a theatrical gesture that seems at first to turn spectatorship back to involved participation and direct communication only further bears out distance and separateness.

Li Yu will offer one more twist in scene 28. A year has passed, and Miaogu's mother Jiangxian takes her daughter's place to perform a ritual drama on the same festive occasion. She does not realize that Miaogu and Tan have been rescued by the water god—who transformed them temporarily into a sole and had a hermit-fisherman save them from the river—and are now watching nearby. Tan, a newly appointed magistrate, deliberately commissions another scene from *The Thorn Hairpin*, in which Jiangxian has to play the male protagonist Wang Shipeng 王十朋 holding a mourning ceremony for his wife Qian Yulan 錢玉蓮, the female character that Miaogu played one year before. The purpose is to see whether Jiangxian would show any remorse onstage. Only in front of the spectators (Miaogu and Tan) and in the awkward role as a heartbroken *husband* does the mother finally repent and reform.

Here again ritual is displaced by theater, but in a much more radical sense. The comic confusion of Jiangxian, the mother character (which belongs to a *xiaodan* 小旦 or secondary female lead type), playing the husband character in *The Thorn Hairpin* (which belongs to a *sheng* or male lead type), cannot be fully appreciated only in terms of the plot or its enactment; rather, one must look at the printed text of *Sole Mates*. Just before the play-within-a-play begins, a stage direction refers to her as a *xiaodan*: "Gong and drum played in backstage; the secondary female lead in a male cap and clothes enters." But once the scene begins, the stage directions designate her as "the male lead" (*sheng*). Further down, "the male lead" conducts a mourning ritual and wails, and Miaogu, now a member of the audience, reacts with tears. Her response, which should not be part of the text of *The Thorn Hairpin*, now paradoxically infiltrates its stage directions. The hitherto neatly upheld boundaries between the play-within-a-play and what should be outside of it break down. The stage direction begins to refer to the mourning husband not as "the male lead" but as "the secondary female lead," signifying the collision between the identities of Miaogu's mother and the mourning husband she is playing. In addressing the departed soul as "my wife," this "female lead" refers to herself as "your husband," before finally calling out the name "Miaogu" and referring to herself as "your mother." A voice from backstage reminds her that the name should be "Qian Yulian," not "Miaogu." She acknowledges her mistake and returns to singing about resuming their "matrimonial bond" (*yinqi* 姻契) in her dream, while the stage direction continues to label her as "the secondary female lead" (see figures 3.3 and 3.4).[48]

A live performance can act out the mother/husband, daughter/wife, Miaogu/Yulian confusion, but only the published text with its interlineal stage directions can fully reveal the deeper confusion over the type casting system that breaks out from the spatial split between the enveloping and embedded plays. In other words, emotion goes astray from this double ritual context (a rite of mourning conducted within a ritual drama) and reveals itself to a much more remote audience—a reader sitting in a secluded study trying to imagine a performance from which she or he is entirely separate. If the first play-within-a-play bifurcates the total participation of ritual into acting versus viewing, the second play-within-a-play further clarifies such bifurcation as an effect of printed text on the spectator *as a reader*.[49] No matter how much Li Yu emphasized actual practices of stage performance in sharp contrast to his distaste for scholarly playbooks,[50] the playfulness of *Sole Mates* can be fully appreciated only when theater intersects with print, when we read the play text like a full-length fiction.

And yet, if we simply resort to ritual—the point of reference for early drama studies—to explain the difference between *The Wrong Career* and *Sole Mates*, we fall into a methodological trap. By distinguishing ritual from theater, and by asserting the former as atheatrical in the sense that it demands total participation as opposed to passive viewing, Turner's anthropological account actually reinvokes theatricality at a still higher level. When all members of a community are absorbed into the ritual and posited as "insiders," the "position of the other in theater"

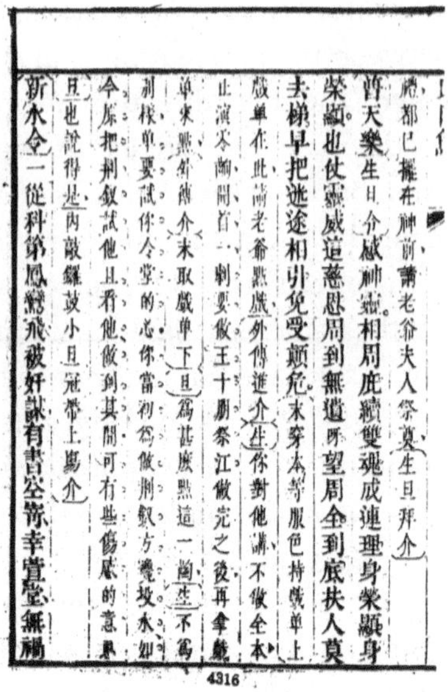

FIGURES 3.3 AND 3.4 Spectator as reader: facsimiles of Kangxi edition of *Sole Mates*. *Source*: Ma Hanmao (Helmut Martin), ed., *Li Yu quanji*.

is reserved for the outsider-ethnographer. This separation between the "natives" and the ethnographer, which mirrors the classic separation between performers and audience, resurrects the structure of theater. The natives' ritual is regarded as a performance soliciting the gaze of the ethnographer in a strictly theatrical sense, rendering native culture visible, exhibitionist, and communicable to the observer. But also, paradoxically, to overcome their outsider status, ethnographers also try to identify with the ritual participants through the trope of "performance" that helps make the cultural performance of the natives and the "ethnographic performance" of the anthropologists commensurable. Unifying things in their separateness, as Weber, borrowing Guy Debord's diagnosis of spectacle, points out, is precisely how theater operates.[51] This double operation of likening and differentiating theater and ritual, oscillating between an aloof view and a desire to join, between separation (theory vs. action, observer vs. the observed) and integration facilitates a self-serving discourse that allows ethnographers to shape and appropriate their object. As Catherine Bell argues, "ritual" has been elevated as a privileged object of study, and "performance" has become a privileged trope to describe ritual because scholars take "ritual performance" as the clearest form in which a culture becomes displayable to itself and to outsiders.[52]

This fantasy of another culture as "performance" is expressed in a theatricalistic structure. Theater, thanks to its presumed association with the spectator, turns out to provide the most powerful underpinning for ritual studies. Bell's critique of the discipline would therefore be better served if we qualify the "essence of theater" by tracing out its historical limits so as to have its transparency forfeited. Reading *The Wrong Career* in the context of its *yuanben* double embedded in ritual is *not* to assert any ritual origin/function of drama, or conversely, the theatrical/performative nature of ritual; neither does it purport to delineate the distinction between ritual and theater. Any orchestration of the relationship and distance between "ritual" and "theater" that does not involve questioning the "essence of theater" leaves intact the problematic theatrical framing of ritual studies, safeguarding the privileged position of the spectator-participant vis-à-vis his object. Instead, my reading of *The Wrong Career* in connection to ritual is meant to blast open this framing by questioning theater's naturalized correlation to spectatorship and conceiving of an alternative that does not presume the alterity of the audience—that is, an earlier theater without theatricality.

We can see such a possibility in the early fourteenth-century *The Wrong Career*, or perhaps its *zaju* antecedent *Wind and Moon in the Courtyard of Purple Clouds*, but we have also seen how easily this alternative can be obscured by two interrelated operations. First, we tend to fill in the "blank" with what we expect to see so as to put ourselves in the spectatorial position best served by the play-within-a-play device. Second, in order to explain why this absence of metatheater is not a sign of lacunae or naiveté, I have referred to ritual or ritual drama not only as a context within which a certain version of *The Wrong Career* had been regularly staged but also, more broadly, as the model of performance in which the spatial divide between production and reception, performing and viewing are irrelevant. But this explanation leaves unchallenged the theatrical framing of our discourse about ritual.

In order to put the radically different nature of Song-Yuan theater in perspective, we need to see *The Wrong Career* not as a ritual drama in opposition to a universal essence of (secular) "theater" but as an instance of theater characterized by a historically different mode of spatiality than that of theatricality represented by *Sole Mates*. This kind of theatrical performance has little to do with playing a role (separate from the actor's real body) under the gaze of the audience. Rather, as I will show in the next two sections, it is a magical invocation of beings into the world, a process of *transformation* that exposes the actor's body as just another ephemeral entity, at once instigating and deferring the real-unreal division, and rendering irrelevant the break between actor and role and between the audience's space and the imaginary space onstage that is constitutive of theatricality.

5. FROM METAMORPHOSIS TO METATHEATER

How can we trace the complicated transposition between *The Wrong Career* and the metatheater of Li Yu, which brought about such a drastic shift not simply in the art of performing but also in the way we perceive space, personhood, and alterity? One useful point of entry is to look at how actors assume and relate to their parts—under what conditions, and by whose authority. Too often we take it for granted that acting involves role-playing, which implies an inner distance from one's role and an outsider's gaze. That assumption becomes problematic when we examine *Top Graduate Zhang Xie* (*Zhang Xie Zhuangyuan* 張協狀元), the earliest extant southern drama dating from the thirteenth century, which was rediscovered along with *The Wrong Career* in 1920. Here we see the male lead (*sheng*) enter the stage and assume his role as the protagonist Zhang Xie:

[The *sheng* enters and speaks:]
Are you ready yet?
[The troupe assents (from backstage). *Sheng*:]
I've bothered you so much to send me on my way (*laode xie song dao* 勞得謝送道).
[Troupe:]
It is we who are troubling you, fellow gentleman.
[*Sheng*:]
Fellow gentlemen at the back, please perform a "Candle Shadow Waving Red" to send me off.
[Troupe members play the instruments and the *sheng* dances following the tune. The *sheng* declaims:]
. . . .
When we enter or leave the stage, we need a song to send us off.
In between we are full of gag and jest,
To make the audience wallow in delight.
Just now, I heard some notes of a song but I don't know what tune it is?
[Troupe:]
"Candle Shadows Waving Red."
[*Sheng*:]
Let me have the troupe's help for a minute.
[Troupe:]
We're here.
[*Sheng*:]
Very well. I shall assume the likeness of Top Graduate Zhang.⁵³

The actor begins not by facing the audience but by conversing with the backstage music troupe. This is because role-playing is a matter of crossing the threshold of the "ghost gateway" (*guimendao* 鬼門道) and emerging from the underworld. What is needed is a musical routine called "sending-off" (*duansong* 斷送) that functions both as a rite of passage and a device for reincarnation. That is why upon his entry the male lead lavishly thanks the troupe for escorting him or conjuring him with music.⁵⁴ With the help of the musicians, the male lead assumes "the likeness of Top Graduate Zhang," as he proclaims, and the cheers of his troupe follow. Only after these elaborate exchanges with the troupe does the actor turn to address the audience members briefly to ask for quiet, flatter them a bit, and promise pleasure and originality. The ontological foundation of playacting lies obviously in the musical troupe rather than the audience, with role-playing as magic incantation.⁵⁵

We can further contrast the first character's entrance to the opening of the play, which is in effect a "prologue." The prologue features a *mo* (extra male role in southern drama), who directly addresses the audience: "Let this hubbub rest for a while,/Hold your laughing banter,/And pay attention to this distinctive performance." He boasts that this production is better than what other troupes have done with the same story, and then describes how Zhang Xie, the male protagonist, sets off to take the examination, only to run into a mountain bandit.⁵⁶ Clearly, the prologue is not a drama performance but an act of storytelling; the direct address to the audience sets up the primary condition of communication, reminiscent of the oral embedment that channels the Yuan-dynasty "Water Margin" plays as shared dreams with the audience.⁵⁷ The presentation using the *mo* in the prologue therefore makes perfect sense, since, as Regina Llamas argues, the *mo* is the particular role type mediating other comic characters and the audience.⁵⁸ In contrast, playacting, as the ensuing entrance of the first character makes clear, has to be based on a totally different condition: the passage facilitated by the sending-off tune from one side of the ghost gateway to the other.

In reference to the ghost gateway, Jeehee Hong connects this spectral connotation of theatrical performance as summoning spirits from the past to the theater images carved on Jin-Yuan tombs. Stepping outside her subject matter of tombs, she makes a more general observation that "the doorway [of theater] is thus transformative by nature . . . located midway . . . between the fictive world and the real world."⁵⁹ At issue is not only a "theater of the dead," to use Hong's term, but a theater predicated on the principle of metamorphosis that is pertinent to the spatiality of dreamscapes, where the conjuration of the dead into the living world is part of what Zhuangzi has identified as the "transformation of things" that occurs during the deliverance from one dream to another. Three observations can be made here. First, the notion *wuhua* acknowledges that, between a dreamer and the dreamed, there must exist ineradicable differentiation (*bi you fen* 必有分), so it is not the case that the actor playing the male lead (*sheng*) *is* really Zhang Xie.[60] Second, because every reality to which one awakens will be quickly unmasked as another layer of dreams, however, the differences between real and unreal, self and other are forever deferred. Third, thanks to this interminable suspicion of the very ground one is standing on, the staging of transformations of things in theatrical performance entails moments of self-reflexive exposure.[61]

This explains why such an early play includes so many intriguing moments of self-mockery that expose the artificiality of dramatic conventions, especially with regard to the role-type system (which prescribes cross-dressing and requires one actor to play multiple roles) and the barebones stage (which requires the human body to turn into various props), each related to a certain kind of transformation. Commenting on how *Top Graduate Zhang Xie* makes fun of role-playing, Llamas observes:

> Roles on stage are well aware of their position in front of the audience and make no attempt to disguise the fact. On the contrary, jokes about the gender of the actor behind the role (for example, a male role being played by a female actor) or the duplicity of roles playing several types (the allusions by other roles to the different types a *jing* plays) are commonplace.[62]

To this acute observation I would add two important points. First, the self-reflexive exposure is not based on a mode of spatiality that stresses the locus of playacting "in front of the audience." Nor does exposure necessarily imply what Llamas calls "a distance between the spectator and the stage."[63] The direct address to or interaction with the audience is a legacy of oral storytelling, which obliterates such a critical distance: a storyteller, as emulated in vernacular tales, can mock and criticize anything except the authority of his own voice magisterially describing how the society works, which one is the good guy, and what one desires and deserves.⁶⁴ The exposure of one's own artifice in this play therefore comes from a mode of spatiality predicated neither on one's position in front of the audience and distance from them (as in the mode of theatricality), nor on the immediate engagement with the audience (as in the mode of winds); rather, it comes from the mode of the dreamscape, which, by delivering us across the layered boundaries of dreams, keeps unmasking what one takes for granted or what has been naturalized and rendered transparent.

This brings us to our second point: the unmasking in the dreamscape does not expose "the facts," such as "the gender of the actor behind the role," to a spectator; rather, it pulls the rug out from under factuality itself by repeatedly dissolving reality into another layer of dreams. Now that the differences between real (*zhen* 真) and unreal (*jia* 假) are deferred and suspended, one can only be sure about the phenomenon of transformation alone.⁶⁵ Thus the question about self-exposure in *Top Graduate Zhang Xie* should be whether we really know exactly what the actor exposes. Is it the actor's naked body, which the spectator glimpses through the thin veil, or is it an unexpected metamorphosis resulting from a "double exposure," a bizarre overlap between the actor's body and the role he crosses the threshold to play? Such a moment of exposure comes in scene 35,⁶⁶ when the gate guard calls out the unbound feet of the female lead playing Poorly (Zhang Xie's wife), which betray her as a "false madam" (*jia furen* 假夫人). This presents a hybrid figure conjured up in the realm of ephemerality, an unsightly, grotesque body marked with contradictory features that threaten both class and gender boundaries.⁶⁷

The metamorphosis through hybridization is especially relevant to this theatrical space, which is so barebones that the actors' bodies occasionally function as props. For example, in scene 10, two assistants of the temple god played by the *mo* and the *chou* "pose as door panels." Each "ties a hand" to the (invisible) frame to make a hinge. The humanoid doors open automatically and emit squeaks. Indeed, the doors cannot stop chatting even though they are told to shut up; one of them groans loudly in response to a knock. They even start to *think* like wooden doors: when the god threatens to hit his two assistants with an iron hammer if they fail to do a good job playing the doors, the *chou* asks the god if he will use "only the iron hammer, or will you use nails?" When the job is done, the god commands, "You two doors, come inside the temple."[68] Even more hilarious is the hungry singing table in scene 16, in which a neighboring old couple Grandpa (*mo*) and Grandma Li (*jing*) decide to throw a wedding party for Poorly (*dan*) and Zhang Xie (*sheng*) but find no table on the empty stage. That is when they find their imbecile son Xiao'er (*chou*) handy:

> [JING:] Son, you look like....
> [CHOU:] What do I look like? I look like a bridegroom!
> [MO:] What a nerve! You look just like a table!
> [CHOU:] I'm a man and you take me as a table?
> [JING:] I'll get you some fruit.
> [MO:] And I'll get you some wine.
> [CHOU:] I'll do it!
> [MO:] How generous!
> [CHOU:] If you are getting some wine, bring some over.
> [MO:] Sure!
> [CHOU:] If you are getting some meat, bring some over.
> [MO:] Sure!
> [CHOU:] When I shout for you, it's because I am hungry.
> [MO:] I know, but just act the table.
> [THE CHOU BENDS OVER. SHENG:] Grandpa Li, where did you get the table?
> [CHOU:] I'm the table.
> [MO:] Be quiet!
> [THEY PLACE SOME PLATES AND FOOD ON THE CHOU'S BACK. THE JING PICKS UP THE WEDDING CUP, THE DAN PICKS UP THE BOTTLE OF WINE, AND THE CHOU EATS THE FOOD. THEY MAKE GESTURES. THE SHENG SINGS:] (To the tune "Pai ge")
> I thank you,/Grandma and Granpa Li, for coming.
> ....
> [THE CHOU CONTINUES THE SONG:]
> To act as a table,/I have to bend my waist and my head is low down./
>   If there is any wine, pass me a cup./And give the table a drink.
> [THE MO SPEAKS:] Quiet!

What Is Wrong with The Wrong Career? 115

[THE *DAN* SINGS:] (To the tune "Hong xiuxie")
Where is Xiao'er speaking from?
[*CHOU*:] Below the table.
[*JING*:] I'll pick up the table and have a look. Oh! How odd!
[THE *CHOU* STANDS UP. THE *JING* ASKS:] Where has the table gone?
[THE *CHOU* CONTINUES THE SONG:]
Mother, the table/Has been borrowed by someone else.⁶⁹

A human is not a table, as Xiao'er complains, but he does function as a table anyway, supporting the meal. His "magic" gestures of bending over and standing up straight conjure up and away not an ordinary table, but a human table or a table human that talks, sings, steals food, and demands a drink.

Xiao'er's punchline, "Mother, the table/Has been borrowed by someone else," deserves special attention. Playacting in the dreamscape involves transforming oneself by being delivered across from another realm, and forms change because things are all ephemeral. That means, ultimately, that one is not so much transforming as taking out a kind of short-term form-loan. This shifts our sense of illusion, falsehood, and faking—all expressed by the Chinese word *jia*, as in playacting (*jiazhuang* 假裝 or *jiaban* 假扮) or "false madam" (*jia furen*). Since the real-unreal difference is forever deferred in the dreamscape, where even the real is evanescent, what is foregrounded is another connotation of *jia*, namely, "to borrow something for temporary use" (as in the ancient linguistic term *jiajie* 假借 or "loan character") and hence "provisionary."⁷⁰ In this context, hybrid-morphosis does not mix up true and untrue; rather, it happens when someone takes out two mortgages at the same time, which is perhaps a more precise description of playacting in the dreamscape.

We are now in a position to identify significant differences between Song-Yuan theater and what Egginton calls "Real Presence," the regime of spatiality in medieval Europe before the rise of theatricality. According to Egginton, Real Presence describes a magic world that goes beyond the Christian context of communion and covers ancient cultures across the globe. In his account, magic is not superstition or mystification but an underlying episteme in which beings, however far apart, are conceived as unmediatedly connected by resemblance, analogy, telepathy, and mutual attraction. The drug or operation administered to a witch doctor has a direct impact on his patient's body. By the same token, an actor in a passion play does not play the role of Jesus; rather, he *becomes* Jesus by way of magic gestures, and ancient and present become contemporaneous. Role-playing has no place in this kind of performance, just as the sign *is* what it signifies. This changes in the sixteenth century, Egginton argues, when theatrical performance in Europe begins to assume the separation of the actor from the character he plays, mirroring the separation between the spectator's real world and the virtual reality onstage. Performance thus becomes a business of make-believe: the double separation has to be "suspended" in the mind of both the actor and the spectator in order for the performance to become credible.[71] Signification becomes possible when one consents to the conventional reference of a sign without taking the signifier as the signified.

The Song-Yuan theater, in contrast, operates not in the mode of Real Presence or theatricality, but in dreamscapes. Magic transformation during the deliverance presupposes the distinction between identities but collapses any solid foundation of reality, not because disbelief is suspended for the sake of make-believe, but because one thing is metamorphosing into another, or, more precisely, one loan is taken out to pay for another loan, one signifier in deferral to another. No one naively believes that a male actor literally *is* a door, a table, or a woman; rather, the actor becomes an indeterminate neither-nor or simply both. The spatial division stressed here is not the separation of the spectator from the stage but the threshold across which playacting as transformation becomes possible.[72]

What we have gleaned from the thirteenth-century *Top Graduate Zhang Xie* is the insubstantiality of the "spectator." Now we should not be surprised not to find any plays-within-a-play in *The Wrong Career* or *Wind and Moon in the Courtyard of Purple Clouds*. Why would the father in the former play have keen enough eyes to recognize his son even before the show starts? And would it have been more interesting for the woman in the latter play to see her father-in-law among the spectators only after she finishes performing? Those questions are not even thinkable because the spectatorship enjoys far less authority in Song-Yuan theater than we habitually assume, so that both fathers find it unnecessary to become audience members before having their family reunion.

There is an apparent exception that could testify to this paradigm. Idema and West find in the last, fourth act of a fourteenth-century *zaju* drama *A Peddler, Imitating Sounds in Storm and Rains* (*Fengyu xiangsheng huolangdan* 風雨像生貨郎旦) "a remarkable parallel" to *Courtyard of Purple Clouds* (*The Wrong Career*'s *zaju* double), except that "the situation is reversed: it is now the son who summons some artists to perform before him, who turn out to be his long-lost father and wet nurse."[73] The most radical difference, however, is that the son fails to recognize the two until he hears the wet nurse's chantefable, through which she tells their life story. This prosimetric oral narrative is not a play but a kind of conversation between the wet nurse and the son. At first, as the wet nurse sings and narrates the story, the son only bravos a couple of times; as he becomes more and more curious, he raises questions each time the woman shifts to prose narration. Finally, realizing that he is probably the child in the story, he interrupts her singing line by line. With these intrusions the son becomes more of an interlocutor, or interrogator, than a spectator; conversely, the wet nurse no longer seems like a performer; she has become the subject of an interrogation. The theatrical framing, which could have differentiated the levels of the play-within-a-play, is no sooner established than dissolved. And it is thanks to his disqualification as a spectator that the son manages to rejoin his old family.[74]

The preeminence of interlocution rather than spectatorship in a scene that falls short of becoming a play-within-a-play reinforces my argument that the Song-Yuan theater challenges our underlying assumption of theatricality. The "spectator" was probably on the verge of appearing only when the early Ming theater started to turn recycled *yuanben* farces into early instances of a play-within-a-play. It was heretofore a common practice for a Yuan-dynasty *zaju* play to incorporate a brief *yuanben* as a comedic set piece at the same level as the rest of the play—in one play, an ailing character is visited by two awful doctors whose jests are taken from a *yuanben* performance called *Shuang dou yi* 雙鬥醫 or *A Pair of Battling Quacks*.[75] It is not until the early fifteenth century that we find a couple of examples of a *yuanben* being staged within another play as a second-degree theatrical performance supposedly being watched by other characters. A case in point is the *zaju* play *Misstress and Maid* (prefaced 1435), attributed to Liu Dui 劉兌, which showcases both uses of *yuanben*, testifying to a twilight era when the spectator appeared paradoxically as a *nonbeing*. The play ushers in its first *yuanben* when Shen Chun 申純 (played by the male lead *mo*) visits his future parents-in-law (played by the old man and woman types *gu* 孤 and *bu* 卜), and the old man welcomes him with an unspecified *yuanben* performance:

> You came but we have nothing to treat you. We have called upon several performers to serve us wine with their music.
>
> [*Mo* thanks him and says:] I feel grateful to both of you. How could I, a junior like your son and daughter, ever deserve this?
>
> [*Yuanben* enters, deploys, and exits; *zaju* enters (*yuanben shang, kai, xia; zaju shang* 院本上，開，下；雜劇上).][76]

At first glance it is in the presence of Shen Chun and his future parents-in-law that the *yuanben* is staged, but the stage direction takes the trouble to clarify that the *zaju* play resumes or "enters" (*shang*) again only after the *yuanben* has finished and "exited" (*xia*). By implication, the *zaju* play has to exit right before the "*yuanben* enters."[77] In other words, strictly speaking, there is no play-within-a-play here; the *zaju* play *Jiao Hong ji* never embeds the *yuanben* but instead alternates with it. Shen Chun and his parents-in-law do not stay onstage to watch the *yuanben* performance. In terms of actual theatrical practice, none of them is ever presented as a spectator. Once again, the spectator fails to appear precisely when we expect him to be there.

That same year (1435), one of the first plays-within-a-play did appear in *Lü Dongbin huayue shenxian hui* 呂洞賓花月神仙會 (Flowers and moon in Lü Dongbin's congregation of immortals), the last deliverance play written by Zhu Youdun 朱有燉 for festive occasions in the palace. In the second act, the immortal Lü Dongbin 呂洞賓, disguising himself as a brothel visitor, has four professional actors—actually his immortal fellows—perform a *yuanben* in celebration of his "birthday." This is the first time that a *yuanben* is not just mentioned (as in *The Wrong Career*) or incorporated into the dramatic action (*The Story of the Western Wing* and *Mistress and Maid*) but performed within a play. The *yuanben*, called "Deities of Longevity Present Fragrance to Prolong Your Life" ("Changshou xian xianxiang tianshou"

長壽仙獻香添壽), is a birthday show that ends with a blatant celebration of "wealth, beautiful women, drinking parties in the raised tower—all these serve a good time in this world!" The targeted spectator is Zhang Zhennu 張珍奴, a courtesan of celestial origin whom Lü Dongbin and his colleagues plan to deliver with this birthday show. The courtesan's response is far from enthusiastic: "I don't really like watching this. What I do every day is burn incense and pray I can learn the Way of Immortality. That is why I have never spent one single day practicing performance."[78] In this sense, the deliverance-play-within-a-deliverance-play succeeds—the courtesan apparently rejects the false talk about worldly desire in that birthday show and devotes herself to the Way. But this success is predicated on an uninterested spectator turning away her eyes.[79]

The play thus finds itself on a threshold: it contains a play-within-a-play that establishes the spectator as its raison d'être, but that nascent spatial structure seems haunted by a detached spectator who does not care. Equally disruptive is the enjoyment on the actors' side, which is expressed when one of them sings: "All these are the immortals' play" (*zongdoushi shenxian zuoxi* 總都是神仙作戲)![80] The actor-immortals insist on their autonomy by enjoying their own reincarnation onstage without much caring about the spectator, although the foundation of that autonomy has been compromised by the theatrical framing that is shifting power to the spectator.

The work that probably did the most to situate the spectator in the metatheater is Xu Wei's 徐渭 (1521–1593) *The Mad Drummer's "Thrice-played Yuyang"* (*Kuanggu shi Yuyang sannong* 狂鼓史漁陽三弄), one of the four *zaju* dramas he wrote in the late sixteenth century under the title *The Gibbon's Four Cries* (*Si sheng yuan* 四聲猿).[81] In *The Mad Drummer*, the Netherworld Judge summons Mi Heng 禰衡 and Cao Cao 曹操 to restage a famous historical episode in which Mi loses his life after cursing the evil minister at the banquet. Yuming He has recently shown that "the narrative structure of the 'play within a play' of *The Mad Drummer* mirrors the structure of the desire of such drama connoisseurs as Xu Wei for private spectacles of this sort"—that is, the desire to bring home the performance of northern-music *zaju* drama which was disappearing from public theater in the late sixteenth century.[82] To this insightful observation, I would add that one of the most peculiar aspects of the staging of this play-within-a-play is the unprecedented prominence of the spectator. Mi Heng agrees to perform but on one special condition:

> Your Honor, you have been always humble and I see you would not agree to take a seat and watch. That would never make it a play, however. In the past when I cursed at the banquet, there were guests in their seats. Today please put up with being Cao Cao's guest, sitting there to watch. Then this will form a scene.[83]

The Judge occupies a crucial position in the play: He is the host and is therefore in charge of the theatrical space; he is the initiator of the show and its director, with the power to interrupt the performance, add new elements, and order it to be resumed—in short, he stands in for Xu Wei the playwright. But at the same time, the host assumes the status of a guest; Mi Heng requests that he sit and watch, because without him as the spectator, the actors "would never make it a play."

This scene altered the dynamics of theater in several ways. First, unlike the early-fifteenth-century *Congregation of Immortals*, in which the spectator cannot wait for the forced encounter with the theater to end while the performance just stays in play (*zuoxi* 作戲) on its own, in *The Mad Drummer* the spectator is the very condition for the performance (*xishua* 戲耍). Second, in contrast to the fourteenth-century *A Peddler*, in which the interior spectator is dissolved into an interlocutor and the levels of action that would have been kept apart in a play-within-a-play simply collapse, *The Mad Drummer* keeps its interior spectator in the third-party position vis-à-vis the two performers. Therefore, although the Judge comments from time to time, he functions as a stand-in for the audience outside the play, channeling their opinions. More important, when directly addressing Cao Cao, the reluctant actor who is always trying to leave the show, the Judge is coercing him to continue to play the part. The direct address in this case does not break down the spatial split and collapse the action levels; rather, it maintains the theatrical framing of the play-within-a-play by forcing the actor back into the show. Finally, unlike the thirteenth-century *Top Graduate Zhang Xie*, where acting is predicated on being delivered into another realm rather than role-playing in front of the audience,

The Mad Drummer heralds a reconceptualization of playwriting and acting through the eyes of the spectator.

This last point requires further elaboration. The superimposition of the playwright and spectator in *The Mad Drummer* is ambiguous. One could say that it was the persona of the literatus writer with a heightened individualized subjectivity that established the equally respectable persona of the spectator. And yet the historical trajectory proves that it was the other way around: the playwright was caught up in the mindset of spectatorship. At the turn of the seventeenth century, it was no longer enough for a playwright to just know about metrics and diction. According to Wang Jide's 王驥德 *Rules of Opera* (*Qulü* 曲律, posthumously published in 1624), in order to write a self-introductory aria (*yinzi* 引子) for a character, "I postulate my body in their position" (*wo she yi shen er chu qi di* 我設以身而處其地) so as to see what the character would say in their very first song.[84] In so doing, Wang Jide in fact situated himself in the first place as a spectator vis-à-vis the character and then tried to project further into the character's situation and identify with him.

No doubt Wang Jide is alluding to Zhu Xi's twelfth-century commentary to the *Doctrine of the Mean*, where Zhu uses an almost identical expression—"to postulate one's body in another's position in order to know his heart" (*she yi shen chu qi di er cha qi xin*)—to talk about the emperor's compassion for his courtiers. However, as I argued in the previous chapter, Zhu's formulation—a revisionist reading of the phrase *ti qunchen* (to incorporate the flock of officials) in the *Doctrine of the Mean*—had largely to do with his attempt to reconcile the anxiety of contamination by winds and the dreamscape paradox of enlightenment-through-illusions by rendering emotion exterior while at the same time subjugating emotion to the bipartite structure of the heart. Zhu was concerned with delimiting and segregating the exterior aspect of the heart (*xin*), not with establishing the particularity of the other's "situation" (*di* 地) and the paradoxical way for one to enter the other's position without actually being there. In the final analysis, he was responding to the challenge of the dreamscape without genuinely heralding the advent of theatricality. That explains why Zhu himself almost immediately shifted back to the traditional reading of the phrase *ti qunchen* in his own commentary, and why his revisionist formulation lay dormant for another three hundred years and remained within the strictly exegetic context related to the discussions of the *Doctrine of the Mean*.[85]

It was not until the sixteenth century that Zhu Xi's formulation was picked up and condensed into the idiomatic expression *she shen chu di* in political discourse, which generalized the ethical issue of the lord's compassion for his courtiers into compassion across the bureaucratic system, high and low, close and far.[86] To my knowledge, Wang Jide was the first to take Zhu Xi's words out of political context and inject into them the new sensibility in drama criticism. After that, the floodgates opened wide and *she shen chu di* spread into literary commentary,[87] poetic discourse,[88] critical essays,[89] interpretations of history,[90] and exegeses of other Confucian classics.[91] In short, since the turn of the seventeenth century, the urge to put oneself in the other's position in order to imagine how the other feels has reverberated across a wide range of fields.

Still commonly used in writing and conversation, *she shen chu di* is the closest Chinese expression to the English term "sympathy," whose original meaning in the eighteenth century was at once broader and more specific than its modern meaning as something akin to pity and compassion. According to Adam Smith, sympathy hinges on the spatial specificity of another person's situation, which means that one has no direct access to the other's feeling. To feel what the other feels requires one to put oneself in the other's position, and to put oneself in a position that one does not actually occupy necessitates imagining or postulating (*she* 設) that one's body is somewhere else.[92] To distinguish this early modern form of fellow feeling from the ancient sense of natural sympathy based on presumed harmony among humans and things in the universe, James Chandler calls the former "imaginative sympathy" and aligns it with "the fundamental psychological necessity of commercial translations," in which "two agents keen to strike a bargain must each, in order to serve his or her own interest, be able to imagine what it might be in the interest of the other to do or have done."[93]

In the wake of Wang Jide, the discussion of *she shen chu di* in drama criticism continued to expand, but it took some time for it to migrate from the context of playwriting to that of playacting, probably because it was easier for a playwright to see himself as a spectator/reader.

Zhang Dai's mid-sixteenth-century memoir *The Dream Recollection of Tao'an* (*Tao'an mengyi* 陶庵夢憶) praises a late Ming great performer, Peng Tianxi 彭天錫, for his intense acting, which tended toward over-the-top villainy: "I postulate myself in that situation (*she shen chu di*), and I am afraid even Zhou [the notorious tyrant] would not have been that evil!"[94] For Zhang as a spectator, *she shen chu di* had become a natural way to appreciate performance, not in the sense that the performer also designed his portrayal of the character by *she shen chu di*, but in the sense that the spectator could admire the performance that actually exaggerated a spontaneous reaction in an emulated situation. In a nutshell, the spectator followed the principle of *she shen chu di* so that he could appreciate how the performer deviated from it.

Eventually, actors began to follow the principle. In his popular manual of connoisseurship, *Random Repository of Idle Sentiments* (*Xianqing ouji*, 1671), which was published a decade after *Sole Mates*, Li Yu applied the principle of *she shen chu di* not just to introductory arias but to the whole play. We have seen him claim he could impersonate whomever he wrote about by a change of heart. More than that, he was the first to extend the reach of *she shen chu di* to theatrical performance, thereby defining acting as sympathetic identification with the role, in the context of a discussion of the physical difficulties that limit female actors' ability to play *sheng*, *jing*, and *chou*. Gender disadvantage, he suggests, can be ameliorated through imaginary identification with the characters.[95] During the eighteenth century, when male actors came to dominate the Qing theater, Li Yu's gender-specific advice was extended to female impersonators, as recorded by Ji Yun 紀昀 (1724–1805):

> In the year 1747, a dignitary once asked an actor whom he really admired: "There are so many of you in your profession; why are you the only one who is really good on the stage?" The actor replied: "When I impersonate a female on the stage, I not only try to look like a female in my physical appearance; I also try to turn my heart into female. It is the tender emotions together with the sweet and delicate demeanor that enthralls the viewers. If I retain just one bit of my male heart, that bit of me will disrupt my female resemblance. How can I compete for the audience's affection for feminine

beauty and guile? . . . When I play a chaste woman, I keep my heart rectified and would not lose my chaste manner even when having fun joking and laughing. When I play a dissolute female, so, even if I am sitting still, I cannot hide my dissolute nature . . . As for happiness, anger, sorrow, or joy as well as kindness, resentment, love, or hate, for each one of these sentiments I put myself in the position of my character (*she shen chu di*). When I am no longer simply playing but experiencing the real, the audience accepts me as such too.⁹⁶

At the turn of the nineteenth century, both acting per se and spectatorial amusement were defined in terms of sympathizing with the other's feeling in the professional actor's hand-copied manual *Pear Garden Basics (Liyuan yuan* 梨園原; prefaced 1819) as a general principle not only on the occasions of cross-dressing but for any kind of role-playing: "In any male or female role, and for whatever kind of person you are costumed to play, you should posit yourself as that very kind of person. Happiness, anger, sorrow, or joy as well as separation, reunion, sadness, or jubilance—all should then come from within yourself, so that spectators will be deeply moved upon seeing your performance."⁹⁷ What comes "from within yourself" (*chu yu jizhong* 出於己衷) therefore neither belongs to oneself nor originates within; rather, it is the other's feeling that one cannot access without putting oneself in a position that one actually does not occupy. The spectatorial pleasure derived from watching an actor's *she shen chu di* is explicable only when we realize that spectatorship per se operates according to the principle of *she shen chu di* and makes it the model for playwriting and role-playing.⁹⁸

This paradigm of the spectator was first completed in Li Yu's hands.⁹⁹ Ten years before he established *she shen chu di* as an acting principle, he conceived a perfect example of an actress (over)identifying with her role. As we have seen, in his first play, *Sole Mates*, Miaogu's mother Jiangxian plays a mourning husband crying over his/her wife/daughter in the second play-within-a-play. Her acting might be over-the-top and confused—but it is not grotesque, because the self-reflection on the arbitrary role-type attribution does not create a bizarre body as it does in *Top Graduate Zhang Xie*;¹⁰⁰ rather, the excess and confusion stem from a totally different issue that is absent from *Top Graduate Zhang Xie*: namely, sympathetic identification with the character. The identification becomes way too powerful not just because Jiangxian and her character—Wang Shipeng, the husband—get into similar situations, but also because her daughter previously played the wife and "died" in her role.

At the end of her 1661 preface to *Sole Mates*, Wang Duanshu remarked: "My hometown predecessor Xu Wenchang 徐文長 [Xu Wei] composed the unrivaled *The Gibbon's Four Cries*. Isn't *Sole Mates* its worthy companion?"[101] In a profound sense, Li Yu did bring to completion what Xu Wei started—the transition to a regime in which the spectator is the necessary condition, without which a scene could not have formed.

6. FROM BACKSTAGE TO BALCONY

The emergence of the spectator, as examined through textual analysis of the play-within-a-play and the principle of *she shen chu di*, does not remain textual. Indeed, the history of the spatiality of emotion has been inscribed in performance venues and embodied by theater architecture. Despite the brevity of stage directions vis-à-vis the set for the play-within-a-play scenes—in scene 15 the directions read "Build a stage first" (*xian da xitai* 先搭戲台)—*Sole Mates* provides some interesting details about the spatial features of the temple theater where Miaogu and later Jiangxian perform. For Miaogu, the temple's location and stage structure are instrumental in her public suicide: "That Lord Yan's Temple lies opposite a broad stream, and the stage has been erected outside the temple gate, with its back resting on the bank and its front extending out over the water. Let me pick a play of martyrdom and act it out for real. Up to the point I will suddenly jump to the river."[102] The short story version further distinguishes the way Miaogu makes use of the stage:

> Other actresses, in doing this scene, would jump from the back of the stage into the greenroom, pretending to jump into the river but actually jumping on to dry land. But Miaogu . . . went straight to the front of the stage, from which, as she concluded her song, she gave a mighty leap—right into the river. She had acted out a real play, just as she had promised. Shocked almost to death, the audience clamored for someone to rescue her.[103]

What seems to distinguish Miaogu's performance from that of other actresses is the river as a liminal zone dividing the performance space from the audience. Miaogu's leap comes close to traversing the boundary and taking the play into the crowd, making it "real." And yet the breakdown of the theatrical framing stops right on the border since her performance ends with the pronouncement of her "death." The "reality" that emerges—Scholar Tan announces his "husband and wife" relationship to Miaogu, and the agitated crowds chase the villain—lies outside the play-within-a-play. The separateness of the spectator is reasserted rather than forfeited. This division is further stressed in the two-volume novel titled *Xi zhong xi* 戲中戲, or *A Play-within-a-Play* (the second volume is also titled *Sole Mates* [*Bimuyu*]), a prose fiction adaptation of Li Yu's play published around the eighteenth century. The novel now explains why the stage has to be built above the water: "It was only because this was a play performed by a female troupe. Were the stage not built over the water, those shameless beasts would have made tons of trouble. Built this way, the stage was over the water, four to five feet away from the spectators, who could only watch from afar but not get any closer."[104]

Strangely, the illustration of the play-within-a-play in scene 15 in early editions of *Sole Mates* contradicts the play text by depicting the audience not as gathered on the other side of the river but surrounding the stage, watching the actress being taken away by the river. An illustration to scene 28 similarly shows the performer and the audience on the same side of the river, with the latter rather unnaturally bumping up against the left rim of the stage (see figures 3.5 and 3.6).[105] We might be tempted to ascribe these discrepancies between text and pictorial representation to the difficulty of articulating this spatial separation of the spectator in premodern Chinese theater. Some might argue that the figment of imagination in literary texts has exaggerated the spatial divide while oversimplifying the much more complex theater practices in Chinese history, or that we have mistakenly read a modern, "westernized" sensibility into the past and disfigured the essential character of the Chinese theater. In the West, the emergence of the spectator culminated in the nineteenth-century proscenium stage, which featured a receding platform and an invisible "fourth wall" delineating a clear-cut boundary between the audience and the stage—an architectonic that

FIGURE 3.5 Illustration to scene 15, facsimile of 1661 edition of *Sole Mates*. *Source*: Liao Ben, *Zhongguo gudai juchang shi*.

FIGURE 3.6 Illustration to scene 28, facsimile of 1661 edition of *Sole Mates*. Source: Liao Ben, *Zhongguo gudai juchang shi*.

hypostatizes the spectator as a separate entity so thoroughly that he is rendered absent. This development seems irrelevant to China, since archaeological findings show that protruding stages surrounded by audiences on three sides coexisted with "mirror-framed" stages receding from the audience across most areas and types of performances.[106] Only in Northern China was there a discernible shift away from early three-sided stages, which were outnumbered by and/or converted to one-sided stages in the course of the Qing Dynasty.[107] That trend was counterbalanced by the predomination of the three-sided stage in the South, and both types of stage can be found in both Northern and Southern China.[108] Given the wide variety of spatial layouts of pre–twentieth-century Chinese theater that hardly impose a rigorous onstage/offstage separation, as the proscenium stage would do, it is difficult to pin down any decisive architectural marker for the historical emergence of theatricality in the Chinese context.

However, the fact that emergence of the spectator in early modern China did not culminate in the proscenium stage tells us that the proscenium stage is *not* the essential embodiment of theatricality. Rather, as will be shown, theatricality as a global category actually opens up a unifying field for pre–twentieth-century Chinese theater and the Western proscenium stage, however different they look. Unfortunately, the treatment of the proscenium structure as the privileged counterpoint to the character and development of Chinese theater—ultimately the reification of the difference between Western and traditional Chinese theater—has obscured the historical emergence of spectatorship. Just as the anachronistic juxtaposition of spatial modes of emotion propels us to look for theatricality where it does not belong and to explain theatricality in terms of what it is not, the anachronism of theatrical space (the nonlinear distribution of protruded and mirror-framed stages) seduces us into misidentifying and essentializing the "spectator" as a universal category. The two fallacies may seem to be parallel, but we will soon see that they actually go in opposite directions.

One way to scrutinize this misidentification and essentialization is to examine the contrast frequently made nowadays between the Western proscenium stage—which seals off spectators from the fourth wall, silencing them in the dark and focusing their attention on the lit-up mirror-framed stage—and the Chinese "teahouse theater," the major commercial venue from the mid-eighteenth to early twentieth centuries, where spectators on three sides of the stage ate, drank, chatted, and never shied away from expressing their responses to the performance. Amid the hubbub, tumult, and distraction, Joshua Goldstein notes, the audience and stage spaces appeared "mutually permeated, or continuous": "Rather than pretend that the audience did not exist, the actors often addressed them directly . . . and the audience reciprocated, communicating with the actors (and each other) through shouts of 'Hao!' (lit. Good! Bravo!)."[109] We could say that this noisy presence of the spectator represents an alternative to Western-style theater;[110] still better, the heat and noise of teahouse theaters signals an outpouring of the "energy of disorder," subverting the capitalistic logic of commodification by way of festive, excessive consumption.[111] Characterized in this way, the Chinese teahouse theater seems to epitomize the power and agency of the spectator-consumer.

The implications of this characterization go well beyond mid- and late Qing teahouse theater. Scholars tend to see this form of theater as simply inheriting defining features—structural openness, multifunctionality, spectatorial participation—from temple theaters, features that are the essence of Chinese performance arts. As Che Wenming, a leading theater historian, writes:

> The temple theater was not a specialized theater. . . . A temple's main function was sacrifice offering (commonly known as *yingshen saishe*), and dramatic performance comprised only parts of it. . . . From the mid-Qing on, the teahouse theater emerged in Beijing and other big cities as a kind of specialized, indoor theater and should have been more "purified." Regretfully, it was just as noisy and chaotic as the temple's open courtyard. Tables were placed in the audience's area for tea and dim sum. People watching plays here were at the same time socializing, feasting, playing games, and fooling around with prostitutes. . . .
>
> Multi-functionality or non-specialization constitutes the very Chineseness, while structural openness also distinguishes [the Chinese theater] from European mirror-framed stages and facilitates better the communication between the audience and actors. . . .

> The sense of universal participation and equality [in *saishe* activities] made spectators not just spectators but the subject and agent (*zhuti* 主體) of the sacrifice offering activities. Drama in essence was no more than one among the myriad items that worshippers offered to gods and spirits (though it usually was the most significant one). Just as in the case of other items, the subject had absolute power and control over the dramatic performance being offered. From this perspective, performers were hardly on equal footing with spectators.
>
> The openness and multi-functionality of theater, along with the subject status (*zhuti diwei* 主體地位) of the spectator, facilitates the spectator's strong consciousness and actions of participation.[112]

Tracing the spectator as the "subject" of the theater back to the ancient origins of ritual performance, this account of Chinese drama ultimately posits spectatorship as a priori for drama of any kind at any time: "any kind of dramatic form must consist of actors mimicking (performing) a role in front of people (spectators)."[113]

Ironically, at the very moment the spectator is elevated to the status of *total* presence—both because its sonic vigor abolishes the onstage/offstage separation and because it is ubiquitous—it is erased as a historical and spatial category. If it is true that "universal participation and equality made spectators not just spectators but the subject and agent of the sacrifice offering activities," they were active participants, not "spectators" in the first place. It is categorically confusing to maintain that those who "are not just spectators" turn out to be *super-spectators* with "strong consciousness and actions of participation," by which they have determined every aspect and level of Chinese theatrical aesthetics.[114]

This ambiguity cuts in both directions. On the one hand, modern audiences, for whom theatricality has been very much naturalized, tend to anachronistically project spectatorship back to the regime of the dreamscape, leading to our misapplication of the play-within-a-play to early theater. On the other hand, anachronism can go in the opposite direction, when people project the dreamscape down the road into theatricality, leading to a paradoxical category of Chinese "spectators [who] are not just spectators" but also something else. That something else, I would say, is the lingering figure of the dreamer, which was still prominent as theatricality emerged in late Ming and Qing China. This is why, whenever Tang Xianzu is mentioned, the first thing that comes to mind is "Four Dreams." The most memorable thing about Du Liniang, as the playwright himself acknowledges, is that she dies of a dream. The most famous Chinese masterpiece, which repeatedly alludes to *The Peony Pavilion*, is called *The Dream of the Red Chamber* (*Honglou meng* 紅樓夢, a.k.a. *Story of the Stone*). Judith Zeitlin notes "the surge of interest in the dream among literati circles during the sixteenth and seventeenth centuries," with an "emphasis on synthesizing dream materials." Before and after the fall of the Ming, diaries of dreams and memoirs as dreams were quite common, and the mid-sixteenth to mid-seventeenth centuries witnessed what Lynn Struve calls the efflorescence of dream culture.[115] Under these circumstances, the nascent spectator passed for a dreamer, and the restructuration of the dreamscape, epitomized by the position in front of the dream, manifested itself as an occasional hiccup that briefly interrupts but then dissolves into the endless deliverance through layers of dreams.[116] That is why even Li Yu, who did more than anyone to expand the notion of *she shen chu di*, articulated that notion in terms of the dreamscape: "How can one put oneself in the other's position if not by dream travel and spirit roaming?"[117]

Departing from other scholarly works, Sophie Volpp contends that, with the introduction of the fixed stage in late seventeenth-century wine shops (*jiulou* 酒樓), what she calls "participatory spectatorship" (characterized by mobile spectators and spectacle with the boundaries between them in flux) started to give way to the segregation between audience and performer, as reflected in the 1699 play *The Peach Blossom Fan* (*Taohua shan* 桃花扇).[118] Her insight helps us complicate the homogeneous, continual historical account of spectatorship throughout Chinese history. A historical and conceptual question that Volpp has helped open up then follows: How should we explain the specificity of theatricality in the seventeenth century (to which Volpp devotes her pioneering study) if participatory spectatorship is hardly pertinent to that period of time but is alleged by other scholars to be the essential feature of the Chinese theater from the very beginning? If participatory spectatorship defines theatricality until the later part of the seventeenth century, it can only be assumed that theatricality existed in the early theater. If that is the case, we would have to presume that theatricality is a preexisting essence of theater (which becomes more manifest than ever and spreads out to the society at large in early modern times), and spectatorship remains an essential component for all theater even though it can be classified into different historical species.

Yet one way to further historicize theatricality is to put it in the genealogy of emotion-realms, to see how spectatorship came into being only when the preceding mode of spatiality was transformed. The increasingly reified break between performance and spectators detected in the late seventeenth century therefore can be regarded as the precipitated effect of fundamental changes I have tried to pinpoint between the late sixteenth century and the first half of the seventeenth century, when performance was made possible by the "one mind" of the audience vis-à-vis the theater of doubling (*Journey to the West*), by the presence of an onlooker for which a show was staged (Xu Wei), by the position of a postdreamer who found herself *in front of* her dream (Tang Xianzu, Xie Zhaozhe), by *she shen chu di* as a principle that required the playwright to situate himself as a spectator in order to identify with a character (Wang Jide), and by a spectator incapable of intervening the performance (Dong Yue).

Conversely, the fixed stage did not first appear in the late seventeenth-century wine shop; it was from early on a fixture of temple theaters, even though the majority of the audience there was mobile. Without reifying the gap between performance and audience, the very existence of these temple theaters was based not on role-playing *in front of* the spectator (or bringing things *before* one's dream)—but, first of all, on the permeation of boundaries by "sonic" winds.[119] Early Chinese performance venues—plazas for Han-dynasty variety shows, or roofless raised platforms (*lutai* 露台) and dancing pavilions (*wuting* 舞亭) in Tang-Song temples—opened up on all four sides for this omnidirectional flow of affective forces pervading the realm.[120] This relatively free structure of playgrounds—characterized by a directly addressed audience with vocal presence and mobile orientation—continued to inform certain layers of latter-day stage performance in various formats (full play, extracted scenes, pure singing) and settings (public/domestic, ad hoc/permanent).

FIGURE 3.7 Early example of the backstage structure (only two ghost gates remain), in Yedi Village, Shanxi, 1157(?)–1274. *Source*: Feng Junjie, *Shanxi shenmiao juchang kao*.

However, the topos of winds does not explain a new demarcation in twelfth- or thirteenth-century theater, a division not between audience and performance or onstage and offstage, but between stage and backstage (see figure 3.7). It has been generally noted that the rise of the backstage marks the moment when drama parted ways with other kinds of performance such as dancing and acrobatics. But the significance of this change is never fully explained. Scholars have fallen back on an evolutionary narrative of technical progress (the maturation of drama was characterized by an increase in props and preparation, which made a backstage necessary) or invoked the unexamined category of spectatorship (obscuring the backstage with a curtain or wall positions the audience on three rather than four sides of the stage, restructuring the spectator's orientation to the performance).[121] And yet this transition from four-sided to three-sided viewing is at best nominal because long before the appearance of the backstage, the performer in a temple theater by default had to face the main hall where the god was worshipped, and therefore viewers standing behind the stage would be behind the performers.¹²² The advent of the backstage actually introduced something that had little to do with spectatorship. Dividing the rear parts from the stage did not restructure the audience's orientation to the performance, as some theater historians have assumed. Instead, it created additional layers of reality by marking out a *threshold* across which characters were transported from an otherworldly realm (represented by the backstage) into the community. Acting did not entail playing a role in front of spectators but embodying a spirit delivered—usually by way of music, as in *Top Graduate Zhang Xie*—across the threshold to join the ritual participants. In this context, drama did not rely on spectators as its prior condition; rather, even what we often misrecognize as the most privileged "spectators"—namely, the gods being worshipped and entertained—were actually posterior effects of the threshold-crossing ceremony. Not only did the "guest" gods have to be invited to the occasion,¹²³ but even the temple gods, who were supposedly "in residence," had to be conjured (*qishen* 起神) into the dreamscape shared with the human hosts, and conjured away (*xiashen* 下神) at the end of the performance.¹²⁴

Temple theaters continued to prosper in the Ming and Qing Dynasties, with the proliferation of ritual dramatic performances paying tribute to Buddhist, Daoist, or other unofficial local deities. Another new cluster of architectural features that proliferated in the mid-Ming drives home further the threshold-crossing in dreamscape. The "passage stage" (*guolu tai* 過路台) or the "gateway dancing tower" (*shanmen wulou* 山門舞樓), which was first described on record around the Chenghua 成化 era (1465–1487),¹²⁵ functioned as a performance venue, green room, and, most peculiarly, the gateway into the theater (see figure 3.8). It comprises an elevated stage and its backstage—very often with additional green rooms on the left and right sides of the stage (the so-called *erfang*, "ear chambers")—all of which are constructed on top of a passage and usually integrated into the upper story of the lofty gate to the main worship hall's courtyard, which accommodates hundreds to more than a thousand people.¹²⁶ Worshippers would pass through the gateway toward the main worship hall across the courtyard, but music and singing coming from behind would motivate them to turn to see the performance on stage towering over their heads. By mounting the stage on the entrance, this composite structure literally causes the two

FIGURE 3.8 Early extant passage stage, in Hejin City, Shanxi, late fifteenth century. *Source*: Feng Junjie, *Shanxi shenmiao juchang kao*.

thresholds that characterize the theater as dreamscape to overlap with each other—the threshold crossed by the actor delivering a character on and off stage, and the threshold crossed by worshippers (often mislabeled as "spectators"), and indeed the temple god himself to enter and leave the theater. The performer, the "spectator," and the god—none of them actually constituted the vantage point around which the spatial configuration of the temple theater was structured; quite the contrary, each was structured by—in being invoked into presence across—the overlapping thresholds whose prominence is underscored by the architectonics of the passage stage.

It is not entirely clear when the "passage stage" originated. Feng Junjie refers to a carved picture discovered on the stone coffin of the Daoist priest Pan Dechong 潘德冲 (d. 1256) in a Shanxi Daoist temple, which seems to depict a performance on top of an arch that apparently also serves as a passage underneath the stage. Feng suggests that this is a representation of the way performance was conducted in the temple (see figure 3.9).[127] Without material evidence, this is difficult to prove. But we can at least say a "blueprint" for a passage stage appeared

What Is Wrong with The Wrong Career? 137

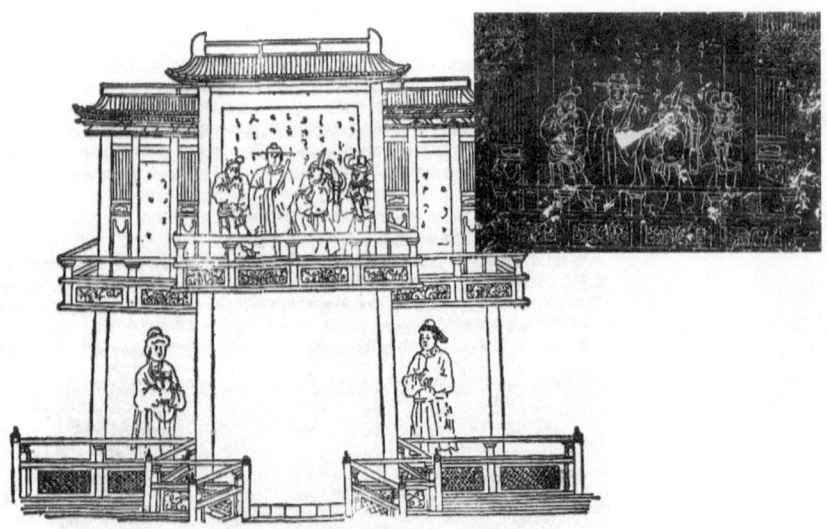

FIGURE 3.9 Passage stage "blueprint" (?) carved on Daoist Pan Dechong's stone coffin, Shangxi, mid-thirteenth century. *Source*: Feng Junjie, *Shanxi shenmiao juchang kao*.

around the same time that the backstage emerged in thirteenth-century China. I would argue that a slightly earlier and more concretely executed design that combines the passage and the stage, again in a funeral context, can be found in the twelfth-century Jin-dynasty tombs unearthed in Jishan 稷山, Shanxi. Some of these tombs feature a sepulcher with carved images of a "dancing pavilion" on their southern walls. These images, which show *zaju* actors performing, face the northern wall, which features the images of the entombed couple, as if they are watching the performance.[128] It has been pointed out that this kind of dancing pavilion image closely resembles the actual architecture around the same period.[129] What is usually overlooked, however, is that the chamber entrance (*mumen* 墓門) is built into the center or the left corner of the southern wall. In other words, the doorway to the sepulcher is either under the carved stage or underneath what would be the left greenroom. The tomb chamber corresponds to the courtyard of a temple theater: the representation of the buried couple occupies a position equivalent to the temple's worship hall (see figures 3.10 and 3.11), and the entrance to the sepulcher replicates the structure of a "gateway

138 *What Is Wrong with* The Wrong Career?

FIGURE 3.10 Passage stage carved on the wall of a Jin-dynasty sepulcher, in Jishan, Shanxi, twelfth century. *Source*: Shanxi sheng kaogu yanjiusuo, *Pingyang jinmu zhuandiao*.

FIGURE 3.11 Carved audience couple (center) on the wall opposing the sepulcher passage stage, in Jishan, Shanxi, twelfth century. *Source*: Shanxi sheng kaogu yanjiusuo, *Pingyang jinmu zhuandiao*.

dancing tower." Following the spatial logic of the dreamscape, this kind of tomb construction foreshadows the passage stage.[130]

The number of passage stages increased over the course of the sixteenth century, and they were widespread throughout the Qing, which would seem to testify to the dreamscape's status as the spatial mode for the Chinese theater. But the passage stage turned out to be a transitional passage into another regime of spatiality. At the turn of the seventeenth century, an add-on to its composite structure marked a subtle shift of emphasis away from threshold-crossing toward viewing from afar. A pair of buildings with what theater historians have dubbed "second-floor balconies" (*erceng kanlou* 二層看樓)—the earliest surviving example dates from 1625[131]—were added along the courtyard's east and west borderlines, rivaling the passage stage in height. The south ends of the balconies intersect with the ear rooms at the east and west ends of the passage stage (see figure 3.12). The balconies accommodated one to two hundred women, who (along with children) were segregated from the men down in the courtyard. As Che Wenming points out,

FIGURE 3.12 Earliest extant passage stage with second-floor balcony, "Qingyun lou," Gaoping City, Shanxi, 1625. *Source*: Feng Junjie, *Shanxi shenmiao juchang kao*.

balconies became the distinctive feature of Qing theater architecture, and temple stele inscriptions started to emphasize their construction.[132] But the fact that such an emphasis came so late runs counter to Che's assumption that that spectatorship is the initial and essential element for drama. The belatedness reveals spectatorship as a category that arose with theatricality and became an important principle for theater architecture in the seventeenth century.

Rather than seeing the discrepancies between different spatial logics, theater historians tend to see balconies as extensions of the passage stage, as final steps in the continual evolution of traditional theater architecture toward its telos. Once the square is seamlessly enclosed by the balconies in the east and the west, the passage stage in the south, and the main hall in the north, the temple theater is deemed "complete," with all the functions of staging performances, resting actors, and accommodating spectators. This configuration allegedly laid down the blueprint for the commercial teahouse theater after the mid-Qing, which retained such architectural features as the left and right balconies.[133] Replacing the temple courtyard where the audience stood in the open air was the dining hall of the teahouse, topped with a ceiling and equipped with tables (*sanzuo* 散座), where the "tea fee" was affordable for plebeians. (Clients at the tables closer to the three sides of the stage paid more than those sitting farthest away or in the middle of the hall called *chixin* 池心.) The stage no longer sat over the gateway but was relocated to where the temple's main worship hall had been. Above the gate was the extra, "main balcony" (*zhenglou* 正樓), which directly faced the stage and was reserved for special guests. The Qianlong Emperor (r. 1736–1795), who was rumored to have visited a teahouse theater once without warning, ended up here. The teahouse balconies, known as *guanzuo* 官座, no longer segregated the genders but instead enforced class distinctions.[134] The tea fee was highest in the balconies over the stage (particularly the ones in the left tower that were closest to the stage exit)—where moneyed clients could flirt and rendezvous with actors and courtesans.[135]

We have come full circle, returning to the claim that the teahouse theater inherited the temple theater's audience distractions as well as its permeable boundaries between stage and audience spaces. These characteristics seem to be foregrounded in Shen Taimou's 沈太侔 (d. 1926) description of Beijing teahouse theaters circa 1880:

> During the daytime performance, after finishing the first three plays, young actors from the Sanqing 三慶, Sixi 四喜, and Chuntai 春臺 Troupes would all gather behind the curtains at the stage entrance and exit, spying on the balconies above. If any old client was spotted, they immediately climbed up the tower to attend him. Very often the client and his guests totaled only two or three people, but surrounding them were as many as twenty to thirty young actors. That made onlookers envy and feel strongly jealous, while the ones inside the circle appeared downright conceited. In effect, the latter couldn't care less about plays. Even before the feature play was staged, they had already departed with their actor-lovers for a wine shop. A poem about balconies reads: "Sitting with both legs crossed,/He was presented a narrow red sheet of play titles./To his left and right were persons as beautiful as jades,/And in the entire theater no one was ever looking at the stage."[136]

With actors partying offstage with clients who pay no attention to the performance, the Chinese theater and its participants could not be more remote from the proscenium stage, it seems. Forging a grand narrative of continuity from temple to teahouse performance, scholars have managed to secure a national identity for the Chinese theater in opposition to the nineteenth-century Western realistic playhouse. But what Shen's remark actually evidences is not a transhistorical Chineseness but a historically specific mode of spatiality—namely, theatricality—that emerged at the turn of the seventeenth century and flourished into the late nineteenth century.

The claim that Shen Taimou's description pertains to spectatorship might sound counterintuitive. "No one was ever looking at the stage," after all, and the onstage/offstage distinction blurred when actors left the stage for the balcony. Yet overemphasizing the permeability of onstage/offstage boundaries and the inattention on the part of the viewer has obscured how the deeply engulfed boundaries crisscrossing clusters of audience members actually determine the insurmountable distance among them, hence instigating the circuit of attention toward one another and—by way of the others—back toward the self. In this particular spatial mode of emotion, one feels in the position of the other placed ahead at a distance. The wealthy client's self-regard feeds on the envious gaze of the people below, for whom he has staged a flamboyant scene with actors and courtesans. Just as the plebeians try to identify sympathetically with the unattainable pleasure he is enjoying in his privileged position, the rich man can only savor his own rapture by "sympathizing" with the poor's envy and despair.

It is the emotional structure of *she shen chu di* in this more general sense—in which a spectator feels sympathetically not necessarily in the position of the performer/character onstage, but in the position of *another spectator who acts just like a performer staging a performance*—that characterizes the spatial mode of theatricality pertaining to early modern China. As Laikwan Pang observes about late Qing teahouse theaters:

> Seeing was not unidirectional from the viewers to the performance—it also took place among the audience. Seeing was connected to and supported class segregation so that the rich presented themselves proudly before the poor and watched the poor as a way to justify their pride. . . . The few females openly seen in the [teahouse] theater were courtesans, whose presence was meant to attract the eyes of the audience and increase people's admiration for their patrons. It is clear that people of different classes and sexes were watching the same performances, yet they were also watching and recognizing each other.[137]

Pang's insight into the diverse viewing perspectives among segregated audiences highlights the specific historicity of a spatial layout that emerged much later in the history of the Chinese theater. More precisely, the partitioning of spectators was not experienced as such until the introduction of balconies into early seventeenth century temples and then into wine shops and teahouses in the Qing. Though there were spatial forms of audience division before the addition of balconies, none of them ever had the same effect. These configurations usually involved local officials and community leaders (or, on some occasions, women) seated on a platform, surrounded by the common folk in the courtyard or inside the main hall and largely out of sight.[138] Both configurations lacked the circuit of attention and sympathetic identification that accompanied the topographical rupture and unevenness introduced by the balconies.

Once we focus on this more pervasive and fundamental spatial split from which the spectator emerged rather than on the narrowly, rigidly defined onstage/offstage division (which was only one of the contingent inflexions of the general split), the opposition of the Chinese stage and the Western proscenium stage is revealed as misleading. Instead of dichotomizing the proscenium stage and the teahouse theater (which is too often taken to represent the eternal essence of Chinese dramatic performance), we should see both as derived from the common ground of theatricality. Both can be articulated only within this shared mode of spatiality, and even their conspicuous divergence makes sense only in terms of spectatorship, determined by the audience's distance from and orientation toward what is being performed, be it onstage or off. The "domination" of the proscenium stage in twentieth-century China should not be reduced to a tale of Western hegemony; rather, the modern Chinese receptivity to this supposedly "alien" form of theater has actually been long prepared—yet not teleologically determined—by the rise of theatricality since the late Ming.

To argue that theatricality underlies and traverses the opposition between Western and Chinese theaters and thereby points toward a global history is not to say that it designates the universal for theater in all times and all places. Rather, Chinese theaters and performance venues before the turn of the seventeenth century operated within very different modes of the spatiality of emotion—namely, winds and dreamscapes. These early instances, one can say, present an oxymoron of "theater before/without theatricality." Just as the balconies built alongside the passage stage restructured the spatiality of the entire site around spectatorship, theatricality was superimposed on the dreamscape, reworking timeworn elements with new implications. The topographical overlap, however, has induced what I have called the anachronism inherent to the historical phenomena, resulting in a no less anachronistic account of history that either projects theatricality where it does not belong or codifies it as what it is not exactly.

As we have seen, our anachronistic understanding of theatricality has driven us to fill in the "blank" in *The Wrong Career* with plays-within-a-play that did not belong there; in the opposite direction, anachronism also tends to obscure the spatial structure pertaining to theatricality with other spatial modes—sometimes with winds but especially with the topos of dreamscapes that were still influential in early modern China—which explains why the original illustrations to *Sole Mates* dissolve the problem of distance (figured as the running river) by showing the crowd already mysteriously delivered across the river and surrounding the stage. In either case, anachronism camouflages itself with the illusion of continuity—by tracing spectatorship all the way back to the origin of time, by glossing theatricality in terms of winds and dreamscapes and therefore obscuring the discordance among them, and ultimately by representing the architectural history of Chinese theaters as a teleological evolution that culminated in functional completeness driven by pragmatic necessity.

Writing against this telos, I have reinterpreted the archaeological findings of theater architecture in light of the textual genealogy of the "spectator" (or his absence) within dramatic works. I adopted this approach, which combines textual analysis and archaeological research, to drive home the intermedial nature of theatricality, which, as we have seen, signifies not a quintessential feature of theater but a decentering of theater per se. Complementary to "theater without theatricality" is this notion of "theatricality beyond theater," in the sense that theatricality as the very mode of spatiality underlies the possibility of cross-media interfacing between stage and book, performance and reading, orality and print.

So far, we have come across a number of cases that illustrate this dimension of theatricality beyond theater: the late Ming "Journey to the West" novel, rather than the early drama cycle, presaged a "one-minded" audience looking at the theater of doubling; Xu Wei's *The Mad Drummer*, itself an effort to bring back a dramatic form largely disappearing from public theater, announced its indispensable reliance on the gaze of a spectator and hence the final mature form of a play-within-a-play by representing a spectator onstage; *The Peony Pavilion*, the bookish play alleged to be aurally incomprehensible for stage performance, carved out the position for a postdreamer as spectator finding herself *in front of* her own dream; and *The Sole Mates*, which Li Yu envisioned as much in printed format as performed onstage, established the centrality of spectatorship to every aspect of theatrical production. Historically, the rise of spectatorship did not start with the construction of the balcony, which only expressed what had been in the making for several decades. The architectural overhaul in the 1620s embodied the precipitated effect of the advent of the spectator since the late sixteenth century.

CHAPTER FOUR

"Not Even Close to Emotion"

A Genealogy of Knowledge

1. A VISION APART

The projection of spectatorship into the dreamscape of *The Wrong Career* is not an empirical mistake. Instead, as Catherine Bell has argued about the "performance" fallacy in ritual studies, this projection is the very condition of our supposedly infallible knowledge production. According to this fallacy, we are not voyeurs violating the integrity of another culture; rather, the people we are observing always already presume someone is looking at the culture they perform; hence, the ethnographer's spectatorial position is justified.[1] Here we see how ritual studies and drama studies work together to create a comfortable position from which to look.[2]

That is what happens when Claude Lévi-Strauss describes an anthropologist as a spectator by alluding to the oft-cited notion of *riken no ken* 離見の見 (Vision of a Distant View) from the treatise "A Mirror to the Flower" ("Kakyō" 花鏡, 1424), by which the Noh-drama master Zeami 世阿弥 (1363–1443) means "taking on the same vision as the audience and learning how you look in places where you cannot yourself see."[3] Naming a book of his (*Le regard éloigné*) after Zeami's notion,[4] Lévi-Strauss sums up the anthropologist's uncanny position as that of the spectator under whose gaze even one's own society—which was initially considered less worthy of study because of its proximity—can turn into an ethnological object.[5] Later, citing Lévi-Strauss's citation of Zeami, Antony Tatlow uses the embedded Zeami quote to depict the mutual appropriation between Brecht and Chinese opera.[6] Underlying the excitement over cultural self-otherness is the spectatorial position that every party presumes and occupies in turn.

Except, perhaps, for Zeami himself. Although *riken no ken* has been seen as a testimony to theatricality and spectatorship in fourteenth-century Noh theater,[7] a close reading of the related passage in the context of the entire essay, other treatises by Zeami, and the stage architecture makes clear that Zeami was describing something utterly different. The only other part of his oeuvre where *riken* can be interpreted as something seen by the audience from afar is a treatise titled "Goi" 五位 (Five ranks), in which the "effect of excitement" (*kanpū* 感風) that startles the audience's "minds and eyes" is thus also named "the visual excitement of a Distant View" (*riken no kenkan* 離見の見感). What is at issue here is not the spectatorial position as the vantage point, but rather the overwhelming power of "excitement" (in the form of *ki*), which is so pervasive that it can be felt by the audience even at a distance, creating a strong sense of immediacy (*soku* 即).[8] He continues to explain "excitement" by citing the "Great Preface": "'Rectifying gain and loss, budging heaven and earth, exciting demons and gods'; this we call excitement."[9]

The direct reference to the "Great Preface," from which the terms *fū* 風 (Chinese: *feng*) and *kan* 感 (Chinese: *gan*) are borrowed, signposts the spatiality of winds that permeate the realm and arouse instant sensation.[10] The Distant View (*riken*) arouses the startling excitement that hits home in the audience's senses. This overwhelming effect—or one could say "affect"— encroaches on one's eyes and mind and, no matter how far away one is seated, eliminates any sense of distancing implied by the term *riken*. And yet, even this spatiality of winds appears only transiently in Zeami's oeuvre, just as in the hierarchy of "Five Ranks," the "effect of excitement" is subsumed under the highest "effect of wonder" (*Myōfū* 妙風). It is this topos of wonder that we should turn to for the more significant mode of spatiality in which *riken* is ultimately framed and determined. This spatial mode is referred to as the "realm of *yūgen*" (*yūgen no sakai* 幽玄の境) and "wondrous places" (*myōsho* 妙所), both introduced just pages later than *riken* in "A Mirror to the Flower." *Yūgen* 幽玄 (Chinese: *youxuan*), originally a term in Chinese Daoism and

Buddhism for profound, unknowable mystery, first appeared in Japanese Buddhist literature at the turn of the ninth century. In Zeami's hands, it turned into a balance between the gentle elegance of gracefulness (which he took over from the *renga* poetics in the early fourteenth century) and the beauty of nothingness (*mu* 無, which reflected the convergence of Zen Buddhism under the influence of Song and Yuan China and the early Muromachi samurai culture).[11]

This duality can be detected in "A Mirror to the Flower" and raises further conceptual issues. On one hand, Zeami advises actors to take on the "the Vision of a Distant View" (*riken no ken*) in order to see the "graceful posture" (*yūshi* 幽姿) or "the graceful dance of the flower posture and jade virtue" (*kashi gyokutoku no yūbu* 花姿玉得の幽舞) in its complete form.[12] This emphasis on gracefulness is in line with a later section on "the realm of *yūgen*" that promotes "the basic style of *yūgen*," the greatest achievement in acting, as "a beautiful and gentle style," or as "beauty and palpable quality" made manifest to the audience's eyes.[13] On the other hand, when Zeami turns to discuss the "wondrous places," which are constituted by "the virtuosic fulfillment of *yūgen*," *yūgen* in this context no longer entails the beauty of gracefulness that is palpable to the audience's eyes (and accessible to actors themselves when they adopt the spectatorial perspective) but "a visual style that reaches the rank of no-mind and no-style" (*mushin mufū no i ni itaru kenpū* 無心無風の位に至る見風).[14]

What is missing in this discussion is how *riken* and *riken no ken* can fit in with this more profound reading of *yūgen* as the beauty of nothingness in wondrous places. It might be easy to see that a spectator is in a position to see the palpable grace of the actor's posture, but this hardly helps the spectator perceive the rather abstract, transcendent quality of no-mind and no-style. The apparent slippage between *riken* as something seen from the spectatorial position and *riken* as something abstractly perceived through the transcendence of the mind has puzzled acute readers.[15]

"The Mirror to the Flower" seems to remain silent on this problem, making no linkage between *riken* and wondrous places. But perhaps the link is always already there only if we realize that our initial grasp of *riken* as a distant view seen by the audience offers only a truncated understanding of the term. *Riken*'s broader scope, which cannot be tied down to the spectatorial position in the first place, is revealed on all other occasions when Zeami mentions *riken* or *riken no ken* again; in each case, the term is much more clearly centered on the topos of wonder. His treatise titled "Nine Ranks" ("Kyūi" 九位), for example, places the "Effect of the Wondrous Flower" (*myōkafū* 妙花風) at the peak of artistic accomplishment and ascribes it directly to *riken*:

> What I mean by wonder pertains to "the path of language severed, the locus of thinking destroyed." Is the sun at midnight a matter to which language can aspire? How does that happen? So then, the sublime effect of a true master in this vocation is beyond the reach of appreciation, and a Distant View (*riken*) of an excitement of no-mind (無心の感 *mushin no kan*) and a ranked effect of no-rank (無位の位風 *mui no ifū*) must most surely be the wondrous flower.[16]

This passage intimates a subtle shift from the ancient spatiality of winds to the wondrous places opened up by medieval Buddhism. The spatiality of wonder is elaborated as "the path of language severed, the locus of thinking destroyed" (*gongo dōdan shingyō shometsu* 言語道断、心行所滅), which is a quote from a Tendai Buddhist text that Zeami identifies as *The Tendai Interpretation of "Wondrous"* (*Tendai myōshaku* 天台妙釈) in "Five Ranks."[17] This peculiar focus on the problematic of language calls our attention to the Zen rhetoric of negation and paradox (an excitement of no-mind, a ranked effect of no-rank, the midnight sun) that embeds and reflexively sheds new light on the linguistic construction of *riken* in "Nine Ranks."[18] In a similar passage from another treatise, *An Effective Vision of Learning the Vocation of Fine Play in Performance* ("Yūgaku shudō fūken" 遊楽習道風見), which cites the same Tendai Buddhist quote, Zeami explains "the wondrous" in terms of "an excitement of no-excitement [無感之感 *mukan no kan*, which] becomes apparent in the *riken no ken*."[19] In this light, *riken* means not things seen from afar but a negation of seeing by departing (*ri* 離) from it; by the same token, *riken no ken* ultimately does not suggest adopting the other's vision apart from one's own, but a paradoxical Vision Apart from Vision per se,[20] which is constructed linguistically in the same unconventional manner as a ranked effect beyond any rank, an excitement felt by no-mind, or an excitement that is at the same time a no-excitement.

Lining up with all these other similar oxymoronic expressions, a Vision Apart from Vision does not recommend taking on the audience's viewpoint but instead instances an aporia that interrupts any artificially defined positions, mindsets, and categories, which—so often reified by language and one's partial perception—hinder our ability to access the wondrous. Therefore, as Zeami illustrates in *A Course to Attain the Flower* ("Shikadō" 至花道), a spectator does not really occupy any vantage point from his own perspective; the vantage is not gained until he starts to reflect upon and synthesize what he has just seen and to come up with a transcendent vision of the *yūgen* that an extraordinary actor has tried to present. Only in this sense does the vision that separates from vision (contra the spectator's own perspective) deliver him into the wondrous.[21]

Neither the spatiality of winds (in which the viewer is embedded with pervasive affect that short-circuits any distance) nor the spatial mode of theatricality (underscoring one's alienation from the other's position that one has to imaginatively identify with, the dominant mode of spatiality that Zeami traced in the early fifteenth century) approximates what we have called the dreamscape. It is no coincidence that Zeami invented the genre called *mugen* 夢幻—the Noh play of dreams and apparitions—which comprises the majority of his dramatic oeuvre, often featuring a priest who encounters in his dream a disguised being that actually comes from another world.[22] Although Steven T. Brown reminds us that *mugen* was a term retrospectively coined more than two hundred years after Zeami's time, what he sums up about "Zeami's theory of acting with its immanent ontology of the other's body"—which involves the actor *becoming* the other's body as if possessed by going through "the paradramatic space of the 'mirror room' (*kagami no ma*)"—actually suggests the spatiality of dreamscape rather than theatricality.[23] Correspondingly, in terms of aesthetic form (or no-form), the realm of *yūgen* and ultimately the wondrous places (that are constituted by the fulfillment of *yūgen*) represent the topography of layered demarcations, where one aspires to a higher plane of existence that is inaccessible to sense and language. In this topos of the dreamscape or the wondrous, the vision apart implies neither the immersion of affect nor sympathetic identification, but the *aporia* of both sense and language that delivers us to the other side paradoxically by severing the path (*dōdan* 道断).

"Not Even Close to Emotion" 151

Frequently cited out of context to mean the actor adopting the audience's viewpoint,[24] the notion of *riken no ken* from "A Mirror to the Flower" turns out to depict just a transitory point within an extensive interruption of sense and language routines. Adopting a vision apart from one's own paves the way to the ultimate Vision Apart from Vision. As a matter of fact, the discursive flow of "A Mirror to the Flower" does not stop at the vantage point of the spectator but rather takes it into the broader realm of *yūgen* and the wondrous places, already suggesting the implied association of *riken no ken* with "a visual style of the rank of no-mind and no-style." Isolating the *riken no ken* passage there and singling out the audience's viewpoint as the vantage for the Noh theater would obscure the more complete picture of the dreamscape in which the vision operates ultimately *apart* from the audience's eyes. The obscuration has led us to mistake the mode of spatiality at issue for theatricality, as seen in the case of Lévi-Strauss. In terms of the spatiality of emotion, anthropology reconfirms its ontological ground by misrecognizing in the Other the dreamscape as theatricality so that the spectatorial position for ethnographers to occupy can be shown as already furnished by the observed culture itself.

In the cases of the Song-Yuan and Noh theaters, I have attempted to redress this misrecognition by uncovering the historical mode of the spatiality of emotion that distinguishes them from theatricality. And yet, the most cunning aspect of this self-legitimation of knowledge production is its ability to turn the whole set of historical findings that the dreamscape is not based on spectatorship into an object for spectatorial consumption. A regime of spatiality without spectatorship turns out to be a product of the self-legitimization of theatricality. To revise Bell's diagnosis, one has to say that anthropology reconfirms its ontological ground by recognizing its cultural Other, whether *accurately or not*. There is no otherness beyond the gaze of the spectator; every reality is eroded by its infectious scan.

Lest we slip into Orwellian paranoia (which is more resonant than ever when these lines are being typed), we should remind ourselves that erosion has always occurred in both directions. We have seen this in the ambiguous notion that the Chinese "spectators are more than spectators." Not only is the dreamscape inevitably marked by the framing of theatricality, despite all the effort of historicization, but theatricality itself is seen as the dreamscape from time to time, especially in the Chinese context. This double anachronism, if it is illuminated rather than blindly practiced, is a good thing. It shows that the epistemological fear that we can never reach the thing-in-itself without any distorted intervention is actually invalid. It is utterly misleading to say that we can never understand another era, another culture (say, the dreamscape) because we are forever trapped in our own era. If this is so, why do things from the past constantly come back to haunt us, catch us off guard, and distort the mirror we look into for a straight image of ourselves? It is precisely in the ghostly distortion of the mirror reflection that we know *something else has left its trace*,[25] or we have left ours in something else. A trace is not a compromise, falling short of immediate presence—because presence by itself would be just ours, leaving no room for the Other.

We are about to enter the deepest understanding of theatricality, in which the spectator who can only imaginarily be transposed to another's position actually is at the same time already there, being absent from his own position. The knowledge of the Other is therefore presented through this divide of the spectator, which is not the splitting of the ego in the Freudian interior, but the exteriority expressed through distancing as hypostasized and foregrounded in theatricality.[26] To understand the trace of the dreamscape as something knowable in theatricality, therefore, we have to scrutinize how theatricality misunderstands itself as caught between two competing sets of knowledge production it has generated: namely, anthropology (in the eighteenth-century sense), which grasps the wholeness of an object paradoxically through its disintegration, and case history, which facilitates the disintegration of the object when supposedly delving into its particularity.

The divide of knowledge production in theatricality takes the form of self-misrecognition, which is further dramatized by the cross-cultural misreading among traditions that have reached the common ground of theatricality from different trajectories. To further extend my revisionist reading of Zeami, this divide of knowledge production in theatricality is "a vision apart from itself" neither in the sense that it takes the vantage point of the spectator from afar nor in the sense that it transcends every single perspective and departs from vision per se, but in the sense that a two-eyed skull can never generate a unitary perspective,[27] doubled by the confrontation between the spectator's simultaneous presence in and absence from both her own position and the position of the other.[28] Cross-cultural misreading testifies not to the incommensurability of China and the West but to the incommensurability within the incongruous landscape of theatricality that both traditions have come to share.

The case in point is the *Haoqiu zhuan* 好逑傳 (The fortunate union; also, The pleasing history). Published between the late seventeenth and early eighteenth centuries,[29] it is one of the first Chinese novels translated into Western languages. In its first European readers' eyes, the novel epitomized the "whole system of manners" in China, in which order and disorder paradoxically overlapped, showing at once the orderly civility *and* the unruly excess of the Chinese. These notions of wholeness and the simultaneity of order and disorder constitute the anthropological turn, which predicates Western knowledge on the finitude and perversity of humanity. Against this order-disorder totality as the foundation for the modern human sciences and hence modern interpretations of the *Haoqiu zhuan*, I propose to read the novel as the late Edo writers Kyokutei Bakin 曲亭馬琴 (1767–1848) and Hagiwara Hiromichi 萩原広道 (1815–1863) did.

My reading focuses on one particular aspect of the novel: *kyō/xia* 俠 ("knight-errantry"), a term prominent in the Chinese text but missing from the Western translations. Rather than serving as the final piece of the puzzle that we could simply put back in order to render the Chinese picture complete, *kyō/xia* here signifies an extreme case in which the norm is exerted beyond recognition. This points to a new mode of knowledge based on case thinking, which entails neither compliance with nor infringement of "the Chinese order," but a rupture in the very idea of the "whole." However, instead of reifying the East/West differences in knowledge production, I will show that both anthropology and case thinking invoke the more fundamental structure of spatiality, namely, theatricality, which ontologically grounds both modes of knowledge.

2. IN THE ORDER-DISORDER DOUBLET

Translated in 1719 by James Wilkinson, an employee of East India Company, as a kind of language exercise, the *Haoqiu zhuan* was the first Chinese novel rendered into English; it was translated into other European languages after its publication in London in 1761.³⁰ A relatively minor work at home, it was perceived abroad as "a piece of considerable note among the Chinese," taken by Western readers to represent, in its British editor Thomas Percy's words, "the *intire* manners of the Chinese" or still better, "the *whole system* of manners of a people [that] can only be *thoroughly known to themselves*."³¹ Superior to any of the Westerners' travelogues or missionary reports then available, a popular novel by a Chinese author—a native informant, as it were—was believed to present "the object in action" and relay thorough knowledge of the entire structure of the cultural order (P1.xv–xvii). This "whole system," as Percy mentioned in one of his footnotes, included "3000 rules of civility" that were "looked upon by [the Chinese] as essential to the good order and peace of the state" (P1.141–42). Out of a vain effort to exhaustively explain the system, Percy showered his readers with excessive commentary, comprising hundreds of extended notes (some of which overflow onto several pages) giving abundant examples illustrating various aspects of this system of Chinese order.

This whole system of manners, ensuring seamless order for the eternal being of the Empire and recounted by the Chinese themselves, was meaningful and conceivable only in a global context. Hence the famous conversation of January 31, 1827, during which Goethe related to Eckermann his ideas about "world literature" by way of his reading experience of "a Chinese novel." To Goethe, the novel represented a people "more clear, pure, decorous" than Europeans. "With them all is orderly, citizen-like, without great passion or poetic flight."³² While an entry of Goethe's diary shows that he might have mistaken a Cantonese chantefable, *Story of the Flowery Notepaper* (*Huajian ji* 花箋記), for a novel, what he continued to say in the conversation with Eckermann unmistakably refers to the *Haoqiu zhuan*, which was translated from English into German in 1766 and recited by Goethe to his friends at a literary salon in 1815:³³ "Another of two lovers who showed such great purity during a long acquaintance that, when they were on one occasion obliged to pass the night in the same chamber, they occupied the time with conversation and did not approach one another." Thanks to such "severe moderation," Goethe inferred, "the Chinese Empire has sustained itself for thousands of years, and will endure hereafter." His admiration of the Chinese novel inspired him to put forth the notion of "world literature": "National literature is now rather an unmeaning thing; the epoch of world literature is at hand." In the same breath, however, Goethe insisted that "while we thus value what is foreign, we must not bind ourselves to one particular thing, and regard it as a model." To him, it was only in ancient Greek literature that "the beauty of mankind is constantly represented," whereas "all the rest"—including the Chinese novel he had just mentioned—"we must look at only historically; appropriating to ourselves what is good, so far as it does."[34] World literature therefore implies not a carnival of multicultural texts but a hierarchical global order under which select tokens of foreignness are decontextualized and reappropriated for one's *national* interest.[35]

The ambiguity underlying Goethe's cosmopolitanism takes us back to the more dubious project of Percy, whose curiosity about the Chinese order represented by *Haoqiu zhuan* was matched by a compulsion to cast this order in an unfavorable light. Percy's preface and commentary to the novel fell in line with the trend in eighteenth-century English learned circles, thus turning against the sinophiles among the general public in England and intellectuals in continental Europe.[36] Despite or perhaps precisely because of the Chinese insistence on order, Percy looked down upon them as a timid and mediocre people with "a littleness and poverty of genius": "The abjectness of their genius may easily be accounted for from that servile submission, and dread of novelty, which inslaves the minds of the Chinese, and while it promotes the peace and quiet of their empire, dulls their spirit and cramps their imagination" (P1.xii–xiii). Such disparaging remarks were not negated by Goethe's positive appraisal; rather, Goethe, in asserting that the Chinese were orderly "without great passion or poetic flight," unwittingly echoes Percy's derision.

According to Percy, the Chinese order was not just debilitating; the entire edifice, in its minute elaboration of rules of etiquette, was also absurd, excessive, and perverse. The "3000 rules of civility" to which "is owing in great measure the wonderful stability of the Chinese empire" appeared now to be a bunch of "ridiculous" punctilios (P1.142). Chinese laws, previously seen as "utterly reasonable," were now dismissed as pointless because of failures of implementation; they "rather create[d] an appearance of virtue, than the reality" (P2.166–69). The virtue of filial piety was carried to "an idolatrous excess" (P1.163); no less "a ridiculous excess" were the myriad forms of address (P2.150–52). The "severe moderation" in sexual conduct that Goethe praised was labeled an "affectation" leading to "absurdity" (P1.116). With minds enslaved and spirits dulled under this senseless order, the only kinds of genius left to Chinese people were "acuteness and cunning" (P1.228) or "subtleness and craft," the very qualities embodied in the novel by the female protagonist Shui Bingxin, who, as Percy noted, "is set forth by the Chinese author, as the perfect exemplar of all virtue." Yet for him, this "virtue" quickly degenerated into "guile" (P1.219).[37]

The point here is not to take an easy shot at Percy's chauvinistic prejudice against China while praising Goethe's cosmopolitanism. Instead, I would argue that Percy and Goethe both operate within a common discursive field, which bestows their opposite appraisals of China with uncanny similarities. First, both perceive the burden of the Chinese order to be crushing creativity and imagination. Second, when Goethe elevates Greek literature to the status of the *universal model* and sees Chinese literature as just *historical*, something to be *appropriated*, he is echoing Percy's recommendation that the "Chinese people 'would be gainers by the exchange' of their own language for Greek."[38] Third, both have to be contextualized in a global picture, in which the Chinese order is resituated and ambiguously transvalued. Before Goethe talked about "world literature," Percy had already cited a "pleasant story" about the shock of the Chinese at finding that their great country was in a corner of a world map (P1.66–67). What unites Percy and Goethe in spite of their different attitudes toward China is the peculiar discourse of "order," which is not so much the opposite of "disorder" as an expanse of excesses, dysfunctions, and perversions. Disorder designates not the lack, loss, or absence of order but that which is coextensive with order. One might dismiss such a perverted vision of the Chinese order as just another example of how the Oriental Other is denigrated by a Eurocentric global mapping.[39] Yet this dubious account of order overlapping with disorder runs much deeper. It indexes a profound restructuring of what can be known by and about humans—a new condition of knowledge that the West imposes on itself as well in the advent of globality.[40]

Between 1760 and 1790, Europe was turning to "man" as both the object and the foundation of knowledge. At its outset, anthropology took the route of empirical psychology to explore the emotive and cognitive functions of the (Western European) individual. These were then used to measure the world-historical progression of various other peoples: hence the emergence of a modern global consciousness that was, initially at least, provincially Eurocentric.[41] Immanuel Kant's *Anthropologie in pragmatischer Hinsicht* (begun in 1772 and published in 1798) is one example of this anthropological turn. Through Foucault's scrutiny of Kant's anthropology, three characteristics can be extracted: (1) anthropology strives to capture the *whole* of the complex of human existence, the world that serves as the source, domain, and limit for what humans can know, should do, and would hope for; (2) this knowledge of the world can be discovered through native, everyday language, which now displaces "Latinicity" and serves to inform the universal philosophical language; and (3) a study of not "what man is" but "what man can and should make of himself" in the concrete existence affected by time. This anthropological knowledge takes note not of the positive attributes of human faculties and power but of the "illegitimate" deviance from their central principles and justification; an entire cultural order is therefore manifested in its *pathology*. The whole of human existence ultimately refers not to an empirical collection of customs but to this co-extensiveness of order and disorder, which means there is no exteriority to order.[42] Defining the structural whole of a people's existence as an order-disorder doublet, these terms of anthropology set the parameters of Percy's and Goethe's reading of the Chinese novel. This anthropological turn of knowledge in the eighteenth century formed the matrix of modern human sciences, which still govern our discursive production. And the order-disorder doublet accompanying the modern epistemic shift has resulted in the political problematic of containment.[43] If, in our political defeatism, containment forecloses any way out of the system, it is because at the epistemological level the order-disorder doublet has always already figured as a totality of coextension eliminating genuine oppositions. It is against this epistemological background that we should reconceptualize the predicament of "containment" in Foucault's political analysis, which, mediated through the new historicism, has influenced the study of late imperial Chinese fiction.

The modern discipline of anthropology, which inherited its name from this paradigm, articulates most clearly the order-disorder doublet in its characterization of society. In Claude Lévi-Strauss's words:

> A society is at once a machine and the work done by that machine. As a steam-engine, it produces entropy, but if we look upon it as a mechanism, it produces order. This dual aspect—order and disorder—corresponds, in the language of anthropology, to two ways of looking at any civilization: there is, on the one hand, culture, and on the other, society. . . .
>
> This being the case, we might say that any social field—if we call a society a social field—produces entropy, or disorder, as a society, and creates order, as a culture.[44]

Order and disorder are therefore not mutually exclusive; rather, they are two sides of a coin called the social field, with their coextension governed by the rules of a zero-sum game: the more order is produced in culture, the more disorder is generated in society.[45] This disorder—which Lévi-Strauss calls entropy, a term in physics for chaos and randomness in a thermodynamic system—also becomes the very focus of the anthropological study of the human order. That is why Lévi-Strauss, playing with the pun, suggests that entropology is a better name than anthropology for the study of the process of disintegration.[46]

We have therefore missed the point in accusing Lévi-Strauss's structural anthropology of being ahistorical; his notion of entropy has already opened up any cultural system, however static, to diachronic change. The "structural, historical anthropology" put forth by Marshall Sahlins, which strives to bring historical contingency back to the synchronic account of culture (and at a higher level, indigenous agency back to the world system), is tautological. Not surprisingly, Sahlins arrives at almost the same typology of societies as Lévi-Strauss did: some societies more "performative" and malleable by practices and events, some others less so;[47] in other words, the former experience higher levels of entropy than the latter. Sahlins's mediation between system and event, culture and history, is therefore one more incarnation of the order-disorder doublet. The desire to grasp the "whole" of a cultural system is driven, not mitigated, by incorporating historical contingency, since, as Sahlins claims, "from the standpoint of a diachronic structure," even what seems like "permanent ambiguity" or "inherent contradiction" in a synchronic order will be "at once resolved and rendered intelligible" by "a more general notion of structure, [which is] necessarily temporal."[48]

It is precisely this notion of temporal or diachronic structure that thrusts us directly into, rather than liberating us from, what Foucault calls "the anthropological circle"—in which the humankind reaches its truth only through the objectified knowledge of its madness[49]—or what I call the order-disorder doublet. It is because the doublet is predicated on human existence that is affected and corrupted by time. Yet, it is always a matter of entering the circle in a right way. To disrupt the "whole" from within, I propose to reverse Sahlins's formulation and explore the "permanent ambiguity" or "inherent contradiction"—the aporia of temporality—at the heart of diachronicity. Thanks to its aporetic structure, diachronicity casts light on the rupture of the whole in the order-disorder doublet. This allows us a glimpse of the association between the spatiality of emotion and the issue of time.

3. A TERM MISSING FROM THE WHOLE

Nowadays, readers East and West still look for "order" in *Haoqiu zhuan*. Though few see the novel as a comprehensive repository of eternal Chinese customs, it appears to our inquisitive eyes as representative of the sexual economy of Qing China. Introductions to modern Chinese editions of the novel either defend or debunk the traditional virtue of chastity ("severe moderation" in Goethe's words) with which the novel has been identified.[50] Scholars have commended the partaking of individual characters in the social models advocated in the novel,[51] or critiqued the conservative domestication of desire through the desexualized notion of *qing*.[52] What remains intact is the presupposition of an encompassing cultural order—presented in the novel "in a nutshell"—wherein the virtue of chastity and neurotic repression coexist.

Ubiquitous though it is even today, this mode of reading is historically bound rather than universal and inevitable—this becomes clear when it is compared to the reception of the *Haoqiu zhuan* in Japan. The novel first appeared on the Japanese import records in 1731, and one century later, Kyokutei Bakin expanded elements taken from the first three chapters of *Haoqiu zhuan* into his novel *Daring Adventures of Chivalric Men* (*Kaikan kyōki kyōkaku den* 開卷驚奇俠客伝, 1832–1835). Hiromichi Hagiwara (1815–1863), who supplemented Bakin's unfinished novel with a fifth volume in 1849, went on to translate the first five chapters of the *Haoqiu zhuan* into Japanese.[53] What attracted these men to the Chinese novel, however, was not the system of customs that Percy and Goethe found there. In a letter dated 1830, Bakin expressed amusement with the *kyō* 俠 or *ninkyō* 任俠 (Chinese: *xia* or *renxia*, meaning chivalry, knight-errantry, heroism, valiance) shown by both the male and female protagonists; otherwise, the novel was "nothing special."[54] At issue for Bakin is not a pervasive cultural system or its derangement—that would not be a concern until the first full-version Japanese translation came out, with a reference to Goethe's appraisal, in 1942.[55] Bakin, instead, zeroes in on one peculiar mode of conduct: *renxia/ninkyō*, an "amusing" motif that would make the novel profitable in the late Edo book market.[56]

But it is tempting to put *xia* back in "the Chinese order," especially since the twentieth century, when *wuxia* 武俠 ("martial arts") fiction and movies became quintessentially "Chinese" in both local and global markets of mass culture.[57] Either a liminal guardian for an endangered order that marginalizes it in the first place[58] or an unruly expression of sadism, misogyny, and cannibalism,[59] Chinese knight-errantry seems to be a good fit for the order-disorder doublet.[60] The fit might appear even better when we examine the specific articulation of *xia* within the eighteenth-century *Haoqiu zhuan*. The action-packed early parts of the novel, which interested late Edo readers most, depict the talented and stalwart hero Tie Zhongyu 鐵中玉 storming a marquis's mansion to rescue a kidnapped girl, while the shrewd and audacious heroine Shui Bingxin 水冰心 avoids one trap after another laid by her wicked uncle and suitor. When Bingxin is in danger and Zhongyu intervenes, the two storylines merge. On several levels, their chivalry seems to reconfirm the discourse of (dis)order: First, both are fighting the abusive power that threatens the family (thus correlatively the state) order. Second, however, the practical ways in which they achieve their noble goal of defending the family/state order are dubious: Zhongyu's impetuous violence shatters the social hierarchy, and Bingxin's cunning manipulation nullifies the marriage agreement she pretends to comply with.[61]

"*Not Even Close to Emotion*"

Third, these deviant behaviors call for a theoretical justification based on the dichotomy of norm (*jing* 經) and expedient (*quan* 權), the key terms in Confucian casuistry, which applies general and theoretical principles to particular situations by comparing and contrasting various cases. The fundamental distinction between the terms is invoked very early in the novel. In chapter 2, when being queried about whether he should have gone through the normal legal procedure instead of beating up the marquis, Zhongyu retorts:

> "What you say is the norm (*jing*), but still you have to know about the expedient (*quan*). The atrocity of that man's conduct requires another mode of proceeding. The case is too urgent to apply common rules." "Your heroic action (*yingxiong zuoyong* 英雄作用) is beyond our comprehension," said the others, "and we beg to ask whether you came hither to revenge some injury as a great knight-errant (*daxia* 大俠), or to right some other person."[62]

In this way chivalry becomes meaningful—and problematic—at the point of convergence and divergence between *jing* and *quan*. Ever since they were raised as a pair of significant categories in the *Gongyang Commentary to the Spring and Autumn Annals* (*Chunqiu Gongyang zhuan* 春秋公羊傳), the ambiguous nature of *quan*, which depends on how one looks at its varying relationship to *jing*, has caused much debate. Does *quan* mean the *opposite* (*fan* 反) of *jing* and therefore amount to out-and-out guile? Or is it just a detour leading *back* to (*fan* 返) the constant of *jing*? In the name of what—goodness, the Way, or righteousness—and under what conditions can this suspension of *jing* be justified?[63] Due to these ambiguities, chivalry as expediency in the *Haoqiu zhuan* is both the fail-safe mechanism that kicks in to restore order when the system fails *and* itself a kind of system failure. That is why Zhongyu's father, the imperial censor, tells his son to prepare for the civil examinations rather than "straying into knight-errantry" (*liuru youxia* 流入游俠), even though without the latter's heroic feat the censor would have failed to capture the lawbreaking marquis (H2.14b).

This problematic of knight-errantry was what fascinated Bakin. His preface to book 1 of *Daring Adventures of Chivalric Men* (hereafter *Daring Adventures*) cites the controversial "Biographies of Knights-Errant"

("Youxia liezhuan" 遊俠列傳) from Sima Qian's 司馬遷 (145-ca. 86 BCE) *Records of the Grand Historian* (*Shiji* 史記) to celebrate borderline criminal conduct in the cause of righteousness.[64] The novel is set in the politically ambiguous aftermath of the civil war between the Southern and Northern Courts (1336–1362). The twenty-six-year conflict broke out when the Muromachi shogunate replaced the venerable Emperor Go-Daigo 後醍醐天皇 with a puppet monarch under his own control. By the time the story proper starts, the country has been reunified under the third-generation shogun Ashikaga Yoshimitsu 足利義滿 (r. 1368–1394), who appropriated from Go-Daigo's successor the "three divine tokens" that traditionally symbolize legitimacy. Here Zhongyu and Bingxin are reincarnated as Koroku 小六 and Komahime 姑摩姬, descendents of the famed royalist Nitta 新田 and Kusunoki 楠木 clans, respectively. Determined to avenge their families and the fallen Southern Court against the evil yet "legitimate" shogun by whatever means necessary, these two young rebels quickly confront the need to measure expediency against norms in their initiation into knight-errantry.

A discussion of *quan* (Japanese: 權 *ken*) comes up for the first time at the beginning of book 2 of the novel, when Koroku sets off to assassinate a powerful vassal of the shogun, Fujishiro Yasutomo 藤白安同, who has murdered Koroku's father and is now bent on entrapping his surrogate father, Nogami no Fuhito Akinobu 野上史著演. A rural samurai who formerly served the Nittas, Akinobu is established from the very beginning of the story as "the one knight-errant of the realm" (*kaidai ichi no kyōsha* 海內一の俠者, K1.36), praised for his "valor" (*kyōki* 俠気, K1.16) and "righteous heroic deeds" (*giki ninkyō* 義気任俠, K1.46). The acts that earned him this exalted reputation are not at all unconventional, but rather very much in conformity with ordinary notions of charity: repeatedly we are told that he is a *xia/kyō* because he has sponsored the proper burial of thousands of war victims' remains. Despite the fact that Akinobu is presented as *the* model for the young Koroku, it is only by breaking with Akinobu's kind of socially sanctioned knighthood that the boy is able to claim the lofty status of "lonely hero" (*kokyō* 孤俠) in his own right (K2.154). Upon learning Yasutomo's plot against his surrogate father, Koroku decides to dispatch the evil vassal and his numerous bodyguards without implicating Akinobu. In a startling feat, Koroku suddenly feigns madness, storming Akinobu's house before vanishing in a torrential stream, faking his own death. In disguise, he launches a surprise raid on Yasutomo. Right before the venture, Koroku explains his guileful act (to a collaborator whom he deems a *xia/kyō*), highlighting the dubious nature of "expediency" (*quan/ken*) but also justifying it in the name of adapting flexibly to contingent situations. Rather than moral principles of charity and righteousness, the hallmarks of his surrogate father, it is this "expedient maneuver" (*quanmou/kenbō* 権謀) that characterizes Kokoru's debut as a knight-errant and launches the main course of action in the novel.[65]

The same applies to the initiation of Komahime, the "female knight-errant" (*jokyō* 女俠, Chinese: *nüxia*, K4.554, 5.655) whose case will be examined more closely in the next section. Interestingly, the issue of expediency, in terms of which we specifically understand the notion of *xia/kyō* here, is self-consciously presented as a matter of cultural translation in the case of the woman warrior. Book 5, authored by Hiromichi, largely expands on chapter 3 of the *Haoqiu zhuan*, where Bingxin demonstrates her appreciation of expedient means at times of crisis: she seems to agree to a marriage to a villainous suitor, promoted by her self-serving uncle, by submitting the "eight characters" (*gengtie bazi* 庚帖八字); but it turns out that the eight characters actually belong to the uncle's own daughter and thus change the identity of the bride. In the *Daring Adventures*, Komahime plays a similar trick on her estranged uncle when she is asked to provide her "eight characters" in return for some lost hereditary possessions, including a brocade banner conferred by the late Emperor Go-Daigo. When it is discovered that, employing exactly the same strategy used by Bingxin, she has substituted the eight characters of another woman for her own in an effort to evade an unwanted marriage, she not only evokes expediency (*ken*) to justify herself but also reflects upon the particular cross-cultural context in which it is operating. Since the "foreign" (Chinese) custom of submitting one's "eight characters" in matchmaking has no sanction in Japanese tradition, Komahime argues, it is therefore legitimate for her to respond to such an "abnormal rite" (*hijō no rei* 非常の礼) with an "abnormal maneuver" (*hijō no hakarigoto* 非常の籌策) (K5.635).[66] Allegorically speaking, the unconventional import of a foreign custom parrallels the cultural transplantation of the notion of expediency. At issue, however, is not the trafficking of an idea from one cultural system to another; rather, expediency is not part of any system of customs that either Percy or Goethe was looking for, but rather a function of the contingency of this cross-cultural transaction.

In fact, *xia* or chivalry, through the grid of *jing* and *quan* (which presents the dilemma that order finds its support in disorder), would have been most relevant to the order-disorder doublet through which the *Haoqiu zhuan* was understood in eighteenth- and nineteenth-century Europe. Paradoxically, however, the notion of *xia* (or its proximate equivalents in Chinese: *yingxiong* 英雄, *haojie* 豪傑) simply failed to come through either in the Wilkinson-Percy edition of *The Pleasing History* or in the later translation made by John Francis Davis in 1829 under the title *The Fortunate Union*.[67] (Like its predecessor in 1761, Davis's new translation was the version on which the second wave of *Haoqiu zhuan* translations in nineteenth-century continental Europe was based.) Every time the notion appears, it mutates into something else. In place of "*da xia*" 大俠 ("great knight-errant") (H2.14a), for instance, the Wilkinson-Percy edition gives "wisdom and courage" (P1.61), while Davis's choice is "a superior, or a god!" (F1.46). A reference to the couple as "the wonderful man and woman in righteous chivalry" (*yixia qi nannü* 義俠奇男女) (H6.10b), is diluted to "so virtuous a pair" in the Wilkinson-Percy edition (P2.37) or, even worse, "fam'd characters" in Davis (F1.143). When the narrator praises Shui Bingxin for her "chilly bones of knight-errantry" (*xia gu lingling* 俠骨泠泠) (H5.11a), the Wilkinson-Percy edition oddly supplies "Her countenance bespeaks a disposition as sweet as the most odoriferous flowers" (P1.212),[68] and Davis does not fare any better with "the cold and rigid strictness of her *manners*" (F1.119, my italics) (see the following list).

Given the intention of capturing "the whole system of *manners* of a people"—which Davis inherited from the 1761 translation and expressed in his numerous footnotes—why was the term *xia* systematically ignored or radically mistranslated? "Bad translation" or "ignorance of Chinese culture" (compared to the supposedly better Edo readers) explains little and begs more questions. What makes the question more pointed is that Percy seemed to be aware that an important value or ethical debate in the novel had been elided from Wilkinson's translation. In one of his notes, Percy stumbles on the word "gallantry," a possible translation for *xia*. But he rejects the possibility that this quality has any place

"Not Even Close to Emotion" 165

METAMORPHOSES OF *XIA* IN ENGLISH TRANSLATIONS OF THE *HAOQIU ZHUAN*

Chinese original	Wilkinson-Percy (1761)	John Francis Davis (1829)
大俠 (H2.14a)	Wisdom and courage (P1.61)	A superior, or a god! (F1.46)
流入游俠 (H2.14b)	That extravagance of warmth, to which your temper is addicted (P1.64)	Let the impetuosity of your temper betray you into trouble (F1.47)
俠骨泠泠 (H5.11a)	Her countenance bespeaks a disposition as sweet as the most odoriferous flowers (P1.212)	The cold and rigid strictness of her manners (F1.119–20)
義俠奇男女 (H6.10b)	So virtuous a pair (P2.37)	Fam'd characters (F1.143)
俠烈 (H7.)	The sport of passion (P2.87–88)	Impetuosity (F1.165)
英雄豪傑 (H7.12b)	Virtue and greatness of soul (P2.98–99)	Persons of their superior characters (F1.172)

in the story. After toying with the term, he pronounces it irrelevant to the male protagonist, because "gallantry" has no place "among a people, who admit of no intercourse between two Sexes; whose Marriages are contracted without the consent of the Parties, and even without their personal knowledge of each other; and who by being allowed a plurality of Women lessen their attention to any one" (P2.127–28).

In focusing exclusively on one sense of the word—that is, emphasizing attentive treatment of women rather than great bravery in war or danger—Percy manages to deny the existence of "gallantry" in the novel. Of course this is particularly interesting because the novel—as he must have known—in fact depicts just the sort of male-female relationship that he identifies as "gallant": a monogamous relationship growing out of frequent interactions between the male and female protagonists. But Percy does not recognize his own contradiction, and the untranslated term *xia* was left aside as neither order nor disorder, a ghostly absence from the whole system.

Percy's emphasis on "intercourses between two Sexes" as the condition for gallantry suggests an explanation for the failure of not only Percy but also Davis, who knew Chinese, to engage with the notion of *xia*. One might be tempted to say that unlike the Western chivalric hero, for whom "love of a beauty is a great honor and an inspiration to prowess," the traditional Chinese *xia* feels threatened by erotic attraction, which is seen as compromising the stoic heroic code.[69] But before we yield to general perceptions of East-West cultural differences, which are usually too reductive to clarify concrete situations, we should take a closer look at the peculiar way the chivalry in the *Haoqiu zhuan* insists on sexual abstinence by modifying the meaning of the *jing-quan* tension, which suggests a possibility to get out of the order-disorder doublet.

4. ECSTATIC TEMPORALITY OF CASUISTRY

The domestic order delineated by the supposedly rigid Chinese gender segregation, on which Percy and Davis comment repeatedly,[70] is thrown into chaos when, in chapter 6, Bingxin offers to shelter the ailing Zhongyu, who has been poisoned by their enemies. Bingxin legitimates her "heroic undertaking" (*yingxiong zuoshi* 英雄做事) by invoking a precedent from Confucius—"even the Sage, when finding himself in danger, could not walk away without resorting to expediency" (*shengren zhi chu huannan weichang wu quan* 聖人之處患難，未嘗無權). This speech and behavior make her, in Zhongyu's eyes, a "magnanimous hero" (*da haojie* 大豪傑) (H6.6b–7a). When confronted by her uncle, who takes issue with her accommodation of a young man, she gives him a long lecture, unpacking Mencius's famous statement that a man *should* expediently violate the rule of sexual segregation in order to save a sister-in-law from drowning (H6.14a–16a). To eliminate any ambiguities in her practice of *quan*, however, Bingxin watchfully stays in the dark behind a curtain when chatting and drinking with Zhongyu,

"Not Even Close to Emotion" 167

who sits under a light on the other side of the curtain (H7.5b–6a).⁷¹ The scene stages their innocence for the eyes of a thief on the roof, sent by the magistrate to spy on the couple. Here it takes a new expedient—the magistrate's employment of a thief—to demonstrate the legitimacy of a previous expedient act—Bingxin's violation of the norm of sexual segregation.⁷² Conversely, with Bingxin's inappropriate conduct now justified, the thief's "break-in"—*zuan kui* 鑽窺, a term that had a strong connotation of illicit intercourse since the time of Mencius—is pronounced a "nice business" (*meishi* 美事) by the narrator.⁷³ In this double movement, *quan* reinforces its own authority by way of itself.

Upon verification of their spotless virtue, the magistrate (who had been conspiring with Bingxin's wicked suitor) miraculously reforms and, along with Bingxin's uncle (whose plan has also changed), advocates the union of Bingxin and Zhongyu. Yet precisely at the moment when expediency is fully accepted by the society, it is abruptly discredited, if not entirely discarded. Against everyone's expectation, both Bingxin and Zhongyu violently dismiss the idea of marrying; even when, in the face of another crisis, Bingxin pretends to wed Zhongyu, they refuse to consummate the marriage. In Bingxin's words, "We may at least remain as we are, with the name of marriage, and the reality of friendship and esteem." And the narrator reports that even though their marriage "was confined as yet to its external forms, their esteem and attachment for each other exceed those of an ordinary couple who intimately share their bed" (H15.16b, 16.1a; F2.135–36, translation modified). Modern readers tend to read this infamous episode of sexual denial in Chinese literary history as reflective either of the worship of the chaste body in the Qing⁷⁴ or of the projection of male homoerotic "friendship" onto a heterosexual relationship (a characteristic of chivalry-love tales since the late Ming).⁷⁵ Instead of taking the order or disorder of the sexual economy as the ultimate point of reference, I propose to step back and scrutinize the logic of the narrative—or more precisely, the mode of temporality underlying this logic—that leads to the characters' ascesis.

In other words, we have to ask why the idea and practice of *quan*, which by chapter 7 has reached its zenith of power in authorizing the protagonists' heroic undertaking with a double movement of self-authorization, would suddenly be inadequate to justify the marriage of Zhongyu and Bingxin. That is exactly what Bingxin's uncle complains about in chapter 8 when Bingxin cites the irregular situation in which she and Zhongyu had met (in states of emergency without proper ceremonies or go-betweens) as the reason they should not get married:

> "Remember," said her uncle, "what you observed the other day, about expediency (*quan*) afforded by such exigencies as a man giving a hand to the drowning sister-in-law. [So it won't be a problem if you two get married even in an irregular situation.]"
> Bingxin, the young lady, retorted: "Expediency is just a matter of the moment. It would be absurd if, after pulling the sister-in-law out of the water, the man pulled her again even though she was not drowning. Moreover, expediency can be applied to anything—except for marriage, which is the chief of human relations, and therefore should be scrupulously regulated from the beginning to the end—it does not allow for any intervention by expediency."
> "There is no need to talk about the regulated end," cried the other; "just look at the beginning of your acquaintance: although it started in a situation of crisis that did not allow any orderly procedure, yet everybody knows that neither of you has ever slipped into dissipation, and accordingly we won't call the beginning unregulated."
> "The proof that we began without dissipation," replied the young lady, "depends on our not concluding this acquaintance by marriage. Only that would reveal our innocence thoroughly. Were we to finish with wedlock, who would believe that we began without dissipation?" (H8.4a; F2.183, translation modified)

To her uncle's suggestion that Bingxin and Zhongyu can get married under the auspices of expediency, Bingxin makes three counterarguments. The first one, that expediency is just "a matter of the moment" (*yishi* 一時), is inconclusive, because it cannot foreclose any future exigency—the man still can and should give help if his sister-in-law is drowning *again*. The second one, that marriage is beyond the sovereignty of expediency, is simply unsustainable, because expediency, according to its formal definition, means noncompliance with the norm, regardless of what content the norm bears. Even overthrowing a ruler was already included as an example of *quan* among Confucian scholars;[76]

"*Not Even Close to Emotion*" 169

the exceptional status Bingxin grants marriage to protect it from any arguments from expediency is therefore hardly defensible.

Bingxin's third argument, the only genuine one, introduces an extra factor that complicates the *jing-quan* coordinates: the diachronic relationship of expedient acts. Bingxin is not saying that one has to remain pure and virtuous from beginning to end—that "pedant's talk," using the uncle's words, is nothing new. What Bingxin really tells us is that she and Zhongyu started their acquaintance during an emergency, without following proper procedures; they had to resort to a chivalric expediency that violated the norm, but at least were able to avoid dissipation. Once this first expedient act is carried out, however, its moral purchase necessarily conditions their ensuing course of action, and any consideration of future expediency has to revisit this previous act. Conversely, what they take liberties to do in the future would threaten what they accomplished in the past. They cannot authorize themselves to get married in the name of *quan* without destroying the knight-errantry of the *quan* they established in the first place. Or, to use Zhongyu's succinct expression, "Should we eventually contract marriage, our former acts of knight-errantry will turn into something performed with an ulterior view" (F2.101, translation modified).[77]

Underlying Bingxin's diachronic thinking of expediency are Heidegger's so-called "ecstasies of temporality." "As the *ekstatikon par excellence*," temporality is "the primordial 'outside of itself' in and for itself,"[78] in the sense that "each dimension of time is treated or aimed at as something other than itself."[79] Not only does the past condition the present, leading to a certain future, but a projected future retrospectively revises our understanding of the past that is in turn factored into how we adjust our course of action at present. In Bingxin, we start to see the issue of expediency become temporalized in such a way that her actions (and nonaction) at various moments are related, bearing on one another's meaning. Considerations of expediency are thus tantamount to a narrative of the self built on what Paul Ricoeur calls the "interconnectedness of life." The ecstatic unity of moments supporting such a narrative, however, is as much disjunctive as interconnected. As Ricoeur points out: "Heideggerian repetition reveals itself to be the emblematic expression of the most deeply concealed figure of discordant concordance," because the "unity [of coming towards, having-been, and making present] is said to be undermined from within by the dehiscence of what Heidegger henceforth calls the ecstasies of time. . . . Whence the surprising assertion: temporality is the primordial 'outside of itself' [*Ausser-sich*] in and for itself."[80] Any sense of the "interconnectedness of life" can only be a fictive organization through narrativization, which tries to bestow concordance upon the discordant. The dehiscence is manifest in Bingxin's struggle with the expedient decision she made in the past: rather than seeing past, present, and future cohesively come together, reinforcing one another in repetition, Bingxin can only preserve the legacy of her expedient act she took in the past by denying expediency per se in the future.

This discordant connection between expedient acts is precisely what underlies—and almost undermines, in the sense of pulling it all the way down to earth—the knight-errantry of Bingxin's Japanese counterpart, Komahime. Unlike Koroku, who remains an unfledged youth under the wings of his surrogate father for the first fifth of the novel, Komahime soars with exuberant powers not long after her first appearance at the end of book three of *Daring Adventures*. A blend of Bingxin and magic swordswomen from other medieval and late imperial Chinese stories,[81] Komahime undergoes supernatural training in her childhood. Casting a spell of invisibility, she fatally shoots Shogun Ashikaga Yoshimitsu at his headquarters and walks away under everybody's nose. But when she asks permission to kill off other Ashikaga kinsmen, her immortal mentor Kurohime 九六媛 curbs her powers by adducing the principle of expediency and, more important, by appraising expedient acts in their diachronic relationship.

At this point, Kurohime explains that lending the young girl the swordplay skill of knights-errant (*kenkyō no jutsu* 剣俠の術) was done only expediently (*shibaraku jutsu o kashitaru nomi* 権且術を借したるのみ): "in China, for those swordswomen (*kenkyō no onago* 剣俠の女子), once the revenge has been achieved, this skill should not be used again; otherwise, calamity would befall."[82] She further warns that, as powerful as the magic (*genjutsu* 幻術) is, it will be overcome by a forthright, heroic enemy (*hōsei eiyū no teki* 方正英雄の敵). This discussion of the nonrepeatable expedient reverses the black-and-white moral judgment well established until now. Up to this point, it has been unthinkable that an opponent on the Ashikaga side could be "forthright" and "heroic," but now Kurohime reminds the girl that the Ashikagas have got the three divine tokens in their possession and that the puppet emperor they crowned has therefore become the orthodox (*seitō* 正統) ruler (K3.323–24). Predictably, Komahime fails to heed the advice and tries to assassinate the new shogun, only to be defeated by the famous "little monk Ikkyū" (*ko oshō* Ikkyū 小和尚一休), who humbles the recalcitrant Komahime by arguing that she should have challenged the shogunate openly on the battlefield rather than making clandestine raids (K3.337).[83] Here Komahime bears out Bingxin's worst fears that a later expedient act could ruin the meaning of an earlier act; through her rash attempt to destroy her enemy by stealth, she ends up lending legitimacy to his regime (see figure 4.1).[84]

Thanks to ecstatic temporality, which subjects the meaning of actions to discordant diachrony, the casuistry in the *Haoqiu zhuan* and *Daring Adventures* become radically different from traditional

FIGURE 4.1 "Regretful over not heeding the advice, the female knight-errant is ensnarled in a bitter battle." Illustrated by Ikeda Eisen in 1831–1835. *Source: Kaikan kyōki kyōkaku den.*

discussions of *quan*. The latter concentrate only on contemporaneity—the timeliness of taking action vis-à-vis a particular situation at present. Zhu Xi, who wrote in the era in Chinese cultural history when publications of legal casebooks first thrived,[85] would call the action proper to its time *"yishi zhi zhong"* 一時之中.[86] The only diachronic relationship Zhu Xi perceives is not that between an individual's expedient acts but that between the norm and the expedient: *"Jing* is the *quan* that has already been institutionalized; *quan* is the *jing* that has not yet been so" (*jing shi yiding zhi quan, quan shi weiding zhi jing* 經是已定之權，權是未定之經).[87] In so saying, Zhu Xi envisages not the qualification or negation of expediency by the sedimentation of preceding actions but exactly the opposite: the universal confirmation of expedients by putting them on equal footing with the norms, which turn out to be the institutionalization or fossilization of expedient acts. This drive toward extricating universal meanings from a particular instance went in line with the rise of a general thinking in cases during the Song period. Robert Hymes finds this "cross-case comparative urge at work" not simply in what are formally recognizable to us as casebooks but also in a wide range of "cultural practices—the Imperial Seminar, the examinations, memorials, philosophical dialogue, petty-religious pedagogy, the teaching of letter-writing—that constructed knowledge at least in part out of the interaction of general principles, recurrences, or maxims with concrete instances of historical or personal experience."[88]

Later, these two notions of temporality in Zhu Xi—timeliness and institutionalization of *quan*—merged to define the legal system and fictional discourse of the Qing. The hierarchy of statutes (*lü* 律), substatutes (*li* 例), and leading cases (*cheng'an* 成案) implied an effort both to close the gap between laws and myriad circumstances (by comparing a lawsuit at hand with leading cases) *and* to generalize from specific events (by institutionalizing practical cases into substatutes).[89] In the novel *Shiyuan huanjian* 世緣幻鑑 (The illusory mirror of fates in the world) attributed to a Guanwu'an 觀物庵,[90] there is an episode in which the protagonist Lu Yicheng 呂頤誠 debates with the School Superintendent about a "public case undecided for hundreds of generations" (*baishi gong'an* 百世公案): why did the Sage King Shun 舜 (who lived in the twenty-second century BCE according to the legend) and the Sage

Duke of Zhou (a historical figure in the eleventh century BCE) treat their rebellious brothers in totally opposite ways? Yicheng wins with Zhu Xi-style reasoning, emphasizing the universal nature of expediency:

> As to whether to follow the norm or take the expedient, the Sages are forced to make decisions that differ from those of other Sages—that is what we call timeliness; but the Sages do not actually differ—that is what we call the Way. If Shun had had two elder brothers who, like the Duke of Zhou's brothers Guan 管 and Cai 蔡, wreaked havoc in the world, then he would have sentenced them to death, just as the Duke of Zhou did; if the Duke of Zhou had had a brother like Xiang 象, the brother of Shun, then he would have granted him titles and territories, just as Shun did. (Interlinear commentary: Here we see the Sages do not actually differ.) Xiang, Guan, and Cai—they all were sinful men of the world, but since Shun was the king and the world was Shun's world, he had the power to assign Xiang titles and land; but the Duke of Zhou was only a prime minister, and the world was not the Duke of Zhou's world, so the Duke of Zhou had no choice but to execute Guan and Cai. (Interlinear commentary: Here we see the Sages cannot help but do things differently.) Though their deeds are different, their Way is the same. *Jing* is the *quan* that has already been institutionalized; *quan* is the *jing* that has not yet been so. The constant norm and common righteousness is what the Sages have institutionalized; the expedient made according to the circumstances is what the Sages have not institutionalized yet. People only know that [the Duke of Zhou's] execution of Guan and Cai is expediency, but they don't realize that [Shun's] granting Xiang titles and land is an institutionalized expedient; people only know granting Xiang titles and land follows the norm, but they don't realize that executing Guan and Cai is the not-yet-institutionalized norm.[91]

Expedient acts, despite their time-place specificity, are thus universalized: the comparison between Shun and the Duke of Zhou places them in two parallel worlds, and we are allowed to freely hypothesize that if their positions were swapped, Shun would have behaved as the Duke of Zhou did and vice versa. In this sense, their actions are less bound to time or place than universal to *anybody* who happened to land in their circumstances. Supplementing this universality is a tamed sense of diachronicity, which is evoked only to render an expedient as a norm-to-be, implying that expedients are *not* fundamentally different from norms in terms of universal applicability.

Hence there is a sea change from the *Shiyuan huanjian* to the *Haoqiu zhuan*. In the *Haoqiu zhuan*, a similar situation would not yield a similar judgment and reaction, because people here are determined as well by their whole trajectories, which are open-ended and never the same.[92] That explains why we find the female and male protagonists so difficult to relate to—not because they are too affected or uninteresting, but because we are as confounded as all the other characters in the novel (the magistrate, the uncle, their parents, even the villains) by this couple's apparently senseless course of action. Their obstinate refusal to get married or—even after their forced wedding ceremony—to consummate their relationship mystifies the world around them.

The collapse of universality is not tantamount to the privileging of individuals (or of indigeneous cultures over globality, of contingent events over cultural systems, etc.). As seen above, the "interconnectedness of life" highlighted in the diachronicity of expediency does produce a narrative of the self, but that narrated self is at the same time dismantled by the dehiscence of ecstatic temporality. The practice of *quan* is centered not on the ultimate authority of the individual moral subject who is supposed to have the power to arbitrate between abstract principles and concrete situations; rather, *quan* now predicates the harshest critique of such a sovereign subject, who is unmasked as no more than an unintended, alienated effect of the sedimentation of—among many other things ever receding in the ungraspable given of one's existence—his or her own actions. The misnomer for the sediment of givenness in which the subject is thrown is *fate*; the mood of this subject, battered and betrayed by its own action, is *regret*.[93] But the strange situation in which our ill-fated protagonists find themselves also ironically yields surplus pleasure: if fate does not allow them to live together as husband and wife, they can live together as "friends" (*fufu wei ming, pengyou wei shi* 夫婦為名，朋友為實) and pursue a "lifelong pleasure" in this friendship (*le ci zhongsheng* 樂此終生) (H15.16a), which exceeds even what one can get from sex (H16.1a).[94]

Putting in tandem the two points made above—namely, the collapse of universality and the evacuation of the moral subject—we have a radicalized casuistry that disfigures the two poles of individual and community, with both moral subjectivity and universality dismantled.[95] Here the case reasoning is centered neither on the idiosyncratic qualities inherent to the individual nor on communal values that speak across the individual cases. Eventually, neither expediency nor the norm makes sense, and the whole classical language of *jing* and *quan* is rendered obsolete. Bingxin dispenses with expediency to uphold the sacred order of marriage, but what she actually does in her own marriage—her decision not to sleep with her husband in order to stay "chaste"—is too bizarre to be called a norm agreed upon by society. Instead, people surrounding her, virtuous or sinister, keep urging her to do otherwise. As a romantic comedy, the *Haoqiu zhuan* has Bingxin and Zhongyu consummate their relationship in the last few lines of the book, thanks to the unsurprising intervention of a deus ex machina (that is, the Emperor's verdict). However, the female protagonist of another early Qing novel, *Jin Yun Qiao zhuan* 金雲翹傳, persists to the very end in a no less bizarre project of chastity, presenting the case of a former prostitute who keeps her body "chaste" by denying access to no one except her husband.[96]

5. A CASE OF PLEASURE

Imagining and watching the *case* of the other whose action makes no sense to outsiders, or makes sense only if the spectator imaginatively puts his or her self in the case of the other—this case thinking should now be further explained as a spatial function derived from early modern theatricality, as embodied by the thief on the roof as the spectator to Bingxin and Zhongyu's staging of moral sentiment in the *Haoqiu zhuan*. Theatricality is here understood not as the universal essence of any form of theater but a historically specific mode of the spatiality of emotion in late sixteenth-century China modified from the medieval spatial structure of the dreamscape. In spatial terms, theatricality arose when the dreamer was sidelined as an onlooker, taking the position of an "idiot" who could only stay *in front of* rather than traveling in or through the dream. The medieval metaphor of character-as-dreamer or performer-as-sleepwalker was hence displaced by a new trope of (post)dreamer-as-spectator, testified to by Xie Zhaozhe's innovative use of the world-dream-drama analogy at the turn of the seventeenth century.[97]

A parallel development occurred in seventeenth- and eighteenth-century Japan when various notions of communality cemented by emotion were conceived in reaction to the fragmentation of the commercialized society of the early and mid-Tokugawa era. The result was a reinterpretation of the ancient Confucian term *shu* 恕 (Japanese: *jo*) to mean considering "what situation [others] are in and what they do. . . . as if their hearts are our own hearts," or later by way of the nativist poetics of *mono no aware* 物の哀れ, which at once problematized and necessitated the emotive communication and connection between self and other.[98] Either way, the universality and transparency of emotion was elided by a spatial problem of distance and discrepancy, which was encapsulated in the rise of spectatorship in the commercial Kabuki theater. If the Noh audience was evoked only to be transcended for the production of the dreamscape, it was with the Kabuki theater in the seventeenth century that the spectator truly emerged as a central category. That explains why a Noh performance almost never directly addresses the audience whereas Kabuki frequently does—not because the former hypostatizes the spectator watching from afar while the latter dissolves the onlooker into a participant, but because the audience position is so insubstantial in Noh that it is not even the counterpoint of the performance, whereas in Kabuki the direct address calls into being the spectator as a distinct component on which the whole performance pivots.[99]

It is no coincidence, therefore, that in a preface dated 1820, Bakin implicitly alludes to Xie Zhaozhe when applying to novels these related notions of theatricality and spectatorship that had subtly shifted the meaning of the dreamscape:

> Bitterness and pleasure in dreams—these are not real emotions, but can be more real than real. Those who love reading unofficial history and fiction also have similar experience. Browsing through a title, we would grasp our wrists, sigh and weep whenever we see a worthy man in mishap, a petit knave holding sway, a talented scholar mismatched with his times, or a beauty married to a dumb husband. Or, instead, we would elatedly toy with the tome and

"Not Even Close to Emotion" 177

laugh for a whole day whenever we see a treacherous scoundrel chastised, a worthy talent promoted, or filial piety and chastity commended at the city gate. *These matters, upon a closer look, have nothing to do with me, but I could not help but being intent upon them.* Why? It is because human nature is bestowed by heaven, and heaven is fond of life and cordial to goodness. *If one browses through a title and enters its magnificent world so as to understand its circumstances, then one can shed any selfish idea.* Thereupon even a woman or child can understand clearly the principle of righteousness and the distinction between good and evil, right and wrong. This is what nature bestowed from heaven enables one to do. Therefore it was really profound for eminent and talented writers in the past to promote goodness and admonish evil by way of unofficial history and fiction. Dogmatic pedants blame unofficial history and fiction for confounding laymen by deviating from official historiography. But isn't there any difference from accusing a dream for failing to tell us our fortune accurately when we fail to understand what a dream as a dream is actually about? . . . The way unofficial history awakens the unenlightened is just like the way an empty dream startles an idiot. In the past people had the drama-as-dream metaphor. Not only does a theatrical stage look like a dream, but unofficial history and fiction can also be likened to dreams.[100]

Echoing Xie Zhaozhe, Bakin here also talks about the insubstantiality of emotion in dreams, the pedantry of scholars who measured such illusoriness against historical facts, and ultimately the dream-drama analogy.[101] Whereas Xie views any emotional attachment to dreams/dramas as misguided and chided the "idiot" (*chiren* 癡人; Japanese: *chijin*) who mistook illusions for reality, Bakin finds the idiot's attachment vital for didactic purposes. Traversing this apparent divergence in opinions, what Xie and Bakin share is the theatricalistic structure of emotion, within which the feeling subject was constituted as a spectator to its own dream. Not only does Bakin further underscore the profound connection between spectatorship in theater and readership of the novel, but he also clarifies the general operation of feeling as sympathy in this theatricality of emotion. In other words, as spectators in front of the dream, readers are not simply being moved by the sentiments found in a fictional narrative. First of all, they find that those sentiments "have nothing to do with" them (*sono koto gōmo waga mi ni nashi* 其事毫無與於我身) unless they project themselves over there into the circumstances (*sono kakyō ni hairi, sono jōjō wo u* 入其佳境，得其情狀) in which they could sympathize with what the characters feel. Rather than conveying any particular kind of moral sentiment to the reader, it is this general operation of sympathy that carries the ethical significance in reading novels. Only by way of getting into the other's case, where one does not belong, and by sharing feelings that are not one's own in the first place can we shed our selfishness (*shi'i* 私意).

The case thinking derived from this spatiality of theatricality found a concrete expression in the discourse of *she shen chu di* in the sixteenth and seventeenth centuries. If, as Haiyan Lee argues, in the Confucian structure of feeling arising in this period the moral subject assumes the social mores as one's own by investing them with one's *personal* feeling,[102] preceding and underlying that structure is another *theatricalistic structure of feeling* in which what I personally feel actually takes a detour through what the other feels in his or her particular (bodily) case in the first place. Through this trope of theatricality, our discussion can move away from the hypothesis of "containment" (which presumes an essential, "ownmost" interior being exploited or restrained) toward the issue of exteriority articulated in early modern theatricalistic culture. And yet in the case of *Haoqiu zhuan*, the peculiar temporality of casuistry results in a strange course of action with the most bizarre interpretation and modification of the norm—and therefore not supposedly recommendable for others to follow; it signifies the breaking point of sympathetic identification. In this sense, the *Haoqiu zhuan* sums up the paradox of the theatricality of emotion.

Postulating a bizarre situation that tests the limits of the audience's sympathy also accounts for the charismatic and baffling qualities of such Qing novels as the *Humble Words of an Old Rustic* (*Yesou puyan* 野叟曝言, ca. 1767–1772) by Xia Jingqu 夏敬渠 (1705–1787).[103] It is probable that the first time the title of *Haoqiu zhuan* was mentioned on Chinese record was in Xia's novel. In chapter 31 of *Humble Words*, Xuangu 璇姑, the future concubine of the protagonist Wen Suchen 文素臣, is held hostage by a seducer. The method of seduction is so elaborate

"Not Even Close to Emotion" 179

that it involves all four aspects of speech, sound, reading, and painting, appealing to both visual and aural senses (*er tingzhe yinyu yinsheng, yan kanzhe yinshu yinhua* 耳聽著淫語淫聲，眼看著淫書淫畫). Xuangu is entertained with a licentious talk and the hubbub of coition on the other side of the wall. On top of this, she is given several high-end illustrated imprints of pornographies, among which she finds the *Haoqiu zhuan* printed on glossy white paper—a muted tongue-in-cheek self-mockery, since *Humble Words* looks more like porn for all its explicitness and indeed was officially listed as such by a Qing censor.[104]

Needless to say, our virtuous heroine is unmoved by this sensorial bombardment. What enables her to resist, however, turns out to be more dubious than it seems. Back in chapter 7, in order to thank Wen Suchen for rescuing her sister-in-law from a licentious Buddhist temple, Xuangu actually plays the role of seducer, sneaking onto his bed, pressing against his body, intertwining her legs with his. Fearing that his rejection would result in her suicide, Suchen thinks, in terms we should now be familiar with: "Liuxia Hui 柳下惠 let an eloped woman stay on his lap, and he was consecrated as a sage for posterity. What I can do now is to *forsake the norm and adopt the expedient* (*she jing xing quan* 舍經行權). Just let it be tonight."[105] He ends up making out with Xuangu in bed one night after another, but they always stop short of coitus, which he insists can only be sanctioned by marriage with his mother's approval. In chapter 8, on the third night they spend together, their bodies are merged in tremendous delight—though without penetration—and Suchen explains:

> The pleasure (*le* 樂) between man and woman arises from emotion (*qing*). The love we show each other eroticizes our whole bodies (*bianti ju chun* 遍體俱春).... Moreover, the pleasure between man and woman takes place only prior to coitus, and they acquire inexhaustible pleasure right at the moment when their affection (*qingsi* 情思) for each other imbues them thoroughly. Once the coitus is finished, what remains is just something left over.[106]

Far from dogmatic, Suchen's suspension of penetration for prolonged pleasure is more like an extreme form of the *ars erotica*. Here pleasure (*le*) figures as the third term subordinating both emotion (*qing*) and

180   *"Not Even Close to Emotion"*

desire (*yu*) and determining their split, hence rupturing their holistic union in intellectual discourse since the late Ming.[107] In short, by not submitting to the teleology of sexual desire, pleasure retains its full potential of extension and metamorphosis. Carnal desire is unpleasant not because it is indecent by orthodox standards but because consummation brings about an end to pleasure too quickly. In contrast, emotion between man and woman is cherishable, not because it is pure and platonic, but because it is the source of endless erotic pleasure—or what could be called "forepleasure"—which trivializes the telos of copulation. Pleasure can be limitless with emotion, not only temporally (thanks to the deferral of the orgasm) but also formally because, compared to desire in this context, emotion with all its semantic ambiguity can imply any protean form of sexual act other than intercourse. To lament the "suppression" of desire in the allegedly conservative Qing novels is to endorse the normative model or "common sense" of genital sex.[108] But, Suchen retorts, who would exchange the so much more intense pleasure of emotion for the satiation of just one tiny part of the flesh? As he and Xuangu graphically show, pleasure runs pervasively over the body, over whose surface an indefinite number of ever-divisible erogenous zones still await their exploration and reinvention as they press and rub against each other with their limbs twisted together to the melting point.[109]

Two observations can be derived from this discussion. First, it is only within Suchen's case reasoning (*she jing xing quan*) that this critique of desire and genital sex from the standpoint of emotion and its highly charged erotic pleasure can be made. Here pleasure cannot be abstracted as a universal principle; rather, through the theatricalistic structure of feeling, pleasure must be produced within a particular case.[110] Pleasure in each case is contingent on a peculiar set of circumstances; what feels pleasurable in one case might amount to displeasure in another. But this does not mean that pleasure can only be reserved for the experiencing subject (and therefore underscores the subject's privilege access to its own experience that in turn defines its identity); rather, no more or less than an outsider, the subject has to be displaced from itself so that it looks back on the case of pleasure from a spectatorial position. It is through the theatricalistic structure of feeling underlying each case that pleasure is generated and mediated.

This is exactly the point that queer studies touch upon and yet fall short of explicating. In an attempt to replace the theory of gender performance, the queer theorist Tim Dean places emphasis on "outside sexual" pleasure. Since the 1990s, performance theory has subverted the essentialism of sexual difference and heterosexual orientation, unmasking them as cultural constructs resulting from repetitive practices of the body and hence susceptible to mistaken or parodic appropriation.[111] According to Dean, performance theory overemphasizes the mimesis of gender identification and the determinative effect of language upon the body, failing to see that the cause of desire and pleasure—namely, the partial object or the so-called *object petit a*—actually transcends gender identities and the signifying system of language.[112] Fragmentary and apersonal, partial objects can be as conventional as the "mammilla" or the "phallus," but can also be as abject as "feces" and "the urinary flow"; Lacan offers "an unthinkable list" that includes such intangible things as "the phoneme, the gaze, the voice—the nothing."[113] Proliferating along with the ever-divided multitude of erogenous zones, these objects—and the desire and pleasure they arouse—can hardly be classified along the fault line of gender difference and sexual orientation.

In Lacanian terms, Dean takes issue with performance theory for being stuck in the "imaginary" of gender mimesis and the "symbolic" of language and hence failing to account for the "real" cause of desire and pleasure, namely, the partial object, a nongendered leftover after the "cut" of language. Yet at the same time, Dean acknowledges that the desiring subject can never directly relate to a partial object; rather, the desire for and pleasure derived from the object must be generated through the mediation of "fantasy" that constitutes what Dean calls "the *mise-en-scène* of desire" into which the subject is "desubjectivized"—that is, "decomposed" into a sequence of images it seems caught up with. Facing this "*mise-en-scène* of desire," the subject is displaced to the position of the spectator and identifies with various images in the scenario. This "fantasmatic identification," Dean argues, "furnishes an important raison d'être for sympathies and allegiances that otherwise might remain unaccountable" and makes possible "queer theory's identificatory alliances and its effort to connect queerness with categories of social exclusion that aren't obviously grounded in sexuality."[114] Despite his critical attitude toward mimesis, performance, and imaginary identification,

Dean's theory of pleasure with its political radicality ultimately relies on the theatricalistic structure of feeling. Today's Lacanians tend to critique the shortcomings of the imaginary (almost a synonym of misrecognition and facile understanding) from the perspective of the real. Taking the theatricality of the case of pleasure as our vantage point, however, we have to argue that the critical value of the real is actually predicated on the imaginary.

Dean stresses the subversion of the subject in his discussion of partial objects: the subject does not pursue and dominate the object but is decomposed and desubjectivized in the *mise-en-scène* of desire. We have just clarified that this critique of subjectivity should be grounded in the theatricality of case thinking. More precisely—and this is our second observation—such desubjectivization arises from the correlation between theatricalistic spatiality and ecstatic temporality in case thinking, to the point that the subject is decomposed in the sedimentation of expedient acts. Feeling in the other's case only becomes problematic and has to be mediated through sympathetic imagination when the meaning of a case is no longer determined fully by its synchronic commensurability with the exemplar but also by its diachronic connection to actions taken at other points of time. If theatricality as a mode of the spatiality of emotion emerged in the late sixteenth century, which then gave rise to the discourse of sympathy (putting oneself in the other's case) from the early seventeenth century on, then the correlation between theatricality and diachrony in case thinking became manifest in late seventeenth- and eighteenth-century novels.[115] It is thanks to her experience in chapters 7 and 8 that Xuangu later rejects all the sensuous temptations in chapter 31 based on sounds and images of copulation, something that she and Suchen have dismissed not as immoral but as simply too boring to pursue. What was forged as an expedient act in the earlier moment—namely, the nongenital lovemaking—conditions a later moment of exigency. The ecstatic temporality in case reasoning that we have seen in the *Haoqiu zhuan* is also exercised in *Humble Words*.

The ambiguous place occupied by the *Haoqiu zhuan* in this context can now be clarified. Presented to Xuangu as one of the seductive tools, the *Haoqiu zhuan* is dismissed as just another distasteful artifact capitalizing on conventional desire. And yet, making its first known appearance in Chinese—or indeed, world—literature through chapter 31 of

Humble Words, the *Haoqiu zhuan* implicitly prefigures for eighteenth-century novels the radicalized mode of casuistry and pleasure, which has been unfortunately misrecognized as the suppression or containment of emotion. To put this in the *Haoqiu zhuan*'s own terms, it is tempting to take at face value the poem in chapter 14: "Reconcile emotion and nature;/only by then would the Confucian teaching of rectified names be established" 調乎情與性，名與教方成 (H14.15b). Yet in the wake of this reconciliation between emotion and nature—a typical characteristic of Qing-dynasty fiction in which emotion is interiorized into nature with desire excluded—emotion and its resulting pleasure turn into something unrecognizable. Contradicting "the Confucian teaching of rectified names" (*mingjiao* 名教), emotion and pleasure in Zhongyu and Bingxin's bizarre case go awry against any normative definition of their names, as the end of the same chapter suggests: "The pleasure is not any normal pleasure; the emotion is not even close to emotion" (*xi fei chang xi, qing bu jin qing* 喜非常喜，情不近情) (H14.16a).

This brings us to the most bizarre case in all of eighteenth-century fiction, Jia Baoyu 賈寶玉, whose famous characterization is precisely "emotional yet unemotional" (*qing bu qing* 情不情). The characterization *qing bu qing* is from the Red Inkstone (*Zhiyan zhai* 脂硯齋) Commentary, which in turn quotes a lost manuscript of the final chapters of *The Story of the Stone*. Traditionally, it has been given two definitions: it means that Baoyu's affection indiscriminately embraces all beings, even those without emotion; it also refers to a process of his enlightenment—from enchantment to disenchantment, from emotional to emotionless.[116] But no one seems to have explained *qing bu qing* in light of the phrase *qing bu jin qing* from the *Haoqiu zhuan*. Here we see a third possible definition: the radical disfiguration of emotion due to experiments of pleasure in a specific limit case. Emotion is still named, but it is no longer close to the word's semantic meaning. As should be clear to us by now, it is only in this alternative reading that we glimpse what lies beyond—or better, right within—the notion of containment, which should no longer be understood as the limit of conservative sex economy but as a productive site of pleasure, or its impaired version, interiority.

We are now in a better position to appreciate the beauty of the misunderstanding by which the *Haoqiu zhuan* was assigned the historical mission of revealing the entire system of Chinese customs in the natives' own terms. Thematizing the feat of chivalry in terms of *norm and expedient*, the novel almost invites readers to satiate their curiosity about man's order-disorder doublet, which was the primary object of the emerging anthropological project in the eighteenth century. Everything goes awry, however, when the *Haoqiu zhuan* deprives expediency of subjectivity and universality, in effect exiling the "whole" from both the individual and the collective levels. The idiosyncratic case of Bingxin and Zhongyu is never meant to represent the whole of Chinese order or disorder, because this case is incomprehensible and inapplicable to the characters around them; nor does it illustrate a secret, individual psychological order or disorder—indeed, the absence of any such interiority has frustrated the twentieth-century Japanese translator of the novel.[117] This homeless whole, which loses its way at every level of the *Haoqiu zhuan*, proleptically says less about the enigma of the Chinese empire than about the hollowness underneath the edifice of modern knowledge concerning humankind. Founded on a peculiarly reoriented temporality of expediency, the missing term *xia* from Western translations of the novel should therefore be understood not as the piece that, once restored to these translations, will provide a full picture of Chinese culture, but rather as a nodal point that paradoxically rejects the very possibility of wholeness.

How can we explain the European reception of the novel in the eighteenth and early nineteenth centuries as expressive of the "whole system of manners" of China, whether orderly or excessive, repressive or emancipative? Should we assume that the radicalized case thinking represented in the work, with its ecstatic temporality and spatial mode of theatricality, is so uniquely Chinese that cross-cultural misreading is inevitable? This assumption of Chinese exceptionalism is neither conceptually sound—it tends to reconfirm Chinese culture as a distinctly unfathomable system—nor historically sustainable. In the Western context, case studies emerged from Jesuit casuistry in the late sixteenth century and proliferated through the eighteenth and nineteenth centuries, concurrent with the rise of theatricality in Europe.[118] Theatricality as a mode of spatiality underscores the alienating distance between audience and performance, readers and the text, the market and producers, subjects and emotion, hence dismantling the "wholeness" on both the collective and individual levels. The same spectatorial distance constitutes the anthropological structure of Western knowledge.

In the preface to *Anthropology from a Pragmatic Point of View*, Kant enumerates three inherent limitations of anthropological knowledge:

1. If a human being notices that someone is observing him and trying to study him, he will either appear embarrassed (self-conscious) and cannot show himself as he really is; or he dissembles, and does not want to be known as he is.
2. Even if he only wants to study himself, he will reach a critical point, particularly as concerns his condition in affect, which normally does not allow *dissimulation*: that is to say, when incentives are active, he does not observe himself, and when he does observe himself, the incentives are at rest.
3. Circumstances of place and time, when they are constant, produce habits which, as is said, are second nature, and make it difficult for the human being to judge how to consider himself, but even more difficult to judge how he should form an idea of others with whom he is in contact; for the variation of conditions in which the human being is placed by his fate or, if he is an adventurer, places himself, make it very difficult for anthropology to rise to the rank of a formal science.[119]

This threefold problem is linked to the spatial structure of theatricality, characterized by the distance between the spectator and the object. The pretense under the Other's gaze underscores the presence of the spectator in one's consciousness; the discord between affect and self-reflection reveals the paradox of being the spectator to one's own emotive experience; the divergence of circumstances leading to prejudice necessitates the ethical positioning of oneself in the other's place. Kant never tries to resolve these limitations, because to him they arise from human nature as such; rather than being obstacles to what is knowable, they constitute the structural possibility of anthropological knowledge, which takes human nature as both its object and foundation. And yet from the perspective of historical ontology, what determines the limit and possibility of anthropological knowledge is not the man per se but the spatiality of theatricality that dictates this distancing of the spectator in the first place.

China, the exemplar of orderly civility *and* unruly excess, was literally staged in English operas as a spectacle around this time.[120] When the modern discipline of anthropology embraces ethnography as its methodology, this sense of distance becomes even more prominent, prompting ethnographers to construct the Other as a reified object of study, so that the Other's culture turns into a "performance" of self-display while ethnographers put themselves in the position of the spectator, blessed with the power of seeing, the authority of interpreting, and the freedom to get involved or remain detached. It is from this spectatorial position that Lévi-Strauss regards every society as an "entropological" system presenting the order-disorder doublet.

In this light, theatricality should never be confused with any "whole system of manners." It is not another example of cultural order/disorder; rather, it is a historically specific spatial structure in which the "whole system" of cultural order/disorder can be construed under the anthropological gaze, yet at the same time dismantled in radicalized, diachronic case thinking. The *Haoqiu zhuan* has been regarded as the epitome of Chinese order-disorder since the eras of Percy and Goethe, whereas for Bakin it was a strange case of knight-errantry defying generalization. This divergence in reading is not an expression of essential cultural differences between East and West; rather, it is the result of the paradoxical structure of theatricality underlying both readings.

CHAPTER FIVE

Time-Space Is Emotion

In reconceiving emotion as exterior and spatial, this study has turned overfamiliar notions inside out. In their place, it has foregrounded three fundamental topoi, each marking a distinct regime of spatial organization in the Chinese history of emotion. In place of the stirred heart as the origin of emotion, I have traced the stirring motion of "winds" in ancient poetics permeating and traversing the interior that is only secondarily produced; in place of oneiric fantasies residing only in one's mind, I have mapped medieval "dreamscapes" through which one is incessantly delivered back to the exterior; in place of the absolute ipseity according to which a theatrical other is explained away as a projection of oneself, I have introduced early modern "theatricality" in which the dreamer turns into a spectator watching emotion from afar that is hardly reducible to "one's own" and can only be imaginably identified with.

This topological schema reveals the spatiality of emotion to be less a universal and univocal edifice than a site of sedimentation where one historically specific structure builds on and reconfigures preceding structures over time. The genealogy of emotion-realms lays the foundation on which to revise Chinese histories of morals (from the anxiety of things and the annoyance with illusions to the agony in identification), drama performance (from a theater of metamorphosis upon the passage between backstage and stage to a metatheater that hinges on the distance from the balcony), and knowledge production (from the traditional discourse of norm and expediency, which are treated as interchangeable, to a radicalized casuistry that threatens even the wholeness of the particular as its object of study). All of these histories converge at the emergence of sympathy, or *she shen chu di*, as the distinctive symptom of theatricality.

To grapple with the broader implications of this genealogical study, however, we need to return to the basics, to examine every crucial term we have invoked or assumed to construct this genealogy and historicize the spatiality of emotion in the Chinese context. We will see how our historical consideration of Chinese materials casts new light on each of those terms, realigning and retooling conceptual frameworks in a way that will benefit Chinese studies and beyond.

The first term to scrutinize is precisely "space." The main thrust of this study, the reconceptualization of emotion as spatial, has postponed rethinking space itself up to this point. And yet, modern critical reflections on space cannot help but gesture toward rethinking the relationship between space and emotion as well, only in light of which can the meaning of space be illuminated. Two such approaches—the phenomenology of worldliness and affect theory—merit our attention, not only because they present the most radical potentialities for overcoming the habitual division of emotion from space, but also because, in a way reminiscent of the Chinese poetics of "emotion-landscape mingling," these approaches fall back on the division if we do not push them to confront their own limits.

Walking the fine line between phenomenology and affect theory, we can clarify the spatiality of emotion not just as a kind of spatiality among myriad others but as spatiality per se, which is derived neither from the orientation to the world nor from the affective body, but from the emotion-realm. Based on this understanding, we can retrace the genealogy of spatiality from dreamscapes to theatricality, this time as an unfolding in which the three dimensions of the emotion-realm—i.e., embedment, deliverance, and faceoff—are organized variably from one historical regime of spatiality to another. Rather than following an inherent, universal trajectory, the unfolding proves to be culturally diverse when we compare the genealogies of the spatiality of emotion in China and the West. It is from this comparative perspective that we will overturn the understanding of the two key terms we have so far adopted without adequate reflection—namely, theatricality and sympathy. It is not so much that their meaning is completely different in China and the West as that they take rather different trajectories in their respective contexts. What each genealogy reveals is not a linear, teleological progression from primitive to advanced but rather a set of dynamics marked by misrecognition and anachronism among these regimes, which is then carried over and blown up in cross-cultural perceptions. In the end, the fate of the modern Chinese nation, which has been accused of lacking sympathy, will be explicated in revised terms we develop in this concluding chapter.

1. THREE WAYS TO THE BRIDGE

We started by arguing emotion per se is spatial. But what does this imply about space? Space seems conceivable without regard to emotion. What is space, if not the most basic *ground* of reality that is elementary enough to stand alone? If that is the case, the spatiality of emotion would not throw any new light on space as such—we have simply applied what we already know about space to one more area.

Ironically, in the Chinese field, the question "what is space as such" is seldom pursued for the opposite reason: space always messes about with other things, we are told; at least that is the way it is in Chinese culture, where "space and time are not to be separated from the actual content or happenings of the world,"[1] and therefore "the traditional Chinese rarely discussed space and time in abstract terms. They utilized practical temporal and spatial concepts close to everyday human life."[2] This claim is problematic on various levels. First, being "abstract" has nothing to do with the distinction between theory and practice but with the one-sided understanding of a notion at issue.[3] Second, in our case, the notion that is incompletely understood is space itself, because to understand space exclusively in terms of inextricable involvement in the "happenings of the world" neither discloses what constitutes the world nor exhausts other dimensions of space. Finally, ancient Chinese texts do discuss space and time in the least "pragmatic" way; if they never elaborate, it is because they belong to a different kind of writing economy, in which a text presents a "condensed summary of speech" rather than mimicking the conversation itself.[4]

Two fragmentary discussions from the Warring States Period showcase the depth in brevity; together, they trace out the aporia of time and space. From the Mohist Canons (fourth to third century BCE), we have the definitions of time and space—"Duration is pervasion of different times. Space is pervasion of different places"—which entails the paradox that the oneness of space or time is composed of infinitesimal differentials.[5] How could the increment of differences ever turn into something that is identical in itself? This paradox is highlighted when differentiated places and moments collapse to one another, as in another remark left behind by the Logician sophist Hui Shi 惠施 (370–310 BCE): "[one would] set off for [the state of] Yue *today* but have arrived *yesterday*" (*jinri shi Yue er xi zhi yi* 今日適越而昔至矣). Hui Shi's warped itinerary is dismissed as vain talk of absurdity, quite prematurely, by his friend and competitor Zhuangzi.[6] To reopen the Hui Shi case, we need to ask: How could one be already over there even before departing from here, or how could what is yet to happen already take place yesterday?[7] Only by bringing together near and far, past and future, can we conceive of space and time in their respective oneness, a oneness that can only be as warped as Hui Shi's itinerary.

Hui Shi is not alone in entertaining a warped itinerary. A similar trip appears in Heidegger's 1951 essay "Building Dwelling Thinking," which queries the way "we speak of man and space . . . as though man stood on one side, space on the other. Yet space is not something that faces man. It is neither an external object nor an inner experience."[8] In other words, space is neither an "extended thing" (*res extensa*) standing over against the cogito, as Descartes sees it,[9] nor a mental representation—whether based on Leibniz's ideal "relations" or Kant's "pure intuition"[10]—through which the monadic subject approaches the external world. Rather, intrinsic to the existential structure of human activities, spaces are generated for "dwelling" (*Wohnen*)—our daily practice of preserving and staying (*Aufenthalt*) with things-as-locations (*PLT* 145, 149, 155–56). And the way we orient ourselves in spaces is not by facing them but by *pervading* and *persisting through*. It is in this context that

Heidegger envisages the scenario in which one reaches a bridge before traveling to it:

> Even when we relate ourselves to those things that are not in our immediate reach, we are *staying with the things* themselves. We do not represent distant things merely in our mind. . . . If all of us now think, from where we are right here, of the old bridge in Heidelberg. . . . In itself thinking gets through, persists through, the distance to that location. *From this spot right here, we are there at the bridge*—we are by no means at some representational content in our consciousness. . . . To say that mortals *are* is to say that in dwelling they *persist through spaces* by virtue of their *stay (Aufenthaltes) among things and locations*. . . . When I go toward the door of the lecture hall, I am already yonder, and I could not go to it at all if I were not such that I am yonder. *I am never here only, as this encapsulated body; rather, I am yonder, that is, I already pervade the room, and only thus can I go through it*. (PLT 154–55, translation modified, italics mine)[11]

Three correlated questions are raised here: (1) How can we pervade space so that we are always already *over there* staying with things when we are just thinking of them? (2) How does each possible answer to this question clarify or obscure the nature of spatiality? (3) If I am *already* yonder even *before* getting there, the paradox is as much temporal as spatial. So how does a discussion of spatiality throw light on temporality? In this regard, Hui Shi's itinerary, which was prematurely foreclosed in early Chinese philosophy, is a condensed expression of issues that are central to the paradox of what we will call time-space below.

The first answer to the question of how one reaches the bridge before getting there has to do with a radicalized notion of "intentionality," originally a psychological term characterizing the "self-directedness" of mental activities toward its object. From Brentano to Husserl, insofar as intentional acts were deemed psychological and immanent within the subject, there has always been the issue of "transcendence": How could the mind ever reach a thing outside of it? Understood in this way, intentionality could not have brought the early Heidegger to the bridge,[12] until 1927, when the notion of "staying" began to emerge in his discussion of the ontological structure of human existence (Da-sein), namely, "being-in-the-world." For Da-sein to be, it must always be absorbed in everyday coping with things, which it associates with one another in a total network of purposes, and "world" is the name for this totality of useful things lying around us.[13] Intentional acts are therefore never just mental but "comportmental," as practical behaviors in utilizing things more or less handy to us in the environing world.[14] Even when just *thinking* and *looking*, Da-sein is a mode of "staying *(Sichaufhaltens)* together with beings" (*BT* 57–58, translation modified).[15] Right in its inner sphere, Da-sein is "*outside* in the world" (58).

Heidegger then dissects the structure of "being-in-the-world" by breaking it into two kinds of spatiality. What is familiar to us is the spatiality of useful things: we find them available in *places* over there, the "yonder" to which they belong, characterized by nearness and remoteness (*BT* 94–97).[16] Yet things are "close" or "far" not objectively but only as concerns us. Hence the spatiality of things ("the world") is "oriented to" the existential spatiality of Da-sein as such ("being-in"). Since Da-sein constantly intends toward and stays with things, it "is initially never here, but yonder. From this yonder it comes back to its here" (*BT* 100, translation modified). Derived from this primary character of Da-sein's spatiality is its tendency of "dis-tancing" (*Ent-fernen*), which initially means "nearing" (*Näherung*), to bring things-over-there closer to here; more precisely, it means bringing things to presence by making room for them so that they can encounter us nearby or remotely (97–102).[17] Hence the first explanation for why we are already outside on the bridge just in thinking of it: the intentional Da-sein is constantly with things before getting back to its here and in so doing becomes the condition for the bridge to be "over there" in the first place.

In this light, we should reexamine the most quoted tenet of Chinese poetics from the "Great Preface": "Poetry is that to which the intent goes. Inside the heart is the intent; when expressed it becomes poetry." Traditional reading has it that poetry originates in what lies inside the human psyche, and poetic expressions thus serve to communicate one interior to another. Modern scholars started to explore the rich meanings of the ideographic component 之/㞢 that is shared by "intent" (*zhi* 志/㦃) and "poetry" (*shi* 詩/䛥). Reading 㞢 as a foot moving or pausing, they re-interpret poetry as an expression moving outward from the intent that remains in the heart, or emphasize the poetic rhythm punctuated by the movement and stasis of the foot.[18] But this etymological reimagination has been devoted to asserting the relationship between *shi* and one's inner feeling (*neixin ganqing* 內心感情).[19] One more counter-reading is available, however: without presuming some *interior* origin that has to communicate itself to the outside world, the intent (*zhi*) per se is always already going toward something rather than residing inside the heart.

By subjugating Da-sein's "here" to things' "yonder," *Being and Time* invalidates the Cartesian division between mind and space and decenters the interior subject. However, the division is re-erected within Da-sein, thanks to Heidegger's vigilance in differentiating the spatiality of Da-sein per se ("being-in") and that of things ("the world"), out of the fear that Da-sein would "lose itself in what it encounters within the world and be numbed by it" (*BT* 71). More important, the centrality of Da-sein is reconfirmed two chapters later, under the heading of "Being-in As Such," where being-in is glossed as Da-sein's being "there" (*da*) underlying both "here" (*hier*) and "yonder" (*dort*). Whereas the totality of useful things and hence the complete formation of the world are mapped out along the here-yonder axis, the "there" features a "current situation" or "subworld," shaped by the pragmatic activities of a particular Da-sein as "a moving center."[20] Da-sein decentered in the previous reading of being-in as "outside in the world" ends up being recentered as being-*there*. In upholding its integrity and primacy contra the world, Da-sein turns out to be just another version of the subject. Underlying this anxiety about falling into the world is the distrust of space per se: in the second half of the book, Da-sein's entanglement with the world is revealed as the loss of this past-present-future unity to the inauthentic "making present" (*BT* 337–38).[21] Spatiality may be the most proximal dimension in the existential structure of the everyday Da-sein, but for that very reason it allegedly hampers the self-understanding of Da-sein in time.

To unseat Da-sein from its centrality, Jean-Luc Marion rereads "dis-tancing" from the opposite direction. Rather than the intentional Da-sein letting something present near or far, Marion argues, it is something he calls a "saturated phenomenon" that *gives* not only itself but the very being of the recipient in the first place.[22] Dis-tancing here is reinterpreted as a constitutive distance over which givenness reaches out and makes us what we are only by withdrawing itself.[23] This rereading might have been found within the late Heidegger himself—if not explicitly in "Building Dwelling Thinking," then certainly in another essay, "The Thing."[24] Whereas the former article still talks about humans who "preserve and care for things" in staying with them (*PLT* 145), the latter clarifies that it is *thingness* that *stays* various elements and *brings them near* to one another in the formation of a thing. Thus dis-tancing is now attributed not to the spatiality of Da-sein but to the nature of things itself (175) and is rebranded as "appropriating" (*Ereignen*). Instead of seizing for one's own interest, appropriating here pairs with the idea of the "gift": a thing "gives" in the way that it appropriates and "entrusts" elements (sky, earth, divinities, humans) to one another so that they are gathered "into the light of their mutual belonging" in the form of a thing (171).[25]

This "appropriative" giving completes the reversal of the relationship between time and space in the 1962 article "Time and Being,"[26] which suggests that even time and Being do not stand on their own but have to be *given* by a self-withdrawn origin, which Heidegger now names "appropriation" (*Ereignis*). "The unity of true time" itself also results from the event of appropriation as "giving," which "brings future, past and present near to one another by distancing them" or, in other words, "holds them apart thus opened and so holds them to one another in the nearness" (*T* 13–15). What is thus opened up for the three dimensions of time to be together from afar is the underlying fourth dimension, "time-space." Heidegger now concedes that his previous attempt "to derive human spatiality from temporality is untenable." In his revised picture, the focus shifts from human spatiality to that of "site" (that is, the things as locations discussed in the "Building" article), and both spatiality and temporality, analogous to each other, are derived from "appropriation" as its "gifts" (*T* 23). But with appropriation understood as "nearing nearness" (a.k.a. dis-tancing), spatiality is all that appropriation consists of, not some secondary derivation from it; space is not analogous to time, but is the very *ground* (the time-*space*) that unifies temporality by way of holding its dimensions apart so as to bring them near to one another. Here comes the second way to be on the bridge before even reaching it: it is not because as Da-sein I am already yonder with things before coming to myself, but because the bridge as a location-thing bridges and brings into a mutual belonging those lying near and far—including the "me" who is thinking of the bridge.²⁷ By the same token, the future in which I anticipate myself over there is already here right now, as the two moments are entrusted to each other in their separation over the time-space offered by the bridge. The warped itinerary that Zhuangzi considers to be absurd—to "set off for Yue today but have arrived yesterday"—turns out to be a given bestowed in the mutual giving among past, present, and future that is called for by the spatiality of things.

Spatiality so defined could not belong to the bridge itself; the latter only channels what it receives from that which gives in withdrawal. That which gives withdraws itself and never presences as a thing. Staying ever unrepresentable and unthinkable, it can only be referred to by provisional names (dis-tancing, nearing, thingness, gift, appropriation), echoing the notable dilemma that inaugurates the *Daode jing* 道德經. The late Heidegger is historically distinguishable from Laozi, however, in the former's immersion in "the age of the world picture," the modern regime of representation (*Vor-stellung*). By setting things *before* the mind as "something standing over-and-against," representation turns them into objects for exact sciences and "anthropology," with the latter term designating the "interpretation of man which explains and evaluates beings as a whole from the standpoint of, and in relation to, man." With everything we see, touch, and envisage turned into research data, world views, cultural values, and life experience angled toward our subject "position,"²⁸ the Heideggerian call for letting the thing be thing (*PLT* 178) sounds already impossible. A "poetic" solution, he suggests, is riding this tide of subjectivity and retreating to the very "heart's space" of the innermost interior that cannot be revealed by representation.²⁹ Having relegated spatiality to things, we come a full circle, back to the monadic, interior subject in the world picture, which as we have seen informs the dominant psychological reading of the "Great Preface" as a eulogy of the interior origin of poetry in the "heart."

Our contemporary obsession with "material history," governed by an impulse of "going to the things," should now be clarified as an attempt to capture the ever evasive givenness—a more fundamental sense of spatiality than the spatiality of Da-sein in the early Heidegger. However, because of the vulnerability of things to representation, we need to preserve givenness by way of a better term. Such an alternative term turns out to have been buried deep in *Being and Time*—not undiscovered in oblivion but covered up by a deceptive familiarity and structural misplacement. To retrieve it we need to take apart and reassemble the components of Heidegger's magnum opus. The notion of being-in-the-world is dissatisfying, as we recall, since it grounds the spatiality of useful things (aroundness) in the spatiality of Da-sein (being-in), the moving center—a local "there"—around which the world of things is constellated. Against such a centripetal picture, we should first regard both the spatiality of useful things and of Da-sein on the same level. When we refer to either the things that lie close and remote or Da-sein, which initially stays with things before coming to itself, we are actually referring to the same totality of the world structure coordinated in terms of "here" and "yonder" and under the operation of dis-tancing.[30] Underlying "here" and "yonder," however, the "there" should not be understood as the "moving center" where Da-sein is. The locality of "there" intimates neither centrality nor periphery but a singular modality through which the overall world structure is concretely realized so that "here" and "yonder" are charted, related, and experienced in a historically specific fashion. "There" constitutes the most fundamental level of spatiality not because the world of things depends on the spatiality of Da-sein, but because anything, including Da-sein, enters the world in a particular way that is never neutral but always already "affected." "There" in this sense is an entry point in a shifting itinerary and at a varying angle into a decentered world for things to be given to one another. This partiality of entering the world, as we will see, is described as *being-in-a-mood*.

Separate from the sections on spatiality, Heidegger's discussion of "there" is articulated with Da-sein's situatedness (*Befindlichkeit*)—an ontological term characterizing Da-sein as always finding itself "affected or moved" in a situation (*BT* 129)—and hence with its ontic manifestation, mood, or attunement (*Stimmung*).[31] In line with the radicalized notion of intentionality, mood is understood not in psychological terms as "a state of mind" that would have to be transmitted from one individual's interior to another's, but in terms of our situationally modified "way and manner" of comporting ourselves with one another.[32] Far from being immanent, mood serves as the primary condition for transcendence: without mood we could hardly find anything in the world that matters to us and would not have been directed to anything (129). Yet it is no less problematic to say mood is a "connection" between the world and us, since Heidegger invalidates all three perspectives on mood that try to posit it, respectively, within the subject, within the object, or somewhere in between, since mood is not a "being" present anywhere.[33] More fundamentally, this withdrawal has to do with the ultimate characteristic of mood, namely that in being in a mood Da-sein is first of all delivered back to grounds that are already given to it, situating it but ever escaping its cognition. Being delivered over, by, and into mood is a primordial way to confront (and turn away from) the fact that one has always been delivered over or thrown into some inexplicable givenness, which he calls "thrownness" in this context (*BT* 126–28).[34] "Precisely because [mood] leads us back into the grounds of our Da-sein, the essence of [mood] remains concealed or hidden from us."[35]

Mood thus gives us to ourselves only when its essence withdraws itself from us. This notion of mood in the early Heidegger would make a better candidate than the thing or thingness to stand for that which gives in withdrawal, which is pivotal to his rethinking of spatiality in his later years. Yet in what sense is mood *spatial* on top of all the varied descriptions (dis-tancing, bringing near, appropriating, and so forth) pertinent to the here-yonder axis in the totality of the world but not to the particular situation of there?[36] Though they are scattered and undeveloped, some remarks from Heidegger's works during the late 1920s and the mid-1930s introduce nuances that have to do with the subtly differentiated dimensions of moodlike situatedness.

First, in the dimension of being situated along with other people (and things as well), mood is described as an atmosphere, which covers and saturates a sphere of clearing so as to constitute a current situation. Being attuned is not just being directed to a situation but being immersed in mood. Mood does not reside inside the subject; it is the latter that is embedded in it.[37] Second, before being embedded, *Da-sein* has to be "trans-posed" into mood,[38] disclosing the existential structure that we are always already "delivered over" to the "there" (*BT* 127). And since Da-sein is always being in a mood, it must have already been thrown into one mood *from some other mood*; or, conversely speaking, "we never master a mood by being free of a mood, but always through a counter mood" (*BT* 128). This implies the fickleness of mood change that shapes and differentiates situations not through saturation but through demarcation and trespass. The so-called thrownness—some deep "background" that has been shaping us but can never be fully penetrated—therefore is expressed in the deliverance through evanescent moods. Each time, only in *belatedness* does one come out of a mood and try to figure out what it has actually been about (unwittingly in light of another mood).

Meanwhile, this enigmatic having-been stays just ahead of us in its self-withdrawal, leaving us in anticipation of its suspended disclosure. Just as embedment entails deliverance, deliverance in turn leads us to a third dimension of moodlike situatedness, which I have called faceoff. Mood discloses Da-sein to itself by bringing it in front of itself, letting Da-sein realize its own nature as having been thrown into a certain "there." Since thrownness could show only in withdrawal, Heidegger stresses the precognitive character of this disclosure against and beyond any representational knowledge based on objectification. Contrary to knowing, seeking, and seeing oneself (*BT* 127–28), self-disclosure takes place when we find ourselves affected or attuned by mood. In so arguing, he leaves a paradox of this spatial dimension unresolved: "In situatedness, Da-sein is always brought before itself, it has always already found itself, not as perceptional finding-itself-ahead (*wahrnehmendes Sich-vorfinden*), but as attuned finding-itself (*gestimmtes Sichbefinden*)" (*BT* 128, translation modified). Here disclosure in finding oneself (*Sichbefinden*) "moody" or "attuned" is cautiously distinguished from self-reflection, finding oneself *in front of* oneself (*Sich-vorfinden*), as objective presence for perception. What makes the latter suspicious manifests in the prefix *vor* shared by "representing" (*Vor-stellen*)—the "setting before"[39]—which, as we recall, has the world stand over and against us in the form of an objectified "picture." That is also the problem we have seen in the vulgar understanding of space as something set before us, something external to and therefore mentally represented by the interior subject. Substituting *gestimmtes befinden* for *wahrnehmendes vorfinden* can be seen as a move to keep these misleading notions of mental representation at bay. But this does not entail falling back on a naïve notion of mood or feeling as a kind of immediacy to oneself, which would erase any sense of spacing;[40] rather, the trace of *vor* remains, casting its long shadow from the beginning of his statement: "Da-sein is always brought before itself" (*das Dasein immer schon vor es selbst gebracht*). A dilemma now stares at us: How could mood bring one before oneself without setting one forth as mental representation?

To surmount this paradox, we need to bring to light the notion of mood as space in its third dimension—the faceoff—which has been almost rigorously denied owing to its dubious vicinity to the "setting before" of representation.[41] Mood does not bring me in front of myself in the sense that a "tranquil" state of mind brings about self-reflection—in which case we would still be reducing the spatiality of mood to something interior.[42] Rather, what I am brought in front of is mood per se. Mood is not just what embeds me or a series of demarcated layered realms I have been delivered through, but also what lies ahead of and encounters me. Instead of pitting an interior subject against the external space, the dimension of faceoff inserts the subject in the midst of a sprawling structure of spatiality that is discordant with and yet inseparable from the other two dimensions, embedment and deliverance. Being brought in front of mood does not render it an object for scientific investigation; rather, the "being brought in front of" itself is one of the inseparable dimensions constitutive of the spatiality of mood. Being in a mood therefore entails a threefold experience that is irreconcilably concurrent with me, stretched from the past to me, and yet to be fully assumed and identified with as mine. What "Time and Being" calls the time-space, which gives past, present, and future to one another by holding them apart, should therefore be understood as a function ascribed to the "discordant concordance" among the spatial dimensions of mood.[43] What preserves givenness as the condition of dis-tancing is mood, not the thing.

These spatial dimensions of mood (embedment, deliverance, faceoff) ground the temporal dimensions of making present, having-been, and coming-toward, respectively. Mood—or, to go back to the term developed in this book, the emotion-realm—is therefore a structure of time-space. And since the spatial dimensions themselves do not separate from but refract one another, each of them articulates and informs with its primary tendency an interconnection among the moments of time. Atmospheric embedments of mood primarily make present to us a current, ongoing situation in which we find ourselves, and yet only through this making present does *reliving* a bygone sentiment or experience also become possible (as when an audience is overpowered by and totally immersed in a spellbinding performance of an old song, for instance), which in turn gives rise to the anticipation of future generations perceiving what we perceive as *today*. Yet if we turn to the dimension of deliverance, the deep background of a current mood remains concealed until we are transposed into another mood. What one can anticipate is therefore the necessity of constant retrospection, and any hindsight, belated by default, is again afforded by some no-less-dubious background conditions, the understanding of which is subject to further rear vision. From the vantage point of faceoff, however, both the mood in which we find ourselves embedded and the preceding moods we have been thrown through are primarily experienced as facing us at a distance. It is not that past and present, unfulfilled, await teleological closure in the future; rather, it is that past and present are posited as "future" that the future itself has to look forward to. The three moments stand in the face of, move toward, and forever miss one another.

Our analysis of the spatiality of moods as withdrawn givenness therefore determines that moments of time give themselves to one another in multifarious ways, depending on which one of the spatial dimensions—embedment, deliverance, faceoff—is being stressed. By contrast, Heidegger, in isolating moodlike situatedness from spatiality as if they were two unrelated matters, arbitrarily determines the dominant mode of temporality for each of them, thus reducing spatiality to "making present" while characterizing situatedness and mood as "having-been." In a section titled "The Temporality of Situatedness," he shows how each kind of "mood temporalizes itself" in such a way that having-been "modifies" its unity differently with future and present (*BT* 313). Such a taxonomy of moods only serves to reveal how Da-sein takes its stance toward the having-been differently within the leeway of its existential structure. My own study, on the contrary, compensates for "the spatiality of mood" that is missing from both the early and late Heidegger and scrutinizes how over time various modes of this spatiality—each privileging one spatial dimension over the other two and thus articulating a distinct kind of time-space—unfold, interact, and generate different regimes of domination in certain historical contexts.

Rather than one kind of spatiality among others, "the spatiality of mood" is spatiality per se not only because the situated "there," with which mood is closely associated, underlies both "here" and "yonder," but also because mood is more fundamental than the intentional Da-sein in making possible transcendence and more secure than the thing in hosting givenness.⁴⁴ The stark absence of the notion of "the spatiality of mood" in Heidegger reveals the difficulty in bringing together space and mood. In launching its powerful critique of the split between subject and space, phenomenology stumbles upon the issue of landscape and emotion I have highlighted in Chinese poetics: how to wrap one's head around "mood" and "situation" as a unitary structure of space. Given that Heidegger himself stresses the spatial connotation of "situation" as a "clearing" in the forest (*Lichtung*),⁴⁵ how should we add the intangible mood to the equation?

The effort to systemize the spatial tropes (along with the temporal implications) in Heidegger is just a first step toward dealing with this question. Yet they are more than tropes, or rather they are tropes in the dynamic and physical sense: they *turn*, exert force, move things, and change the ground. In spreading out, shuttling through, and encountering ahead, mood generates and defines a situation with *movements* rather than just registering or reacting to it. I prefer the term *emotion* to *mood* not just because Heidegger himself uses mood to refer to emotion as well⁴⁶—or because this phenomenology of mood fits in with the appraisal theory of emotion in cognitive psychology⁴⁷—but because in the basic connotation of emotion, we are emotional in motion when we are being moved,⁴⁸ and there is no need to endorse the term's psychological meaningfulness in contrast to feeling and affect. By being moved, I refer not to a stirred state of mind but rather at turns to a universal motion within which my body is immersed and swayed as one of the relay spots, or to an endless trajectory through which one is transported from one realm of existence to another, or to the remove at which we are distanced from ourselves as well as the others. It is these three different ways of being moved, not the static measurements (length, width, height), that constitute the three "dimensions" (embedment, deliverance, face-off) of an emotion-realm.

This takes us to the final sense in which situation and mood (from now on, emotion) should come together—and this is the third way to reach the bridge just by thinking of it—a possibility revealed by Wang Guowei's subversive "landscaping" of emotion and appropriation of the Chinese term *qingjing*$_2$, which suggests emotion is a "realm" in itself, with a genuine sense of spatiality. Yet the "emotion-realm" or *qingjing*$_2$ is just an expression for "situation," along with other colloquial expressions such as *qingxing, qingkuang,* and *qingshi*. This meaning is reminiscent of the nonpsychological connotations of *qing* in ancient Chinese text as essence and reality. *Qing* as situational without psychology—that is what brings us to the bridge as part of the emotion-realm.

2. AFFECT, BODY, AND HISTORICAL ONTOLOGY

This counter-psychological critique, which opens up a spatial understanding of emotion, is at once informed by and critical of recent discussions of "affect." A physiological force and a sensation running through the body, affect is envisioned as preceding, underlying, and never entirely subsumed and captured by the cognitive and emotive consciousness of the person. In contrast to emotion, which is allegedly imbued with psychological content, affect remains impersonal and pre-individual, calling attention to its immersion in the embedding environment.[49] That explains why affect has been referred to as a circuit *in* which we find ourselves,[50] a profuse atmosphere, a dream. As Kathleen Stewart puts it:

> Everything depends on the feel of an atmosphere and the angle of arrival. Anything can feel like something you're in, fully or partially, comfortably or aspirationally, for good or not for long. A condition, a pacing, a scene of absorption, a dream, a being abandoned by the world, a serial immersion in some little world you never knew was there until you got cancer, a dog, a child, a hankering . . . and then the next thing—another little world is suddenly there and possible. Everything depends on the dense entanglement of affect, attention, the senses, and matter.[51]

Taking the forms of atmosphere and dream, which denote not inner states of mind but "some little world" we are in, this "dense entanglement of affect" is clearly conceivable only in terms of spatiality and exteriority.

And yet in counteracting cognitive psychology, this discussion of affect is heavily invested in neuroscience, according to which affect is as much hardwired biologically as capable of altering the biochemistry and neurology of one's sensorium. Defending cognitive and intentional values of emotion, Ruth Leys accuses affect theory of restaging the old body-mind dichotomy in privileging the corporeality of affect over consciousness.[52] But a more profound problem lies underneath the shared ground of cognitive psychology and affect theory. Just as the feeling-thinking subject discounts impersonal environments precisely when affirming entanglement with them, the affective body—though itself designated as "impersonal"—eventually shifts our focus away from the entanglement per se to the sensorium as the quintessential foundation of affect. The spatial experience of "something we're in" is drowned out by the physiological issue of how one body neurologically affects and is affected by another. Once the atmosphere of emotion is pinned down to pheromones—once the spatial configuration of thresholds, surfaces, layers, and mediation becomes linearized as the "projector and receptor structure" of hormonal secretion[53]—spatiality is short-circuited by signals that literally get on my nerves. Catherine Malabou introduces a certain spatiality back to the innermost "auto-affection" by arguing that "self-encounter always occurs as a spacing" and therefore "the reflexivity of essence over and on itself is never immediate, but creates a material and spatial surface." However, in her own words, the spacing of affect is just a neural mapping "formed in populations of neurons that constitute neural networks or circuits."[54]

Traversing and connecting bodies through neural stimuli, affect debunks the myth of the self-contained subject whose emotional experience is inherent. The paradigm of this trans-subjective affective process is sympathy, which the neurosciences now explain in terms of mirror neurons: "when we see an action performed, the same neural networks that would be involved if we were to perform it ourselves are activated," so that "we may actually experience something of what it feels like to perform the action."[55] On the one hand, this conception discredits the belief that affects are just "private obscure internal responses," because they travel socially among bodies that share feelings by mimicking one another. On the other hand, any spatial setting and perception in which bodies find themselves in mutual relation is again rendered irrelevant since "at the heart of mimesis is the *immediacy* of what passes between bodies," which "cognitively mediated representation . . . does not ever entirely replace or supersede."[56]

The way the affective body at once facilitates and undercuts a radical rethinking of space is demonstrated in Henri Lefebvre's seminal study *The Production of Space*. Against the fragmentary reification of space as a bunch of different objects and commodities, Lefebvre seeks to recover a unified understanding of spatial practices as both means and ends of the relations and forces of production.[57] A house is deceptive in its reified form unless we unravel it into "streams of energy" ("water, gas, electricity, telephone lines, radio and television signals") that permeate it, so that the so-called immovable property can be unveiled as "a two-faceted machine analogous to an active body," which is at once an energy-guzzling beast for busy activities and an information-based device hypersensitive to low-energy signals (*PS* 93). Just like a house, the body, which can act and can be acted upon, is not self-contained and separate from its milieu but "immediately subject to that space" onto which it is grafted; its "material character derives from space, from the energy that is deployed and put to use there" (195).

Here lies the centrality of the affective body to Lefebvre's theory of space. The body not only provides an analogy to space as a field of relations and forces; it also constitutes in his analysis the fundamental stratum, "the affective level, which is to say the level of the body" (224), at which space is lived and produced. At this level of "affective, bodily lived experience," the body grounds its "immediate relationship" to space: "body *is* space and *has* its space" (170). "Places" are marked out with the body's rhythms, gestures, and "indicators of affect" (saliva, urine, odors), in such a way that space "comes into being as an extension of the space of bodies" (172, 174, 198, 207).[58] We misconstrue spatial categories as purely abstract only when we overlook "the core and foundation of space," namely, "the total body" (200). He concludes that "the whole of (social) space proceeds from the body, even though it so metamorphoses the body that it may forget it altogether—even though it may separate itself so radically from the body as to kill it. The genesis of a faraway order can be accounted for only on the basis of the body itself" (405).[59]

Most paradoxically, not only is the immediacy of space derived from the body, but the very possibility of confronting space as an opaque medium or imaginary representation riddled with "gaps and tensions, contacts and separations" is "intrinsic to lived experience itself," because the body inherently entails duality in "its mirror-image and shadow" (*PS* 182–84). Despite all the distortion and concealment, such representational space is "mediated *yet directly experienced.*" One example of this oxymoronic area is "theatrical space," a sphere of doubling where the real and the imaginary interact without becoming one (188). An even better example is the "space of the dream," which Lefebvre also sees as a theatrical space—"a putting into images of oneself, for oneself"—and yet it is a theatrical space of a special kind that is not only "at once imaginary and real," but also "strange and alien yet at the same time as close to us as is possible," in which the body shuts down and pulls itself together in "its own truth"—"building up its energy reserve by imposing silence on is information receptors" (208–9).

But doesn't this oxymoron—"mediated yet directly experienced"—signal the dubious short-circuiting of spatiality by the neurology of affect? This reduction of space to the body per se is particularly surprising since, we may recall, Lefebvre started with the house-body analogy, breaking down reified images into "waves and currents." To counter reification is to recognize that the body's "material character derives from space, from the energy that is deployed and put to use there," not the other way around (*PS* 195). Such advice is turned on its head halfway through his argument when he takes the body as the privileged origin from which all properties, determinants, and principles of space, immediate or mediated, have to derive.

This startling reversal reveals the inherent tendencies of affect theory and foreshadows where they have led us in recent discussions of object-oriented ontology. Originally a critique of "correlationism"[60]—the tendency to boil all philosophical problems down to the relationship of objects to human subjects, who always occupy the implied privileged position—object-oriented ontology in its most prominent and controversial vein ultimately dismisses *relations* in the object universe.[61] Instead, it deems the substance that defines an object as intrinsic to the individual form—the *body*—of the object.[62] More precisely, it is argued, objects must be "thought in terms of their endo-relations or intra-ontic structure as radically *independent* of their exo-relations or inter-ontic relations," no matter how ephemeral this independence is, given "the endurance of a substance need be no greater than the smallest possible unit of time." Affect—"the capacity for acting and being acted upon"—no longer de-territorializes the body; rather, it now *belongs* to the bodily interior of the object, which withdraws from extrinsic relations and stands in opposition to other bodies.[63] Since objects retire into their interiors, space can only be understood as external to all of them, that is, as "the mutual exteriority of objects and their partial contact with images of one another."[64] The very thing that affect theory sets out to dissolve—the body external to space—comes around to haunt it.

For Lefebvre, the temptation of the body comes from his Hegelian search for the "concrete universal": as the third moment of the dialectic, "the lived" (bodily experience of representational space) sublates both "the perceived" (particular day-to-day spatial practices) and "the conceived" (general representation of space) (*PS* 15–16, 38–39).[65] Against what he sees as the capitalistic abstraction of space that threatens to kill off our lived experience, the body, with its "biologico-spatial reality," is valorized as the "foundation" for revolt, pitting "life" against "the space of 'no' " (*PS* 171, 208–9).[66] Falling prey to this biopolitical agenda, Lefebvre inadvertently follows the logic of what Foucault calls "incorporation": the reification of the body as the primary source of what had been located in the social or cosmological nexus.[67]

This reification is in line with the tendency of post-Enlightenment biomedicine to posit the ultimate truth of the body *inside* the body per se and, more generally, the anthropological turn of knowledge in Europe that positions mankind as both the object and the foundation of knowledge.[68] As late as the Renaissance, by contrast, Versalius, the alleged father of modern anatomy, found not self-evident biomorphical facts inside the body but "shapes" that could not be seen without the lens of cosmology.[69] Versalius's anatomical science resembles the vision of traditional Chinese medicine, in which the body is a series of coordinates drawn on, mapped by, and correspondent to the macrocosm of *qi, yin-yang*, and the Five Phases, whose valuation does not reside in the naked biological body itself.[70]

This observation is confirmed in Mark Lewis's seminal study of the ancient Chinese construction of space. On the one hand, Lewis finds in Chinese texts the idea that "establishing body as a center and a center within the body are pivotal to self-perfection and spatial organization." He compares this idea to "a major theme of Western philosophy" since Kant and Husserl: the body's role "in fixing the center around which people structure space."[71] Uncannily echoing object-oriented ontology, he further argues that in China "the body became problematic as one spatial unit defined in opposition to others," or as "a central self set against external objects."⁷² On the other hand, these arguments, apparently in line with the reification of the affective body, must be qualified by the premise and overall trajectory of Lewis's discussion. What Lewis actually argues is that this body-centric view arose in response to the primal chaos, a state in which "all spatial units were temporary and unstable conflations of disparate elements that tended to dissociate."⁷³ The body is neither a unitary module nor the centerpiece from which space is derived; rather, the body's transient formation is at the mercy of the same chaos from and against which the bodily order has to be conceived in the first place. The primacy of spatiality should therefore be located in this primal chaos rather than in the body per se.⁷⁴

To fulfill this vision would require us to invert Lewis's emphasis on the ancient Chinese creation of "structured space out of [the primal] chaos" that "separated a structured human world from raw nature."⁷⁵ Such an opposition between an essentially human spatial order and the chaos of "raw nature" raises a series of conceptual issues. As a primordial condition of "raw nature," out of which humans create a structured world, even chaos must be a kind of space. Following Leibniz, Lewis views space as "the relations between things, relations expressed by oppositions between inside/outside, center/periphery, superior/inferior, that defines space."⁷⁶ How then can "raw nature" be characterized as "the primal chaos" devoid of spatial order while at the same time such chaos, as a space, must be governed by various relational demarcations that remind us of the way the ancient Chinese structured the human world? Among these relational demarcations, the opposition between the structured human world and chaotic raw nature is too tidy for that primal chaos to have a place in it. Instead of focusing on how the ancient Chinese constructed orderly spatial systems that were derived from the body amid and against the chaos, we need to go behind the overtly "structured space" and pinpoint the spatiality of chaos—not "the primal chaos" per se but chaos as culturally understood and pertinent to its time: namely, the Warring States discourse on the cosmological forces *qi* or "winds." Saturating an area and permeating porous boundaries, winds motivated the earliest efforts to conceptualize the integrity of the body. Eliminating any distance from what they directly impact, winds resemble what we now call affect, but these affective winds actually configured in antiquity China an ancient regime of spatiality founded not on the body but on the dimension of atmospheric embedment in the spatiality of emotion.

The spatiality of emotion is therefore irreducible to the spatiality of the affective body; rather, the former accounts for the varied conditions of the latter. This does not mean that the spatiality of emotion is ever disembodied; instead, at the initial level, it is all about the varied relationship between the body and the milieu it produces. The nature of that relationship, however, cannot derive from the body itself, no matter how de-territorialized the neurochemical model of the affective body is conceived to be. To the contrary, it is the self-relationship of the body—the way the body perceives itself in making, becoming, moving, projecting forward, gazing back—that has to derive from the emotion-realm, which, as an ontological structure, is not biomorphically determined but emerges from the daily practice of coping with things and is hence open and subject to historical modifications.[77]

The slippage from spatiality to neurology nowadays, however, suffers a kind of self-obliteration in which the historical status of affect theory itself is obscured. The notion that affect traverses individuals, traveling from one body to another and moving them in sync, becomes poignant only when the distance between bodies, between what one and the other feel, and even between the subject and its own emotion, is a problem yet to overcome. This problematic of distance should not be brushed aside as a "deviation" from the essential nature of human bodies always being affectively interconnected. Rather, it should be regarded as a recent historical episode in which the exteriority of emotion has taken the form of spectatorship to one's own feelings and the feelings of others. We have identified this historical mode of the spatiality of emotion as "theatricality"; affect theorists tend to obscure its pertinent logic of distancing, mediating, projection, and reconnection by citing the *direct* experience of mediation or the *immediacy* of what passes between bodies. Just as essentializing the affective body forecloses a historical understanding of theatricality, affect theory evokes alternative spatial tropes—notably, atmospheres and dreams, as seen above—in an anachronistic fashion. Whether this anachronism can chart a genuine way out or is itself the dynamic from which theatricality was constituted—this question cannot be fully answered without reference to a genealogy of emotion-realms—that is, without clarifying the complex, nonlinear relationship between theatricality and the regimes of spatiality that preceded it in both European and Chinese contexts.

In short, the notion of affect simultaneously moves us toward and farther away from the spatiality of emotion. It turns the body into a medium of immediate self-affection in an attempt to obliterate the spectatorial distance characteristic of theatricality. In order to recapture emotion as spatial, we need to work through rather than deny or evade theatricality, still the predominant mode of spatiality today. In order to understand theatricality, we need to trace a genealogy of theatricality's emergence from a dynamic with other historical modes of the spatiality of emotion. And in order to fully illuminate time-space in terms of the different dimensions of the emotion-realm, we need to understand theatricality as *the* mode of spatiality that foregrounds the dimensional incongruity through the prism of faceoff. The intertwined issues of theatricality, emotion, and time-space therefore cannot be unraveled without one another.

3. THEATRICALITY AS ITS ANTONYM

Our description of theatricality as featuring a distanced beholder runs counter to a strong disposition in theater studies to celebrate participatory spectatorship. The belief that audiences should be hurled into the thick of the action is traceable to early-twentieth-century avant-garde theatricalism, which sees theatricality as the direct engagement and provocation of the masses. That understanding informs Martin Puchner's historical account of its mirror opposite, "modernist anti-theatricality," embodied by the closet drama for "a small coterie audience . . . as much as for solitary reading." Spurred by a distrust of theater and its mobs, modernist drama "becomes a literary genre directed at a reader as well as at an audience," and anti-theatricality is made possible by the alienating effect of print that creates a nonpublic audience as private readers.[78]

Etymological scrutiny of the word "theatricality" suggests that Puchner has the map upside down. When Thomas Carlyle coined the term in the 1830s to characterize French Revolution commemorations, he was not simply describing histrionic staginess (which would just be "theatrical") or "an instance of the spectator 'acting back' reciprocally within a spectacle" (the participatory spectator), but the way such reciprocity is mediated through "the narrative interpretive agency of being the historian," i.e., Carlyle himself.[79] From its earliest usage, theatricality has underscored what is beyond the theatrical, beyond the involved audience immersed in the social theatrics. It highlights an overall structure that is perceived only by a somewhat detached spectator whose experience is marked by reading and writing. What Puchner sees as anti-theatricality turns out to be theatricality as it was originally defined. Instead of prescribing a quintessential identity for theater to become "theatricalized," the term "theatricality" was coined ex post facto registering the effect of print displacing theater from itself, which began not with modernism or with Carlyle but, as Puchner points out, as early as the Renaissance.[80]

To add further confusion, scholars have used "theatricality" to cover such incompatible tenets as Artaud's avant-garde theater of presence and Brecht's modernist aesthetics of estrangement.[81] But instead of slipping into notions of indeterminacy and fueling talk of cultural relativism, we should recognize that the reversibility of theatricality's meaning traces the contour of a broader structural issue: the spectator as a spatial category. As Jacques Rancière notes:

> Such are the basic attitudes encapsulated in Brecht's epic theater and Artaud's theater of cruelty. *For one, the spectator must be allowed some distance; for the other, he must forego any distance.* For one, he must refine his gaze, while for the other, he must abdicate the very position of viewer. Modern attempts to reform theater have constantly oscillated between two poles of distanced investigation and vital participation, when not combining their principles and their effect.[82]

Traversing the Brecht-Artaud disagreement, spectatorship presents itself as a problematic of *distance*, which underscores the spectator's historically acquired alterity. Whether perceived as too intrusive or too aloof, either way the spectator has already been a figure of otherness, whose inappropriate distance is perceived as a rupture to be mended or exploited. The spatiality of human existence has always been about alterity: Da-sein initially stays yonder with things before coming back to itself here, and its constant concern with things becomes the condition for dis-tancing, which allows them to be close or far. But only in theatricality would the spectator put herself in the yonder position of the Other and *at the same time* confront it from here. Theatricality, governed primarily by the dimension of faceoff, reifies dis-tancing as the distance from the Other. But "the distance from the Other" is not quite the right description, since it is in the position of the Other over there that the spectator has always already been staying with other things and people. What stands ahead of the spectator is neither an objectified Other nor a mirror reflection of the self, but the very "situation"—what we have glossed as "emotion-realm"—in which the spectator finds herself staying with others. Yet the reason she is not just *embedded in* or *delivered through* that situation but is also encountering it ahead of herself is precisely that she conjoins the same situation *in its faceoff dimension*. Paradoxically, the spectatorial position is separate and distanced from the emotion-realm under her gaze—but only to the extent that the position remains part of that realm as one of its dimensions. Conversely, only in preserving this ineradicable distance between the viewer and the viewed can the dissonance among the dimensions of the emotion-realm be fully appreciated. By identifying theatricality with this spatial problematic of distance rather than with any of the performance styles or relationships to the audience circumscribed within that problematic, we can explain why contradictory meanings have been ascribed to the term.

The referential oscillation of "theatricality" mirrors the historical dynamic that brought the spectator into being *through negation* in the Western context. In the eighteenth century, such negation took a fierce form in Diderot's anti-spectatorial aesthetic, which prescribed for theater and painting a fictional, self-absorptive world, as if beholders never existed.[83] As Michael Fried points out, "only by establishing the fiction of [the beholder's] absence or nonexistence could his actual placement before and his enthrallment by the painting be secured."[84] Fried calls the awareness of the spectatorial gaze "theatricality," and explains Diderot's notion of "absorption" as its antidote. Fried's dichotomy between theatricality and absorption unfortunately veils their shared ontological foundation: the being of the spectator, whose position in front of the artwork is ironically further confirmed in any disavowal of it through absorption.[85] In the Western context, absorption has been the repeated operation through which theatricality has become more and more irrefutable.⁸⁶ If theatricality is taken to mean opposite things—to the extent that it is mixed up with the "theatrical"—it is because theatricality feeds on its apparent opposite,⁸⁷ namely, the dreamscape as a state of absorption.

Dreams have been invoked by affect discourse to overcome the alienation associated with theatricality. Lefebvre's "space of the dream" as a superior kind of "theatrical space" turns the "strange and alien" into the body's "own truth." So does Stewart's mention of dreams in tandem with "a state of absorption." The invocation of dreams in order to reinstate Lefebvre's biologico-spatial reality is traceable to Diderot's biological philosophy. Still an emerging fantasy back in the eighteenth century, biology takes the form of "dream-fiction" in his oeuvre. As Aram Vartanian notes, Diderot explored the automatism of the body that was not yet captured by Newtonian-mathematical physics but was revealed in "the autistic condition of sleep." Once the distracting senses turn off, "the consciousness mirrors more passively and faithfully the biological reality."⁸⁸ Only when the senses are dormant can we suspend disbelief and accept what is perceived in dreams:

> Thus the *naïveté* of the dream restores the cognitive conditions of an original materialism—of a primitive receptivity by which the mind accepts things *as they present themselves vividly to it*, overcoming through the immediacy of perception—by an act of visual faith—the overlucid subtleties of dualistic or subjectivistic metaphysics.⁸⁹

Expanding on this observation, Fried argues that the "primitive receptivity" Diderot attempted to retrieve through dream is "the cognitive condition of a pre-theatricalized mode of perception," by which Fried means pre-theatricality.⁹⁰ Nothing could be more remote from Diderot's theater of absorption than Artaud's theater of cruelty, but the latter pursues exactly the same dream. In Derrida's words, Artaud protests "against a certain Freudian description of dreams as the substitutive fulfillment of desire" and tries to "return their dignity to dreams"—that is, to restore them as a topos of "force, presence, and life" through "the present tense of the stage."⁹¹

However, theatricality and pre-theatricality are differentiated not by "the cognitive condition"[92] or by the body as the precogitive stratum, but by their modes of spatiality. In historicizing the emergence of theatricality in sixteenth-century Europe, William Egginton contrasts it to its predecessor, "Real Presence," in which miracle plays *make present* Jesus Christ—just as the sacrament in the Eucharist is treated literally as his body and blood—rather than having an actor create an illusion of the "character" on the spectator's mind. Since the double distance between actor and character and between the performance and the audience is irrelevant, all things performed are essentially *present*.[93]

Egginton's Real Presence is the regime to which Diderot retrospectively refers by the more general name of "dream." Using Paul Valéry's words, "essentially a dream belongs to the *present*," and "it turns [past and future] into the present—the here and now."[94] Theatricality emerged in this context by creating the spectator as a separate spatial entity, under whose gaze the actor-character split comes into being. Egginton complicates the otherwise linear narrative from Real Presence to theatricality by introducing a psychoanalytic analogy to the drive-desire relationship: "with desire we seek the directness of a contact with the world that we believe we have lost with the primary repression of our drives; in theatricality, we search endlessly for the little pieces of the real that constitute our only experience of presence."[95] This "return of the repressed" model, however, does not exhaust the dynamic in the Western context. Theatricality is intensified in an incessant process of self-negation, that is, in reconfirming the spectator only through negating it by way of "the *naïveté* of the dream." Despite the referential oscillation that reflects the paradoxical dynamic, Egginton upholds a stable meaning for theatricality without justifying his use of the term. This has to do with his understanding of theatricality just as a historical variation of Da-sein's existential spatiality. Following the early Heideggerian definition of spatiality,[96] he reconfirms the disconnect between spatiality and mood by deliberately excluding the issue of "emotiveness."[97] Hence, his analysis does not explore the way Real Presence and theatricality draw on different *yet interconnected* dimensions of the spatiality of emotion—namely, making present (or in my terms, embedment) and faceoff—and how embedment is invoked in the service of faceoff in the regime of theatricality.

Only by recognizing that spatiality and emotiveness are the same issue can we do justice to the complex genealogy of theatricality. David Marshall touches on the dynamic between theatricality and dreamscapes in a discussion of sympathy. Unlike the recent neurological essentializaton of sympathy as an effect of firing up mirror neurons across individual bodies, Marshall argues that eighteenth-century thinkers like Adam Smith turned away from views of sympathy as natural fellow feeling and redefined sympathy as an emotive structure made possible by spectatorship. Being sympathetic means that I become a distanced viewer of another's feeling, which cannot be felt by my natural senses but is shared only when I put myself in that person's position. Marshall contends that the paradoxical "dream of sympathy" is meant to "cancel out the theatricality of the most theatrical situations," or, in other words, to cancel out the spectatorial distance that is the very condition of sympathy. Spectators can somehow "stop being spectators" by entering into "the sentiments of the person they are beholding."[98] In another discussion, Marshall turns to Diderot's "dream of theater," where the spectator "suddenly forgets theater in the transport of sympathy" when actors forget themselves in their performance. "In this dream, theater would not represent absence, alienation, difference, and distance." But here comes a further twist:

> It is precisely at this moment of forgetting that the spectator must remember that he is a *spectateur ignoré*: that he will always be unknown and ignored by characters who will never allow him to feel present. The most successful theatrical illusion must end in disillusionment by leading us to knock up against the stage's fourth wall, to discover ourselves *here* instead of *there*. . . . Both the forgetting and the remembering of this position are crucial for Diderot. The spectator must forget theater in order to remember it. Indeed, the only way for the spectator to remember theater is to forget it; the moment of forgetting is what forces the spectator to remember his place—which he might otherwise forget.[99]

The trope of dreams, where the double distance between actor and character and between stage and audience is obliterated, only reconfirms the position of the spectator. It is because the spectator immersed in the actor's performance of absorption ultimately finds herself *ignored* and left aside in the position of an onlooker. Rather than nullifying theatricality, the dream of sympathy recertifies it. Once again, the dynamics that reinforce theatricality are misrecognized as its undoing, and the word "theatricality" is used as its own antonym.

In China, a different dynamic underlies the emergence of theatricality. Theatricality, to be sure, is a Western term with no Chinese equivalent. Even the modern Chinese neology *juchang xing* 劇場性, which means the nature or defining features constitutive of theatrical performance, elides the distinction between theatricality and the theatrical.[100] However, this does not mean that theatricality is irrelevant in the Chinese context or that Western theatricality is the norm. Nor does it lend itself to a general critique of equivalence in translingual practice and symbolic economies.[101] On the contrary, the absence of a Chinese equivalent is as suggestive as theatricality's referential oscillation in the West. Just as the ambivalence of the Western term reveals the paradoxical dynamic constituting spectatorship by way of negation, theatricality's "transparency" in the Chinese lexicon has to do with the camouflaging of the spatial restructuring toward spectatorship as a continuation of the preceding regime of spatiality. These diverse symptoms—oscillation and transparency—bespeak the different historical unfolding of theatricality in Europe and in China, which foreground two different ways of misrecognizing the relationship between the dreamscape and theatricality.

Whereas in Western discourse the dreamscape is often deemed the opposite of theatricality—despite or precisely because of the fact that it becomes the driving force behind theatricality in consolidating the spectatorial position—that opposition has never been felt and established in the Chinese context. Just as there is no neology in Chinese that differentiates theatricality from theater, theater itself is still described as an ephemeral, illusory dream. Unlike the dreams in the history of Western theater, which are often invoked as a topos of *presence*—or, to speak in terms of the dimension of the emotion-realm, as an atmospheric embedment that makes things present to those immersed therein—what is present in the Chinese dreamscape is subsumed by another dimension, namely, the incessant *deliverance* from one mood to another. Presence is constantly displaced with the never-ending uncertainty of the "having-been," the ever receding background to which one keeps awaking but of which one never gets to the bottom, hence the unresolved oscillation between illusion and the real. What is ultimately left of the "embedment" dimension is not the immediate presence of things therein (since no sooner are things made present than they unravel as illusions) but one's own being-ever-present-in-a-dream per se.

If Western theatricality is driven by its misleading "antagonism" with the dream of presence, the displacement of presence with deliverance in Chinese dreamscapes, from which one can never become *absent*, prescribes a different trajectory: the emergence of theatricality in camouflage as just another episode of ephemerality. The *mise en abyme* of ephemeral moods into which the dreamer is delivered would remain a prominent topos for the rest of the imperial history, but a subtle reconfiguration at the interstices of dreams: the incessant falling through layers of dreams was now punctuated with fleeting moments when the dreamer is arrested in a pause standing *in front of* a dream. Transpiring at the liminality between dreams and suspended beyond the cycle of enchantment and disenchantment, this strand of the "front" where the dreamer confronts the dream and turns into the spectator of her own emotion easily passes for part of the structure of the dreamscape.

From the historico-ontological perspective, among the three dimensions of the emotion-realm, it is deliverance from one ephemeral mood to another that reveals most conspicuously that we have always been in a certain mood, and that moodlike situatedness is not happenstance but an existential structure. Likewise, in the Chinese dreamscape, the historical mode of spatiality governed by deliverance, there is no flight from dreams since the awakened keeps slipping into another oneiric layer, although precisely because of that the enlightened one would never get stuck in any one of them. With just a slight slippage of perception, however, the historical regime that envisages *no outside of dreams* would tend to be regarded as *a regime without an exit*. Conceived as having no beginning and no end, the dreamscape thus *has no history*. However, this is a mirage that arises when we project only one dimension of the emotion-realm (namely, deliverance) onto the entire genealogy of emotion-realms.[102]

That is why, despite its modern association with *spectacularity*, theatricality in early modern China was actually qualified by its discursive *transparency*. The blank created by such transparency has been filled with anachronistic languages not only from the medieval and Song-Yuan dreamscape, but also, still further back in the genealogy, from the atmospheric immersion of "winds" in antiquity. In Zou Diguang's 鄒迪光 (1550–1626) notable essay, "Guan yanxi shuo" 觀演戲說 (On watching dramatic performance), *theatrum mundi* (*rensheng yi yi xichang ye* 人生亦一戲場也) is explained in terms that sway back and forth between atmosphere (flickering weather, auratic effluvium) and deliverance (illusion, dream, suppositionality). What is missing, however, is an explanation centered on the titular notion of spectating (*guan* 觀) per se.[103]

Thus far, we have come to grips with the specificity of theatricality by two steps. In the first step, the spatiality of emotion appears in historically diverse ways when the general condition of dis-tancing (at the level of "world" formation that underlies all human practices) is singularized in different "dimensions" (at the level of "situation" as emotion-realm). In other words, staying in the yonder—before coming here—can be alternately expressed as being *embedded* in an environing ambient (in ancient Chinese terms, "winds"), which constitutes and makes present the subject in body and soul, or as having been *delivered* across thresholds of layered realms (in medieval Chinese terms, "dreamscapes") through which the constituted subject is always to be seen retrospectively as unraveled and transformed. In contrast, what qualifies dis-tancing in early modern theatricality is the dimension of faceoff, where deliverance is interrupted by the extradition of the subject to the spectatorial position, on the one hand, and being-embedded-in is inverted as being-watched-from-without, on the other. Split over the distance between the viewer here and the viewed in the yonder, subjectivity remains an unfinished project in the sense that the emotion-realm at once embedding and lying ahead of the spectator calls for and yet eludes complete identification.

In the second step, we see that the specificity of theatricality is not exhausted by these dimensional differences across embedment (making present), deliverance (having-been), and faceoff (lying ahead); rather, it is further enriched by the trajectory extended from its antecedents—from other historical regimes of the spatiality of emotion. This account of diverse trajectories in China and the West suggests that we have reached a shared regime of theatricality in the wake of the early modern, and yet the way we enter, inhabit, experience, and misrecognize it can significantly vary from one tradition to another, since the preceding regimes in their respective traditions organize the dimensions of the emotion-realm in such different fashions that the ways these regimes are reorganized into theatricality also differ significantly. Determined by the dimension of embedment, the medieval dream of presence in the West haunts and negates theatricality, only to reconfirm its face-off dimension by excluding the spectator from the dream. Embedment itself is absorbed into the grand movement in the dimension of deliverance—which alternates between dreaming to presence and awaking to one's own absence from the dream—a "dialectic" movement that ultimately strengthens the faceoff dimension through the negation of it, leaving the impression that theatricality is increasingly prominent and irrefutable.[104] In the Chinese context, the predominant regime of dreamscapes defined by deliverance in China renders theatricality "transparent" under the grand illusion that one is delivered from one dream to another and continues to be embedded therein without any way out, although the spectator emerges at the interstices and thresholds between layers of the dreamscape. In both cases, theatricality is misidentified as its opposite, or as what it is not, but for different reasons and with contradictory effects.

4. AN ARCHAEOLOGY OF CHINESE SYMPATHY

At issue is not that the Western tradition naively believes a dream is *real* presence whereas the Chinese fails to draw any substantial knowledge other than seeing the world as a big illusory dream. The difference drawn here concerning the prehistories of theatricality in China and the West is not about the truth values of the dream's content (real or unreal) but about the spatial structure of the dreamscape conceived in different traditions, and the determination of truth values is just one of the effects of that spatial structure.

In the European context, whether a dream is a *real* presence (as in medieval drama) or just an *ideal* presence—a theatrical illusion predicated on the spectator's suspended belief and doomed to be demystified (as in Diderot's dream-fiction)—is a secondary question, because in either case the dreamscape is primarily characterized by its making

Time-Space Is Emotion 219

things *present* in an atmospheric embedment.[105] What defines the outside of the dream is not "reality" but *absence*—the dreamer's own absence from the dream. The awakening of Diderot's dreamer in the spectator's seat, which renders her absent from the dream, continues to solicit the dream as a recalcitrant *ex*ponent that supports the regime of theatricality by opposing it. It is the spatial relationship of the dreamer to her dream that determines whether its presence is real or unreal: in real presence, things are conjured up in the presence of the dreamer; in what is called "ideal presence," the conjured things are made present in her absence.

By the same token, in the Chinese context, the division and interplay between real and unreal should not be taken as a fundamental issue, a starting point, or even an essential feature for us to understand dreams and theater, because the spatiality of the dreamscape—namely, deliverance, instead of making present—is the condition for the problematic of real and unreal. Much like the Diderotian dreamer-turned-spectator, a Chinese dreamer comes to distinguish real from unreal upon awakening. Unlike the former, she never finds herself "outside" and therefore absent from the dream; rather, in the dimension of deliverance she is thrown into and through layers of the dream, and the ever-shifting distinction of real and unreal is just one of the corollaries in her crossing the layered demarcations of the dreamscape.

Yet, as long as its ontological ground in the spatiality of emotion remains covered up, the question of real and unreal is reduced to what takes place within one's own mind. This reduction of spatiality to psychology, unfortunately, has shaped the way we understand theatricality. When Egginton differentiates theatricality from Real Presence as a specific kind of spatiality, he predicates the former on the mental activity of the spectators. It is allegedly in the audience's "imagination" that the "character" comes into being as distinct from the person doing the play-acting, and the physical site of the stage turns into a virtual reality.[106] Such an account falls back on the supposed confrontation between an interior subject and the external space mediated by mental representation: the spectators are said to "see themselves represented by characters on the stage," and to experience those characters as "representatives of complex and mostly concealed psychologies and desires, motivations that they, like the other characters up on the stage, must interpret and explain."[107] A similar return to representation takes place when Derrida deconstructs Artaud's dream of presence, which looks most remote from Egginton's Diderotian theater but ends up inducing the same mistake: "Presence, in order to be presence and self-presence, has always already begun to represent itself."[108] Derrida comes close to seeing that theatricality is complemented rather than subverted by the dreamscape as presence, but he misunderstands the faceoff dimension of theatricality as representation only.

The psychologizing of theatricality is most obvious in the way we misconstrue "sympathy," the notion that should have preserved the distinctiveness of theatricality as a historical mode of spatiality of emotion. Unfortunately, sympathy is more often tied up with a debilitating question—how to relate oneself to another person's feelings—that presumes an epistemological gap between one and the other and hence leads to a dubious answer: the transport to the other's feelings happens through imagination as a kind of mental representation. For Henry Home, sympathizing with someone absent (the long deceased) or distant from us (a stranger) is utterly difficult unless "bolder fictions" are employed to bring his suffering into "ideal presence," "till [the reader] be thrown into a kind of reverie; in which state, losing the consciousness of self, and of reading, his present occupation, he conceives every incident as passing in his presence, precisely as if he were an eye-witness." Despite the approximation to "real presence" in terms of affective power, "ideal presence" is characterized as what a man imagines "in his mind."[109] These bold fictions are products of "imagination," likened to a "reverie" or a "waking dream,"[110] terms that his protégée Adam Smith also uses to describe sympathy.[111] Coming from this eighteenth-century Scottish Enlightenment tradition, Marshall stresses that sympathy is an "imagined representation."[112] Calling this "the dream of sympathy" does not actually help Marshall examine sympathy in terms of the interaction between historical modes of the spatiality of emotion (namely, dreamscapes and theatricality). Rather, his conventional usage of the notions of dream, fiction, and imagination threatens to reduce sympathy to a matter of mental representation. The bipartite premise that one's senses only feel what one feels *and* what one takes as the other's feeling turns out to be just one's imagination doubles down on the interiority of a monadic subject.

Like Egginton's account of theatricality, Marshall's account of sympathy ends up resurrecting the split between the interior subject and external space. In his words, the ultimate truth to which the spectator should awake is that his position is "*here* instead of *there*." That helps us understand why Heidegger, who rejects the picture of man standing in the face of space by arguing that one always *stays with* things and others in the yonder, also dismisses the entire question of *Einfühlung* (empathy):[113]

> The apparently presuppositionless approach which says, "First there is only a subject, and then a world is brought to it," is far from being critical and phenomenally adequate. So is the assumption which holds that first a subject is given only for itself and the question is, how does it come to another subject? Since only the lived experiences of my own interior are first given, how is it possible for me to apprehend the lived experiences of others as well, how can I "feel my way into" them, empathize with them? It is assumed that a subject is encapsulated within itself and now has the task of empathizing with another subject. This way of formulating the question is absurd, since there never is such a subject in the sense it is assumed here.[114]

Yet, just as Heidegger falls short of reaching the spatiality of mood, so does he prematurely dismiss sympathy as a symptom of the monadic subject; as a result, just like Marshall, he fails to understand sympathy in terms of its own spatiality. This mistake can be averted if we read Marshall and Heidegger in light of one another. Isn't Marshall's sympathetic spectator—who dreams his way into the other over "there" before waking up in his position "here"[115]—also a manifestation of what Heidegger has called Da-sein's spatiality, which "is initially never here, but yonder" and only "from this yonder comes back to its here" in the sense that the here is always interpreted in light of the yonder? This is the same paradoxical logic Marshall detects in Adam Smith, whose initial premise that one can only feel what one feels but not the feeling of the other is reversed when Smith realizes that he must sympathize with the way the other feels about him before he can know what to feel about himself. Sympathy is *the* foundation feeling, rather than a secondary projection of what one feels onto what others might also feel.¹¹⁶

This view of sympathy sheds new light on a comparable notion of fellow feeling in ancient China: *shu* 恕, which Confucius defines as "never inflicting upon others what one does not want" (*ji suo bu yu, wu shi yu ren* 己所不欲，勿施於人). Despite the impression left by later interpretations of *shu* as "taking oneself as the yardstick to measure others" (*yi ji liang ren wei zhi shu* 以己量人謂之恕) or "extending oneself to things" (*tui ji ji wu* 推己及物),¹¹⁷ *shu* does not imply that I arbitrarily project my idiosyncratic liking or disliking onto others, or that the knowability of what others desire all depends on the palpability of my own preference. Rather, my capacity to extend myself to others is rooted in what I have in common with others. The radiation from near to afar—typical of Confucian spatial thinking—presupposes a more primordial trajectory from yonder to here; I stay with others before I can "extend" to them. What I extend is applicable beyond me only because it has been assigned to me from elsewhere. By extending what did not originate in me, I am helping fulfill the shared potential bestowed on everybody.¹¹⁸ The ethics of "extending" as fulfillment testifies to the existential structure in which we are feeling along with one another in the first place.

However, this general structure of intentional Da-sein as dis-tancing (that is, as an existence directed initially toward the yonder before coming to itself) does not exhaust the modern notion of sympathy. The Confucian notion of extending in the discourse of *shu*, which predicates the ethical obligation of action on a shared nature and feeling—"that which all hearts would affirm in common" (*xin zhi suo tong ran* 心之所同然), as Mencius says—does not treat accessing what others feel *as a problem*.¹¹⁹ Feeling at a distance becomes a poignant issue only when theatricality puts in perspective the distance between here and yonder *through the prism of faceoff*—that is, by arresting Da-sein's itineration from yonder to here into a confrontation between the spectator's position here and the position of the Other with which she has always already been staying in the yonder.¹²⁰ Conversely, other historical regimes of spatiality that privilege dimensions of the emotion-realm other than faceoff entail different modes of fellow feeling from "sympathy." A study in the spatiality of emotion in China ultimately brings the genealogy of these modes of fellow feeling to light.

I have identified a close match between Smith's description of sympathy ("by the imagination we place ourselves in his situation") and the Chinese idiom *she shen chu di* (to postulate/imagine one's body in another's situation), but in order to fully capture the specificity of "sympathy," I need to look at the meanings of "imagination" (*she*) and "situation" (*di*). The first step is to trace the idiom back to the genealogy of fellow feeling in China. As seen in chapter 2, the precursor of *she shen chu di* appears in the comments of the twelfth-century Neo-Confucian Zhu Xi on a phrase from the *Doctrine of the Mean*, *ti qunchen*, which describes one of the "nine cardinals" that a ruler must fulfill. The classical explanation given by Zheng Xuan 鄭玄 (127–200) glosses *ti* 體 (originally a noun, meaning "body") as *jiena* 接納, "to incorporate," which is further elaborated by Kong Yingda 孔穎達 (574–648): "To incorporate the flock of officials and become one body with them" (*jiena qunchen, yu zhi tong ti* 接納群臣，與之同體).[121] This notion of incorporation as forming one body with others was preserved among the eleventh- to twelfth-century Neo-Confucians, who further explain it as a particular way of being concerned (*tixu* 體恤 or *xu* 恤) with others in the yonder. Gu Yuanchang 顧元常, for instance, suggests the following exposition:

> The realm under heaven, the state, and the family are relegated to the [lord's] body, which is taken as their bearing. So how could the body not be cultivated? . . . In regard to the lord's relationship to the flock of officials, when the power difference sets them afar, and the status distinction divides them apart, even to just a slight extent, he would tend not to understand their well-being and hardship. The lack of understanding then leads to the lack of concern (*xu*) for them. That is why "to incorporate them" is of utmost importance. "To incorporate" implies that well-being and hardship are considered evenly shared within one single body (*shijun yiti* 視均一體).[122]

The body is an initial point of cultivation not because it is a primordial entity, the "ground zero" for all human practices and edifices, but because the yonder ("the realm under heaven, the state, and the family") has bestowed itself upon it to begin with. Incorporation as a concern for others therefore does not entail extending what I know about my idiosyncratic self from which I come to understand other people otherwise unknown to me; rather, incorporation is dis-tancing *of a singular kind*: the general structure of "staying with the yonder before coming to the here" is *singularized through the prism of embedment* in the ancient regime of "winds" lingering into the eleventh-century exegesis of *ti qunchen*.[123]

Departing from this enduring tradition, Zhu Xi reinterprets *ti qunchen* as "to postulate one's body in another's position in order to know his heart" (*she yi shen chu qi di yi cha qi xin*). But in the same breath, he falls back on the old reading of *ti* as "incorporation," citing Lü Dalin's 呂大臨 (1046–1092) notion of "regarding courtiers as my own four limbs" (*ti qunchen* means *shi qunchen you wu siti* 視群臣猶吾四體).[124] This oscillation does not indicate that he is really adhering to the ancient regime of winds; nor is he heralding the advent of theatricality. Instead, by bringing together the incompatible interpretations and invoking both dimensions of embedment and faceoff, he is addressing the paradox of dreamscapes that had complicated the ethics of emotion. As seen in chapter 2, in addition to the classical anxiety about external contamination by the unruly "winds," from which one was advised to untie one's emotion, eleventh-century Neo-Confucians were trying to sort out another annoying ambiguity typical of dreamscapes—namely, that emotion was both susceptible to deception and necessary for enlightenment—by meting out contradictory admonitions either to insulate one's inner "nature" or to let emotion follow through on its entanglement with the outside world. Zhu Xi embraces both: on the one hand, he marginalizes emotion in the exterior; on the other hand, he subjugates it within the composite entity called "heart," which "integrates (inner) nature and (exterior) emotion." That is why, for the lord to understand the courtier's heart, the premise that all humans share the same nature is no longer adequate, since the heart has an exterior aspect, the attachment of emotion to things, which can be clarified only if the lord postulates himself in the courtier's situation.

However, Zhu Xi's formulation of the lord's concern for the courtier, in its recourse to postulation or imagination (*she*), does not foreground the indelible distance between the former in here and the latter over there; rather, it highlights their *commensurability*. As discussed in chapter 4, his maxim "*jing* (norm) is a *quan* (expedient) that has already been institutionalized; *quan* is the *jing* that has not yet been so" elides the distinction between universal constancy and circumscribed particularity. Hence, casuistry in the Zhu Xi style reaches the conclusion that, however exceptional, expedients are ultimately equivalent to the norm and therefore to one another. Imagining oneself in the case of another is mutually substitutable with imagining another in one's own case, in the sense that both would have felt and acted as the other did if their circumstances were swapped—or, in terms of the dreamscape, if each had awakened to the other's dream. In other words, being delivered through layers of the dreamscape highlights not the distance but the incessant replacement of dreams.

Just as theatricality emerged as a "transparent" modification of the dreamscape without a proper discursive expression, the sixteenth-century idiom *she shen chu di* might seem to be just a short version of Zhu Xi's gloss to the *Doctrine of the Mean* (*she yi shen chu qi di yi cha qi xin*). But the fact that Zhu Xi's formulation never circulated beyond the exegetic discussion of the *Doctrine of the Mean* until the condensed expression appeared three hundred years after his death (at first in official discourses of governing) indicates a new sensibility. Since then, *she shen chu di* quickly gained popularity across the domains of drama, fiction, poetry, history, and, coming full circle, canonical exegesis, where it spread into the commentaries to other Confucian classics, as discussed in chapter 3. The replacement and substitutability of dreams was now reconfigured into reified distance that took the form of the confrontation and hence incommensurability between yonder and here. Whereas postulation (*she*) in Zhu Xi as one way to understand the other was made *possible* by the presumably interchangeable nature of situations (*di*), postulation in the idiom *she shen chu di* was made *necessary* because situational commensurability was crumbling in the era of theatricality.

Even though what was crumbling was still habitually presumed, thanks to Zhu Xi's continued influence in official learning, the unsettlement could be sensed at three levels. First, *she shen chu di* suggests that one cannot exactly feel what the other feels since every party is trapped under their own skin.[125] The bodily incommensurability was often expressed in terms of gender, which was determined not by anatomy but by cultural inscription, most visually evident in women's bound feet. Gender-crossing identification, especially on the part of women, necessitated the invocation of *she shen chu di* as an *imaginary* slipping into the opposite gender's body (chapter 3).

Second, the facile notion of monadic subjects defined within their bodies is disrupted by a more profound sense of distance and incommensurability located not between my body (*shen*) and the other's situation (*di*), but right at the "heart" (*xin*)—the very component eclipsed by and yet still underlying the condensed expression. While Zhu Xi invoked the composite nature of the heart to account for the exteriority of emotion, which he reductively understood as emotion's subjection to the outside world, the late sixteenth-century *Journey to the West* and its early seventeenth-century *Supplement* turned the composite heart into a topos of spectatorship, where one faced off with an uncanny double unassimilable to oneself (chapter 2).

Third, the moral and aesthetic imperative to imaginatively put oneself in another's situation was necessitated by the precondition that identifying with oneself had become as problematic as identifying with the other, as a result of dis-tancing mediated through the prism of face-off. But we should push further and argue that this faceoff is neither an encounter with someone whose interior is unknown to me nor an internal drama within my split consciousness; it takes place between me, the spectator in here, and the emotion-realm in the yonder, where I am already staying with the other. What I am confronting and challenged to identify with is less the psychological state of myself or someone else but the *"situation" as an emotion-realm* that involves both myself and others and at the same time lies ahead of me. How to access what others feel and, conversely, how to dip into the underside of the self—these psychological questions can be raised only secondarily within the spatial problematic by asking how to "imaginatively" have oneself already *delivered through* a situation that one is *embedded in* and at the same time *distanced from*. "Imaginatively" is used here not in the sense that sympathy happens only immanently as a mental representation but in the sense that sympathetic identification with regard to emotion-realms can never take place in any logical or pragmatic fashion because it signifies the aporia of spatiality. Distending over the productive incongruity among embedment, deliverance, and faceoff, spatiality opens up multifarious possibilities of social relations to others and multiple historical trajectories relating past and future. And yet it aporetically leaves unresolved the paradox between the oneness of "time-space" and the discordance among its three dimensions.[126]

This dimensional discordance of the emotion-realm—the same aporia that plagues time-space—lies at this third and deepest level of incommensurable situations, as dramatized by the radicalized casuistry in the early eighteenth-century *Haoqiu zhuan* (chapter 4). Spatially, characters and readers are like the spying thief on the eaves who is drawn toward the chivalrous heroes only to find their perverted principles unapproachable. But this double movement of drawing toward and holding apart (called "appropriation") also takes the form of ecstatic temporality. Recall that the contemporaneity in Zhu Xi's casuistry exclusively emphasizes the situation *at present* that calls for a "timely" action, and that, given the presumed interchangeability between norms and expedients regardless of their temporal discrepancies, he puts virtually all ethical cases, despite their historical distance, on the same time plane, an eternal present. By contrast, ecstatic temporality requires one to evaluate another person's ethical decision by putting it in diachronic context that runs through its agent's whole course of life, so that even similar situations bear incommensurable meanings thanks to their unique positions in the life stories of their authors.

It may seem that individuality (as a distinct "whole") is reified as the natural fault line, which would only reproduce the commonplace that I can never feel what another body feels. But ecstatic temporality fractures the wholeness of the self, with the eternal present where ideal timeliness resides blasted open in opposite directions toward past and future. On the one hand, the inadvertent effects of an expedient act from the past come to haunt the heroes so that they no longer feel free to take timely actions in response to new situations; on the other hand, the meanings of their past expedients are always susceptible to potential subversion by their future decisions. While awakening to another layer of deep background that sheds light on one's existence is a signature aspect of deliverance, that aspect is inverted into the dimension of face-off through which the past now figures less as a preordinance than as a precarious project set ahead of oneself, such that one is constantly in danger of either falling short of it or, even worse, parodying the project by overreaching it. Forging wholeness out of an individual life story by giving its moments to one another, the radicalized casuistry ends up staging the incongruous juxtaposition of deliverance to the past, embedment in the present, and faceoff with the future.

As a distinctive symptom of theatricality, sympathy can now be redefined fully in terms of the spatiality of emotion: *the dimensional discordance highlighted by the historical regime of theatricality in the confrontation between the spectator and the emotion-realm she is simultaneously involved in and excluded from.* The discordance is expressed through the Chinese idiom *she shen chu di*, which harbors in a compressed form its sprawling origins from earlier regimes. The philological entanglement of *she shen chu di* (predicated on reified distance) with *ti qunchen* (predicated on a shared body) and *she yi shen chu qi di yi cha qi xin* (predicated on the interchangeable situations) lays traps of anachronism that threaten to obliterate the distinction between the regimes of winds, dreamscapes, and theatricality. But such anachronism can now be seen as an effect derived from the aporia of spatiality—that is, from the dimensional discordance within the oneness of the emotion-realm (time-space) itself, which I am *already delivered through*, *always being embedded in*, and at the same time *distanced from* (and thus *not yet* there). That effect is magnified by the foregrounding of dimensional discordance through the prism of faceoff in theatricality. If our impulse to "historicize" is sustained by the spectatorial distance that puts historical and cultural differences in perspective, that does not mean that our historical consciousness is more advanced or that history is the ultimate form of knowledge in the era of theatricality. Rather, it means that historicization is a secondary reaction to the newly heightened sensibility of anachronism, which has a primordial connection to the aporia of spatiality.

This anachronistic effect was especially prominent in the early modern Chinese context, where theatricality, following its peculiar trajectory, always proceeded in discursive transparency. As I have argued, to fill in its blanks, terms garnered from other historical modes of spatiality of emotion have been mobilized and misapplied. As a result, *she shen chu di* is understood in terms of the dreamscape rather than recognized as a distinct symptom of theatricality; worse still, it is considered absent from traditional drama.[127] Discussions of Chinese fellow feeling have largely focused on the much older discourse of *shu*, which is, as aforementioned, not quite the same as sympathy. Historically, this discursive blindness to Chinese theatricality was coupled with a malignant ethico-political charge that emerged in the nineteenth century: the Chinese have no sympathy. On this contentious site of absence, the interplay between dreamscapes and theatricality entered a new phase at the dawn of modern China. Again, as in the case of theatricality, it is not enough to redefine sympathy in terms of the aporia of the spatiality of emotion. We now need to lay out the varied trajectories in which sympathy emerged as a symptom of theatricality from the dreamscape structured differently from one tradition to another.

5. AT THE DREAM'S END

Overlaying the aporia of spatiality, the most common misunderstanding of sympathy positions the subject exclusively in the "here"; sympathy is thus reduced to a private fantasy cementing—in both senses of covering and hardening—the break between self and others. Detachment from the yonder is overcompensated for by the privileging of the interior herein as the natural locus of feeling to such an extent that my inability to access what others feel is turned into their own deficiency of feeling.

For this reason, the remote "China" as a signifier has doubly functioned as an ideal Other in the Western discourse of sympathy for two contradictory reasons. Smith writes that one hardly feels as strongly for the entire population in China killed in an earthquake as for the prospect of losing one's little finger. But such mitigating effects in sympathizing with the remote Other, Smith maintains, furnish the rational foundation of moral sentiment for Western civil society, because they prove that sympathy is founded not on natural feelings (which would never defeat selfishness) but on a deeper, stronger power of principle and conscience.[128] On the other hand, as Eric Hayot shows, this Scottish Enlightenment project of sympathy reached a bizarre conclusion in the nineteenth century: it was the Chinese who appeared indifferent to self-inflicted cruelty and failed to feel pain in their stricken bodies (and, by extension, in their own countrymen); it took a Western spectator to feel on their behalves, and compassion comingled with condemnation.[129]

This notion of Chinese unfeelingness tends to reduce spatiality to a nervous system, as propagated in Arthur Henderson Smith's infamous *Chinese Characteristics*, which alleges "the absence of nerves" in the

Chinese body and relates this to "the absence of sympathy." The two absences overlap in the exemplary instance of public gazing. On the one hand, Reverend Smith, a nineteenth-century missionary, claims that "the lack of sympathy" is most clearly manifested in the "general indifference to the feelings of the poor child thus exposed to the public gaze." On the other hand, those feelings are put in doubt because the Chinese subject demonstrates indifference to any "observation without sympathy," no matter "how many people see him, nor when, nor for how great a length of time," precisely thanks to his lack of nerves.[130] Reversing the premise of the Scottish Enlightenment that my senses allow me no immediate access to what another body feels (and thus I must use my sympathetic imagination to put myself into another's position in order to feel), the nerveless Chinese body does not feel itself.

We will return to this unfeeling body in a moment; but first we must unmask the fundamental issues of spatiality it has displaced. We need to detail how the two contradictory accounts of China in the modern discourse of sympathy could work together. How could China be too remote for Westerners to sympathize with but also completely at the mercy of Western sympathy (since it fails to feel for itself)? The apparent incoherence is dissolved once we recall the dream of sympathy we have seen in Diderot and Adam Smith, which is supposed to annul the reified distance in theatricality so that feeling is made present for me to share—until I wake up and find myself "absent" from the dream. These cycles of immersion in and excommunication from the dream of sympathy, which oscillate around the axis of presence and absence, perpetuate theatricality along with its spectatorial distance.

Yet what confronts Arthur Smith is quite another dynamic, owing to a different structure of dreamscapes and an alternative trajectory toward theatricality in the Chinese context, even though the Chinese themselves internalize the Western gaze. Lu Xun 魯迅 (Zhou Shuren 周樹人, 1881–1936)—a keen reader of *Chinese Characteristics*[131]— diagnoses "the masses, especially the Chinese ones," as a swamp of "spectators" who take in the "sacrifice" on display as no more than a fleeting, forgettable amusement.[132] According to the fable in his 1922 preface to *Call to Arms* (*Nahan* 吶喊), his writing career was launched by a primal scene of his own spectatorship when he was studying medicine in Japan. In a class he saw a slideshow during the Russo-Japanese War featuring a public execution, with the Chinese convict and his countrymen audience wearing no expressions but numbness and indifference. Thereupon Lu Xun famously declared that the Chinese soul mortally needed a cure that is available only in literature.[133]

Behind this apparently uncritical reproduction of the Western prejudice, scholars have perceptively detected an introspective reflection on literary style (the "violence of observation" in realism),[134] media culture (the "immobility" imposed upon the image of "Chineseness" in film or photography),[135] the politics of witnessing (a reported beheading scene was probably fictive),[136] and the validity of the entire symbolic order (haunted by the somatic of the grotesque decapitalized body).[137] To Haiyan Lee, Lu Xun's critique turns the imperative to sympathize on its head. By exploring the mutual victimization so deeply entrenched in the Chinese society, Lee contends, he is poised to "question the tendency (including his own) to attribute historically and socially generated problems to the absence of sympathy or lack of emotion, and to suggest that without radically transforming the basic structures of society, sympathy will always be out of place, so to speak, and remain a sentimental solution."[138] I would add that Lu Xun rejects sympathy as a solution not because it is secondary to other social issues; rather, he does so because he does not share the particular kind of "dream of sympathy" based on the presence-absence oscillation with which Adam Smith addresses the crisis of theatricality. The dreamscape Lu Xun engages is structured not in terms of presence but of deliverance, which provides the context for the issue of watching and being watched.

That is why Lu Xun's preface has to open with a series of "dreams" he was delivered through during his youth. He first relates a "beautiful dream" of rescuing the nation with modern medicine, which is superseded by a grimmer dream of rescue through literary writing, which in turn gives way to disillusionment when the abortion of his stillborn journal *New Birth* mortified him so much that he withdrew into resignation. In response to a friend petitioning him to write again, he describes the current situation of both the country and himself as one spatial setting:

> Imagine an iron house without windows and doors, absolutely indestructible, with many people fast asleep inside who will soon die of suffocation. But you know since they will die in their sleep,

they will not feel the pain of death. Now if you cry aloud to wake a few of the lighter sleepers, making those unfortunate few suffer the agony of irrevocable death, do you think you are doing them a good turn?[139]

To defamiliarize this oft-cited scenario from the inception of modern Chinese literature, one has to start by asking an obvious question: Why would an unbreakable iron house, a topos of an absolute dead end, be considered possible? The unprecedented national crisis withstanding, hasn't the preface thrown Lu Xun from one short-lived illusion to another, as traditional dreamscapes are always supposed to do? So why does the ceaseless motion of deliverance suddenly glide to an abrupt halt, and why is ephemerality put on hold between the sealed walls of finality?[140]

Without seeing that the traditional dreamscape is at odds with the image of the iron house, we take the iron house as an image of the dreamscape and of "tradition" per se. It is tempting to see the "awakening to the reality of the daylight world" in traditional dream-fiction as "an awakening to a universal moral order from which there was, in effect, *no 'way out.'* "[141] However, in misconstruing the dimension of deliverance—where incessantly being thrown into one illusion after another is actually *the very way of getting out* of each one of them—as a cul-de-sac, modern readers themselves become trapped in the Enlightenment discourse of awakening. Only under the imperial eyes of the West, which sees itself as the only awakened agent of "rationality, autonomy, and progress," would the Chinese dreamscape appear to be a realm of stagnation.[142] In our earlier discussion (section 3), we saw how the dimension of deliverance—the endless itinerary through oneiric layers—tends to be misplaced onto the genealogy of emotion-realms as a whole, bringing about the grand illusion that there is no exit from (and hence no history for) the historical regime of dreamscapes. Now, through the distorted lens of Western awakening as linear progression, that grand illusion is refracted to the level of dimension, misrepresenting the course of deliverance as a blind alley.

We need to go beyond this geopolitical critique to a critique of spatiality. Underneath the characterization of China (and Asia in general) as stagnant lies a more profound misunderstanding of the waking world *as external*, as exemplified by Hegel's stigmatization of "the dreaming Indian":

> In a dream the individual ceases to be conscious of the self as such, in contradistinction from objective existences. *When awake, I exist for myself, and the rest of creation is an external, fixed objectivity, as I myself am for it.* . . . [But in the Indian dream,] things are as much stripped of rationality, of finite consistent stability of cause and effect, as man is of the steadfastness of free individuality, of personality, and freedom.[143]

This returns us to the ambiguities of Lu Xun's iron house. Where does its despairing sense of finality come from? For Enlightenment observers, it is a product of the traditional Chinese dreamscape with "no way out." But what sounds more vicious a trap than "an external, fixed objectivity" that claims to grant you freedom? What entraps Lu Xun is not the cannibalistic tradition he famously attacks but the objectification of space set before the "awakened" one.

Such objectification is not unique to Hegelian thinking (with Descartes, Leibniz, and Kant already perpetuating it in one way or another) and is hardly even modern. It is rooted in the easy slippage from the dimension of faceoff, in which I am confronted with the emotion-realm that involves me in the yonder, into a reductive scenario where what I face off with is a world picture. The misguided effort to "mingle" emotion and landscape in Chinese poetics and the Hegelian dialectic to unify subject and object stem from the same confusion.[144] The confusion would grow most severe under the advancement of theatricality centered on that particular dimension. It is no coincidence that sixteenth-century Europe witnessed both the rise of theatricality and the naissance of the "pure landscape," a homogenized space emptied of historico-religious meaning and detached from the inwardly turned human figure in the foreground.[145] Karatani Koji argues that, at the inception of modern Japanese literature, this imported notion of "landscape" epiphenomenal with the "discovery of interiority," marked a paradigmatic shift underlying such diverse or contradictory tenets as realism, romanticism, and proletarian literature.[146] Given the Japanese connection among the May Fourth writers, Karatani's insight helps us look across the artificial schism between Lu Xun's realistic "depiction" (*miaoxie* 描寫) and Yu Dafu's 郁達夫 romantic "expression" (*biaoxian* 表現), and later between the bourgeois "literary revolution" and proletarian "revolutionary literature."[147] As Karatani contends, once pure landscape—a modern invention—took over, it was "inverted" and essentialized as something that has been around since the beginning of time—a homogeneous, empty stratum on which culture and history are inscribed. Lu Xun's iron house as pure landscape, however, inscribes its essentialized homogeneity back onto the entire history of Chinese civilization, and that is why he can condemn the nation as a whole (or make up a "nation" to condemn).

Before he hits the iron walls, Lu Xun contextualizes the homogeneous picture of space and civilization within a very different kind of topos: the topos of the dreamscape. He is delivered into the iron house through a series of dreams, and, absent the misguided modern notion of the outlying world as fixed and external, the iron house would have dissolved into just another layer of dreams. This subjunctive mood ("would have") brings to mind an overlooked lineage with which Lu Xun would probably be a better fit than with the May Fourth generation: the lineage of dream masters. His enunciative position as the awake one and his speech act of sentencing a whole civilization to a horrid end could bring Lu Xun into the line of magicians like Zhongli Quan and Lü Dongbin, and the iron house could be an instance of "dreadful realms" conjured up in a deliverance play. As we recall, the sense that there is "no way out" is just a trick played by the dreamscape to shock the uninitiated *out* of their self-absorbed existence.

Under the sway of the Enlightenment, Lu Xun's dreadful realm is reified as an absolute fixture of objectivity with no hope of jailbreak. Accordingly, the emergence of theatricality from the dreamscape also takes a different turn. What had been, in sixteenth-century China, a moment punctuating the ongoing course of deliverance, an interstitial strand for Du Liniang to tiptoe in front of her dream, a quick glimpse of the burgeoning topos of theatricality still obscured by the dreamscape, has become the boxed-in destiny of an entire people. With deliverance frozen up—that is, with awakening no longer relativized as another ephemeral dream[148]—spectatorial distance is entrenched between the awakened one and the masses.[149] In this changing topos of heightened theatricality, the dreamscape is not tossed aside but revamped. Once the dimension of embedment is liberated from deliverance now stalled, the dreamers become thoroughly exposed to the inundation of presence, to the winds of agitation in the form of mass passions that threaten to collapse distance and height—except for the newly entrenched distance between awakening and dreaming, which motivates the makeover of the Chinese dreamscape on the basis of presence in the first place.[150]

Eugenia Lean offers a vivid picture of a full-blown culture of "popular sympathy" in Republican China by the 1930s as a media sensation that generated a civil society of spectators who maintained a critical distance from the spectacle they themselves formed. But she points out that collective sentiment lost its "autonomy" to government control during the war and became susceptible to manipulation in Communist China.[151] This less egalitarian trend might have started in the 1920s, as John Fitzgerald notes, when the division between the awakened one and the sleeping masses ran deeply into the modern Chinese polity; the awake circle became ever smaller within the modern intelligentsia, then became ensconced in a political party, and eventually was limited to the supreme leader. Springing directly from this "Machiavellian" aspect of awakening were political regimes whose self-legitimacy depended partly on the sympathetic power of the awakened one, who claimed to feel the grief of which the unaware majority themselves had yet to become conscious.[152]

Since awakening now means coming to a world that is "an external, fixed objectivity," the awakened one finds himself outside of and *absent* from the dream that is accordingly defined by *presence*. To compensate for the lost immediacy of embedment, he can transport himself back to the dream of sympathy, where the spectator ceases to be one by sharing others' emotion—until he wakes up in the spectatorial position, reconfirming the distance from the emotion-realm he has already shared with the others in the yonder. In contrasting "the dreaming Indian" and the awakened (European) individual, Hegel never means to segregate them; rather, the dream revamped as presence is preserved and sublated (*aufgehoben*) into awakening, just as enlightened Spirit (the human mind) keeps perfecting itself by reproducing within it the antithesis of its own, a procedure Hegel formalizes as the universal program of "dialectics" through which rational thinking progresses and synthesizes its object at all levels of sublation.[153]

Adorno rebukes the Hegelian self-affirmative drive toward synthesis for overlaying a semblance of identity on the contradiction between the thinking subject and the thing opposing it, which eventually comes down to social contradictions. Adorno's "negative dialectics" draws consciousness to the nonidentity that crisscrosses thinking itself between concepts used to comprehend things and things—"the nonidentical" (*das Nichtidentische*)—that are at once comprehended in and lying outside of them.[154] To follow Adorno, one might say that the totalitarianism that accompanies the "awakening" in modern Chinese politics results from the imposed synthetization of the revamped dreamscape into the totality of theatricality, empowering the awakened one as the supreme spectator by way of the dream of sympathy. However, the "nonidentity" Adorno champions is constituted by the distance between the spectatorial subject in the here and the emotion-realm she is at the same time involved in along with others in the yonder. Whether affirmative or negative, dialectics is a generalization of the historically specific trajectory in which theatricality emerges from and reinforces itself through the dreamscape-as-presence. It is this trajectory of Western history that embodies the dimension of deliverance, by means of which presence is brought into the service of faceoff. Neither a teleological program prescribing history (Hegel) nor a critical theory overcoming it (Adorno), dialectics owes its validity to that very course of history. That is tantamount to saying that its validity is doubly limited, since the particular historical trajectory of theatricality's self-affirmation, from which dialectics is abstracted, itself draws on but hardly exhausts the aporetic structure of theatricality.

Dialectics, even with Adorno's retooling, misses the kernel of that aporia. Despite the appearance of specular symmetry, the Adornoian object (which lies simultaneously inside and exterior to the concept) and our spectator (who stands simultaneously ahead of and within an emotion-realm) do not share the same universe. To redress the self-aggrandizing synthetic power of the Hegelian subject, Adorno upholds the priority of the thing over conceptual thinking on the one hand and explores nonidentity cutting through both subject and object on the other, at once demystifying the hypostasis of the subject-object distinction and maintaining its necessity for epistemological reasons.[155] But nonidentity does not really take place at the level of subject-object relationships, nor does it privilege the latter over the former. Rather, it should be traced back to the aporia underlying the spatiality of emotion, namely, the dimensional discordance among embedment, deliverance, and faceoff that is foregrounded by the structure of theatricality and expressed as the problematic of sympathy.

Sympathy turns out to be the issue on which either version of dialectics runs aground. To Adorno, it is suffering that registers social contradictions—the negative nonidentical that no concept is ever able to assimilate and transcend. The self-expression of a body in pain is taken for granted as "a condition of all truth," just because, in his words, "suffering is objectivity that weighs upon the subject."[156] Yet the modern discourse of sympathy has been built on the Chinese body that fails to suffer because it is unable to feel at all. The body is therefore not a privileged ground for the negativity of dialectics; it is the unfeeling body itself that is invoked to necessitate "positive" preservation and sublation. In other words, having classified the Chinese body as unable to feel, the Western subject feels on its behalf by way of the dream of sympathy—making present the pain that is absent in that body before waking up in the spectatorial position. However, even such an affirmative dialectics breaks down in face of this anesthetic body, since nothing could be more remote from self-legitimate regimes of sympathy than Lu Xun's economy of unfeelingness. If, as noted, the dream of sympathy has no place in his writing, it is not just because he is skeptical about any medium at his disposal and about his own position of authority vis-à-vis the sympathetic object, but also because he has followed a different trajectory without recourse to the dream as making present. It is through the dreamscape centered upon deliverance that he ends up in the iron house, and the house's historical significance resides in bringing an end to the otherwise endless process of deliverance. The postdreamer Lu Xun emerges as a lone spectator facing a full house of bodies that feel no pain from suffocation.[157] Infamously, he would have kept it that way, if he had not been persuaded by his friend to give awakening his countrymen one more shot. But he warns us that by calling them to arms, he is probably costing everybody a good eternal sleep for nothing.[158]

In Lu Xun, the unfeeling bodies belong to unawaken social spectators who fail to feel for one another, much like the nerveless bodies without sympathy in Arthur Smith's work. But the analogy stops here:

sympathy is never "absent" from Lu Xun because he rejects both the spontaneity of bodily affect and the dream of presence, both being the dialectic condition for sympathetic identification and based on the embedment dimension of the emotion-realm. By riding the dimension of deliverance till the last layer of the dreamscape, he finds himself facing the unfeeling bodies, which he is aporetically forever stuck with and alienated from. As long as the aporia of spatiality persists, so too does sympathy as a heightened expression of that aporia through the prism of faceoff. What he sympathetically identifies with is strictly speaking not the bodies, but unfeelingness per se.

In the second half of the "Preface," as Eileen Cheng points out, "his earlier dismissal of the inconsequential lives of certain others [as unfeeling onlookers] comes back to haunt him full force as Lu Xun *depicts himself after this second conversion as numb and soulless as the bystanders he condemned*," which leads to a self-critique of his "textual authority."[159] We should delve into the paradox that Lu Xun's belated identification with unfeelingness becomes the way for him to sympathize. Unfeelingness designates not an abstract nonexistence of feeling but an elaborate spatial structure that gives the relationship to one's own emotion-realm in the yonder an ironic twist under the regime of theatricality. If one always stays and feels along with others over there in the emotion-realm before coming to the here, as the intentional dis-tancing generally prescribes, the other side of the picture—namely, that one necessarily *unfeels* in the here without coming from the yonder—now comes to the forefront precisely when what is between here and yonder is reified through the prism of faceoff into a distanced confrontation, with one simultaneously unfeeling here and feeling along with others over there. The Chinese unfeeling body is not an essential organism without access to sympathy, nor is it subsumed under the Western spectator who alone is capable of sympathizing. Rather, the body without nerves is a figure of *spectatorship on the part of the Chinese* facing off with the emotion one at once has shared in the yonder and is yet to feel in the here.[160]

Hence, the Victorians encountered in China not an exotic or inferior Other but the common ground of theatricality that both parties have come to cohabit, by different trajectories, since the sixteenth century. Without acknowledging the fact of already being with the Other in the same regime of theatricality, the Western spectator repeats the structural "failure" of the allegedly unfeeling Chinese to recognize himself always already in the Other's position, which is less a "defect" than the constitutive character of spatiality in the dimension of faceoff underlying relationships between self and other, here and yonder, past and future. The "ancient civilization" of China—in which Arthur Smith claimed to find the complementarity between a merciless public gaze *and* "nerveless" immunity to being watched—turns out to be not that "ancient"; rather, through a warped journey of time-space, he reached the land of a dystopic future promised a century before by Adam Smith, who foresaw the gravest nightmare of theatricality: a spectatorship incapable of and in no need of fellow feeling.[161]

Treating the nerveless Chinese as an apocalypse of theatricality would perpetuate the bias of the affirmative and negative dialectics according to which either the unfeeling body has to be sublated or all bodies are assumed to be able to feel. But that amounts to saying that the unfeelingness in the here as the negativity of spectatorship—resulting from the heightened aporia of spatiality in the distanced confrontation between here and yonder—is the ultimate nonidentical that evades even negative dialectics itself. Exploring history through the spatial structure of unfeelingness entails following an unbeaten trail without recourse to the self-confirming subject or the self-affecting body. Such an approach to history is made possible not by anachronistically rejecting theatricality in favor of some phantomic immediacy but by engaging unfeelingness as the most unsettling moment of negativity underlying the spectatorial position.

Ironically, the normative imperative to sympathize—that is, to *feel* what another *feels*—fails to consider the possibility of unfeelingness without losing consciousness in a different cultural context, as exemplified by the anesthetic body in Chinese acupuncture, which Hayot calls "a spectacle that showed Europe the possibility of an 'alternatively' modern future."[162] What Arthur Smith misrecognizes as a nerveless body turns out to be a body with intricate channels, pinpointed nexuses, and pressure points that are well charted under the needles.

The way forward does not involve the substitution of one body for another; that would still reduce sympathy to an issue of the nervous system. An anesthetic body from an immemorial past lies ahead as the future for another culture (for "us") because the spatiality of emotion is now so warped that what is supposed to have been remains unfulfilled through the prism of faceoff and, more important, because even in this dimension of faceoff, however strongly the distanced confrontation is felt, the fact that one is always already staying with others and sharing the emotion-realm in the yonder is so firmly in place that the equiprimordial unfeeling in the here remains inconceivable and bizarre. In a last twist to the spatiality of emotion, that which has ever stayed ahead and beyond our reach is not the yonder but this futuristic "here," the iron house of unfeelingness. We have thus mistaken the challenge of theatricality *outside in*. We are never trapped in an iron house with no way out; rather, we are being locked out and are in need of another dream-ride into it.

Notes

PROLOGUE: WEATHER AND LANDSCAPE

1. Norbert Schwarz and Gerald Clore, "Mood, Misattribution, and Judgments of Well-Being: Informative and Directive Functions of Affective States," *Journal of Personality and Social Psychology* 45, no. 1 (1983): 513–23.
2. Richard S. Lazarus, "Cognition and Motivation in Emotion," *American Psychologist* 46, no. 4 (April 1991): 352–67; Brian Parkinson, *Ideas and Realities of Emotion* (London: Routledge, 1995), 27–68; David Konstan, *The Emotions of the Ancient Greeks: Studies in Aristotle and Classical Literature* (Toronto: University of Toronto Press, 2006), 20–40.
3. If the moods aroused by memories of a life event are more personal and hence informatively more valuable than the moods driven by rain or an unappealing room, the quintessential locus of emotion is clearly assumed to be in the interior, not in an entanglement with the exterior.
4. The inner-over-outer hierarchy proves more tenacious than the reason-emotion dichotomy. It is perpetuated not only through mid-twentieth-century cognitive science, which sees the mind as a software program in charge of the hardware, but also through more recent "postcognitive" approaches, which supposedly integrate the mind with its environment, only to relegate the world to the "perceiver-dependent" status. The world is relevant only insofar as it is related to the subject's concern and purpose. See David Herman, "1880–1945: Re-minding Modernism," in *The Emergence of Mind: Representations of Consciousness in Narrative Discourse in English*, ed. David Herman (Lincoln, NE: University of

Nebraska Press, 2011), 254–57; W. Teed Rockwell, *Neither Brain nor Ghost: A Nondualist Alternative to the Mind-Brain Identity Theory* (Cambridge, MA: MIT Press, 2005), 86–90.

5. Cai Yingjun, *Bi xing wuse yu qing jing jiao rong* 比興物色與情景交融 (Taipei: Da'an chubanshe, 1986), 138–39, 1–17. See also Cecile C. Shun, *Pearl from the Dragon's Mouth: Evocation of Scene and Feeling in Chinese Poetry* (Ann Arbor, MI: Center for Chinese Studies, 1995); *The Poetics of Repetition in English and Chinese Lyric Poetry* (Chicago: University of Chicago Press, 2011).

6. François Jullien, *Detour and Access: Strategies of Meaning in China and Greece* (New York: Zone Books, 2000), 152. In other words, at the fundamental level of its own language, the "emotion-landscape mingling" discourse defeats its mission of mingling by naming two separate things in the first place. Notably, the discourse reached its breaking point by reflecting upon this paradox in the seventeenth century; to this we will return at the end of chapter 2.

7. Jullien, *Detour and Access*, 152, 180. This explains why, historically, the Six Dynasties notion of "natural scenery" felt dubious to later critics for its stress on the resemblance of landscape in its own right over expressive values. See Cai, *Bi xing wuse*, 168–221. By the same token, it is against things considered "external" (narratives, arguments, descriptions) dominating the Song poetry that the notion of "emotion-landscape mingling" was coined to uphold the primacy of interiority rather than really transcending the interior-exterior duality. See Gong Pengcheng 龔鵬程, *Shishi bense yu miaowu* 詩史本色與妙悟 (Taipei: Taiwan Xuesheng shuju, 1986), 14–15.

8. Wang Guowei, *Renjian cihua huibian huijiao huiping* 人間詞話彙編彙校彙評, ed. Zhou Xishan 周錫山 (Taiyuan: Beiyue wenyi chubanshe, 2004), 165, 201, emphasis added.

9. "詩者，志之所之也。在心為志，發言為詩。情動於中而形於言。" See *Mao shi zhengyi* 毛詩正義, in Ruan Yuan 阮元 (1764–1849), comp. *Shisanjing zhushu* 十三經註疏 (Beijing: Zhonghua shuju, 1977), 1:270; Stephen Owen, *Readings in Chinese Literary Thought* (Cambridge: Council on East Asian Studies, 1992), 41, translation modified.

10. Wallace Stevens, "To Hi Simons," in *Letters of Wallace Stevens*, ed. Holly Steven (Berkeley: University of California Press, 1996), 348–49.

11. Jullien, *Detour and Access*, 164.

12. Debates over whether or how weather affects our mood therefore miss the point. It is not that our mood is inside us and under the yet-to-proved influence of weather; rather, we are *under* the weather as much as we are *in* the mood that is in the air.

13. Its modern social-science version would be "topophilia," which studies "all of the human being's affective ties with the material environment" on the one

hand, and how "environment provides the sensory stimuli, which as perceived images lend shape to our joys and ideals" on the other. See Yi-Fu Tuan, *Topophilia: A Study of Environmental Perception, Attitudes, and Values* (New York: Columbia University Press, 1974), 93, 113.

14. Wang Guowei twice compiled and published materials from his *Treatise on Song Lyrics* manuscripts in 1908–1909 and 1915. The two entries cited above were never sent to press, however, until Wang's disciple Zhao Wanli 趙萬里 published them along with forty-two other entries in "Renjian cihua weikangao ji qita" 人間詞話未刊稿及其它, *Xiaoshuo yuebao* 小說月報 19, no. 3 (February 1928): 376.
15. Wang Guowei, *Renjian cihua huibian*, 26.
16. Scholars have been tempted to see Wang Guowei as further developing traditional discussions of "emotion-landscape mingling" with his Schopenhauerian philosophy. Zhou Zhenfu 周振甫, *Shici lihua* 詩詞例話 (Beijing: Qingnian chubanshe, 1962), 73–77.
17. Xu Fuguan, "Wang Guowei *Renjian cihua* jingjie shuo shiping" 王國維《人間詞話》境界說試評, in *Zhongguo wenxue jingshen* 中國文學精神 (Shanghai: Shanghai shudian chubanshe, 2006), 74. Other scholars take the mid-Tang (eighth century) as the turning point at which the word $jing_2$ in discussions of poetry "no longer referred to demarcations of space in the objective world but phenomena undetachable from perceptions" under the influence of Buddhism. See Xiao Chi 蕭馳, *Fofa yu shijing* 佛法與詩境 (Taipei: Lianjing chuban shiye gufen youxian gongsi, 2012), 138. Although Xiao more cautiously regards sentiments in Buddhist poetry as transcendent rather than subjective and therefore warns us not to read it in terms of "emotion-landscape mingling" (181), I would argue that turning landscapes into phenomena dependent on the mind, Buddhist discourse exhibits the same symptom as other, more general "emotion-landscape" discussions.
18. Xu Fuguan, "Wang Guowei *Renjian cihua*," 72, emphasis added.
19. The second- to third-century philology associates the two words together by their connection to "light," which is the original meaning of $jing_1$, while $jing_2$ means the lighted area. See Ogawa Tamaki 小川環樹, "Chūgoku bungaku ni okeru fūkei no igi" 中国文学における風景の意義, in *Ogawa Tamaki chosakushū* 小川環樹著作集 (Tokyo: Chikuma Shobō, 1997), 1:261–62. The words are differentiated by tone in Mandarin but are exact homophones in medieval Chinese and also interchangeable. See Zhou Zumo 周祖謨, ed., *Guangyun jiaoben* 廣韻校本 (Beijing: Zhonghua shuju, 1960), 1:318. Even in late imperial times $jing_2$ *jie* could still be transcribed as $jing_1$ *jie* 景界. See Xu Wei 徐渭, "Du Longti shu" 讀龍惕書, in *Xu Wei ji* 徐渭集 (Beijing: Zhonghua shuju, 1983), 1:678: "Between evildoing and hypocrisy, even though it seems to be inscrutable

slippage, their delimited realms are fundamentally different (*jing₁ jie dunbie* 景界頓別)."

20. The term is traceable to Wang Changling's 王昌齡 (ca. 698–ca. 757) *Norms of Poetry* (*Shige* 詩格), where he understands it as an inner domain "deployed in the thought and posited inside the body" (*zhang yu yi er chu yu shen* 張於意而處於身), as distinct from "the territories of things" (*wujing*物境) and "the territories of thoughts" (*yijing*意境). See *Wang Changling quanji jiaozhu* 王昌齡全集校注, ed. Hu Wentao 胡問濤 and Luo Qin 羅琴 (Chengdu: Bashu shushe, 2000), 316–17. Modern scholars continue to use this term to "highlight 'emotion' as the essence of lyrical literature" despite the talk of unifying the internal and the external. See Wang Wensheng 王文生, *Lun qingjing* 論情境 (Shanghai: Shanghai wenyi chubanshe, 2001), 89–90, 92.

21. This rather colloquial usage of *qing* as situational rather than psychological should be traced back to ancient writings in which *qing* could be used to mean "essence," "reality," or more paradoxically, both "reality input" and "reality response." The ambiguity and even contradiction in the word's connotations shows that the usual reading of emotion as feedback to external stimuli does not really work. In place of the confrontation between emotion and the external world, what we see here are the early signs of exteriority and spatiality underlying the Chinese vocabulary of emotion. For a more detailed discussion, see chapter 2, section 2.

22. See "Minmatsu Shinsho ni okeru 'jinsei wa dorama de aru' no setsu" 明末清初における「人生はドラマである」の說, in *Chūgoku tetsugakushi kenkyū ronshū: Araki Kyōju taikyū kinen*中国哲学史研究論集：荒木教授退休記念, ed. Araki Kyōju Taikyū Kinenkai 荒木教授退休記念会 (Fukuoka-shi: Ashi Shobō, 1981), 625, 629.

23. See Wai-yee Li, *Enchantment and Disenchantment: Love and Illusion in Chinese Literature* (Princeton: Princeton University Press, 1992), 47–48. Zhang Dai was recalling what happened in 1629. See "Jinshan yexi" 金山夜戲, in *Tao'an mengyi/ Xihu mengxun* 陶庵夢憶/西湖夢尋 (Shanghai: Shanghai guji chubanshe, 2001), 12–13.

24. Sophie Volpp, *Worldly Stage: Theatricality in Seventeenth-Century China* (Cambridge, MA: Harvard University Asia Center, 2011), 18–19, 21.

25. Volpp, *Worldly Stage*, 32–36. The episode is from Zhang Dai, "Xihu qiyueban" 西湖七月半, *Tao'an mengyi/ Xihu mengxun*, 111–12.

26. Volpp, *Worldly Stage*, 22, 32, 56.

27. See, for example, *Audience Participation: Essays on Inclusion in Performance*, ed. Susan Kattwinkel (Westport, CT: Praeger, 2003).

28. Chen Jiansen 陳建森, *Song Yuan xiqu benti lun* 宋元戲曲本體論 (Beijing: Renmin chubanshe, 2012), 61–78, 89–104.

29. Jeehee Hong, "Virtual Theater of the Dead: Actor Figurines and Theater Stage in Houma no. 1, Shanxi Province," *Artibus Asiae* 71, no. 1 (2012): 82, 101, 107, 109–111.
30. Michel Foucault, "What Is the Enlightenment?" in *Foucault Reader*, ed. Paul Rabinow (New York: Pantheon, 1984), 46–49. Ian Hacking narrows down the term focusing only on how "the coordinates of 'scientific objectivity'" are singularly "rearranged" over time through "discourse and practice," but that only covers the second field in Foucault's framework. See *Historical Ontology* (Cambridge, MA.: Harvard University Press, 2002), 3–6.
31. Michael Schwartz, "Epistemes and the History of Being," in *Foucault and Heidegger: Critical Encounters*, ed. Alan Milchman and Alan Rosenberg (Minneapolis: University of Minnesota Press, 2003), 179–81.
32. See Hubert L. Dreyfus's "'Being and Power' Revisited" and Stuart Elden's "Reading Genealogy as Historical Ontology," in *Foucault and Heidegger*, 30–54, 187–205.
33. See chapter 5, section 1.
34. See Li Zehou, *Lishi benti lun, Jimao wushuo* 歷史本體論、己卯五說 (Beijing: Sanlian shudian, 2003), 8–20, 35–44, 48–59, 85–119.
35. This misperception is debunked in Jeffrey Nealon, *Foucault Beyond Foucault: Power and Its Intensification Since 1984* (Stanford: Stanford University Press, 2008).
36. As will be argued in chapter 4, Foucault's problematic diagnosis of power derives from the dilemma of his epistemology.
37. Wang, *Renjian cihua huibian*, 11.
38. Zhu Guangqian, *Shilun* 詩論, in *Zhu Guangqian quanji* 朱光潛全集 (Hefeishi: Anhui jiaoyu chubanshe, 1987), 3:59–60.
39. Zhu Ziqing 朱自清, preface (dated 1931) to Zhu Guangqian, *Wenyi xinlixue* (Shanghai: Kaiming shudian, 1936), 4.
40. Gong, *Shishi bense yu miaowu*, 6–7.
41. Yeh Chia-ying, *Wang Guowei ji qi wenxue piping* 王國維及其文學批評 (Taipei: Guiguan tushu gongsi, 2004), 252. For Wang Guowei, in "the realm with me," my existence feels pressured by what is outside me and my will comes into conflict with others'; hence the experience of sublime. In contrast, in "the realm without me" such confrontation is smoothed out; hence the experience of beauty. Wang Guowei explicitly maps the Western categories of the sublime (*hongzhuang* 宏壯) and beauty (*youmei* 優美) onto his two realms (*Renjian cihua huibian*, 20). For the politics of the sublime in Wang Guowei, see Ban Wang, *The Sublime Figure of History: Aesthetics and Politics in Twentieth-Century China* (Stanford: Stanford University Press, 1997), 17–54.

42. Zhu, *Wenyi xinlixue*, 43–44. For this late nineteenth-century German aesthetic movement of empathy and space that Zhu Guangqian introduced into China in the 1930s, see *Empathy, Form, and Space: Problems in German Aesthetics, 1873–1893*, ed. and trans. Harry Francis Mallgrave and Eleftherios Ikonomou (Santa Monica: The Getty Center for the History of Art and the Humanities, 1994).
43. Susan Lanzoni, "Empathy in Translation: Movement and Image in the Psychological Laboratory," *Science in Context* 25, no. 3 (2012): 307–21.
44. Zhu, *Wenyi xinlixue*, 33–70.
45. Translation from Gustave Flaubert, *The Letters of Gustave Flaubert, 1830–1857*, ed. and trans. Francis Steegmuller (Cambridge, MA: The Belknap Press of Harvard University Press, 1980), 203.
46. Zhu, *Wenyi xinlixue*, 39–40.
47. Li Yu, *Xianqing ouji* 閑情偶寄, ed. Jiang Jurong 江巨榮 and Lu Shourong 盧壽榮 (Shanghai: Shanghai guji chubanshe, 2000), 63–64; translation modified from *Chinese Theories of Theater and Performance from Confucius to the Present*, ed. and trans. Faye Chunfang Fei (Ann Arbor: University of Michigan Press, 1999), 81–82.
48. Edward Titchener, *A Beginner's Psychology* (New York: Macmillan, 1915), 198. The same point is repeated in Richard B. Miller's *Friends and Other Strangers: Studies in Religion, Ethics, and Culture* (New York: Columbia University Press, 2016), 114–15: "Sympathy consists in 'feeling for' an individual, typically when she or he is suffering, and often with care or concern. It need not adopt feelings from another's point of view. Parents may feel sympathy for their child's emotional difficulties without participating in those emotions themselves. We sympathize for but empathize with . . . emotively sharing in a misfortune and hoping for the better. But empathy can include feelings other than those associated with suffering with another, and it need not include well-wishes."
49. Andrew James Terjesen, "The Role of Sympathy and Empathy in Moral Judgment" (Ph.D. dissertation, Yale University, 2005), 10–15.
50. See David Marshall, *The Surprising Effects of Sympathy: Marivaux, Diderot, Rousseau, and Mary Shelley* (Chicago: University of Chicago Press, 1988), 3.
51. Such a chronological progression is constructed in Timothy C. Vincent, "From Sympathy to Empathy: Baudelaire, Vischer, and Early Modernism," *Mosaic: A Journal for the Interdisciplinary Study of Literature* 45, no. 1 (March 2012): 1–15.
52. For Flaubert, the highest achievement of art is "to set us dreaming" (*The Letters of Gustave Flaubert*, 198) and the empathetic identification with characters and situations is a fleeting dream for the writer himself. Just above the passage Zhu quotes, Flaubert writes: "But I fear the awakening, the disillusion that may come when the pages are copied. No matter: for better or worse, it is a delicious

thing to write, to be no longer yourself but to move in an entire universe of your own creating" (203). Instead of opposing this empathetic dream to sympathy, we should see the opposition as already articulated within the eighteenth-century discourse of sympathy, which presents a "dream of sympathy" the spectator goes into and awakens from. See chapter 5, section 3.

1. WINDS, DREAMS, THEATER: A GENEALOGY OF EMOTION-REALMS

1. "*Yin qing cheng meng, yin meng cheng xi*" 因情成夢，因夢成戲. Tang Xianzu, "Fu Gan Yilu" 復甘義麓, in *Tang Xianzu quanji* 湯顯祖全集, ed. Xu Shuofang 徐朔方 (Beijing: Beijing guji chubanshe, 1999), 2:1464.
2. Shih-Hsiang Chen, "The Shih-ching: Its Generic Significance in Chinese Literary History and Poetics," in *Studies in Chinese Literary Genres*, ed. Cyril Birch (Berkeley: University of California Press, 1974), 8–41; Earl Miner, *Comparative Poetics: An Intercultural Essay on Theories of Literature* (Princeton: Princeton University Press, 1990), 20–31, 56–60.
3. The quote never appears in Tang's oeuvre. It was widely circulated as hearsay only after 1620. See Cheng Yun 程芸, *Tang Xianzu yu wan Ming xiqu de shanbian* 湯顯祖與晚明戲曲的嬗變 (Beijing: Zhonghua shuju, 2006), 52–53.
4. "情不知所起，一往而深。生者可以死，死者可以生。" Tang Xianzu, "Zuozhe tici" 作者題詞, in *Mudan ting*, ed. Xu Shuofang and Yang Xiaomei 楊笑梅 (Beijing: Renmin wenxue chubanshe, 1997), 1. References to this book below will be indicated by page numbers in parentheses. Ye Changhai 葉長海 calls attention to the inscrutability of *qing* in Tang's foreword, but he falls back on the explanation of *qing* as "subjective emotive thoughts" (*zhuguan qingsi* 主觀情思). See *Tang xue chuyi* 湯學芻議 (Shanghai: Shanghai renmin chubanshe, 2015), 100–101.
5. Pan Zhiheng, "Qing chi: Guan yan *Mudan ting huanhun ji*" 情痴：觀演《牡丹亭還魂記》, in *Pan Zhiheng quhua* 潘之恆曲話, ed. Wang Xiaoyi 汪效倚 (Beijing: Zhongguo xiqu chubanshe, 1988), 72–73.
6. See the discussion in Grant Guangren Shen, *Elite Theatre in Ming China, 1368–1644* (London: Routledge, 2005), 106.
7. Pan Zhiheng, *Pan Zhiheng quhua*, 72.
8. *Mao shi zhengyi*, 269; "The 'Great Preface,'" 38. For winds as a timeworn trope of emotion, see Paolo Santangelo, *Sentimental Education in Chinese History: An Interdisciplinary Textual Research on Ming and Qing Sources* (Leiden: Brill, 2003), 147–48.
9. Mark Edward Lewis, *The Construction of Space in Early China* (Albany: State University of New York Press, 2006), 20–21.

10. Shigehisa Kuriyama, "The Imagination of Winds and the Development of the Chinese Conception of the Body," in *Body, Subject, and Power in China*, ed. Angela Zito and Tani E. Barlow (Chicago: University of Chicago Press, 1994), 23–41; Ogawa Tamaki, "Fū to un: Kanshou bungaku no kigen" 風と雲—感傷文学の起源, in *Ogawa Tamaki chosakushū*, 1:235–58; Zheng Yuyu 鄭毓瑜, "Cong bingti dao geti: 'Tiqi' yu zaoqi shuqing shuo" 從病體到個體：" 體氣"與早期抒情說, in *Ruxue de qilun yu gongfulun* 儒學的氣論與功夫論, ed. Yang Rubin 楊儒賓 and Zhu Pingci 祝平次 (Taipei: Guoli Taiwan daxue chubanshe, 2005), 417–59.

11. Ben Anderson, "Affective Atmospheres," *Emotion, Space and Society* 2, no. 2 (December 2009): 77, 80.

12. For ancient poetics and the cosmology of correspondence, see Gong Pengcheng, "Cong *Lüshi chunqiu* dao *Wenxin diaolong*: Ziran qigan yu shuqing ziwo" 從《呂氏春秋》到《文心雕龍》——自然氣感與抒情自我, in *Shuqing zhi xiandaixing: "Shuqing chuantong" lunshu yu Zhongguo wenxue yanjiu* 抒情之現代性："抒情傳統"論述與中國文學研究, ed. Chan Kwok-kow 陳國球 and Wang Der-wei 王德威 (Beijing: Sanlian shudian, 2014), 592–621. For a summary and critique of the readings of spontaneous or involuntary expression in the "Great Preface," see Martin Svensson, "A Second Look at the *Great Preface* on the Way to a New Understanding of Han Dynasty Poetics," *CLEAR* 21 (December 1999): 1–33.

13. See Owen, *Readings in Chinese Literary Thought*, 39. Critical of the psychological model, Zheng Yuyu radically reinterprets correspondence as "resonance embedded within the entire atmospheric condition," which characterizes the topos of winds as seen above. Yet, despite the atmospheric diffusion, she argues that resonance "takes the body as the core." See *Wenben fengjing: ziwo yu kongjian de xianghu dingyi* 文本風景：自我與空間的相互定義 (Taipei: Maitian, 2005), 326. Fleeing from psychology to physiology, we run into a reified version of the emotive interior. See chapter 5, section 2.

14. Catherine A. Lutz, *Unnatural Emotions: Everyday Sentiments on a Micronesian Atoll and Their Challenge to Western Theory* (Chicago: University of Chicago Press, 1988).

15. William M. Reddy, *The Navigation of Feeling: A Framework for the History of Emotions* (Cambridge: Cambridge University Press, 2001), 21–31.

16. For the application of a sociohistorical approach to the language of emotion in late imperial Chinese context, showing that "cognitive elements" of emotion vary according to different cultural backgrounds, see Santangelo, *Sentimental Education in Chinese History*, 17–18, 50–69.

17. Robert C. Solomon, *The Passions: Emotions and the Meaning of Life* (Indianapolis: Hackett, 1993), 208. See the critique of Solomon's decisionism in Daniel M.

Gross, *The Secret History of Emotion: From Aristotle's Rhetoric to Modern Brain Science* (Chicago: University of Chicago Press, 2006), 3 n. 3.

18. The problem is therefore not that, as Svensson diagnoses it, Sinologists have endorsed too much involuntary, immediate expression over rational restraint and calculated craftiness while the "Great Preface" itself tilts toward the latter. It has long been recognized the entanglement between these opposite drives. In David Schaberg's terms, the Han dynasty poetics takes songs as expressing "emotional intensity" yet in "coded communication." See Schaberg, "Song and Historical Imagination in Early China," *Harvard Journal of Asiatic Studies* 59, no. 2 (December 1999): 328–39. The genuine problem is that no matter which side—emotion or rationality—one chooses to stress, or still better, whether one chooses to reify that dichotomy (as Svensson does) or to tear it down (as seen in the recent cognitive approach to emotion), the interiority of the feeling subject, who is either a passive receptor or an active thinker, remains intact.

19. Steven Van Zoeren, *Poetry and Personality: Reading, Exegesis, and Hermeneutics in Traditional China* (Stanford: Stanford University Press, 1991), 100–102; Ben Anderson, *Encountering Affect: Capacities, Apparatuses, Conditions* (New York: Routledge, 2012), 149–60.

20. Feng Menglong, *Qingshi*, in *Feng Menglong quanji* 馮夢龍全集 (Nanjing: Jiangsu guji chubanshe, 1993), 7:11.376.

21. Feng, *Qingshi*, 10.361.

22. See Judith T. Zeitlin, *The Phantom Heroine: Ghosts and Gender in Seventeenth-Century Chinese Literature* (Honolulu: University of Hawaii Press, 2007), 13–42. Also see Andrew Schonebaum, *Novel Medicine: Healing, Literature, and Popular Knowledge in Early Modern China* (Seattle: University of Washington Press, 2016).

23. *Tang Xianzu quanji*, 2:1188.

24. Winds are unbound but not undifferentiated due to the unevenness of the moving airs, which is cited in the Han discourse to explain differences among local customs (*feng su*). The totalizing ideology prescribes "the same airs (*feng*) for the entire realm" (*liuhe tongfeng*), but at the same time it is conceded that "airs were different every hundred miles, and so were customs every thousand miles." These competing statements are both from Wang Ji's 王吉 memorial to Emperor Xuan 宣帝 (r. 74–49 BCE), included in Ban Gu 班固, *Han shu* 漢書 (Beijing: Zhonghua shuju, 1962), 10:72.3063. See also Lewis, *The Construction of Space in Early China*, 89–244.

25. Tang Xianzu, "Zuozhe tici," 1.

26. See Hong Xingzu 洪興祖, *Chuci buzhu* 楚辭補注 (Beijing: Zhonghua shuju, 2001), 134. Also see Liao Tengye 廖藤葉, *Zhongguo mengxi yanjiu* 中國夢戲研究 (Taipei: Xuesi chubanshe, 2000), 20–24.

27. "Meng you," *Taiping guangji* 太平廣記, comp. Li Fang 李昉 et al. (Beijing: Zhonghua shuju, 1961), vol. 6, 2241–52.
28. See Bai Xingjian 白行簡 (776–826), "Sanmeng ji" 三夢記, in *Tang Song chuanqi zongji: Tang Wudai* 唐宋傳奇總集：唐五代, ed. Yuan Lükun 袁閭琨 and Xue Hongji 薛洪勣 (Zhengzhou shi: Henan renmin chubanshe, 2001), 1:198. For the Buddhist connotation of "shared dreams," which bespeak the permeability of the self that overlaps with the divine and with other people, see Serinity Young, *Dreaming Lotus: Buddhist Dream Narratives, Imagery, and Practice* (Boston: Wisdom, 1999), 87–94.
29. Only two arias of this adaptation have survived. See Shen Jing, *Shen Jing ji* 沈璟集, ed. Xu Shuofang (Shanghai: Shanghai guji chubanshe, 1991), 819–20.
30. Cited in *Taiping yulan* 太平御覽, comp. Li Fang et al. (Beijing: Zhonghua shuju, 1960), 2:397.1835, where the title of the book is given as *Meng shu* 夢書, which should be a short form for the *Jiemeng shu* listed in the bibliography (1:11).
31. "Qiwu lun" 齊物論, in *Zhuangzi jishi* 莊子集釋, ed. Guo Qinfan 郭慶藩 (Beijing: Zhonghua shuju, 1961), 1:104–5; translation taken from *Chuang-tzu: The Seven Inner Chapters and Other Writings from the Book*, trans. A. C. Graham (London: George Allen and Unwin, 1981), 59–60.
32. "Qiwu lun," 105.
33. In *Zhuangzi*, the term *feng hua* (transformations by the winds) is used to describe sexless reproduction of species ("Tianyun" 天運, *Zhuangzi jishi*, 2:532).
34. "Qiwu lun," 112.
35. For a penetrating analysis, see Qiancheng Li, *Fictions of Enlightenment: Journey to the West, Tower of Myriad Mirrors, and Dream of the Red Chamber* (Honolulu: University of Hawaii Press, 2004), 35–43. Also see Jacqueline I. Stone, "'Not Mere Written Words': Perspectives on the Language of the Lotus Sūtra in Medieval Japan," in *Discourse and Ideology in Medieval Japanese Buddhism*, ed. Richard K. Payne and Taigen Dan Leighton (New York: Routledge, 2006), 165–66.
36. Victor Mair, *T'ang Transformation Texts: A Study of the Buddhist Contribution to the Rise of Vernacular Fiction and Drama in China* (Cambridge, MA: Council on East Asian Studies, Harvard University, 1989), 45, 48–49. For the cluster of etymologically related words in Tibetan for transformation, magic, illusion, and dream, see *T'ang Transformation Texts*, 69–70.
37. See Eugene Y. Wang, "Oneiric Horizons and Dissolving Bodies: Buddhist Cave Shrine as Mirror Hall," *Art History* 27, no. 4 (September 2004): 494–521.
38. Eugene Y. Wang, *Shaping the Lotus Sutra: Buddhist Visual Culture in Medieval China* (Seattle: University of Washington Press, 2005), 238–316.
39. Wang, *Shaping the Lotus Sutra*, 296, 310.

40. Liao Zhaoheng 廖肇亨, *Zhongbian, shichan, mengxi: Mingmo Qingchu Fojiao wenhua lunshu de chengxian yu kaizhan* 中邊・詩禪・夢戲：明末清初佛教文化論述的呈現與開展 (Taipei: Yuncheng wenhua, 2008), 435–66.
41. Zibo Zhenke, "Fayu" 法語, in *Zibo dashi quanji* 紫柏大師全集 (Shanghai: Shanghai guji chubanshe, 2013), 153.
42. Zheng Peikai 鄭培凱, *Tang Xianzu yu wan Ming wenhua* 湯顯祖與晚明文化 (Taipei: Yuncheng wenhua shiye gufen youxian gongsi, 1995), 357–444.
43. Tang Xianzu, *Nanke meng ji*, ed. Qian Nanyang 錢南揚 (Beijing: Renmin wenxue chubanshe, 1981), 166-72; *Handan meng ji*, ed. Li Xiao 李曉 and Kin Bunkyō 金文京 (Shanghai: Shanghai guji chubanshe, 2004), 228. Also see Hua Wei 華瑋, "Shijian zhiyou qing nan su: shilun Tang Xianzu de qing guan yu ta juzuo de guanxi" 世間只有情難訴：試論湯顯祖的情觀與他劇作的關係, *Dalu zazhi* 大陸雜誌 86, no. 6 (June 1993): 32–40.
44. For the discussion of this drama genre, see David Hawkes, "Quanzhen Plays and Quanzhen Masters," *Bulletin de l'Ecole française d'Extrême-Orient* 69 (1981): 153–70; Wilt L. Idema, *The Dramatic Oeuvre of Chu Yu-tun (1379–1439)* (Leiden: E. J. Brill, 1985), 63–93; Li Hui-mien 李惠綿, "Lunxi Yuandai Fojiao dutuo ju: yi Fojiao du yu jietuo gainian weiquanshi guandian" 論析元代佛教度脫劇—以佛教「度」與「解脫」概念為詮釋觀點, *Foxue yanjiu zhongxin xuebao* 佛學研究中心學報 6 (2001): 271–316; Li, *Fictions of Enlightenment*, 43–46.
45. Ma Zhiyuan 馬致遠, *Ma Danyang san du Ren Fengzi* 馬丹陽三度任風子, in *Quan Yuan xiqu* 全元戲曲, ed. Wang Jisi 王季思 (Beijing: Renmin wenxue chubanshe, 1999), 2:43; Li Shouqing 李壽卿, *Yueming heshang du Liucui* 月明和尚度柳翠, in *Quan Yuan xiqu*, 2:451; Anonymous, *Han Zhongli dutuo Lan Caihe* 漢鍾離度脫藍采和, in *Quan Yuan xiqu*, 7:120, 122. Sometimes the device is called *xiao jingtou* 小境頭 (small realm), which is occasionally just a marvelous magic show, not necessarily a nightmare. See "Que Li Yue shijiu wan jiangting" 瘸李岳詩酒玩江亭, in *Quan Yuan xiqu*, 7:11.
46. Inoue Taizan 井上泰山, "Shinsen dōkegeki ni okeru Kasenko no kage" 神仙道化劇における何仙姑の影, in *Chūgoku kinsei gikyoku shōsetsu ronshū* 中國近世戲曲小說論集 (Osaka: Kansai Daigaku Chobanbu, 2004), 183–84.
47. *Huijiao xiangzhu Guan Hanqing ji* 彙校詳注關漢卿集, ed. Lan Liming 藍立蓂 (Beijing: Zhonghua shuju, 2006), 1:273; translation taken from *Monks, Bandits, Lovers, and Immortals: Eleven Early Chinese Plays*, trans. Stephen H. West and Wilt L. Idema (Indianapolis: Hackett, 2010), 70. Also see Li Hui-mien, *Xiqu xin shiye* 戲曲新視野 (Taipei: Guojia chubanshe, 2008), 89–138.
48. Wang Shifu. *Xixiang ji*, ed. Wang Jisi (Shanghai: Shanghai guji chubanshe, 1978), 7, 9; translation modified from Wang Shifu, *The Moon and the Zither: The Story of the Western Wing*, trans. Stephen H. West and Wilt L. Idema (Berkeley: University of California Press, 1995), 177, 181.

49. Liang Huang 梁煌, "Yong mu laoren shi" 詠木老人詩. The poem is also attributed to the Tang emperor Xuanzong 玄宗 under the title "Kuilei yin" 傀儡吟. See *Quan Tang shi* 全唐詩, comp. Peng Dingqiu 彭定求 et al. (Beijing: Zhonghua shuju, 1960), 3:2116, 1:42.

50. Wang Anshi 王安石, "Xiangguosi qi Tongtianjie daochang Xingxiangyuan guan xizhe" 相國寺啟同天節道場行香院觀戲者, in *Linchuan xiansheng wenji* 臨川先生文集 (Beijing: Zhonghua shuju, 1959), 156; Hong Mai 洪邁, *Rongzhai suibi* 容齋隨筆 (Shanghai: Shanghai guji chubanshe, 1978), 1:179.

51. For the details of Buddhist circumambulation taught by the Tiantai 天台 master Zhiyi 智顗 (538–97) and its affinity to the "Pacing the Void" (*Ta kong* 踏空, which involved *Yu bu*) in the early fifth-century Lingbao School of Daoism, see Wang, *Shaping the Lotus Sutra*, 381–83.

52. See Jo Riley, *Chinese Theatre and the Actor in Performance* (Cambridge: Cambridge University Press, 1997), 105–10. A Shanxi ritual manual, *Shangu shenpu* 扇鼓神譜, unearthed in 1909 has helped to reconstruct one variation of this kind of choreography dating back to late Yuan and early Ming times, *zou bagua* 走八卦. See Arisawa Akiko 有澤晶子, *Chūgoku dentō engeki yōshiki no kenkyū* 中国伝統演劇樣式の研究 (Tokyo: Kenbun Shuppan, 2006), 296–300.

53. See chapter 3, sections 5 and 6.

54. Stephen H. West, "An Interpretation of a Dream: The Sources, Evaluation, and Influence of the *Dongjing meng Hua lu*," *T'oung Pao* 71 (1985): 63–108. Certain parts of a modern city, like a subway station as a space of transit, still offer a comparable experience of ephemerality. For an interesting case of Lionel Groulx Station in Montreal, Canada, that is taken by performers as a "ephemeral stage," see Amanda Boetzkes, "The Ephemeral Stage at Lionel Groulx Station," in *Circulation and the City: Essays on Urban Culture*, ed. Alexandra Boutros and Will Straw (Montreal & Kingston: McGill-Queen's University Press, 2010), 138–54.

55. Tanaka Issei, *Chūgoku engekishi* 中國演劇史 (Tokyo: Tokyo Daigaku Shuppankai, 1998), 36–40.

56. Mark Elvin, "Chinese Cities since the Sung Dynasty," in *Towns in Societies: Essays in Economic History and Historical Sociology*, ed. Philip Abrams and E. A. Wrigley (Cambridge: Cambridge University Press, 1978), 79–80.

57. Feng Menglong, *Mohanzhai chongding San huiqin fengliu meng chuanqi* 墨憨齋重訂三會親風流夢 傳奇, in *Feng Menglong quanji*, 12:1049.

58. Feng, *Mohanzhai chongding San huiqin fengliu meng chuanqi*, 1054. Also see the remarkable discussion in Catherine Swatek, *Peony Pavilion Onstage: Four Centuries in the Career of a Chinese Drama* (Ann Arbor: Center for Chinese Studies at the University of Michigan, 2002), 56.

59. The woman dreamed by Mengmei promises him the prospect of marriage and high office (3), neither of which ever come up in Liniang's dream. Conversely, in Liniang's dream, she makes love with a young scholar at a peony pavilion (51–53), but the consummation and its singular locale are completely left out of Mengmei's account, in which "underneath a plum tree is standing a beauty of medium build, as if to receive me or to see me off" (3). The plum tree that is so prominently featured in Mengmei's dream does not appear in Liniang's oneiric vision either; she sees the tree only on her second visit to the garden and thereupon decides to be buried underneath it.

60. Though the play never makes this explicit, one can infer that Liniang has been delivered in a similar fashion into Mengmei's dream, which was reported earlier in the play. In this sense, even if they have two different dreams on two separate occasions, they share them by entering each other's dreams.

61. *Qingshi*, 9.312.

62. The *hun/po* distinction originated in antiquity. See Yu Ying-shih, "'Oh Soul, Come Back!': A Study in the Changing Conceptions of the Soul and Afterlife in Pre-Buddhist China," *Harvard Journal of Asiatic Studies* 47, no. 2 (December 1987): 363–95. But Feng Menglong introduced the spectatorial position vis-à-vis one's own soul into the ancient vocabulary..

63. Xie Zhaozhe, *Wu zazu* 五雜組, 1616 ed., *juan* 15, reprint, in *Xuxiu Siku congshu* 續修四庫全書, vol. 1130 (Shanghai: Shanghai guji chubanshe, 1995), 657.

64. The idiom originates in Shi Huihong 釋惠洪 (1071–1128), *Riben Wushan ban Lengzhai yehua* 日本五山版冷齋夜話, in *Xijian ben Songren shihua sizhong* 稀見本宋人詩話四種, ed. Zhang Bowei 張伯偉 (Nanjing: Jiangsu guji chubanshe, 2002), 83.

65. Pan, *Pan Zhiheng quhua*, 73.

66. In Hu Wenhuan 胡文煥, comp. *Baijia cuibian* 稗家粹編 (Beijing: Zhonghua shuju, 2010), 109–114. Also see Xiang Zhizhu 向志柱, "*Mudan ting* lanben wenti kaobian" 牡丹亭藍本問題考辨, *Wenyi yanjiu* 文藝研究 3 (2007): 72–78.

67. "Pursuing the Dream" was as frequently anthologized in Ming-Qing times as "Interrupted Dream." See Yang Zhenliang 楊振良, *Mudan ting yanjiu* 牡丹亭研究 (Taipei: Taiwan xuesheng shuju, 1992), 205. Numerous actresses and female impersonators famous for performing "Pursuing the Dream" before the twentieth century are also well documented. See Li Dou 李斗 (fl. 1764–1795), *Yangzhou huafang lu* 揚州畫舫錄 (Jinan: Shandong youyi chubanshe, 2001), 5.151, 9.239; Zhuquan jushi 珠泉居士, *Xu Banqiao zaji* 續板橋雜記, *juan* 2, in *Xiangyan congshu* 香艷叢書, ed. Wang Wenru 王文濡 (Beijing: Zhongguo shudian, 1991), 9:315; and Jiao Xun 焦循 (1763–1820), *Jushuo* 劇說, in *Zhongguo gudian xiqu lunzhu jicheng* 中國古典戲曲論著集成, ed. Zhongguo xiqu yanjiu yuan 中國戲曲研究院 (Beijing: Zhongguo xiqu chubanshe, 1959), 8:6.197.

68. Translation taken from Tang Xianzu, *The Peony Pavilion*, trans. Cyril Birch, rev. ed. (Bloomington: Indiana University Press, 2002), 60, with modifications to follow as closely as possible the spatial sense of the original text.
69. The sequence of "The Interrupted Dream" and "Pursuing the Dream" is foreshadowed by Su Shi's 蘇軾 song lyric written in 1078: "Three strikes of the midnight drum,/A resounding fallen leaf,/Interrupted the gloomy dream clouds./In the dim of the night,/With nowhere to pursue,/I woke to realize I'd trod the whole garden." See "Yongyule" 永遇樂, in *Su Shi ci biannian jiaozhu* 蘇軾詞編年校注, ed. Zou Tongqing 鄒同慶 (Beijing: Zhonghua shuju, 2002), 1:247.
70. Other translations similarly shift attention to the dream's *inside*: "I still fail to recapture things in dreams" or "I cannot revive the scene in my dream." See Tang Xianzu, *The Peony Pavilion*, trans. Zhang Guangqian (Beijing: Foreign Languages Press, 2001), 88; *Dream in Peony Pavilion*, trans. Xu Yuanchong and Frank M. Xu (Beijing: China International Press, 2012), 67. So does the translation found in Tian Yuan Tan and Paolo Santangelo, *Passion, Romance, and Qing: The World of Emotions and States of Mind in Peony Pavilion* (Leiden: Brill, 2014): "Yet suddenly one can't grasp the soul that once appeared in my dream" (1:514). Here Tan and Santangelo take the "soul" (*hun*) as the object of the verb "grasp," while another translator sees the "dream" (*meng* 夢) as the object and loosely renders the verse as "I fail to see the dreamland sight"; see Tang Xianzu, *The Peony Pavilion*, trans. Wang Rongpei (Shanghai: Shanghai waiyu jiaoyu chubanshe, 2000), 1:165. But "the front of the soul's dream" (*hunmeng qian* 魂夢前) as a whole is a location, not the direct target of Liniang's action. Despite our differences, I side with Birch, Xu, and Zhang in seeing that the object of the line—namely, things that Liniang finds it hard to retrieve—is implicit only.
71. To those who would try to explain away Tang Xianzu's curious word choice (*qian*) by citing the rhyme scheme of the tune, let me just mention Marcel Proust's "good poets whom the tyranny of rhyme forces into the discovery of their finest lines." *In Search of Lost Time*, trans. C. K. Scott Moncrieff, Terrence Kilmartin, and D. J. Enright (New York: The Modern Library, 1992–1993), 1:31.
72. Throughout the scene, making up an ideal image in the self-portrait and doing makeup are deliberately mixed up, based on the ambiguity of the same act of "painting" (*hua* 畫). See also Carlos Rojas, *The Naked Gaze: Reflections on Chinese Modernity* (Cambridge, MA: Harvard University Asia Center, 2008), 36–38. To Rojas, the premodern periods were under the scopic regime of specularity, which features "the closed circuit of specular reflection between the viewer and her own image," whereas the modern regime of spectatorship

heralded by the era of photography presupposes "the insertion of an external gaze." Yet he acknowledges that "the ideal of specularity as representing a direct and unmediated perception of the self is arguably one that never existed except as a retrospective projection of a post-photographic age," and even in *The Peony Pavilion,* Liniang's "specular self-regard is already, from the very beginning, overlaid with the sort of external perspective subsequently embodied by Liu Mengmei," which means "she must first position herself in the space of an imaginary spectator with respect to her own image" (4–5, 26, 36). This shows, I would argue, that the actual "transition" between scopic regimes took place with the emergence of theatricality in the late sixteenth century.

73. See Weihong Bao, *Fiery Cinema: The Emergence of an Affective Medium in China, 1915–1945* (Minneapolis: University of Minnesota Press, 2015), 10–13.

74. Tina Lu, *Persons, Roles, and Minds: Identity in Peony Pavilion and Peach Blossom Fan* (Stanford: Stanford University Press, 2001), 34–35, 38–39, 67.

75. Ellen Widmer, "Xiaoqing's Literary Legacy and the Place of the Woman Writer," *Late Imperial China* 13, no. 1 (June 1992): 111–55.

76. *Wu Wushan sanfu heping xinjuan xiuxiang Yumingtang Mudan ting* 吳吳山三婦合評新鐫繡像玉茗堂牡丹亭, in, *Budeng daya wenku zhenben xiqu congkan* 不登大雅文庫珍本戲曲叢刊, ed. Beijing daxue tushuguan 北京大學圖書館 (Beijing: Xueyuan chubanshe, 2003), 6:23. Also see Judith T. Zeitlin, "Shared Dreams: The Story of the *Three Wives Commentary on The Peony Pavilion,*" *Harvard Journal of Asiatic Studies* 54 (1994): 127–79.

77. Zang Maoxun 臧懋循 is citing Tang Xianzu's friend Shuai Ji 帥機 (1537–1595), who was actually commenting on another of Tang's plays, *The Purple-Jade Flute.* See Xu Fuming 徐扶明, *Mudan ting yanjiu ziliao kaoshi* 牡丹亭研究資料考釋 (Shanghai: Shanghai guji chubanshe, 1987), 114.

78. Cai Mengzhen 蔡孟珍, *Chongdu jingdian Mudan ting* 重讀經典牡丹亭 (Taipei: Taiwan Shangwu yinshuguan, 2015), 1–134.

79. Li Yu, *Xianqing ouji* 閒情偶記, ed. Jiang Jurong 江巨榮 and Lu Shourong 盧壽榮 (Shanghai: Shanghai guji chubanshe, 2000), 34.

80. See Yu Weimin 俞為民, *Ming Qing chuanqi kaolun* 明清傳奇考論 (Taipei: Huazhen shuju, 1993), 138–43.

81. See Swatek, *Peony Pavilion Onstage,* 150–52; Ling Hon Lam, "The Matriarch's Private Ear: Performance, Reading, Censorship and the Fabrication of Interiority in *The Story of the Stone.*" *Harvard Journal of Asiatic Studies* 65, no. 2 (December 2005): 387n. 79.

82. Mao Xianshu, "Yu Li Liweng lunge shu" 與李笠翁論歌書, in *Yunbai* 韻白, the Kangxi (1662–1722) edition, 20b; reprint, *Siku quanshu cunmu congshu* 四庫全書存目叢書 (Jinan: Qilu shushe, 1997), *Jing* 經, 217:454.

1. Winds, Dreams, Theater: A Genealogy of Emotion-Realms

83. Zhang Dafu, *Meihua caotang bitan* 梅花草堂筆談, microfilm of the Qing reprint in the Library of Congress, *juan* 6, "Ge" 歌, 26b–27a.
84. In a letter to Zhang Dafu written in 1616, Tang Xianzu likens him to the blind historian Zuoqiu Ming 左丘明 and praises Zhang for the *brightness* of his aural sense (*tingyong cheming* 聽詠徹明), thus transposing the capacity of sight onto Zhang's ears. See "Yu Zhang Dafu" 與張大復, in *Tang Xianzu quanji*, 2:1520. Zhang is very specific about the time when he lost his sight: on the sixth day of the fifth month in the *guisi* 癸巳 year (June 4, 1593), as soon as he sat down to take a civil exam in Kunshan, he suddenly went blind. See *Meihua caotang bitan*, *juan* 5, "Bingmu" 病目, 16b–17b.
85. See "Ti *Ershou lu*" 題耳受錄, in *Meihua caotang ji* 梅花草堂集, the Chongzhen edition, reprint, *Xuxiu Siku quanshu*, 1380:557.
86. Paize Keulemans discusses how late imperial readers silently read novels but still experienced the "imaginary" sound, which can "project a sense of communality," "to the point where the distinction [between orality and textuality] disappears . . . and the reader is allowed to enjoy them both," see Paize Keulemans, *Sound Rising from the Paper: Nineteenth-Century Martial Arts Fiction and the Chinese Acoustic Imagination* (Cambridge, MA: Harvard East Asia Center, 2014), 9, 268–69. Supplementing these acute observations, my blind spectator who listens as if he were reading goes in a somewhat different direction: under the sway of intermediation, the nature of the sound has to be historicized and is not necessarily communal. As will be argued in chapter 2, rumor, hearsay, and a whole array of oral performances that are featured in a seventeenth-century novel function to interrupt sympathetic identification with others and even with oneself—a primary symptom of theatricality.
87. Min Guangyu, "*Handan meng ji* xiaoyin" 邯鄲夢記小引, in Tang Xianzu, *Handan meng ji*, 1621 ed., reprinted. *Guben xiqu congkan* 古本戲曲叢刊, ser. 1 (Shanghai: Shangwu yinshuguan, 1954), 1a–2b.
88. Min Guangyu, "Fanli" 凡例, in *Handan meng ji*, 1a–1b.
89. In other words, technological determinism is inadequate to explain theatricality; after all, print—if not its inextricable interaction with theater—came into play in China way earlier than the sixteenth century. See Lucille Chia and Hilde De Weerdt, ed., *Knowledge and Text Production in an Age of Print: China 900–1400* (Leiden: Brill, 2011).
90. "The affections are stirred within and take on form in words. If words alone are inadequate, we speak them out in sighs. If sighing is inadequate, we sing them. If singing them is inadequate, unconsciously our hands dance them and our feet tap them." See Owen, "The 'Great Preface,' " in *Readings in Chinese Literary Thought*, 41.

91. For a critical discussion of intermediation of Chinese opera in a modern context, see Weihong Bao, "The Politics of Remediation: Mise-en-scène and the Subjunctive Body in Chinese Opera Film," *Opera Quarterly* 6, no. 2 (Fall 2010): 256–90. This attempt to historicize the questions of media and intermediation through the historicization of theatricality should be differentiated from the discussion of theater and intermediality, which paradoxically recenters theater as essentially a "hypermedium" single-handedly constituting "the stage of intermediality." See Chiel Kattenbelt, "Theatre as the Art of the Performer and the Stage of Intermediality," in *Intermediality in Theatre and Performance*, ed. Freda Chapple and Chiel Kattenbelt (New York: Rodopi, 2006), 29–39.
92. "Given the fundamental structural characteristics of the vast range of aesthetically dominated theater forms, 'theatricality' should be taken, and consequently used, as a concept that relates to virtually any type of socially communicative, constructed ('dramatized') movements and attitude of one or more bodies and/or their audio-visual 'replicants—or their representations, such as masks or technologically objectified images. They have the potential to become semantically charged practices—symbolic actions—and in most cases they do actualize this potential." See Joachim Fiebach, "Theatricality: From Oral Tradition to Televised 'Realities,'" *SubStance*, 31, no. 2–3 (November 2002): 19–20.
93. David Marshall, *The Figure of Theatricality: Shaftesbury, Defoe, and Adam Smith and George Eliot* (New York: Columbia University Press, 1986); Adela Pinch, *Strange Fits of Passion: Epistemologies of Emotion: Hume to Austen* (Stanford: Stanford University Press, 1996); Judith Pascoe, *Romantic Theatricality: Gender, Poetry, and Spectatorship* (Ithaca: Cornell University Press, 1997).
94. William Egginton, *How the World Became a Stage: Presence, Theatricality, and the Question of Modernity* (Albany: State University of New York Press, 2003), 75; "Affective Disorder," *diacritics* 40, no. 3 (Winter 2012–2013): 36.
95. René Descartes, "Preliminaries," in *The Philosophical Writings of Descartes*, trans. John Cottingham, Robert Stoothoff, and Dugald Murdoch (Cambridge: Cambridge University Press, 1985), 1:2.
96. Andrien Bailler, *La Vie de M. Des-Cartes* (Genève: Slatkine Reprint, 2010), 1:80–86.
97. Jean-Luc Marion, "Does Thought Dream? The Three Dreams, or, the Awakening of a Philosopher," in *Cartesian Questions: Method and Metaphysics* (Chicago: University of Chicago Press, 1999), 6–9.
98. As an exception, Hajime Nakatani warns us against misapplying the notion of theatricality to the medieval Chinese phenomena of the gaze. See "The Empire of Fame: Writing and the Voice in Early Medieval China," *positions* 14, no. 3 (Winter 2006): 538–39.

99. Haiping Yan, "Theatricality in Classical Chinese Drama," in *Theatricality*, 67.
100. See chapter 3, section 5.
101. Richard von Glahn, "Myth and Reality of China's Seventeenth-Century Monetary Crisis," *Journal of Economic History* 56, no. 2 (1996): 429–54. Also see Ning Ma, *The Age of Silver: The Rise of the Novel East and West* (Oxford: Oxford University Press, 2017). For the global trafficking of theatricality not just between Europe and China but between China and Japan, see chapter 4.
102. See chapter 5, section 3.
103. Timothy Brook, *The Confusions of Pleasure: Commerce and Culture in Ming China* (Berkeley: University of California Press, 1998), 200–201.
104. Elvin, "Chinese Cities since the Sung Dynasty," 86; William T. Rowe, "Approaches to Modern Chinese Social History," in *Reliving the Past: The Worlds of Social History*, ed. Olivier Zunz (Chapel Hill: University of North Carolina Press, 1985), 272–73. The experience of alienation aggravated by interregional commercial networking is captured by the 1612 classical tale "The Pearl Shirt" ("Zhu shan" 珠衫) by Song Maocheng 宋懋澄 (1569–ca. 1620), whose modified version is included in Feng Menglong's *History of Emotion* and vernacularized by Feng into "Jiang Xingge's Reunion with the Pearl Shirt" ("Jiang Xingge chonghui zhenzhu shan" 蔣興哥重會珍珠衫) as the very first story in his 1620 collection *Gujin xiaoshuo* 古今小說. Both the classical tale and its vernacular adaptation give an account of two itinerant merchants who virtually exchange their wives as result of transgression and coincidence. They map out what Tina Lu has called "the geography of exchange" in which goods, people, and even karma are circulated across a wide span of the country. See Lu, *Accidental Incest, Filial Cannibalism and Other Peculiar Encounters in Late Imperial Chinese Literature* (Cambridge, MA: Harvard University Asia Center, 2008), 22–54.
105. In the famous "madeleines" moment, Proust's character tries to "clear an empty space in front of [the mind]" for recollection. This moment, so close to Liniang's putting things in front of the dream, then lapses into the interior: "I *place in position before* my mind's eye the still recent taste of that first mouthful, and I feel something start *within* me." *In Search of Lost Time*, 1:62, italics mine.
106. It is this keen attention to the construction of the interior through the intermedial encounter between print and theater that makes the eighteenth-century *Story of the Stone* a work in the era of theatricality, even though it still pays tribute to the overarching frame of the dreamscape through which the protagonist Jia Baoyu 賈寶玉 is supposed to be enlightened. See Ling Hon Lam, "The Matriarch's Private Ear."

2. THE HEART BESIDE ITSELF: A GENEALOGY OF MORALS

1. "Pan geting houjiefu fangpai" 判革停猴節婦坊牌, in An Yushi 安遇時, comp., *Bao Longtu pan baijia gong'an*, 1594 edition; reprint, *Guben xiaoshuo jicheng* 古本小說集成 (Shanghai: Shanghai guji chubanshe, 1990), ser. 2, 13:26–32. For the court-crime story collection as a peculiar print phenomenon pertaining to the turn of the seventeenth century, see Robert E. Hegel, *Reading Illustrated Fiction in Late Imperial China* (Stanford: Stanford University Press, 1998), 32–33.
2. Tao Fu 陶輔, "Jieyi zhuan," in Tao Fu and Zhou Shaolian 周紹濂, *Huaying ji, Yuanzhu zhiyu xuechuang tanyi* 花影集．鴛渚誌餘雪窗談異 (Beijing: Zhonghua shuju, 2006), 41–45. Tao claims that he draws on an incident dating from 1428.
3. Patrick Hanan, "*Judge Bao's Hundred Cases* Reconstructed," *Harvard Journal of Asiatic Studies* 40, no. 2 (December 1980): 322–23; Cheng Yizhong 程毅中, "*Bao Longtu pan Baijia gong'an* yu Mingdai gong'an xiaoshuo" 包龍圖判百家公案與明代公案小說, *Wenxue yichan* 文學遺產 1 (2001): 85–86.
4. Tang Xianzu, "Yihuang xian xishen Qingyuanshi miao ji," 2:1188.
5. That is why lesbianism was never an issue in late imperial law. See Matthew H. Sommer, *Sex, Law, and Society in Late Imperial China* (Stanford: Stanford University Press, 2000), 162–63. But Sommer does not mention bestiality. Even with penetration, bestiality seems to be a gray area in the late imperial Chinese legal imagination.
6. The Judge Bao story is also bizarre in the way the official suddenly intervenes. According to Sommer, in late imperial China, "the accuser is an immediate in-law, a stepson, or an adopted heir"; these were the only people who were "qualified to act and also stood to gain from an unchaste widow's exposure." See *Sex, Law, and Society in Late Imperial China*, 195.
7. James St. André argues that *A Hundred Cases* is distinguished from thirteenth-century court-crime stories by its great concern about sexual impropriety. See "Reading Court Cases from the Song and the Ming: Fact and Fiction, Law and Literature," in *Writing and Law in Late Imperial China*, ed. Robert E. Hegel and Katherine Carlitz (Seattle: University of Washington Press, 2007), 193–96.
8. See Ban Gu, *Han shu*, "Gai Kuanrao zhuan," 蓋寬饒傳, 7:3245; Ye Mengde 葉夢德, *Bishu luhua* 避暑錄話, in *Song Yuan biji xiaoshuo daguan* 宋元筆記小說大觀 (Shanghai: Shanghai guji chubanshe, 2001), 3:2648–49. Ren Bantang 任半塘 argues that monkey performance in the Tang already contained dramatic elements and should be regarded as more advanced than puppet theater. See his *Tang Xinong* 唐戲弄 (Beijing: Zuojia chubanshe, 1954), 1:465–79.

9. Shen Defu 沈德符 (1578–1642), *Wanli yehuo bian* 萬曆野獲編 (Beijing: Wenhua yishu chubanshe, 1998), 2:64.670.
10. Zhu Quan, *Taihe zhengyin pu jianping* 太和正音譜箋評, ed. Yao Pinwen 姚品文 (Beijing: Zhonghua shuju, 2010), 90–91.
11. Zhou Qi, *Mingyi kao* 名義考 (originally with 1583 and 1584 prefaces), in *Siku quanshu zhenben* 四庫全書珍本, ser. 5 (Taipei: Shangwu yinshuguan, 1974), 233:5.23b.
12. Chu Renhuo 褚人穫, *Jianhu ji* 堅瓠集, the Kangxi (1662–1722) edition, reprint, *Xuxiu Siku quanshu*, 1261:169; Li Tiaoyuan 李調元, *Yucun quhua* 雨村曲話, in *Zhongguo gudian xiqu lunzhu jicheng*, 8:40; Jiao Xun, *Jushuo*, 8:81–83, 91–92.
13. See Zhou Yude 周育德, "Yihuang xishen bianzong" 宜黃戲神辨踪, in *Tang Xianzu lungao* 湯顯祖論稿 (Beijing: Wenhua yishu chubanshe, 1991), 282–86. Lige Yuweng 笠閣漁翁 (Wu Zhensheng 吳震生, 1695–1769) has highlighted the connection between *The Journey to the West* and *The Peony Pavilion* on the general theme of eroticism. See "Pi *Caizi Mudan ting* xu" 批才子牡丹亭序, in Wu Zhensheng and Cheng Qiong 程瓊, comp., *Caizi Mudan ting*, ed. Hua Wei 華瑋 and Wang Juyuan 汪巨源 (Taipei: Taiwan Xuesheng Shuju, 2003), vii. But perhaps the deeper association between the two lies in the restructuration of theatrical performance in the late sixteenth century.
14. Zhuang Yifu 莊一拂, *Gudian xiqu cunmu huikao* 古典戲曲存目匯考 (Shanghai: Shanghai guji chubanshe, 1982), 1:167, 192–93.
15. *Shuihu xiqu ji* 水滸戲曲集, ed. Fu Xihua 傅惜華 (Shanghai: Shanghai guji chubanshe, 1985), 1:1–15.
16. The novel in 100 *juan* was first registered in the 1540 bibliography *Baichuan shuzhi* 百川書志 by Gao Ru 高儒. See *Shuihu zhuan ziliao huibian* 水滸傳資料匯編, ed. Zhu Yixuan 朱一玄 and Liu Yuchen 劉毓忱 (Tianjin: Nankai daxue chubanshe, 2002), 131.
17. Mei Chun, *The Novels and Theatrical Imagination in Early Modern China* (Leiden: Brill, 2011), 3–4.
18. On record, at least thirty-four "Water Margin" *zaju* plays were produced during the Yuan and early Ming times, and ten of them have survived. For their influence on the content of the novel, see Wang Ping 王平, "'Shuihu xi' yu *Shuihu zhuan* de chuanbo" '水滸戲'與《水滸傳》的傳播, *Dongyue luncong* 東岳論叢 26, no. 6 (November 2005): 113–18. In contrast, we know only seventeen "Journey to the West" play titles up to the early or mid-Ming (five still extant), and they inform the novel version to a much lesser and limited extent. See Wang Ping, "'Xiyou xi' yu *Xiyou ji* de chuanbo" '西遊戲'與《西遊記》的傳播, *Ming Qing xiaoshuo yanjiu* 明清小說研究 80 (2006): 73–84. Wang's article identifies sixteen "Journey to the West" play titles but leaves out the play mentioned below in n. 81.

19. See George A. Hayden, *Crime and Punishment in Medieval Chinese Drama: Three Judge Pao Plays* (Cambridge, MA: Harvard University Press, 1978); Fan Jiacheng 范嘉誠, *Yuan zaju Bao gong xi pingzhu* 元雜劇包公戲評注 (Jinan: Qilu shushe, 2006).
20. "Hundred kinds of animals all dancing" (*baishou shuai wu* 百獸率舞) to the sage king's music is a motif of antiquity traceable back to "Yao dian" 堯典 and "Gaotao mo" 皋陶謨, in Qu Wanli 屈萬里, *Shangshu jinzhu jinyi* 尚書今註今譯 (Taipei: Taiwan Shangwu yinshuguan, 2009), 22, 36–37.
21. In addition to the notable example of the metamorphosis between Zhuangzi and the butterfly, one can refer to the striking Tang-dynasty tale in which a man of letters is mesmerized and transformed into a tiger savoring human flesh. See "Nanyang shiren" 南陽士人, in *Taiping guangji*, 9:432.35041–506.
22. Xunzi, "Zhengming" 正名, in Wang Xianqian 王先謙, comp., *Xunzi jijie* 荀子集解 (Beijing: Zhonghua shuju, 1988), 2:412, emphasis added; "Liyun" 禮運, in *Li ji*, in *Sibu beiyao* 四部備要 (Shanghai: Zhonghua shuju, 1934), *juan* 9, p. 8a; "Xing zi ming chu" 性自命出, in *Guodian chumu zhujian* 郭店楚墓竹簡, ed. Jingmenshi bowuguan 荊門市博物館 (Beijing: Wenwu chubanshe, 1998), 179.
23. A. C. Graham, *Studies in Chinese Philosophy and Philosophical Literature* (Singapore: Institute of East Asian Philosophies, 1986), 59–65.
24. Anthony C. Yu, *Rereading the Stone: Desire and the Making of Fiction in Dream of the Red Chamber* (Princeton: Princeton University Press, 1997), 55–66.
25. Chad Hansen, "*Qing* 情 in Pre-Buddhist Chinese Thought," in *Emotions in Asian Thought: A Dialogue in Comparative Philosophy*, ed. Joel Marks and Roger T. Ames (Albany: State University of New York Press, 1995), 181–203.
26. Without any explanations, Hansen shifts back and forth between "*qing* [reality input]" and "*qing* [reality response]" and leaves the following paradoxical remark: "情 *qing* [reality response] is *input from* reality" (196, italics original). Michael Puett contends, against Hansen's presupposition of "a single, unified meaning" for *qing*, that the character has a broad semantic range in early philosophical debates. See "The Ethics of Responding Properly: The Notion of *Qing* 情 in Early Chinese Thought," in *Love and Emotions in Traditional Chinese Literature*, ed. Halvor Eifring (Leiden: Brill, 2004), 37–68. I would say that semantic heterogeneity underlies Hansen's reading of *qing* itself as covering both reality and feeling, input and feedback.
27. "Qing wei he 'wu'" 情為何"物", in *Wan Ming yu wan Qing: Lishi chuancheng yu wenhua chuangxin* 晚明與晚清：歷史傳承與文化創新, ed. Chen Pingyuan 陳平原, Wang Der-wai 王德威, and Shang Wei 商偉 (Wuhan: Hubei jiaoyu chubanshe, 2002), 526–27.
28. See "Emotion, Knowledge, and the Reconfigured Self in the Tang-Song Transformation," in *Love, Hatred, and Other Passions: Question and Themes on Emotions in Chinese Civilization* (Leiden: Brill, 2006), 167–69.

29. Paolo Santangelo, "A Research on Emotions and States of Mind in Late Imperial China: Preliminary Results," *Ming Qing Yanjiu* 7 (1995): 101.
30. "Zhi beiyou" 知北遊, in *Zhuangzi jishi*, 3:765.
31. He Shao 何劭, "Wang Bi zhuan" 王弼傳, in Wang Bi, *Wang Bi ji jiaoshi* 王弼集校釋, ed. and annot. Lou Yulie 樓宇烈 (Beijing: Zhonghua shuju, 1980), 2:640. See the discussion in Zhang Dainian 張岱年, *Zhongguo zhexue dagang* 中國哲學大綱 (Beijing: Zhongguo shehui kexue chubanshe, 1982), 473.
32. See Ji Kang, "Shi si lun" 釋私論, in *Ji Kang ji jiaozhu* 嵇康集校注, comp. Dai Mingyang 戴明揚 (Beijing: Renmin wenxue chubanshe, 1962), 234.
33. Ji Kang, "Sheng wu aile lun" 聲無哀樂論, in *Ji Kang ji jiaozhu*, 196–225.
34. The connection between "Harmony," the distillation of emotion, and the goal of nourishing one's life through music performance can be seen in such other articles by Ji Kang as "Qin fu" 琴賦 and "Yangsheng lun" 養生論; see *Ji Kang jijiaozhu*, 2.106, 3.143–55.
35. See also Ulrike Middendorf, "Music Without Emotion: Xi Kang Meets Hanslick," in *Power, Beauty, and Meaning: Eight Studies in Chinese Music*, ed. Luciana Galliano (Florence, Leo S. Oischki Editore, 2005), 41–67.
36. Ronald Egan, "The Controversy over Music and 'Sadness' and Changing Conceptions of the *Qin* in Middle Period China," *Harvard Journal of Asiatic Studies* 57, no. 1 (June 1997): 46–52.
37. See Cheng Hao, "Da Hengqu Zhang Zihou xiansheng shu" 答橫渠張子厚先生書, in Cheng Hao and Cheng Yi 程頤, *Er Cheng ji* 二程集, ed. Wang Xiaoyu 王孝魚 (Beijing: Zhonghua shuju, 2004), 1:460. The epistle was written around 1059. Some scholars take it as consistent with the viewpoint of Wang Bi rather than realizing that what Cheng suggests here is diametrically opposite to Wang Bi's advice not to let emotion become "implicated with things." See Zhang Dainian, *Zhongguo zhexue dagang*, 474; Zhu Hanmin 朱漢民, *Xuanxue yu lixue de xueshu sixiang lilu yanjiu* 玄學與理學的學術思想理路研究 (Taipei: Taida chuban zhongxin, 2011), 81–82.
38. For a discussion of Zhu Xi's reading this notion of "heart" into Cheng Hao's letter, see Zhang Heng 張亨, " 'Dingxing shu' zai Zhongguo sixiang shi shang de yiyi" 〈定性書〉在中國思想史上的意義, *Taida Zhongwen xuebao* 台大中文學報 7 (April 1995): 19–20.
39. *Zhuzi yulei* 朱子語類, comp. Li Jingde 黎靖德 (Beijing: Zhonghua shuju, 1986), 1:5.92–93.
40. *Zhuzi yulei*, 4:62.1487–89.
41. Zhu Xi, *Sishu zhangju jizhu* 四書章句集注 (Beijing: Zhonghua shuju, 1983), 29. See also chapter 2, section 5. The significance of this classical exegesis back in the Han and Tang from which Zhu Xi deviates will be fully explored in chapter 5, section 4.

42. Wang Shouren 王守仁 (Wang Yangming), *Chuanxi lu* 傳習錄, pt. 2, "Da Lu Jingyuan shu" 答陸靜原書, in *Wang Yangming quanji* 王陽明全集, ed. Wu Guang 吳光 et. al. (Shanghai: Shanghai guji chubanshe, 1992), 1:64.
43. See Wang, *Chuanxi lu*, pt. 1, 7.
44. Li, *Zhuzi yulei*, 1:5.90, 94.
45. Zhu Xi, "Guanxin shuo" 觀心說, in *Zhuzi wenji* 朱子文集, ed. Chen Junmin 陳俊民 (Taipei: Institute of History and Philology, Academia Sinica, 2000), 7:3389–90.
46. Liu Zongzhou, "Yangming chuanxin lu" 陽明傳信錄, pt. 3, in *Liu Zongzhou quan ji* 劉宗周全集, ed. Dai Lianzhang 戴璉璋 and Wu Guang (Taipei: Zhongyang yanjiu yuan Zhongguo wenzhe yanjiushuo choubeichu, 1996), 4:66.
47. Liu Zongzhou, "Xueyan" 學言, pt. 2, in *Liu Zongzhou quan ji*, 2:489–90.
48. See also chapter 5, section 1.
49. See Liu Zhuo 劉汋, "Nianpu" 年譜, pt. 2, in *Liuzi quanshu* 劉子全書, ed. Dong Yang 董暘, 40b.25a. See the discussion in Cui Dahua 崔大華, "Liu Zongzhou yu Mingdai Lixue de jiben zouxiang" 劉宗周與明代理學的基本走向, in *Liu Jishan xueshu sixiang lunji* 劉蕺山學術思想論集, ed. Zhong Caijun 鍾彩鈞 (Taipei: Zhongyang yanjiuyuan Zhongguo wenzhe yanjiusuo choubeichu, 1998), 167–210.
50. According to Mou Zongsan 牟宗三, Zhu Xi's notion that "the heart integrates nature and emotion" severs the pre-Zhu unity between the heart and nature and makes it necessary for Ming thinkers after Wang Yangming to restore it. But even if one grants that the union between nature and the heart has a solid tradition going back to the mythical past and reacting powerfully to any interruption, the same cannot be said of emotion. To tackle this asymmetry, Mou has to coin a neologism, "originary emotion" (*benqing* 本情), which is not separate from the heart and nature. See *Xinti yu xingti* 心體與性體 (Taipei: Zhengzhong shuju, 1968), 3:233, 270. But even Cheng Hao, the guardian figure in Mou's narrative upholding the traditional unity between the heart and nature does not assign emotion to the heart but to things.
51. For a version of the celebration of Chinese nonduality, see François Jullien, "Did Philosophers Have to Become Fixed on Truth?" *Critical Inquiry* 28 (Summer 2002): 803–24. See the critique of Jullien in Bernard Faure, *The Rhetoric of Immediacy: A Cultural Critique of Chan/Zen Buddhism* (Princeton: Princeton University Press, 1991), 74–75; Haun Saussy, *Great Walls of Discourse and Other Adventures in Cultural China* (Cambridge, MA: Harvard University Asia Center, 2001), 108–14.
52. For the complex relationship between emotion and desire in late imperial intellectual discussions, see Martin W. Huang, "Sentiments of Desire: Thoughts on the Cult of *Qing* in Ming-Qing Literature," *CLEAR* 20 (1998): 170–74.

53. Thomas A. Metzger has detected a strong sense of "predicament" among Neo-Confucians in multiple forms of unresolved notional dyads. See his *Escape from Predicament: Neo-Confucianism and China's Evolving Political Culture* (New York: Columbia University Press, 1977), 49–165.
54. For the bipolarization of *qing* and *yu* in Qing fiction, see Martin W. Huang, "Sentiments of Desire," 179–84; *Desire and Fictional Narrative in Late Imperial China* (Cambridge, MA: Harvard University Asian Center, 2001), 236–70.
55. See chapter 4, section 5.
56. Cao Bingjian 曹炳建, *Xiyou ji banben yuanliu kao* 西遊記版本源流考 (Beijing: Renmin chubanshe, 2012), 92–96. This collaborates Glen Dudbridge's cautious remark that judging from the novel's absence in the bibliography *Baowentang shumu* 寶文堂書目 (c. 1560), it probably belongs to the popular romances of the latter part of the sixteenth century. See "The Hundred-Chapter *Hsi-yu Chi* and Its Early Versions," *Asia Major* 14, no. 2 (1968–1969): 190–91.
57. The syncretic reading is testified to by an essay by Sun Xu 孫緒 (1474–1547) on the "Journey to the West" tales predating the formation of the novel itself. Sun positions himself as a Confucian, but what he actually does is rendering every Buddhist motif inside the tales into a Daoist allegory. See Sun Xu, *Wuyong xiantan* 無用閑談, *juan* 5, in *Shaxi ji* 沙溪集, in *Yingyin Wenyuange Siku quanshu* 影印文淵閣四庫全書 (Taipei: Taiwan Shangwu yinshuguan, 1264:649. This "Daoist turn" was also seen in the popular syncretic sect Luoism, which retold the tales in terms of Daoist Inner Alchemy by using the colloquial poetic genre "precious volumes" (*baojuan* 寶卷). See Ling Hon Lam, "Allegory and the 'World' Formation in *The Journey to the West*," forthcoming in *A Companion to World Literature*, ed. Christopher Lupke (Hoboken, NJ: Wiley-Blackwell).
58. See Anthony C. Yu, "Religion and Literature in China: The 'Obscure Way' of *The Journey to the West*," in *Tradition and Creativity: Essays on East Asian Civilization*, ed. Ching-I Tu (New Brunswick, N.J.: Transaction, 1987), 124–26.
59. Chen Junmin "Lun Quanzhen dao ji qi neidan changsheng sixiang zhi yanbian" 論全真道及其內丹長生思想之演變, *Hanxue yanjiu* 漢學研究 16, no. 2 (1998): 257.
60. See *The Journey to the West*, trans. and ed. Anthony C. Yu, rev. ed. (Chicago: University of Chicago Press, 2012), 2:316. For the Chinese original, see Wu Cheng'an 吳承恩, *Xiyou ji* (Beijing: Zuojia chubanshe, 1954), 541. Hereafter references to *JW* are by volume and page numbers, followed by the page number of the Chinese original.
61. Lin Zhao'en, "Diwang wuwai zhixin," *Linzi quanji* 林子全集, in *Beijing tushuguan guji zhenben congkan* 北京圖書館古籍珍本叢刊 (Beijing: Shumu wenxian chubanshe, 1987), 63:45. For the view that syncretism in the Roman Empire served as an imperialist strategy, see Rosalind Shaw and Charles Stewart,

"Introduction: Problematizing Syncretism," in *Syncretism/Anti-syncretism: The Politics of Religious Synthesis*, ed. Rosalind Shaw and Charles Stewart (London: Routledge, 1994), 4.

62. The anchoring point (*point de capiton*) is the master signifier that "stops the otherwise endless movement of signification," the last term "sealing [the preceding others'] meaning by its retrospective effect." See Jacques Lacan, "The Subversion of the Subject and the Dialectic of Desire in the Freudian Unconscious," in *Écrits: A Selection*, trans. Alan Sheridan (London: Routledge, 1989), 303.

63. On the "inclusivistic" tendency of reducing the other to selfsameness in late Ming syncretism, see Timothy Brook, "Rethinking Syncretism: The Unity of the Three Teachings and Their Joint Worship in Late-Imperial China," *Journal of Chinese Religions* 21 (Fall 1993): 19–27. For a historical account of the variety of Neo-Confucian, Buddhist, and Daoist syncretism in the late Ming and the purist counteraction, see Kai-Wing Chow, *The Rise of Confucian Ritualism in Late Imperial China: Ethics, Classics, and Lineage Discourse* (Stanford: Stanford University Press, 1994), 15–43.

64. Andrew Plaks, *The Four Masterworks of the Ming Novel* (Princeton: Princeton University Press, 1987), 263. It should be added that the title *Duoxin ji* also appears in the ninth-century tale "Xuanzang" 玄奘 from Li Rong's 李冗 *Duyi zhi* 獨異志 and in the thirteenth-century *Da Tang Sanzang qujing shihua* 大唐三藏取經詩話; see *Xiyou ji ziliao huibian* 西遊記資料匯編, ed. Zhu Yixuan and Liu Yuzhen (Tianjin: Nankai daxue chubanshe, 2002), 32–33, 58–59. Neither of these texts, however, associates the title with the colloquial expression *duoxin* as *The Journey to the West* does.

65. The explanation Monkey gives the king for the absence of the black heart—"In priests like us there are only good hearts, but your father-in-law is the one who has a black heart" (*JW* 4:50/901)—can only be taken as self-mockery, because what he presented at court just a moment before were anything but "good hearts." And the novel never tells us the actual color of the monster father-in-law's heart. Zhang Shushen's interpretation of the multiple hearts as one single black heart (*Xinshuo Xiyou ji* 新說西遊記, 1748 edition; reprint, *Guben xiaoshuo jicheng*, ser. 1, 115:2519) obviously runs counter to the text itself.

66. For the proximity of oneself to the Other as irrecoverably archaic, anachronistic, and an(-)archic in oblivion, see Emmanuel Levinas, "Enigma and Phenomenon," and "Substitution," both in *Basic Philosophical Writings*, 69–70, 80–82. Quotation from "Substitution," 80. Zhang Jinchi 張錦池 notices the "discrepancies" in the novel concerning Monkey's relationship to his former sworn brothers but speculates not entirely convincingly that they arise from changes made to an earlier version. See *Xiyou ji kaolun* 西遊記考論, rev. ed. (Harbin: Heilongjiang jiaoyu chubanshe, 2000), 332–34, 383.

67. See Mou Zongsan 牟宗三, *Cong Lu Xiangshan dao Liu Jishan* 從陸象山到劉蕺山 (Taipei: Taiwan Xuesheng shuju, 1979), 14–17; Edward T. Ch'ien, *Chiao Hung and the Restructuring of Neo-Confucianism in the Late Ming* (New York: Columbia University Press, 1986), 200–15.
68. The single mind as surplus is clear in "the gate of Chan." The sixth patriarch Huineng 慧能, in negating the being of the heart in his famous gatha, says, "there is not ever a single thing [*wu yiwu* 無一物]."
69. "No mind" or "no thinking" is an example of Chan Buddhism's denial of its own traces of linguistic and symbolic mediation. See Faure, *The Rhetoric of Immediacy*, 63–64, 112. Taken as a rhetorical device rather than at face value, nonetheless, "no mind" can turn into a highlight of the aporia of language itself. See chapter 4, section 1.
70. The "babe" refers to lead in External Alchemy or the essence of the kidney in Inner Alchemy. The "holy embryo" means realized immortality (*JW* 1: 528n. 11, 3: 387n. 6). The formation of the babe or embryo with the prerequisite of negating the heart here thus disturbs the Neo-Confucian effort of assimilating the Daoist language as seen in Wang Yangming, who likens the "crystallization" of the Heaven's Principle in the heart to the forming of the holy embryo (*Chuanxi lu*, pt. 1, 11).
71. See "Qiwu lun," 79; *Chuang-tzu*, 56.
72. As Bernard Faure nicely puts on another occasion, "Buddhist emptiness remains a structure, and the Chan vision is still 'structured like a language.'" *Chan Insights and Oversights: An Epistemological Critique of the Chan Tradition* (Princeton: Princeton University Press, 1993), 167. Also see *Rhetoric of Immediacy*, 41–44.
73. *Chuang-tzu*, 56: "Take no step at all, and the 'That's it' which goes by circumstance will come to an end."
74. For a fuller discussion of syncretism and the doubleness of the heart, see Ling Hon Lam, "Cannibalizing the Heart: The Politics of Allegory and the *Journey to the West*," in *Literature, Religion, and East/West Comparison*, ed. Eric Ziolkowski (Newark: University of Delaware Press, 2005), 162–78.
75. Iriya Yoshitaka 入矢義高, *Baso no goroku* 馬祖の語錄 (Kyoto: Zen Bunka Kenkyūjo, 1984), 75.
76. Juelang Daosheng, "He Tang Jiyun jushi qing Tianning shang tang yun" 和湯季雲居士請天寧上堂韻, in *Tianjie Juelang Chanshi quanlu* 天界覺浪禪師全錄, reprint., *Mingban Jiaxing Dazang jing* 明版嘉興大藏經 (Taipei: Xinwenfeng chuban gongsi, 1987), 34:18.19.
77. Juelang Daosheng, "Shizhong shi zhu nazi ji zhong jushi" 室中示諸衲子及眾居士, in *Tianjie Juelang Chanshi quanlu*, 7.18. Also see Liao Zhaoheng, *Zhongbian, shichang, mengxi*, 359–60.

78. "Thus the spectator's gaze is double: he sees in the actor both the subject that he is and the fiction that he incarnates (or the action he performs); he sees him as both the master of himself and subject to the other within him. He sees not only what he says and what he does, but also what escapes him—what is said in himself and in spite of himself. The spectacle is the vehicle for all of this, and it is from this ultimate cleavage that one of the spectator's most profound pleasures arises. It is here that the spectator grasps the otherness in the actor—the actor as himself but also as other." See Josette Féral, foreword to *SubStance*, 31, no. 2–3 (November 2002): 12.
79. Zhou Ji 周楫, "Jue Sheli yinian cuo toutai" 覺闍黎一念錯投胎, *Xihu erji* 西湖二集 (Beijing: Renmin wenxue chubanshe, 1989), 99. The story is alluded to in Mei, *The Novel and Theatrical Imagination*, 123.
80. See *Da Tang Sanzang qujing shihua* and the fragments preserved in *Yongle dadian* 永樂大典, *Pak t'ongsa ŏnhae* 朴通事諺解, and *Xiaoshi zhenkong baojuan* 銷釋真空寶卷. The fragments can be found in *Xiyou ji ziliao huibian*, 109–16.
81. See "Erlang Shen suo Qitian Dasheng," in *Guben Yuan-Ming zaju* 孤本元明雜劇, ed. Wang Jilie 王季烈 (Shanghai: Hanfenlou, 1941), 29:3b, 9a, 10a–11b2a–3b.
82. Only in the anonymous Yuan or Ming *zaju* play *Shi Zhenren sisheng suo baiyuan* 時真人四聖鎖白猿 are the trick of doubling and the confrontation between the authentic and the counterfeit fully played out onstage; see *Guben Yuan-Ming zaju*, 29:2a–3b. But this again is only remotely related to the "Journey to the West" story. The White Ape calls himself not Qitian Dasheng but Yanxia Dasheng 煙霞大聖, and his captor is Shi Zhenren rather than Erlang Shen.
83. Shi Nai'an 施耐庵 and Luo Guanzhong 羅貫中, *Rongyu tang ben Shuihu zhuan* 容與堂本水滸傳 (Shanghai: Shanghai guji chubanshe, 1986), 2:74.1093–94; the English translation is from *Iron Ox: Part Four of Marshes of Mount Liang*, trans. John and Alex-Dent-Young (Hong Kong: Chinese University Press, 2002), 214–17. This Rongyu tang edition has recently been confirmed as closest to the partially survived Jiajing 嘉靖 edition (1522–1566), which now consists of chapters 47–55 only. See Ma Youyuan 馬幼垣, *Shuihu erlun* 水滸二論 (Beijing: Sanlian shudian, 2007), 78–79. Ma's conclusion that "the Rongyu tang edition is a late Wanli 萬曆 (1573–1620) product, but its text could not be later than the Jiajing era" can be applied to chapter 74, even though the chapter at issue is not included in the Jiajing edition's fragments.
84. The very brief classroom episode in the novel might have incorporated elements from another lost Yuan *zaju* play by Gao Wenxiu, "The Black Whirlwind Plays the Teacher." The way Li Kui wanders from one performance venue to another is reminiscent of ritual drama, which will be discussed in chapter 2. It is noteworthy that a lost Yuan *zaju* play again by Gao Wenxiu is

titled *Heixuanfeng jieshi huanhun* 黑旋風借屍還魂 (see Zhuang, *Gudian xiqu cunmu huikao*, 1:192), and there is also an episode in the novel about "Heixuanfeng qiao zhuogui" 黑旋風喬捉鬼 (see *Rongyu tang ben Shuihu zhuan*, 2:73.1071–74).

85. *Rongyu tang ben Shuihu zhuan*, chapter 23, 27–28, 31.
86. See Liangyan Ge, *Out of the Margins: The Rise of Chinese Vernacular Fiction* (Honolulu: University of Hawaii Press, 2001).
87. *Rongyu tang ben Shuihu zhuan*, 315.
88. *Rongyu tang ben Shuihu zhuan*, 1093. Conversely, even when a hero himself falls victim to impersonation, the name has never really gone astray from its proper reference. Quite the contrary, such cases show that every person coheres so tightly with his name that the prerequisite to be an identity thief is to have a real name that sounds close enough to the name one is bent on stealing. The famous example is the fake Black Whirlwind Li Gui 李鬼 (chapter 43). More intriguingly, a duo of swindlers simply calls itself "Song Jiang," a medley of their real names "Dong Hai" 董海 and "Wang Jiang" 王江 (chapter 73, page 1079). The episode is based on a survived Yuan *zaju* play by Kang Jinzhi 康進之 (fl. 1264–1294), "Liangshanpo Heixuanfeng fujing zaju" 梁山泊黑旋風負荊雜劇, where the duo's members are named Song Gang 宋剛 and Lu Zhi'en 魯智恩, the impostors of Song Jiang and another hero Lu Zhishen 魯智深. See *Shuihu xiqu ji*, 33–45.
89. *Shuihu xiqu ji*, 1:3.
90. Mei, *The Novel and Theatrical Imagination*, 87–98.
91. A closer analysis into the dreamscape, however, will further specify the condition of its performance as threshold-crossing, whereas the traces of oral storytelling that still seem to frame the dreamscape as a shared dream can be shown as a legacy of the regime of winds. See chapter 3, section 5.
92. *The Journey to the West* has been regarded as another early vernacular novel comparable to *The Water Margin* concerning their oral provenance indicated by recurrent narrative patterns. (See Ge, *Out of the Margins*, 92–93.) But that makes the former a more useful case to illustrate the transition from the early to the late sixteenth century.
93. One example is the eighteenth-century drama *Pigsy Gets Married* (*Bajie chengqin* 八戒成親). Isobe Akira 磯部彰 found this anonymous play in the eighteenth-century dramatic collection *Qingyin xiaoji* 清音小集. Like Yang Ne's *zaju* play *The Journey to the West*, the *Pigsy Gets Married* has Monkey transform into Pigsy's wife and flirt with him. But the latter play obviously was influenced by the novel rather than the *zaju*, because, as Isobe points out, it combines the two episodes from chapters 18, 19, and 67 of the novel. See his *"Saiyūki" kenseishi no kenkyū* "西遊記"形成史の研究 (Tokyo: Sōbunsha, 1993), 426–29.

94. The corresponding part of the novel is in chapter 34. The episode is also included in the early part of Zhang Zhao 張照 et al., *Shengping baofa*, Qing manuscript copy; reprint, *Qinggong daxi* 清宮大戲 (Taipei: Tianyi chubanshe, 1986), vol. 4, scenes 22–23. For an introduction to *Shengping baofa*, see also Su Xing 蘇興, "*Shengping baofa* yu *Xiyou ji* sanlun" 昇平寶筏與西遊記散論, *Luoyang shizhuan xuebao* 洛陽師專學報 18, no. 3 (June 1999): 71–74; Isobe Akira, "*Saiyūki*" *shiryō no kenkyū* 西遊記"資料の研究 (Sendai-shi: Tōhoku Daigaku Tōhoku Shuppansha, 2007) 323–91.
95. *Shengping baofa*, vol. 7, scene 6, 30a. For a general description of this play, see Isobe, "Seidai niokeru 'Saiyūki' no syokeitai tosono juyōshi nitsuite," 494–96.
96. *Shengping baofa*, 28a, 30a.
97. *Shengping baofa*, 31a–31b.
98. *Shengping baofa*, 31b–32a.
99. An alternative attribution of the work to Dong Yue's father Dong Sizhang 董斯張 (1587–1628) and an accordingly different dating of it to somewhere close to 1628 can be found in Li Qiancheng 李前程, foreword to *Xiyou bu jiaozhu* 西遊補校注 (Beijing: Kunlun chubanshe, 2011), 1–23.
100. Dong Yue, *Xiyou bu*, 1641 edition; reprint, *Guben xiaoshuo jicheng*, ser. 3, 125:6. The English translation is from Tung Yueh, *Tower of Myriad Mirrors: A Supplement to Journey to the West*, trans. Shuen-fu Lin and Larry Schulz (Berkeley: Asian Humanities Press, 1978), 25 (hereafter *SJ* followed by the page number of the Chinese original).
101. Christopher Harbsmeier, "Weeping and Wailing in Ancient China," in *Minds and Mentalities in Traditional Chinese Literature*, ed. Halvor Eifring (Beijing: Culture and Art Publishing House, 1999), 317–422.
102. Anne E. McLaren, *Performing Grief: Bridal Laments in Rural China* (Honolulu: University of Hawaii Press, 2008), 17.
103. For the mirror as a figure of gateway to the dreamscape, see chapter 1, section 2. Critics have noted that the novella, with its prefatory materials, makes numerous conspicuous references to dreams. See Fu Shiyi 傅世怡, *Xiyou bu chutan* 西遊補初探 (Taipei: Taiwan Xuesheng shuju, 1986), 124–31. The word "dream" or *meng* 夢 appears at high frequency in Dong Yue's poems, which very often use dreams as devices for traveling to a fantasyland. In 1643, he laid down four "Agreements of the Dream Society," in which he lays out four things to do with dreams: roaming heavens, cruising territories, visiting the past, and seeing the future—all of which are fulfilled by the narrative of *Supplement*. See Dong Yue, "Mengshe yue" 夢社約, in *Fengcao an qianji* 豐草庵前集, in *Dong Ruoyu shiwen ji* 董若雨詩文集 (Wuxing: Liushi Jiayetang, 1914), 15a–16b.
104. Carlos Rojas regards specularity as a primary mode of premodern Chinese visuality; see *The Naked Gaze*, 31–53. Art historians, however, attend mostly

to the symbolism of cast images on the reverse rather than the reflecting side of ancient mirrors. From this discrepancy Paula Varsano captures a phenomenological paradox, namely, the "disappearing" nature of Chinese mirrors, by which she means "what survived of [an] ancient mirror was not its defining, much vaunted reflective powers, but the signs and symbols that vaunted them." See Varsano, "Disappearing Objects/Elusive Subjects: Writing Mirrors in Early and Medieval China," *Representations* 124, no.1 (Fall 2013): 99. This "disappearing," however, itself cannot be explained either in terms of the mirror's reflexivity or by its decorated reverse side, but in terms of an operation of traversing inherent in the mythology of the mirror. Rather than staying with either side of the mirror, the significance lies in traversing from one side to another. While polishing and casting had been mature enough to create the reflecting and decorated sides of mirrors as early as the Shang dynasty, the traversing of the two sides did not become technologically possible until the Han dynasty, when the "light-penetration mirror" (*touguang jing* 透光鏡), "in which the cast image projects its design through the reflecting side." See Michael A. DeMarco, "Mirror Symbolism: A Chinese Bronze Art," *Chinese Culture* 25, no. 4 (December 1984): 61. The mirror in *Supplement* shows no reflection, but the image of the other side should not be mistaken as just a piece of transparent glass (which was not imported to China until the early eighteenth century), but rather a fantastic version of "light-penetration."

105. Robert E. Hegel, *The Novel in Seventeenth-Century China* (New York: Columbia University Press, 1981), 164.

106. Qiancheng Li, *Fictions of Enlightenment*, 107.

107. "A prosthesis is an object that acts as an extension of the body schema . . . The implicit presence of the object-ness of the avatar as prosthesis adopting certain subjective qualities creates a tension or resistance within both the user-avatar relation and the formation of identity in virtual worlds. The user perceives the avatar as being both an object outside of the body and an extension of the same body." See Maeva Veerapen, "Encountering Oneself and the Other: A Case Study of Identity Formation in Second Life," in *Reinventing Ourselves: Contemporary Concepts of Identity in Virtual Worlds*, ed. Anna Peachery and Mark Childs (London: Springer, 2011), 90–91.

108. For prosthesis as a dangerous supplement subversive of the primacy of interiority and the coherence of identity, see Yoshiki Tajiri, *Samuel Beckett and the Prosthetic Body: The Organs and Senses in Modernism* (New York: Palgrave Macmillan, 2007), 40–47; David T. Mitchell and Sharon L. Snyder, *Narrative Prosthesis: Disability and the Dependencies of Discourse* (Ann Arbor: University of Michigan Press, 2000), 6–10. Only through a fantasy of an increasing naturalization of the prosthetic avatar does one get an impression, as celebrated

recently by Jonathan Boulter, that the avatar itself becomes "mathematically less [foreign]," and the space that we experience through avatars also becomes accordingly "our *own*." The avatar, according to Boulter, is therefore "a perfect representation of the uncanny, indeed of the doubled and split interiority." See Boulter, "Posthuman Melancholy: Digital Gaming and Cyberpunk," in *Beyond Cyberpunk: New Critical Perspective*, ed. Graham J. Murphy and Sherryl Vint (New York: Routledge, 2010), 142. Such mathematically increased interiorization of exteriority, however, is precisely what we should resist. To see space become our own through the naturalization of the avatar, which ultimately is just a by-product of our interiority (however complex the interior is), is just to resurrect the opposition between the external world and the interior subject, which is not to be resolved a bit by the mediating avatar.

109. Rune Klevjer, "Enter the Avatar: The Phenomenology of Prosthetic Telepresence in Computer Games," in *The Philosophy of Computer Games*, ed. John Richard Sageng, Hallvard J. Fossheim, and Tarjei Mandt Larsen (London: Springer, 2012), 20.
110. Klevjer, "Enter the Avatar," 20–21.
111. Klevjer, "Enter the Avatar," 33.
112. We will come back to this discussion in chapter 5, sections 3 and 4.
113. As if to anticipate Wu Zhensheng's verdict about the supremacy of Tang Xianzu's play over *The Journey*, *Supplement* turns the tables, suggesting that Tang himself "intends to destroy Form and Passion" with his *Dream of South Branch*, whereas Monkey is the one who proves "Form and Passion can hardly be destroyed."
114. In the play, Monkey flaunts his sexuality, claiming that he has "an asshole hard as brass, a penis that can split tin." In the adventure to the Women Nation, Monkey is awfully aroused until the gold hoop on his head hurts him so much that he cannot get an erection. See Yang Ne, *Xiyou ji*, in *Yuanqu xuan waibian*, 2:654, 679, 683. Monkey as a lewd abductor originates in the "ape tales" dating from the pre–Eastern Han dynasty and was heretofore unrelated to Tripitaka's story until Yang's play. For a discussion of the ape tales, see Wu Hung, "The Earliest Pictorial Representations of Ape Tales: An Interdisciplinary Study of Early Chinese Narrative Art and Literature," *T'oung Pao* 73 (1987): 86–112.
115. Slavoj Žižek, *The Plagues of Fantasies* (London: Verso, 1997), 35–40.
116. The "body outside the body" also appears in chapter 11 of *Supplement*, where Monkey transforms his hairs into a myriad of Monkeys, who are then sent to explore on his behalf the labyrinthine Green Green World. One of them flirts with a woman and gets drunk; Monkey punishes him physically for falling prey to the Demon of Passion. This episode demonstrates how the avatar, far from

being oneself, is an indispensable medium or "prosthesia" through which one can gain access, however problematically, to the phenomena of emotion.
117. Lin and Schulz miss the punchline of calculation here by rendering the last two sentences "I am disembodied; in fact, I've never even been joined with a body."
118. Li Qiancheng, *Xiyou bu jiaozhu*, 192.
119. Alison Black, *Man and Nature in the Philosophical Thought of Wang Fu-chih* (Seattle: University of Washington Press, 1989); Xiao Chi, *Shengdao yu shixin* 聖道與詩心 (Taipei, Lianjing chuban shiye gufen youxian gongsi, 2012).
120. Siu-kit Wong, "Ch'ing and Ching in the Critical Writings of Wang Fu-chih," in *Chinese Approaches to Literature from Confucius to Liang Ch'i-ch'ao*, ed. Adele Austin Rickett (Princeton: Princeton University Press, 1978), 130–131.
121. Xiao, *Shengdao yu shixin*, 69–71.
122. Wang Fuzhi, "Xitang yongri xulun" 夕堂永日緒論, in *Jiangzhai shihua jianzhu* 薑齋詩話箋注, ed. Dai Hongsen 戴鴻森 (Beijing: Renmin wenxue chubanshe, 1981), 55. The translation is from Owen, *Readings in Chinese Literary Thought*, 465. Xiao Chi has insightfully connected Wang Fuzhi's empirical emphasis to his appropriation of the Buddhist notion of *xianliang* 現量 (Sanskrit: *pratyakṣa*), which signifies the immediate, intuitive comprehension of things grasped in a unitary moment of presence (*Shengdao yu shixin*, 69–71).
123. Wang, "Xitang yongri xulun," 52. The translations are modified from Owen, *Readings in Chinese Literary Thought*, 462.
124. Owen, *Readings in Chinese Literary Thought*, 463, 466.
125. Wang, "Xitang yongri xulun," 50, 52, 72, 95.
126. Wang, "Xitang yongri xulun," 74.
127. We have to be cautious about this initial discussion of fiction and imagination, which has not yet challenged the classical view of sympathy as fictive and thus representational. The discussion is deployed this way here so far as it fulfills its purpose to underline the differences between dreamscapes and theatricality as two historical modes of the spatiality of emotion. But it is actually misleading to imply that my being situated in the here is real whereas my being transported to another person's position over there is fictional. I have touched on this when discussing the issue of avatars, but the meanings of fiction and imagination cannot be fully clarified without a thorough understanding of not just emotion as spatial but also of the entire structure of spatiality as emotional—a daunting task we will take on in section 4 of the concluding chapter. Before that, any mentions of "imaginary" or "fictional" in the following chapters should be viewed as tentative and put in brackets.
128. For the notion of problematization as a working category to historicize ethical systems, see Michel Foucault, *The Use of Pleasure: Volume 2 of History of Sexuality*, trans. Richard Hurley (New York: Vintage, 1990), 10–24.

3. WHAT IS WRONG WITH *THE WRONG CAREER*?: A GENEALOGY OF PLAYGROUNDS

1. See Zhao Shanlin 趙山林, *Zhongguo xiqu guanzhongxue* 中國戲曲觀眾學 (Shanghai: Huadong shifan daxue chubanshe, 1990).
2. See *Quan Yuanqu* 全元曲 (Shijiazhuang: Hebei jiaoyu chubanshe, 1998), 10:7114–15.
3. Zhou Yude, "Zhiwuren huanhun" 植物人還魂, *Zhongguo xiju* 中國戲劇 581 (October 2005): 25–26.
4. Wang Haibian 王海邊, "*Huanmen zidi cuo lishen* de juben gaibian yishu"《宦門子弟錯立身》的戲本改編藝術, *Zhongguo xiju* 503 (April 2004): 13. See also Ji Guoping 季國平, "Guju xinbian hua *Huanmen*" 古劇新編話《宦門》, in *Guqiang xinyun: Bei Kun* Huanmen zidi cuo lishen *ping lun ji* 北崑宦門子弟錯立身評論集, ed. Liu Zhen 劉禎 and Xie Yongjun 謝雍君 (Beijing: Zhongguo xiju chubanshe, 2006), 117–18.
5. Dai Hebing 戴和冰, "*Huanmen zidi cuo lishen*: Chuantong xiqu de yizhong chuancheng baohu moshi"《宦門子弟錯立身》：傳統戲曲的一種傳承保護模式, in *Guqiang xinyun*, 159.
6. *Huanmen zidi cuo lishen*, in *Yongle dadian xiwen sanzhong jiaozhu* 永樂大典戲文三種校注, ed. Qian Nanyang (Taipei: Huazheng shuju, 2003), 254. In the *Yongle dadian* manuscript where the play was found, the word 介 is originally given as 个. Qian Nanyang regards the latter as a mistake of copying, but actually 个 and 介 are interchangeable. See Cheng Xueyi 程學頤, "*Huanmen zidi cuo lishen* chongzhu"《宦門子弟錯立身》重注, *Yishu yanjiu ziliao* 藝術研究資料 8 (1984): 157–58 n. 8.
7. "A Playboy from a Noble House Opts for the Wrong Career," in Wilt Idema and Stephen H. West, *Chinese Theater 1100–1450: A Source Book* (Wiesbaden: Steiner, 1982), 235.
8. See Hu Ji, *Song Jin zaju kao* 宋金雜劇考 (Beijing: Zhonghua shuju, 2008), 68, 212–15. At one point, a *yuanben* is staged to entertain the characters of the *Jiao Hong ji*. As I explain below, in section 4, this moment comes close to the play-within-a-play design but does not really become one.
9. An alternative translation without these textual changes to the description of the actions can be found in "Grandee's Son Takes the Wrong Career," in *Eight Chinese Plays: From the Thirteenth Century to the Present*, trans. William Dolby (New York: Columbia University Press, 1978), 51.
10. Shi Junbao 石君寶, *Zhugongdiao fengyue Zhiyun ting* 諸宮調風月紫雲亭, in *Shi Junbao xiqu ji* 石君寶戲曲集, ed. Huang Zhusan 黃竹三 (Taiyuan: Shanxi renmin chubanshe, 1992), 117–80. The translation can be found in Idema and West, *Chinese Theater 1100–1450*, 236–78. See also Li Gang 李鋼, "Shilun *Huanmen zidi cuo*

lishen: Jianji Nanxi yu Yuan zaju de guanxi" 試論宦門子弟錯立身：兼及南戲與元雜劇的關係, typescript, Zhongguo yishu yanjiuyuan, 2001, 7–8. Liao Ben 廖奔 has argued that the southern drama *The Wrong Career* was adapted from other earlier northern *zaju* versions, some of which bear the same or similar titles. See "Nanxi *Huanmen zidi cuo lishen* yuanchu Bei zaju tui kao" 南戲宦門子弟錯立身源出北雜劇推考, *Wenxue yichan* 文學遺產 2 (1987): 97–104. Since all the other three *zaju* versions have been lost, we can refer only to *The Purple Cloud Pavilion* as the possible antecedent.

11. Translation taken from Idema and West, *Chinese Theater 1100–1450*, 275, 277.
12. The same phenomenon occurs in the Yuan *zaju* drama *Zhongli of the Han Leads Lan Caihe to Enlightenment* (*Han Zhongli dutuo Lan Caihe*). When Lan Caihe 藍采和 the actor is asked by the immortal Zhongli Quan 鍾離權 in disguise to perform a few variety plays, he enumerates seven plays he knows. See *Quan Yuan xiqu*, 7:118. Though, after enlightened, Lan performs a Daoist-themed song for his wife, that counts only as "a performance-within-a-play," which differs from a play-in-a-play in that the interior performance "cannot stand on its own because it does not have its own plot" or "characters of its own." See Kimberly Cashman, *Staging Subversions: The Performance-within-a-play in French Classical Theater* (New York: Peter Lang, 2005), 19.
13. See Stephen H. West, "Shifting Spaces: Local Dialect in A Playboy from a Noble House Opts for the Wrong Career," *Journal of Theater Studies* 1 (2008): 89–94.
14. *Rensheng ru xi* is clearly just a variation of another set phrase *rensheng ru meng* 人生如夢.
15. This line is highlighted and favored by Cai Xinxin 蔡欣欣, "Chongsu jingdian: Yongle dadian xiwen sanzhong zhi 'xiangxiang kunju gefan' gaibian yanchu" 重塑經典：永樂大典戲文三種之"想像崑劇格範"改編演出, presented at "Re-reading Classics: International Conference on Traditional Chinese Fiction and Drama," Chinese University of Hong Kong, January 3–5, 2008.
16. Samuel Weber, *Theatricality as Medium* (New York: Fordham University Press, 2004), 4–5, 33, 40–41, 43.
17. William Egginton, *How the World Became a Stage*, 74–75. I differ with Egginton on one significant point. Whereas he regards theatricality as "the essence of theater" and therefore reserves the word "theater" exclusively for the era of theatricality, I apply "theater" to venues of dramatic performance preceding theatricality as well because, as I argue throughout this book, theatricality is all about intermediation that moves us away from theater per se.
18. Lionel Abel, "Beckett and Metatheatre," in *Tragedy and Metatheatre: Essays on Dramatic Form* (New York: Holmes & Meier, 2003), 158.
19. Abel, "Genet and Metatheatre" and "Brecht and Metatheatre," in *Tragedy and Metatheatre*, 154, 164.

20. For a general discussion, see Eric Henry, "Life as Impersonation: *The Paired Soles*," in *Chinese Amusement: The Lively Plays of Li Yu* (Hamden, CT: Archon, 1980), 19–51.
21. *Sheng, dan, jing, chou* (in addition to *mo* and *wai* seen in *The Wrong Career*) are role-types in southern drama and *chuanqi* drama. In Chinese theater, actors are trained to specialize in certain role-types, each with its distinct costumes, makeup, and acting style. In the capacity of a role-type he or she is assigned to play a character. However, traditional theater systematically fosters and deliberately plays on misalignments among actor, role-type, and character. For instance, a male actor can specialize in the "female lead" role-type, and in that role-type he can play an effeminate man. The Chinese script would refer to his part as "female lead" (*dan*) though his character is the male protagonist. See Sophie Volpp, "Gender, Power and Spectacle in Late-Imperial Chinese Theater," in *Gender Reversals and Gender Cultures: Anthropological and Historical Perspectives*, ed. Sabrina Petra Ramet (London: Routledge, 1996), 138–43.
22. See Jing Shen, *Playwrights and Literary Games in Seventeenth-Century China: Plays by Tang Xianzu, Mei Dingzuo, Wu Bing, Li Yu, and Kong Shangren* (New York: Rowman & Littlefield Publishers, 2010), 178–81. The quote is from page 201.
23. As will be seen below, the self-exposure of role-type arbitrariness happens in much older plays and in itself does not distinguish Li Yu's work. Those earlier examples, however, point to a different mode of spatiality than theatricality.
24. Georges Forestier, *Le théâtre dans le théâtre : sur la scène française du XVIIe siècle* (Genève: Librairie Droz S.A., 1996), 11–12.
25. To fully capitalize on the sensation of theatricality, however, the 2007 Cantonese opera version of *Bimuyu* instead starts with a play-within-a-play, and the stage directions highlight the spectators watching the embedded play: "In the center is the stage . . . The clearing in front of the stage is used as a space for performing, where the audience appearing within the play stays." See Li Mingkeng 李明鏗, *Bimuyu*, in Li Long 李龍 and Xu Rongrong 徐蓉蓉, *Xun longyu shuo* 尋龍魚說 (Hong Kong: Hong Kong yishu fazhanju, 2008), 72.
26. Li Yu, *Bimuyu*, in *Li Yu quanji* 李漁全集 (Hangzhou: Zhejiang guji chubanshe, 1991), 2:150. The play retells Li Yu's short story "Tan Chuyu xili chuanqing, Liu Miaogu quzhong sijie" 譚楚玉戲裡傳情，劉藐姑曲終死節 published a few years before. See *Li Yu Quanji*, 5.251–80. This passage appears in the story almost verbatim but in third-person narration. The translation was partially drawn from Li Yu, "An Actress Scorns Wealth and Honor to Preserve Her Chastity," in *Silent Operas*, ed. and trans. Patrick Hanan (Hong Kong: Research Center for Translation, CUHK, 1990), 174.
27. *Bimuyu*, 111.

28. Wang Duanshu, foreword to *Bimuyu*, 107.
29. *Bimuyu*, 152.
30. *Bimuyu*, 132, upper margin. For the identity of Qinhuai zuihou, see Huang Qiang 黃強, *Li Yu yanjiu* 李漁研究 (Hangzhou: Zhejiang guji chubanshe, 1996), 348–52.
31. Rei Terada, *Feeling in Theory: Emotion After the "Death of the Subject"* (Cambridge, MA: Harvard University Press, 2001), 16–47.
32. "生旦演此，非優孟古人，直是我與我周旋，那得草草？" *Bimuyu*, 111, upper margin.
33. According to the stage direction, "Actors play the spectators swarming in. The painted face [*jing*, playing Qian Wanguan] takes a folding chair, sits down and watches, giving a condescending look." *Bimuyu*, 156.
34. The impression of "being more advanced" is perhaps an intended effect pursued by Li Yu, especially with the play-within-a-play device, rewriting and embedding an old play in his own to show off a better self-consciousness of theatricality. Jing Shen detects "Li Yu's intention to make [Sole Mates] surpass *Thorn Hairpin* with respect to theatrical presentation and his gratification over this use of a meta-theatrical device." *Playwrights and Literary Games*, 193.
35. See Hansheng 寒聲 et al., "*Yingshen saishe lijie chuanbu sishiqu gongdiao zhushi*"《迎神賽社禮節傳簿四十曲宮調》注釋, *Zhonghua xiqu* 中華戲曲 3 (April 1987): 51–117.
36. See Liao Ben, *Song Yuan xiqu wenwu yu minsu* 宋元戲曲文物與民俗 (Beijing: Wenhua yishu chuanshe, 1989), 363.
37. Yang Mengheng 楊孟衡, "Pingshunxian Dongyugou Jiutian Shengmu miao sai" 平順縣東峪溝九天聖母廟賽, in *Taihang shenmiao ji saishe yanju yanjiu* 太行神廟及賽社演劇研究, ed. Feng Junjie 馮俊杰 (Taipei: Caituan faren Shi Hezheng minsu wenhua jijinhui, 2000), 332; David Johnson, *Spectacle and Sacrifice: The Ritual Foundations of Village Life in North China* (Cambridge, MA: Harvard University Asia Center, 2009), 189–90.
38. Tanaka Issei argues that romantic comedies such as *The Wrong Career* were performed to console wronged women's spirits. *Chūgoku engekishi* 中國演劇史 (Tokyo: University of Tokyo Press, 1998), 257.
39. David Johnson, "Actions Speak Louder Than Words: The Cultural Significance of Chinese Ritual Opera," in *Ritual Opera, Operatic Ritual*, ed. David Johnson (Berkeley: Institute of East Asian Studies, 1989), 1–45; Qitao Guo, *Ritual Opera and Mercantile Lineage: The Confucian Transformation of Popular Culture in Late Imperial Huizhou* (Stanford: Stanford University Press, 2005), 99–102; Yung Sai-Shing 容世誠, *Xiqu renleixue chutan: Yishi, juchang yu shequn* 戲曲人類學初探：儀式、劇場與社群 (Taipei: Maitian, 1997), 25–57.

40. Hao Yuxiang 郝譽翔, "Cong yishi dao xiju: yige yi Zhongguo minjian yingshen saishe weili de chubu yanjiu" 從儀式到戲劇：一個以中國民間迎神賽社為例的初步研究, *Donghua renwen xuebao* 東華人文學報 1 (July 1999): 221–22.
41. "*Yingshen saishe lijie chuanbu* jianshi" 《迎神賽社禮節傳簿》箋釋, in Liao Ben, *Song Yuan xiqu wenwu yu minsu*, 388, 392, 398.
42. Huang Zhusan 黃竹三, "Woguo xiqu shiliao de zhongda faxian: Shanxi Lucheng Mingdai *Lijie chuanbu* kaoshu" 我國戲曲史料的重大發現——山西潞城明代《禮節傳簿》考述, *Zhonghua xiqu* 3: 145–46.
43. "*Yingshen saishe lijie chuanbu* jianshi," 403, 418.
44. Johnson, *Spectacle and Sacrifice*, 330–33.
45. Victor Turner, "Acting in Everyday Life and Everyday Life in Acting," in *From Ritual to Theatre: The Human Seriousness of Play* (New York: PAJ Publications, 1982), 112.
46. Lord Yan or Marquis Pacifier-of-Waves was the deity who rescued the founder of the Ming dynasty Taizu from a storm. For the origin of Lord Yan's Temple in the reign of Ming Taizu, see Zhao Yi 趙翼, *Gaiyu congkao* 陔餘叢考 (Shanghai: Shangwu yinshuguan, 1955), *juan* 35, 774–75.
47. An earlier work by Li Yu based on the same tale, the vernacular story "An Actress Scorns Wealth" envisages a more direct communication between the actress and the spectator, with an instant didactic effect on the latter: "He knew that her curses were meant for him, but he couldn't help feeling a twinge of conscience and becoming fair-minded." This psychological explanation is omitted from the drama version. See Li Yu, "Tan Chuyu xili chuanqing," 267; "An Actress Scorns Wealth," 183, translation slightly modified.
48. *Bimuyu*, 1661 edition; reprint, *Li Yu Quanji* 李漁全集, ed. Ma Hanmao 馬漢茂 (Helmut Martin) (Taipei: Chengwen chubanshe, 1970), 10:4316–19.
49. As a professional writer, Li Yu composed his plays not only for professional actors whose careers Li apparently set out to redeem with *Sole Mates* but also for commercial publishers; both groups scrambled for his work, he proudly claimed. Later, from 1667 to 1672, he formed a private troupe that performed at home or at his patron's, not without financial interest. It is also well known that he published his own books and even sold paper with his trademark. See Patrick Hanan, *The Invention of Li Yu* (Cambridge, MA: Harvard University Press, 1988), 1–30; Chu-shu Chang and Shelley Hsueh-lun Chang, *Crisis and Transformation in Seventeenth-Century China: Society, Culture, and Modernity in Li Yü's World* (Ann Arbor: University of Michigan Press, 1992), 71–90; Chen Guohua 陳國華, "Li Yu xiqu huodong de shangyexing tezheng" 李漁戲曲活動的商業性特徵, *Xiju wenxue* 戲劇文學 298 (2008): 84–88.
50. See Lam, "The Matriarch's Private Ear," 384–86.
51. Weber, *Theatricality as Medium*, 10–13, 19–20.

52. Catherine Bell, *Ritual Theory, Ritual Practice* (Oxford: Oxford University Press, 1992), 19–54.
53. *Zhang Xie zhuangyuan*, in Qian Nanyang, *Yongle dadian xiwen sanzhong jiaozhu*, 13. The translation is modified from *Top Graduate Zhang Xie*, in Regina Sofia Llamas, "Comic Roles and Performance in the Play: *Zhang Xie Zhuanyuan* with a Complete Translation," Ph.D. diss., Harvard University, 1998, 162–63.
54. For the ghost gateway, see Zhu Quan, *Taihe zhengyin pu jianping*, 91. For "sending-off" and backstage musicians, see Yu Fusheng 余復生, "Song zaju 'duansong' kaobian" 宋雜劇"斷送"考辨, *Tianjin yinyue xueyuan xuebao* 天津音樂學院學報 87 (Winter 2006): 52–68; "Houhang kaoshu" 後行考述, *Zhongguo yinyue xue* 中國音樂學 128 (Fall 2017): 82–87.
55. *Zhang Xie zhuangyuan*, 13 and 16 n. 3.
56. *Zhang Xie zhuangyuan*, 2; *Top Graduate Zhang Xie*, 158, translation modified.
57. This connection to oral storytelling originated in the urban venues of Song-Jin entertainment, where *zaju* players were mixed up with oral storytellers. See William Dolby, *A History of Chinese Drama* (London: Paul Elik, 1976), 18. The convention of self-introduction (*zibao jiamen* 自報家門) upon a character's first entry in Chinese opera is evidently a feature inherited from oral storytelling simply by changing the narration from third-person to first-person. See Xu Dajun 徐大軍, *Huaben yu xiqu guanxi yanjiu* 話本與戲曲關係研究 (Taipei: Xinwenfeng chuban gongsi, 2004), 163–64, 194.
58. See Regina Llamas, *El licenciado número uno, Zhang Xie: Estudio preliminar y traducción* (Barcelona: Edicions Bellaterra, 2014), 49.
59. Jeehee Hong, *Theater of the Dead: A Social Turn in Chinese Funerary Art, 1000–1400* (Honolulu: University of Hawai'i Press, 2016), 129–33, quote from page 130. We will see below that "fictionality" is more complicated than just the opposite to the real world. For the further discussion of theater and tomb architecture, see section 6.
60. See chapter 1, section 3. For the politics of difference in Zhuangzi, see Lai Xisan 賴錫三, *Daojiaxing zhishi fenzi lun: Lun Zhuangzi de quanli pipan yu wenhua gengxin* 道家型知識分子論：論《莊子》的權力批判與文化更新 (Taipei: Guoli Taiwan daxue chuban zhongxin, 2013), 134.
61. Here we need to distinguish self-reflexive moments (in which the theater refers to, queries, or makes fun of its own mechanism and conventions) from metatheater, which we have taken as synonymous with a play-within-a-play, a specific device based on a mode of spatiality that was not available to Song-Yuan theater.
62. Llamas, "Comic Roles and Performance," 34.
63. Llamas, "Comic Roles and Performance," 35.

64. Patrick Hanan, "The Making of The Pearl-Sewn Shirt and The Courtesan's Jewel Box," *Harvard Journal of Asiatic Studies* 33 (1973): 136–38. While Hanan raises the important question of whether vernacular tales (written and circulated in print) reflect the oral tradition or simply present a simulated oral situation, others have found that the overt storyteller who adds intrusive comments is a common feature retained in modern Yangzhou oral storytelling. See Vibeke Børdahl, "The Storyteller's Manner in Chinese Storytelling," *Asian Folklore Studies* 62 (2003): 86–91.
65. Zhao Shanlin captures this *différance* of real and unreal when he points out that the traditonal opera audience "neither take [the performance] as real nor dismiss it as fake." See *Zhongguo xiqu guanzhongxue*, 155–64. What I would like to add is: this is a characteristic of dreams rather than spectators.
66. The *Yongle dadian* text does not divide scenes. The scene numbers are added by the modern editor Qian Nanyang and followed by Llamas.
67. Later in the scene, Zhang Xie, now a freshly minted official, comes out and condemns Poorlass, saying: "Look Poorlass . . . your appearance is squalid, your family poor and your possessions meager. You know nothing of the sacrificial rites. How could we be a couple?" What he confronts is not a false madam as a laughingstock but as an ominous body of socio-physiological nuisances. See *Zhang Xie zhuangyuan*, 160–62; *Top Graduate Zhang Xie*, 336–37, 340, translations modified. The question we ask about scene 35 also applies to scenes 33 and 39 (*Zhang Xie zhuangyuan*, 156, 171) where the *jing* exposes that he (supposedly male) is playing both the temple deity and the old hag.
68. *Zhang Xie zhuangyuan*, 54–57; *Top Graduate Zhang Xie*, 208–14, translations modified.
69. *Zhang Xie zhuangyuan*, 87; *Top Graduate Zhang Xie*, 252–55, translations modified.
70. The fact that *jia* means more "provisional" than "fake" is borne out by another example from the play. In scene 42, when an extra female (*tie* 贴), who has been playing the Prime Minister's daughter Shenghua, shifts to the role of the maid Yefang after Shenghua dies. The stage direction reads as follows: "The female extra, borrowed and dressed (*jiazhuang*) as Yefang, comes out and sings." See *Zhang Xie zhuangyuan*, 182; *Top Graduate Zhang Xie*, 364 (translation modified). Deepening our understanding of the pair of *zhen-jia* in the Song-Yuan theater, Stephen West argues that the *zhen* (real) does not mean mimetic verisimilitude but "genuine essence" based on repeatable types rather than individuality. See Stephen H. West, "Playing with Food: Performance, Food, and the Aesthetics of Artificiality in the Sung and Yuan," *Harvard Journal of Asiatic Studies* 57, no. 1 (June 1997): 105. What we can add to his analysis is that the other half of the formulation, *jia*, means not

just falsehood or artificality; it also means provisionary use or taking out a form-loan.

71. See Egginton, *How the World Became a Stage*, 33–83. In chapter 5, section 4, I offer a critique of this description of theatricality as an effect *in thought*. For now, we will focus only on the historical distinction between Real Presence and theatricality Egginton puts forth. For a more nuanced discussion of the historical specificity of "Real Presence" in comparison with other notions of "representation," see Carlo Ginzburg, "Representation: The Word, the Idea, the Thing," in *Wooden Eyes: Nine Reflections on Distance*, trans. Martin Ryle and Kate Soper (New York: Columbia University Press, 2001), 63–78.
72. This transformation also takes place in the audience, which is delivered across the same threshold. See section 6.
73. Idema and West, *Chinese Theater 1100–1450*, 278.
74. Ibid., 283–98; Anon., *Fengyu xiangsheng huolangdan*, in *Quan Yuan xiqu*, 6:615–23. In comparison, the 2008 production of *The Wrong Career* self-consciously plays with the theatrical framing by having Shouma's father overreact to his son's performance. But his impulse to intrude onto the stage is reined in more than once by his old servant, who keeps reminding him of his role as a spectator: "My lord, just watch the play, watch the play!" "It is a play only . . ." (see figure 3.2). The separation of the spectator is simultaneously made fun of and maintained with a heightened awareness of theatricality.
75. Interestingly, instead of turning any character into a spectator who is in turn watching an embedded play, the survived "A Pair of Battling Quacks" segment from the Yuan *zaju* play *Cai Shun Serves His Mother* (*Cai Shun feng mu* 蔡順奉母) introduces a special role-type called *waicheng* 外呈, who does not really play any dramatic character but functions as an extradiegetic "host." The *waicheng* is not part of the patient's family, nor is he the doctor's companion; he enters the stage from nowhere. He welcomes and chats with the doctors and then, later on, he beats them and ushers them out. Though outside the storyline, the *waicheng* is not an onlooker; he is deeply involved in dialogue and interaction with the *yuanben* characters. See Hu Ji, *Song Jin zaju kao*, 73. For a translation of the segement, see "Appendix I: A Pair of Battling Quacks," in Wang Shifu, *The Moon and the Zither*, 417–28, in which *waicheng* is translated as "someone offstage (the stage manager?)." But from time to time the *waicheng* actually directly intervenes and pushes the action of the two quacks forward, and therefore it would be more reasonable for him to be onstage than offstage, especially at the end when the *waicheng* says "you fucking bastards, beat it," and the two quacks are "beaten off the stage" (428).

76. Liu Dui, *Xinbian Jintong yunü Jiao Hong ji* 新編金童玉女嬌紅記, 1453 ed.; reprint, *Guben xiqu congkan*, ser. 1, 9b. I thank Wilt Idema for calling my attention to this passage.
77. We can therefore insert the omitted "*zaju* exits" at the beginning of the direction. Moreover, very often in the *Jiao Hong ji*, the stage direction only mentions a *zaju* character, who a moment ago ushered in a *yuanben* digression, "enters" (*shang*) after the *yuanben* is finished, with the implication that he went offstage when the *yuanben* took over. In the other six instances where a *yuanben* is incorporated into the storyline rather than being as a play-within-a-play, three of them testify to this rule of abbreviation. For example, Shen Chun goes out and looks around the city. An unspecified *yuanben* set piece is then inserted at this point, supposedly to present the urban scenery he sees on the street. The play text reads: "[*Mo* enters (*shang*) and says] . . . It is still early. Let me go on the street to have fun for a while. [*Yuanben*. *Fu* and *wai* enter. Exeunt (*xia*). *Mo* enters (*shang*) and says] Having fun on the street, I didn't realize it's already that late. Time to go home." See Liu Dui, *Xinbian Jintong yunü Jiao Hong ji*, 34b. As Hu Ji argues, "after the line 'let me go on the street to have fun for a while,' the *mo* should go offstage; otherwise the ensuing direction '*mo* enters' would not make sense. If so, *when staged, this yuanben is entirely treated as another scene*" (emphases original). See Hu, *Song Jin zaju kao*, 213. This observation is applicable to the *yuanben* staged for Shen Chun by his future father-in-law.
78. Zhu Youdun, *Lü Dongbin huayue shenxian hui*, in *Maiwangguan chaojiao ben gujin zaju* 脈望館鈔校本古今雜劇, comp. Zhao Qimei 趙琦美, early seventeenth-century manuscript; reprint, *Guben xiqu congkan*, ser. 4 (Shanghai: Shangwu yinshuguan, 1958), vol. 37, 9a.
79. Idema points out that, according to the convention, there is always tension between "the persistent deliverer and the reluctant object of his attentions," but that this is "defused" or "entirely lacking" in *Congregation of Immortals*. Instead, the dramatic tension is created by "revers[ing] the conventional conflict and mak[ing] the deliverer reluctant to impart the truth." See Wilt Idema, *The Dramatic Oeuvre of Chu Yu-tun*, 90. That explains Zhennu's resistance to the allure of the entertainment staged by the immortals.
80. Zhu Youdun, *Lü Dongbin huayue shenxian hui*, 8b.
81. *The Mad Drummer* has been assigned four different dates: 1559; before 1562; 1573–75; and 1582–88. See Huang Jingxin 黃敬欽, "Tan Xu Wei *Sishengyuan* de sizhong bianxiang" 談徐渭《四聲猿》的四種變相, *Fengjia renwen shehui xuebao* 逢甲人文社會學報 3 (May 2001): 2 n. 5.
82. Yuming He, "Difficulties of Performance: The Musical Career of Xu Wei's *The Mad Drummer*," *Harvard Journal of Asiatic Studies* 68, no. 2 (December 2008): 89.

83. Xu Wei, *Kuanggu shi Yuyang sanlong*, in *Xinjuan gujin mingju leijiang ji* 新鐫古今名劇酹江集, ed. Meng Chengshun 孟稱舜, Chongzhen (1628–44), in *Xuxiu Siku quanshu*, 1764:333. I have provided my own translation to keep intact the motifs of watching and playing. For a full translation of the play, see Xu Wei, "The Mad Drummer Plays the Yuyang Triple Rolls," in Shiamin Kwa, *Strange Eventful Histories: Identity, Performance, and Xu Wei's Four Cries of a Gibbon* (Cambridge, MA: Harvard University Asia Center, 2012), 115–38.

84. "引子，須以自己之腎腸，代他人之口吻。蓋一人登場，必有幾句緊要說話，我設以身處其地，模寫其似。" See Wang Jide, *Wang Jide Qulü* 王驥德曲律, annot. Chen Duo 陳多 and Ye Changhai (Changsha: Hunan renmin chubanshe, 1983), 156.

85. For further discussions of Zhu Xi's position in this genealogy, see chapter 5, section 4.

86. For instance in Liu Lin 劉麟 (1474–1561), "Zhong qi tianen siqiu xiuzhi shu" 終乞天恩四求休致疏, in *Qinghui ji* 清惠集, in *Yingyin Wenyuange Siku quanshu* 景印文淵閣四庫全書 (Taipei: Taiwan Shangwu yinshuguan, 1986), 126:4.359; Hai Rui 海瑞 (1515–87), "Dufu tiaoyue" 督撫條約, in *Hai Rui ji* 海瑞集, ed. Chen Yizhong 陳義鍾, 2 vols. (Beijing: Zhonghua shuju, 1962), 1:254.

87. Jin Shengtan 金聖嘆, *Diwu caizishu Shi Nai'an Shuihu zhuan* 第五才子書施耐庵水滸傳 (Zhengzhou shi: Zhongzhou guji chubanshe, 1985), 1:246, 305, 313.

88. We have seen Wang Fuzhi's use of the idiom in his poetic discussion. See also Shen Deqian 沈德潛's 1764 *Qingshi biecai ji* 清詩別裁集 (Shijiazhuang: Hebei renmin chubanshe, 1997), 1:159.

89. Zhang Xuecheng 章學誠 (1738–1801), "Yangong xia" 言公下, in *Wenshi tongyi xinbian* 文史通義新編, ed. Cang Xiuliang 倉修良 (Shanghai: Shanghai guji chubanshe, 1993), 145.

90. Yun Yuding 惲毓鼎 (1862–1917), "Weiyushi dushu riji" 味腴室讀書日記, in *Yun Yuding Chengzhai riji* 惲毓鼎澄齋日記 (Hangzhou: Zhejiang guji chubanshe, 2004), 1:24.

91. For instance, Bao Yi 包儀, *Yi yuan jiuzheng* 易原就正, in *Yingyin Wenyuange Siku quanshu*, 43:5.32a; Yan Ruoqu 閻若璩 (1636–1704), *Shangshu guwen shuzheng* 尚書古文疏證 (Shanghai: Shanghai guji chubanshe, 1987), 1:5a.416; Jiao Yuanxi 焦袁熹 (1660–1735), *Chunqiu queru bian* 春秋闕如編, in *Yingyin Wenyuange Siku quanshu*, 177:4.18a; Huang Zhongsong 黃中松, *Shiyi bianzheng* 詩疑辨證, in *Yingyin Wenyuange Siku quanshu*, 88:1.64a.

92. "As we have no immediate experience of what other men feel, we can form no idea of the manner in which they are affected, but by conceiving what we ourselves should feel in the like situation. Though our brother is upon the rack, as long as we ourselves are at our ease, our senses will never inform us of what he suffers. They never did, and never can, carry us beyond our own person, and

it is by the imagination only that we can form any conception of what are his sensations. Neither can that faculty help us to this any other way, than by representing to us what would be our own, if we were in his case." See *The Theory of Moral Sentiment*, ed. Knud Haakonssen (Cambridge: Cambridge University Press, 2002), 1.

93. See James Chandler, "Moving Accidents: The Emergence of Sentimental Probability." In *The Age of Cultural Revolutions: Britain and France, 1750–1820*, ed. Colin Jones and Dror Wahrman (Berkeley: University of California Press, 2002), 138 n. 2. Two books on which Chandler bases his argument are especially useful in illustrating the relationship between this new notion of sympathy and commercialization: Albert O. Hirschman, *The Passions and the Interests* (Princeton: Princeton University Press, 1976) and J. G. A. Pocock, *Virtue, Commerce, and History* (Cambridge: Cambridge University Press, 1985).

94. Zhang Dai, *Tao'an mengyi/ Xihu mengxun*, 92. The book was finished some time around 1647. See Hu Yiming 胡益明, *Zhang Dai yanjiu* 張岱研究 (Hefei: Anhui jiaoyu chubanshe, 2004), 185.

95. Li Yu, *Xianqing ouji*, 63–64, 178. See also Prologue.

96. Ji Yun, *Yuewei caotang biji*閱微草堂筆記 (Beijing: Zhongguo wenlian chubanshe, 1996), *juan* 12, 241–42. Translation modified from Fei, *Chinese Theories of Theater*, 89–90.

97. Huang Fanchuo 黃旛綽 and Zhuang Zhaokui 莊肇奎, *Liyuan yuan* 梨園原, prefaced 1819, in *Zhongguo gudai xiqu lunzhu jicheng*, 9:11.

98. Sophie Volpp discusses the passionate attachment and empathetic resonance between actor and spectator that provided a model for literati sociability and readership. See *Worldly Stage*, 173–203, 254–58.

99. It is therefore no coincidence that Li Yu also distinguished himself as a connoisseur who stressed the visual aspect of performance and had a tendency to "pictorize" the world with framing devices in his arts of home decoration. See Patricia Sieber, "Seeing the World Through *Xianqing ouji* (1671): Visuality, Performance, and Narratives of Modernity," *Modern Chinese Literature and Culture* 12 (2000): 1–43.

100. Miaogu's mother mixes up categories of mother/husband and daughter/wife, but she does not transform into a bizarre body; rather, she is manipulated on the symbolic level by Tan, who induces her to play a mourning husband from that particular play and implies that as a good mother/actor she has to sympathetically overidentify with that husband role. The confusion is therefore at the symbolic rather than at the real (body) level. This point is further proved when we recall the issue of print: the confusion of symbolic categories conceived by Li Yu can never be embodied by anyone onstage; rather, it is visible only in the printed play text.

101. Wang Duanshu, foreword to *Bimuyu*, 107.
102. *Bimuyu*, 154. The first sentence of this quote has been modified from Hanan's translation of "An Actress Scorns Wealth," 184.
103. "An Actress Scorns Wealth," 183–84. In the actual staging of the play-within-a-play in *Sole Mates*, the simple design Li Yu prescribes would not allow for a real stream to flow past the little stage. So the play text directs the actress to jump off the little stage and then sneak back to the greenroom (*jitiao xiatai jie, qianxia* 急跳下台介，潛下). See *Bimuyu*, 157.
104. Aiyue zhuren 愛月主人, *Xi zhong xi, Bimuyu* 戲中戲．比目魚, eighteenth-century ed.; reprint, *Guben xiaoshuo jicheng*, ser. 2 (Shanghai: Shanghai guji chubanshe, 1990), 63:81.
105. For a discussion of the illustrations to the early editions of the play, see Wang Shipei 汪詩珮, "Tuxiang, xushi, duzhe fanying: lun Li Yu de 'Tan Chuyu' yu *Bimuyu*" 圖像、敘事、讀者反應：論李漁的〈譚楚玉〉與《比目魚》, *Zhongzheng daxue zhongwen xueshu niankan* 中正大學中文學術年刊 15 (June 2010): 111–48.
106. Liao Ben, *Zhongguo gudai juchang shi* 中國古代劇場史 (Zhengzhou: Zhongzhou guji chubanshe, 1997), 5.
107. Liao Ben's *Song Yuan xiqu wenwu yu minsu* has provided a detailed account of this (125–30).
108. Che Wenming 車文明, *Ershi shiji xiqu wenwu de faxian yu quxue yanjiu* 二十世紀戲曲文物的發現與曲學研究 (Beijing: Wenhua yishu chubanshe, 2001), 43, 47–48.
109. Joshua Goldstein, *Drama Kings: Players and Publics in the Re-creation of Peking Opera, 1870–1937* (Berkeley: University of California Press, 2007), 73. An earlier Chinese scholar expressed a similar opinion: "During a performance of Chinese opera, the onstage and offstage spaces were continual without separation. What is referred to here is reflected not only by the lighting that illuminated both on and off stage and therefore renders irrelevant the notion of the invisible 'fourth wall,' but also by the power of the audience in front of the stage to express at any time their likes and dislikes or even directly intervene the stage performance. The most common way for them to do so was uttering praise or booing. Taking one step further was *dacai* 打彩, which means throwing money or valuable things to the stage as direct encouragement to the actor, or conversely, throwing trash to vent the audience's discontents. Some places even prepared peanut hulls and cypress boughs so that they could be burnt to smoke away lousy performers." See Gao Qihua 高琦華, *Zhongguo xitai* 中國戲台 (Hangzhou: Zhejiang renmin chubanshe, 1996), 101.
110. Nowadays Peking operas are mostly performed on proscenium stage, although in some cases there is table seating reminiscent of the teahouse atmosphere.

See Alexandra B. Bonds, *Beijing Opera Costumes: The Visual Communication of Character and Culture* (Honolulu: University of Hawaii Press, 2008), 22. But some of the traditional temple theaters in Shanxi, Jiangxi, and Shaoxing towns and villages, for instance, are still being used by local communities.

111. Meng Yue, *Shanghai and the Edges of Empires* (Minneapolis: University of Minnesota Press, 2006), 71.
112. Che, *Ershi shiji xiqu wenwu*, 55.
113. Che, *Ershi shiji xiqu wenwu*, 60.
114. Hailing the subjectivity of Chinese spectatorship, Che deduces from it every aspect of traditional drama, which is dictated by the live audience's demand and modified in accordance with local reception; to compete with the tumultuous off-stage atmosphere for the audience's attention, performances featured vibrant colors, sonorous music, painted faces, exaggerated expressions, formulaic gestures, and stereotypical characterization; ultimately, it is the centrality of the spectator that explains every aspect of the expressive, symbolic, or "suppositional" aesthetic of Chinese performance (allegedly in contrast to Western realism) (55–56).
115. Judith Zeitlin, *Historian of the Strange: Pu Songling and the Chinese Classical Tale* (Stanford: Stanford University Press, 1993), 136, 138; Lynn Struve, "Self-Struggles of a Martyr: Memories, Dreams, and Obsessions in the Extant Diary of Huang Chunyao," *Harvard Journal of Asiatic Studies* 69, no. 2 (2009): 343–94; Stuve, "The Dreaming Mind and the End of the Ming World," presented at the Institute of East Asian Studies, University of California, Berkeley, February 8, 2012. Also see Philip A. Kafalas, *In Limpid Dream: Nostalgia and Zhang Dai's Reminiscences of the Ming* (Norwalk, CT: EastBridge, 2007).
116. This obscuration of theatricality by the dreamscape in the Chinese context will be ultimately explicated in chapter 5, section 3.
117. Li Yu, *Xianqing ouji*, 64; see also Prologue.
118. Sophie Volpp, *Worldly Stage*, 77–88. Correlated to the distance between audience and performer is the distance between (social) actors and their roles. See Stephen Owen, "'I Don't Want to Act as Emperor Any More': Finding the Genuine in *Peach Blossom Fan*," in *Trauma and Transcendence in Early Qing Literature*, ed. Wilt L. Idema, Wai-yee Li, and Ellen Widmer (Cambridge, MA: Harvard University Asia Center, 2006), 488–509.
119. The close connection between winds and the voice has been explained by their association with breath. See Owen, "The 'Great Preface,'" 41.
120. Liao, *Zhongguo gudai juchang shi*, 21. The way a roofless platform facilitates the direct communication with and emotive impact on the audience is exemplified by a public performance scene of the First Full-Moon Festival (*yuanxiao*) in Kaifeng, the early twelfth-century capital of the Northern Song: "Under the

[Xuande 宣德] Gate Tower was a roofless raised platform made of square wood pillars piling up" on which various groups of court entertainers took turns performing variety plays. While the emperor was enjoying a separate performance with his consorts on the top of the tower and behind curtains, "tens of thousands of commoners were watching [the variety plays] at the foot of the roofless stage, and the performers from time to time induced them to hurray [for his longevity]." See Meng Yuanlao 孟元老, *Dongjing meng Hua lu* 東京夢華錄 (Beijing: Zhonghua shuju, 2006), 2:542.

121. Chai Zejun 柴澤俊, "Song Jin wutai xingzhi kao" 宋、金舞台形制考, *Hedong xiqu wenwu yanjiu* 河東戲曲文物研究, ed. Fu Renjie 傅仁杰 and Xing Lexian 行樂賢 (Beijing: Xiju chubanshe, 1992), 49–50. The famous example of using a curtain to separate the backstage is provided by the mural on the southeast wall of the Water God's Temple of the Guangsheng Monastery depicting the 1324 performance given by the troupe of Zhong Duxiu 忠都秀, with "a curious back-stage attendant lifts the lower left corner of the curtain and peeps out at the audience." See Anning Jing, *The Water God's Temple of the Guangsheng Monastery: Cosmic Function of Art, Ritual, and Theater* (Leiden: Brill, 2002), 57.

122. "In effect, temple performance was staged to entertain gods. Performance had ever been oriented toward the main hall. Even previously when the stage had no wall at all, still it was not probable to truly realize four-side viewing. Adding a wall to it was therefore simply to comply with the fait accompli." See Liao, *Zhongguo gudai juchang shi*, 22.

123. A modern example of inviting gods from outside the temple is recorded in Willem A. Grooster, "Rural Temples around Hsuan Hua (South China), Their Iconography, and Their History," *Folklore Studies* 10, no. 1 (1951): 37–38.

124. One of the earliest accounts of this ceremony in the fourteenth century, ironically recorded by an official infamous for his harsh suppression of unofficial worship, provides extraordinary details about the case of the God of Putai Mountain 蒲臺山: "The God is received one day before [the ritual dramatic performance at the temple]. People of the six villages parade with ceremonial objects, leading the way with hanging banners, canopies, flags, cymbals, drums, and variety shows, which line up in incessant successions. This is so-called 'conjuring up the God' (*qishen*). The next day sacrifices, wines, and paper money are lavishly presented. Flutes and drums are played and actors present their talents . . . The sun sets, and people again parade. This time they call it 'seeing off the God' (*xiashen*)." See Lü Sicheng 呂思誠, "Putai shan Lingzhan Wang miaobei" 蒲臺山靈贍王廟碑, in Feng Junjie, ed., *Shanxi xiqu beike jikao* 山西戲曲碑刻輯考 (Beijing: Zhonghua shuju, 2002), 127–28. For modern examples receiving and seeing off gods, see Tanaka Issei, "Shinrei kōrin no enshū:

Chūgoku no ba'ai" 神霊降臨の演出――中国の場合, in *Matsuri wa kamigami no pafōmansu: Geinō o meguru Nihon to Higashi Ajia* 祭りは神々のパフォーマンス：芸能をめぐる日本と東アジア, ed. Moriya Takeshi 守屋毅 (Tokyo: Furiki shobō, 1987), 57–85; Johnson, *Spectacle and Sacrifice*, 247–53.

125. Che, *Ershi shiji xiqu wenwu*, 37.
126. Feng Junjie, *Shanxi shenmiao juchang kao* 山西神廟劇場考 (Beijing: Zhonghua shuju, 2006), 249.
127. Feng Junjie, *Shanxi shenmiao juchang kao*, 132–33.
128. Shanxi sheng kaogu yanjiushuo 山西省考古研究所, *Pingyang Jinmu zuandiao* 平陽金墓磚雕 (Taiyuan: Shanxi renmin chubanshe, 1999), 8–9.
129. Luo Deyin 羅德胤, *Zhongguo guxitai jianzhu* 中國古戲臺建築 (Nanjing: Dongnan daxue chubanshe, 2009), 27.
130. Jeehee Hong has also recently related Pan Dechong's sarcophagus to the earlier Jin tomb architecture and images as well as to actual passage stages later appearing in the Ming-Qing period. See Hong, *Theater of the Dead*, 105–35. But to her, all these materials in reference to actual or virtual performance reveal "a tangible sense of theatricality deeply inscribed in the lives of ordinary people during this time period." The main thrust of my argument here is precisely to redress this misrecgonition of dreamscapes as theatricality or vice versa. In question is not just a matter of labelling but a widespread misidentification of dreamers as spectators, which plays a significant role of the historical dynamic between the dreamscape and theatricality.
131. Che, *Ershi shiji xiqu wenwu*, 37–38.
132. Che, *Ershi shiji xiqu wenwu*, 49; Duan Jianhong 段建宏, *Xitai yu shehui: Ming Qing Shanxi xitai yanjiu* 戲台與社會：明清山西戲台研究 (Beijing: Zhongguo shehui kexue chubanshe, 2009), 48–49. Back in the Yuan dynasty, a commercial theater (*goulan* 勾欄) also had a "divine tower" (*shenlou* 神樓), functionally imitating the main hall of the temple theater. But it was not much higher than the audience seated around it. Besides, a balcony called the "dark dragon head" (*qinglongtou* 青龍頭) close to the exit door of the stage could be found in this kind of commercial theater, but again it was rather low and one could easily jump down to the stage. See the discussion in Liao, *Zhongguo gudai juchang shi*, 50–51.
133. See the comparison between temple theaters and teahouse theaters in Che, *Ershi shiji xiqu wenwu*, 48–49.
134. At the turn of the twentieth century, however, mixed seating for men and women appeared in some cities' teahouses, although a Shanghai theater would still insist on gender segregation as late as 1907. See Paola Iovene, "Chinese Opera on Stage and Screen: A Short Introduction," *Opera Quarterly* 6, no. 2 (Fall 2010): 14 n. 3.

135. Aoki Masaru 青木正兒, *Shina kinsei gikyokushi* 支那近世戲曲史 (Tokyo: Kōbundō Shobō, 1955), 803–5. Adrea S. Goldman observes that "even though the commercial theater brought together audiences of the disparate social and occupational backgrounds, status and economic standing within the playhouse were still markedly differentiated by the type of seat purchased." See Goldman, *Opera and the City: The Politics of Culture in Beijing, 1770–1900* (Stanford: Stanford University Press, 2012), 78–79.
136. Shen Taimou, "Xuannan lingmeng lu" 宣南零夢錄, in *Qingdai Yandu liyuan shiliao* 清代燕都梨園史料, ed. Zhang Cixi 張次溪 (Beijing: Zhongguo xiju chubanshe, 1988), 809; also quoted in Che, *Ershi shiji xiqu wenwu*, 54.
137. Laikwan Pang, *The Distorting Mirror: Visual Modernity in China* (Honolulu: University of Hawaii Press, 2007), 141.
138. A platform for women was constructed around 1478. Two early Qing temple theaters with balconies built around 1645–1661 and 1662–1722 seated special guests in the worship hall and on the platform, respectively. A 1719 temple theater features a simplified passage stage without balconies. Women were seated in front of the main hall, surrounded by low walls, while important figures were seated on a temporary platform in front of the stage. See Feng Junjie, *Shanxi shenmiao juchang kao*, 163, 249, 257, 329. In his book *A Residence among the Chinese* published in 1857, Robert Fortune reported a temporary theater built "in the dry beds of streams," presumably without balconies, and his observation of the relationship between the privileged audience seated on the platform and the public standing on the ground around gives a sense of union rather than segregation: "The subscribers or those who gave the play, had a raised platform placed about twenty yards from the front of the stage, for themselves and their friends. The public occupied the ground in the front and sides of the stage, and to them the whole was free as their mountain air, each man, however poor, had as good a right to be there as his neighbour." Quoted in A. C. Scott, *The Classical Theatre of China* (London: Allen & Unwin, 1957), 220.

4. "NOT EVEN CLOSE TO EMOTION": A GENEALOGY OF KNOWLEDGE

1. "[Theodore] Jennings describes ritual as first of all, a display to an observer (god, theorist, etc.) or observers (the community itself) and, second, as an epistemological project.... We need not castigate our pursuit of the meaning of ritual as 'voyeurism or whoring,' Jennings asserts, since our cognitive concerns are simply an 'extension' of those of the ritual we are 'invited' to watch." Bell, *Ritual Theory, Ritual Practice*, 29.

2. See also Pierre Bourdieu, *Outline of a Theory of Practice*, trans. Richard Nice (Cambridge: Cambridge University Press, 1977), 1. As Bourdieu points out, " 'participant' anthropology" does "never more than the inversion of the false objectification performed by colonial anthropology"—namely, "cutting practices off from their real conditions of existence, in order to credit them with alien intentions" (115).
3. "The posture as seen by the audience is my Distant View (*waga riken* わが離見). But what my eyes (*waga manako* わが眼) see is just my subjective view (*gaken* 我見); it is not something seen with the Vision of a Distant View (*riken no ken*). To see with the Vision of a Distant View is, in effect, to see with the same mind as the audience does. . . . For this reason, you need to present a graceful posture through the entire body by seeing with the Vision of a Distant View, taking on the same vision as the audience and learning how you look in places where you cannot yourself see." Zeami, "Kakyō," in *Zeami shū*, 198–99; "A Mirror to the Flower," in *Zeami: Performance Notes*, trans. Tom Hare (New York: Columbia University Press, 2008), 103. Zeami, "Kakyō," in *Zeami shū* 世阿弥集, ed. Konishi Jin'ichi 小西甚一 (Tokyo: Chikuma Shobō, 1974), 198–99; "A Mirror to the Flower," in *Zeami: Performance Notes*, trans. Tom Hare (New York: Columbia University Press, 2008), 103, translation modified.
4. Claude Lévi-Strauss, *The View from Afar*, trans. Joachim Neugroschel and Phoebe Hoss (New York: Basic, 1985).
5. "This title is taken from the Japanese and came to me when I was reading Zeami, the creator of the Noh theater. He says that in order to be a good actor it is necessary to know how to look at oneself the way the audience does, and he uses the expression 'seen from afar.' I found that it summed up the anthropologist's attitude looking at his own society, not as a member inside it but as other observers would see it, looking at it from far off in either time or space." See Claude Lèvi-Strauss and Didier Eribon, *Conversations with Claude Lévi-Strauss*, trans. Paula Wissing (Chicago: The University of Chicago, 1991), 181.
6. Antony Tatlow, *Shakespeare, Brecht, the Intercultural Sign* (Durham: Duke University Press, 2001), 1.
7. See, for instance, Takeyoshi Nishiuchi, "Zeami's Riken and Gadamer's Spiel: A Comparative Analysis of the Bodily Performative Subjectivity," *Proceedings of the Midwest Association for Japanese Literary Studies* 1 (Summer 1995): 54–60.
8. "By excitement, what I mean is what startles minds and eyes in its unexpectedness. In the effect of excitement reside the immediacy to the occasion (*sokuza* 即座), immediacy to the heart (*sokushin* 即心), and immediacy to the eyes (*sokumoku* 即目). When the *ki* has been shifted, the so-called visual excitement of a Distant View will come into being." Zeami, "Goi," in *Zeami shū*, 280; "Five Ranks," in *Zeami: Performance Notes*, 189–90, translation modified.

9. Zeami, "Goi," 280; "Five Ranks," 190, translation modified.
10. In the same treatise, coupling the effect of excitement that somehow stresses the visual aspect is the effect of sound (*seifū* 声風). And another famous passage from the "Great Preface"—"Feelings come forth in the voice, the voice forms a pattern, and one calls this a sound" 情發于聲, 聲成文謂之音—is cited to illustrate how "the excitement of sound will penetrate the mind's ear." See Zeami, "Goi," 281; "Five Ranks," 191. On another occasion, Zeami explains *fū/feng* by citing the *Commentary on the Collected Japanese Poetry of Ancient and Present Times* (*Kokin wakashū chū* 古今和歌集注): "Although neither its form nor its substance is visible, it is concurrent with the phenomenon in question and thus is regarded of as an effect thereof." See "Riku gi" 六義, 297; "Six Models," 199.
11. Andrew T. Tsubaki, "Zeami and the Transition of the Concept of *Yūgen*: A Note on Japanese Aesthetics," *Journal of Aesthetics and Art Criticism* 30, no. 1 (Fall 1971): 55–67; William R. LaFleur, *The Karma of Words: Buddhism and the Literary Arts in Medieval Japan* (Berkeley: University of California Press, 1986), 130–31.
12. Zeami, "Kakyō," 198–99; "A Mirror to the Flower," 103, translation modified. I read *toku* 得 here as the loan character for *toku* 德.
13. Zeami, "Kakyō," 215; "A Mirror to the Flower," 112–13. See also the lucid elaboration of this particular section in Shelly Fenno Quinn, *Developing Zeami: The Noh Actor's Attunement in Acting* (Honolulu: University of Hawaii Press, 2005), 84–88.
14. Zeami, "Kakyō," 223; "A Mirror to the Flower," 117, translation modified: "one does not reply in the slightest on the techniques of performance but aspires to a visual style that reaches the rank of no-mind and no-style—isn't this what constitutes these wondrous places? I would venture to say that the virtuosic fulfillment of *yūgen* in one's manner of expression must be fairly close to these wondrous places."
15. As Tom Hare notes: "[*Riken no ken*] . . . may be read as both concrete and abstract, concrete referring to the actor's body as perceived from front, sides, and back, and abstract as a vision transcending consciousness, linking the actor and audience in a state of wonder. . . . When [*riken no ken*] first appears, it refers to simply the perspective of the audience on the actor's performance, especially in visual terms. It appears later, however, in the description of the top of the Nine Ranks, in a somewhat puzzling way linked with an aesthetic wonder transcending not only vision but also consciousness itself." See glossary to *Zeami: Performance Notes*, 491. What should be added is that even in "A Mirror to the Flower," where *riken no ken* first appears, this puzzling juxtaposition of the "concrete" and "abstract" senses of the term is already established, however indirectly, through the term's association with *yūgen*.

16. Zeami, "Kyūi chū" 九位注, in *Zeami shū*, 288; "Nine Ranks," in *Zeami: Performance Notes*, 193, translation modified.
17. Zeami, "Goi," 280; "Five Ranks," 190, where the quote is given in a fuller form: "There where the path of language is severed, where one cannot fathom the principle, and the locus of thinking is destroyed; that is 'wondrous'" 言語道斷，不思議，心行所滅之処，謂之妙. *The Tendai Interpretation of "Wondrous"* Zeami alludes to has been lost. But "the path of language severed, the locus of thinking destroyed" (with a slight textual difference in the Chinese original that gives *chu* 處 rather than *suo* 所) is a frequently seen couplet in Buddhist literature, traceable to *Foshuo huashou jing* 佛說華手經, trans. Kumārajīva, in *Taishō shinshū Daizōkyō* 大正新脩大藏經, ed. Takakusu Junjirō 高楠順次郎 and Watanabe Kaigyoku 渡邊海旭 (Tokyo: Taishō Issaikyō Kankōkai, 1924–1932), 16:168.
18. For the meaning of *mushin* 無心 in Zeami, see Quinn, *Developing Zeami*, 232–36. The oxymoron *yahan nittō* 夜半日頭 was popular in Chinese Chan Buddhism, starting from Dahui Zonggao 大慧宗杲 (1089–1163). See *Dahui Zonggao zushi yulu* 大慧宗杲祖師語錄, in *Taishō shinshū Daizōkyō*, 47:838. It appeared in the thirteenth-century Japanese Zen text *Chūshinkyō* 注心經, which Zeami probably consulted. See *Zeami: Performance Notes*, 193 n. 2.
19. Zeami, "Yūgaku shudō fūken," in *Zeami shū*, 275–76; "An Effective Vision of Learning the Vocation of Fine Play in Performance," in *Zeami: Performance Notes*, 185–86, translation modified.
20. This is actually what the original discussion of *riken* (Chinese: *lijian*) implies in the *Shurangama Sūtra*, which I believe is the source of Zeami's notion: "When you see your seeing, the seeing is not this seeing [that is being seen]. Since the [former] seeing is beyond the [latter] seeing, the [latter] seeing cannot reach it." 見見之時，見非是見。見猶離見，見不能及。See *Da Foding Rulai miyin xiuzheng liaoyi zhu pusa wanxing shoulengyan jing* 大佛頂如來密因脩證了義諸菩薩萬行首楞嚴經, trans. Pramiti, in *Taishō shinshū Daizōkyō*, 19:113; translation is modified from *The Shurangama Sutra, with Commentary by the Venerable Master Hsuan Hua*, trans. Buddhist Text Translation Society (Burlingame, CA.: Buddhist Text Translation Society, 2003), 2:163–64.
21. "[When you the actor have attained the peak of expertise,] so that your form of expression on the occasion of performance is inexplicably interesting and the audience loses itself in your wondrous appearance; from *the sound vantage point of later reflection, they will then put together in their thoughts all these things that have only now become apparent in their vision separate from vision.* The excitement aroused from your artistic experience in its bones would mean that no matter whatever they look at there isn't a weak spot; the excitement aroused from your artistic experience in its meat would mean that whatever

they look at proves boundless; and the excitement aroused from your artistic experience in its skin would mean that whatever they look at shows *yūgen*." Zeami, "Shikadō," in *Zeami shū*, 148–49. "A Course to Attain the Flower," in *Zeami: Performance Notes*, 135–36, translation modified. In the audience's reflection, images of the performance are put together in such a way that they are no longer viewed from one singular perspective; rather, the composite images provide a virtual, complete form whose perfection can be examined and confirmed from whatever angle is taken in the audience's thought.

22. See Tom Hare, glossary to *Zeami: Performance Notes*, 485.
23. Steven T. Brown, *Theatricalities of Power: The Cultural Politics of Noh* (Stanford: Stanford University Press, 2001), 22–30.
24. See, for instance, Takeyoshi Nishiuchi, "Zeami's Riken and Gadamer's Spiel: A Comparative Analysis of the Bodily Performative Subjectivity," *Proceedings of the Midwest Association for Japanese Literary Studies* 1 (Summer 1995): 54–60.
25. See Paul Ricoeur, *Time and Narrative*, vol. 3, trans. Kathleen Blamey and David Pellauer (Chicago: University of Chicago Press, 1988), 116–26.
26. This complete structure of theatricality will be illuminated in chapter 5, section 3.
27. Tina Lu, *Persons, Roles, and Minds*, 50–51.
28. This aporia of theatricality will be further analyzed as heightening the primordial aporia of spatiality per se, through which the interplay between the dreamscape and theatricality can be further clarified. See chapter 5, section 4.
29. Wen Gehong 文革紅, *Qingdai qianqi tongsu xiaoshuo kanke kaolun* 清代前期通俗小說刊刻考論 (Nanchang: Jiangxi renmin chubanshe, 2008), 472. According to Kwŏn Sŏp's 權燮 *Oksogo* 玉所稿 (dated 1749), the novel had been translated into Korean and circulated in manuscript by 1712. See Suyoung Son, "Transmitting *Haoqiu zhuan* in Eighteenth-Century Chosŏn Korea," *East Asian Publishing and Society* 3 (2013): 3–30.
30. In 1713–1714, Arcade Hoange (Huang Risheng 黃日升, 1679–1716), who served as the Chinese translator and librarian for Louis XIV at the time, rendered into French another scholar-beauty novel, *Yu Jiao Li* 玉嬌梨. But he stopped at chapter 3 of the novel, adding only a couple of poems from chapters 6 and 9. See Xu Minglong 許明龍, *Huang Jialue yu zaoqi Faguo Hanxue* 黃嘉略與早期法國漢學 (Beijing: Zhonghua shuju, 2004), 93–94, 229, 285; Patricia Sieber, "The Imprint of the Imprints: Sojourners, Xiaoshuo Translations, and the Transcultural Canon of Early Chinese Fiction in Europe, 1697–1826," *East Asian Publishing and Society* 3 (2013): 31–71.
31. Preface to *Hau Kiou Choaan or The Pleasing History*, trans. James Wilkinson, ed. Thomas Percy (London: Printed for R. and J. Dodsley, 1761), 1:xi, xix, xvii,

my italics. Hereafter references to this title are indicated with the abbreviation "P" followed by volume and page numbers in parentheses.
32. Johann Wolfgang von Goethe, *Conversations with Eckerman, 1823–1832*, trans. John Oxenford (San Francisco: North Point Press, 1984), 132.
33. Eric A. Blackall, "Goethe and the Chinese Novel," in *The Discontinuous Tradition: Studies in German Literature in Honour of Ernest Ludwig Stahl*, ed. P. F. Ganz (Oxford: Oxford University Press, 1971), 29–53; Tan Yuan 譚淵, "*Haoqiu zhuan de zaoqi xiwen yiben chutan*" 《好逑傳》的早期西文譯本初探, *Zhongguo fanyi* 中國翻譯 26, no. 3 (May 2005), 47–51.
34. Goethe, *Conversations with Eckermann*, 133.
35. Yet David Damrosch also points out that Germany at that time was so disunited, subaltern, and lagging behind as a power that Goethe was prone to being open to foreign cultures. See *What Is World Literature?* (Princeton: Princeton University Press, 2003), 1–14.
36. Qian Zhongshu, "China in the English Literature of the Eighteenth Century," in *The Vision of China in the English Literature of the Seventeenth and Eighteenth Centuries*, ed. Adrian Hsia (Hong Kong: Chinese University Press, 1998), 181–89. It has been noticed that by the beginning of the eighteenth century, "less favorable accounts came from navigators and traders, particularly the Dutch and the English, who were not interested in learning Chinese or accommodating Chinese culture and, accordingly, were far less successful than the Jesuits in gaining entrance to the court and comprehending Chinese ways of doing business." See Marcia Reed, "A Perfume Is Best from Afar: Publishing China for Europe," in *China on Paper: European and Chinese Works from the Late Sixteenth to the Early Nineteenth Century*, ed. Marcia Reed and Paola Demartte (Los Angeles: Getty Research Institute, 2007), 18–19.
37. David Porter explains Percy's contradictory appraisals of China by referring to his conflicting desires "to identify closely with Chinese culture" and "to reaffirm his identity as a Christian" and "as an English writer." Porter further suggests that "the degree of enthusiasm and disdain that animates many of [Percy's] comments on Chinese culture belies his framing assertions of both anthropological objectivity and amateur nonchalance." See Porter, *The Chinese Taste in Eighteenth-Century England* (Cambridge: Cambridge University Press, 2010), 168, 172. I would like to provide another explanation by focusing on how the epistemological frame of "anthropological objectivity," instead of being belied, actually underlies his split identification.
38. Qian, "China in the English Literature," 188.
39. To Chi-Ming Yang, the Orientalist attitude toward China in the eighteenth century is far more complex than downright denigration; rather, the British spectators were more in awe of and confused by the Chinese exemplar of morals,

wealth, and extravagance. See *Performing China: Virtue, Commerce, and Orientalism in Eighteenth-Century England, 1660–1760* (Baltimore: John Hopkins University, 2011). Sieber also calls our attention to the agency of Chinese scholars in making selections of such Chinese novels as *Yu Jiao Li* and *Haoqiu zhuan* for European consumption ("The Imprint of the Imprints," 64–65).

40. At issue is therefore not ethnocentrism per se but how the ethnic differences were constructed by way of the order-disorder doublet in the first place. Percy's case is definitely more complex than the usual Saidian "Orientalist" charge against Western scholars studying the Middle East would have it, because instead of simply constructing China as a despicable Other, the order-disorder discourse with which Percy interpreted the *Haoqiu zhuan* was also applied to his project of compiling ancient English poetry a few years later. On one hand, just as he attempted to extract the Chinese cultural system from the *Haoqiu zhuan*, he looked for distinct native "customs" in his reading of English poetry. On the other hand, Percy implicitly took the elaborate Chinese order that harbored drastic disorder as the inverted, mirror image of ancient England that was comparatively backward yet simplistically beautiful. See Eun Kyung Min, "Thomas Percy's Chinese Miscellanies and the Reliques of Ancient English Poetry," *Eighteenth-Century Studies* 43, no. 3 (Spring 2010): 307–24.

41. Tang Chenxi, "Writing World History: The Emergence of Modern Global Consciousness in the Late Eighteenth Century (1760–1790)," Ph.D. diss., Columbia University, 2000, 107–232.

42. Michel Foucault, *Introduction to Kant's Anthropology*, trans. Robert Nigro and Kate Briggs (Los Angeles: Semiotext(e), 2008), 69–85, 93–103. This anthropological turn of knowledge, however, caused an immense epistemological confusion by assigning mankind the transcendental status. As an "anthropological illusion," the "human" as an unsustainable "empirico-transcendental doublet" is famously said to be dying in Foucault's *The Order of Things: An Archaeology of the Human Sciences* (New York: Vintage, 1994), 381–87. It has been pointed out that the same illusion haunts even Foucault's own working categories as the reincarnation of the transcendental. See Béatrice Han, *Foucault's Critical Project: Between the Transcendental and the Historical*, trans. Edward Pile (Stanford: Stanford University Press, 2002). What has received little attention, however, is that alongside the empirico-transcendental doublet we find the "order-disorder doublet" at the politico-epistemological level. Consecrated as the ultimate source, object, and possibility of knowledge, the finitude of human existence as a whole is now captured in its fallibility, deployed in time and within the limits of language. Hence neurosis outlines the structure of psyche (Freud), the state of exception defines politics (Schmitt), and aphasia holds out

the key to language (Jacobson). We see collapse wherever we pursue order; only in madness do we find the chilly contour of rationality.

43. Jonathan Gil Harris, "Historicizing Greenblatt's 'Containment': The Cold War, Functionalism, and the Origins of Social Pathology," in *Critical Self-Fashioning: Stephen Greenblatt and the New Historicism*, ed. Jürgen Pieters (Frankfurt: Peter Lang, 1999), 150–73.

44. Claude Lèvi-Strauss and Georges Charbonnier, "Clocks and Steam Engines," in *Conversations with Claude Lèvi-Strauss*, trans. John and Doreen Weightman (London: Jonathan Cape, 1970), 40–41.

45. Lèvi-Strauss, "Clocks and Steam Engines," 41: "Primitive peoples produce very little order by means of their culture. . . . But they produce very little entropy in their societies. . . . The civilized peoples, on the other hand, produce a great deal of order in their culture, as is shown by mechanization and by the great achievements of civilization, but they also produce a great deal of entropy in their societies."

46. Claude Lèvi-Strauss, *Tristes Tropiques*, trans. John and Doreen Weightman (New York: Penguin, 1992), 413–14.

47. Marshall Sahlins, *Islands of History* (Chicago: The University of Chicago Press, 1985), xi, xiii, 72.

48. Sahlins, *Islands of History*, xi, xiii, 72.

49. Michel Foucault, *History of Madness*, trans. Jean Khalfa (New York: Routledge, 2006), 522–28.

50. Inspired by the didactic message of the novel, one modern editor writes: "The most reasonable marriage should be the one that combines both blind marriage and free love: the two parties should be introduced to each other by their parents, and the complete consent from the former is also required; if the two parties know each other first, they must still go through the parents, who have the final say. If every couple ties the knot as discreetly as Tie Zhongyu and Shui Bingxin do, there is no reason for them not to enjoy eternal love and intimacy." Mingjiao zhong ren 名教中人, *Tianzuo zhi he* 天作之合, ed. Li Yutian 李毓田 (Hong Kong: Dahua shudian, 1959), 4. Another editor attacks the novel's ideology as feudalistic and challenges Goethe's value judgment. See Mingjiao zhong ren, *Haoqiu zhuan* (Taipei: Heluo tushu chubanshe, 1980), 10.

51. Richard C. Hessney, "Beyond Beauty and Talent: The Moral and Chivalric Self in *The Fortunate Union*," in *Expressions of Self in Chinese Literature*, ed. Robert E. Hegel and Richard C. Hessney (New York: Columbia University Press, 1985), 214–50.

52. Martin Huang, *Desire and Fictional Narrative in Late Imperial China* (Cambridge, MA: Harvard University Asia Center, 2001), 229–35.

53. Caddeau, *Appraising Genji: Literary Criticism and Cultural Anxiety in the Age of the Last Samurai* (Albany: State University of New York Press, 2006), 44–45.
54. Kyokutei Bakin, *Bakin shokan shūsei* 馬琴書翰集成, ed. Shibata Mitsuhiko 柴田光彦 and Kanda Masayuki 神田正行 (Tōkyō: Yagi Shoten, 2002–2004), 1.273; Isobe Yūko 磯部祐子, "Guanyu Zhongguo caizi jiaren xiaoshuo zai Dong Ya chuanbo de tezheng: Yi *Erdu mei* yu *Haoqiu zhuan* wei zhuyao kaocha duixiang" 關於中國才子佳人小說在東亞傳播的特徵：以《二度梅》與《好逑傳》為主要考察對象, *Shanghai shifan daxue xuebao* 上海師範大學學報 34, no. 1 (January 2005): 49.
55. Satō Haruo 佐藤春夫, "*Gokyūden* jo" 好逑伝叙, *Teihon Satō Haruo zenshū* 定本佐藤春夫全集, ed. Nakamura Shin'ichirō 中村真一郎 et al. (Kyōto: Rinsen Shoten, 2001), 34:171.
56. Isobe Yūko, "Chūgoku saishi kajin shōsetsu no eikyō: Bakin no baai" 中国才子佳人小説の影響——馬琴の場合, *Takaoka tanki daikoku kiyō* 高岡短期大學紀要 18 (March 2003): 223–33.
57. For a revisionist genealogy that traces the motif of women warriors in Chinese cinema to American serial queen thrillers and thus challenges the quintessential "Chinese" character of martial arts films, see Weihong Bao, "From Pearl White to White Rose Woo: Tracing the Vernacular Body of *Nüxia* in Chinese Silent Cinema, 1927–1931," *Cinema Obscura* 60 (2005): 192–231.
58. See Chen Pingyuan 陳平原, *Qiangu wenren xiake meng* 千古文人俠客夢 (Beijing: Beijing daxue chubanshe, 1992), 42–59; John Christopher Hamm, *Paper Swordsmen: Jin Yong and the Modern Chinese Martial Arts Novel* (Honolulu: University of Hawai'i Press, 2006), 49–78.
59. C. T. Hsia, *The Classical Chinese Novel: A Critical Introduction* (Ithaca, NY: Cornell University Press, 1996), 106, 114.
60. Roland Altenburger describes the female knight-errant in a seventeenth-century Chinese tale "as both a unofficial guardian of social order and as a potential source of disorder," leaving her male observer in the story "torn between desire and anxiety." See *The Sword or the Needle: The Female Knight-errant* (xia) *in Traditional Chinese Narrative* (New York: Peter Lang, 2009), 182.
61. A similar ambiguity can be found in the medieval and Renaissance European code of chivalry inextricably tied up with the potential of transgression. The new historicism tends to make sense of this order-disorder paradox with the model of "containment," which we have seen is based on an understanding of human existence constantly corrupted by time. In Elizabethan England, the chaos of chivalry was alleged to be aggravated by the aging of the Virgin Queen. See Eric S. Mallin, *Inscribing the Time: Shakespeare and the End of Elizabethan England* (Berkeley: University of California, 1997), 39–44.

62. Mingjiao zhongren, *Haoqiu zhuan*, 1863 Duchuzhai 獨處齋 edition, chapter 2, 8a. Hereafter references to this edition are indicated with the abbreviation "H" followed by chapter and page numbers in parentheses.
63. Lin Yizheng 林義正, *Chunqiu Gongyang lunli siwei yu tezhi* 春秋公羊倫理思維與特質 (Taipei: Guoli Taiwan daxue chuban zhongxin, 2003), 136–55.
64. Kyokutei Bakin, *Kaikan kyōki kyōkakuden*, ed. Yokoyama Kuniharu 橫山波治 and Ōtaka Yōji 大高洋司 (Tokyo: Iwanami Shoten, 1998), book 1, 5. Hereafter references to this edition are indicated with the abbreviation "K" followed by book and page numbers in parentheses.
65. As Koroku explains, "Although cheating one's parents with trickery is close to deceit and a deed of sinfulness, such guile is for the sake of the parents and is not alien from sincere thought—this is an expedient maneuver. Expediency is like the sliding weight of a steelyard. A heavy weight hanging there certainly makes it heavy; a light weight hanging there certainly makes it light. A man who deploys such expediency never inflexibly sticks to the rules but adapts to contingency for what is appropriate" (K2.155).
66. The foreign ritual, deviant from native custom (*fūzoku ōi ni sogo* 風俗大に齟齬), appears so awkwardly in the story that Hiromichi apologizes to the readers in his afterword (K5.709).
67. *The Fortunate Union*, trans. John Francis Davis (London: Printed for the Oriental Translation Fund, 1829). Hereafter references to this translation are indicated with the abbreviation "F" followed by chapter and page numbers in parentheses.
68. This is either due to the liberty the Wilkinson-Percy edition takes in abridging the text, especially in the lyric parts, or to a slightly truncated Chinese version that shortens the original poem. The undated truncated version, also from the same publisher, Duchuzhai, has been reproduced in *Guben xiaoshuo jicheng*, ser. 4, 43:79.
69. Y. W. Ma, "The Knight-errant in *Hua-pen* Stories," *T'oung pao* 61 (1975): 276.
70. There is even a tendency in Davis to smooth out any details in the novel that seem to suggest some flexibility in the rule of segregation of the sexes. For instance, in chapter 3, when a magistrate pays a visit to Bingxin, Davis feels he needs to provide the readers with an explanation: "This may appear a violation of the strict seclusion of females in China: but the Chehëen had a magisterial right to make such a visit which an indifferent person could not have assumed; and this visit would of course be made under the usual restrictions and formalities, a screen being interposed, and the lady being heard, but not seen." But Davis continues with a proviso that undermines the strictness of the Chinese custom he has just tried to reconfirm: "They will sometimes depart from their strict rules in favour even of strangers; and Englishmen have occasionally

been allowed the honour of a visit to ladies of some consideration, when they allowed themselves not only to be heard, but seen too" (F1.53).

71. As we know, this is the scene that left a deep impression on Goethe about Chinese virtue. But the entire setup, constructed by Bingxin, serves only to enable her to see Zhongyu clearly, while he cannot see her at all, hence promoting her voyeuristic pleasure rather than "severe moderation."
72. It is in this marginal figure of voyeuristic thief cum moral messenger, along with the numerous long discourses saturating the novel, that we see the uncanny similarity to chapter 4 of Li Yu's 1670 pornographic novel *Rou putuan* 肉蒲團, 204–9.
73. "Don't say 'break-in' must not be a nice business;/Without it, how can we distinguish chastity from lewdness?" 莫道鑽窺非美事，不然何以別貞淫 (H7.5a). The irony is that the admonition against "breaking-in" (*zuan gui*) is pronounced on the very first page of the novel: "Get rid of any thought of 'break-in,'/And then you will make a good couple" 但須不作鑽窺想，便是人間好唱隨 (H1.1a).
74. Recent discussions of the eighteenth-century cult of chastity through the documents of legal cases have unearthed a picture of conflicting interests, motivations, negotiations, and shifting points of resistance under the umbrella term "chastity." See Janet M. Theiss, *Disgraceful Matters: The Politics of Chastity in Eighteenth-Century China* (Berkeley: University of California Press, 2004).
75. Giovanni Vitiello, "Exemplary Sodomites: Chivalry and Love in Late Ming Culture," *Nan nü* 2, no. 2 (2000): 237–43.
76. The locus classicus on expediency in the *Gongyang Commentary to the Spring and Autumn Annals* is the story of Ji Zhong 祭仲, who deposed his lord Duke Zhao of Zheng 鄭昭公. See *Chunqiu Gongyang zhuan*, 春秋公羊傳, in *Sibu beiyao* 四部備要, 5.5b–6a.
77. "今若到底能成全，則前之義俠，皆屬有心。" (H14.13a).
78. Martin Heidegger, *Being and Time*, trans. Joan Stambaugh (Albany: State University of New York Press, 1996), 302.
79. Maurice Merleau-Ponty, *Phenomenology of Perception*, trans. Colin Smith (London: Routledge & Kegan Paul Ltd., 1962), 448.
80. Ricoeur, *Time and Narrative*, 3:133, 255.
81. For details, see Tokumaru Satoko 得丸智子, "Komahime no adauchi: *Kyōkaku den* no jokyōron" 姑摩姫の仇討――『俠客伝』の女俠論, in *Yomihon kenkyū shinsho* 読本研究新集, ed. Yomihon kenkyū no kai 読本研究の会 (Tokyo: Kanrin Shobō, 1998), 1:165–84.
82. Kurohime does not specify which swordswomen in China she is invoking; instead, she continues by citing a male figure, Huang Gong 黃公 of the Eastern Sea in the Han Dynasty, who had the skill of subduing tigers when he was

young, but was eventually killed in action when he became too old to practice this skill (K3.323). Kurohime seems to imply that Chinese swordswomen had been more prudent and cautious than Huang Gong in not performing their magic twice. That is obviously not the case until the *Haoqiu zhuan* introduces the unprecedented consciousness of diachronically correlating the female knight-errant's expedient acts. Therefore, behind Kurohime's unspecified swordswomen stands the new mode of expediency represented by Bingxin.

83. Henceforth Komahime, whose life is spared thanks to Itsukyu's petition for the shogun's mercy, is placed under house arrest under the surveillance of her estranged uncle, and the story returns from magic fantasy to the mundane world of the *Haoqiu zhuan*, where the female *xia/kyō* does not play with flying swords but fights by outwitting her enemies over the matter of marriage; it is this latter concern that occupies most of the last two books of *Daring Adventures*. Bakin and later his successor Hiromichi, as well as the publisher, repeatedly advertised the long-delayed meeting between Komahime and Koroku, reminiscent of the encounter between Bingxin and Zhongyu, as the major attraction of the work (K3.423, 4.584, 5.714), but the meeting was repeatedly postponed until the end of the incomplete *Daring Adventures*, as attention was drawn to the changed career of Komahime.

84. It has been argued that *Daring Adventures* endorses the notion of "the Southern Court Orthodoxy" (*Nanchō seitō ron* 南朝正統論) with a tragic turn—this was a dominant view from the eighteenth century to the turn of the twentieth century. See Tokuda Takeshi 徳田武, "Go Nanchō hiwa: Teishō, Bakin, Shōyō" 後南朝悲話—庭鐘. 馬琴. 逍遙—, in *Nihon kinsei shōsetsu to Chūgoku shōsetsu* 日本近世小説と中国小説 (Musashimurayama-shi: Seishōdō Shoten, 1987). In this view, Bakin of course has to find a way to explain why, almighty as she is, Komahime still fails to change the course of history. It is interesting to see how this purpose can be fulfilled by the introduction of ecstatic temporality to the female knight-errant's expediency.

85. Charlotte Furth, "Thinking with Cases," in *Thinking with Cases: Specialist Knowledge in Chinese Cultural History*, ed. Charlotte Furth, Judith T. Zeitlin, and Ping-chen Hsiung (Honolulu: University of Hawaii Press, 2007), 6–14.

86. Li Jingde, *Zhuzi yulei*, 3:17.989. See also Lin Weijie 林維杰, "Zhixing yu jingquan: Zhu Xi zhexue de quanshixue moshi fenxi" 知行與經權——朱熹哲學的詮釋學模式分析, *Zhongguo wenzhe yanjiu jikan* 中國文哲研究集刊 27 (September 2005): 185–213.

87. *Zhuzi yulei*, 989.

88. Robert Hymes, "Some Thoughts on 'Thinking in Cases' in the Song," paper presented to the conference "Thinking with Cases: Specialist Knowledge in Chinese Cultural History," University of Chicago, October 12–14, 2001.

89. Pierre-Étienne Will, "Developing Forensic Knowledge through Cases in the Qing Dynasty," in *Thinking with Cases*, 64–65.
90. This work survives only in the form of two Korean manuscript copies. To the best of my knowledge, this novel has never been mentioned in any scholarly work. The bibliographical information in the National Taiwan University Library, which holds the only complete copy, dates the novel to the late Ming, probably because Huang Ruheng (黃汝亨 1558–1626) is listed in the book as the commentator. But judging from the frequent references to Jin Shengtan's commentary to *The Water Margins* in the "General Commentary" (*Zongping* 總評), the novel was more probably produced after the establishment of the Qing regime.
91. "Guanwu'an, *Shiyuan huanjian*, chapter 6, n.p.
92. After the *Haoqiu zhuan*, a similar diachronic tendency can be discerned in the discussion of expediency by Kong Guangsen 孔廣森 (1752–1786), author of *Chunqiu Gongyang jingzhuan tongyi* 春秋公羊經傳通義. Unlike the Han Confucian Dong Zhongshu 董仲舒, who stresses the importance of motivation in appraising an expedient, Kong points to the temporal ambiguity underlying the last part of the definition of expediency given in the *Gongyang Commentary*: "And *then* goodness is produced herein," which means whether an expedient is justifiable depends on the result it brings about at a later point in time. But exactly how late this "then" would be and where the endpoint should be set are questions he never answers persuasively. He ends up arbitrarily limiting his evaluation to the time when the effect of the expedient is still positive, and remaining silent on any negative development beyond this point. In contrast, there is no such endpoint in view when Zhongyu says, "Should we *eventually* contract marriage, our former acts of knight-errantry will turn into something performed with an ulterior view" (emphases added). See Tamura Masaru 田村將, "Kong Guangshen *Gongyang tongyi* ni okeru keiken setsu" 孔廣森公羊通義における経権説, *Chūgoku tetsugaku* 中国哲学 33 (March 2005): 79–106.
93. The mood of regret and the appeal to fate are the two axes of chapter 14: "[Zhongyu sank into a deep reverie:] Thus it turns out that our friendship, our mutual services, and our chances of union, are all frustrated,—Oh, heaven! That we mortals should be so harassed!" (H14.8b, F2:93) "But strange as this may be, it would appear that our mutual services and gratitude are all in vain,—for our ultimate union is impossible! Heaven seems to have a purpose in it, but our crosses and perplexities are sufficiently apparent' " (H14.15b, F2:107).
94. See section 5 for further discussion.
95. For a comparable transition from the generic to the historical in casuistry that happened in early nineteenth-century England, see James Chandler, *England*

in 1819: *The Politics of Literary Culture and the Case of Romantic Historicism* (Chicago: University of Chicago Press, 1998), 225–36.

96. Qingxin cairen 青心才人, *Jin Yun Qiao zhuan*, 1662–1772 ed.; reprint, *Guben xiaoshuo jicheng*, ser. 4, 41:266–69.

97. See chapter 1, section 3.

98. Peter Flueckiger, *Imagining Harmony: Poetry, Empathy, and Community in Mid-Tokugawa Confucianism and Nativism* (Stanford: Stanford University Press, 2011), 3, 54, 178–79.

99. In search of "the broader implication of theatricality" that covers all forms of theatrical performance, Mitsuya Mori recommends the Japanese notion of *geinoh* (*geinō* 藝能) "wherever the Western concept of 'theater' suffers from narrowness and ambiguity." As a result, he regards the Audience, which he argues "is never lost" in any theater, as one of the essential components in the universal "double triangle schemes of theatrical structure," even though, as he notes, "in the koh-joh scene in Kabuki, the actors are directly addressing the Audience," whereas "Noh actors look absolutely indifferent to the audience when performing." See Mori, "The Structure of Theater: A Japanese View of Theatricality," *SubStance* 31, nos. 2–3 (2002): 89, 91. How we conceptualize these two different relationships to the audience, I would suggest, holds the key to a more historically specific notion of theatricality that distinguishes the Noh dreamscape from the Kabuki theater. At the heart of this distinction is Kabuki's immersion in print culture. For the relationship between Bakin's early career and printed guidebooks to the Kabuki theater, see Robert Goree, "Publishing Kabukiland: Late Edo Culture and Kyokutei Bakin's *Yakusha meisho zue*," in *Publishing the Stage: Print and Performance in Early Modern Japan*, ed. Keller Kimbrough and Satoko Shimazaki (Boulder, CO: Center for Asian Studies, University of Colorado Boulder, 2011), 191–213.

100. "Kyokutei Bakin, "*Asahina shimameguri no ki* dai shi hen jo" 朝夷巡嶋記第四編叙, in *Kyokutei Bakin yomihon kanbuntai jijoshū* 曲亭馬琴読本漢文体自序集 (Tokyo: Hōbun Shuppan, 1988), 167–71.

101. The textual connection between Xie Zhaozhe and Bakin was first noted in Nakamura Yukihiko 中村幸彦, "Takizawa Bakin no shōsetsukan" 滝沢馬琴の小說觀, in *Bakin* 馬琴, ed. Nihon bungaku kenkyū shiryō kankō sha 日本文学研究資料刊行社 (Tokyo: Yuseidō, 1974), 78.

102. Haiyan Lee, *Revolution of the Heart: A Genealogy of Love in China, 1900–1950* (Stanford: Stanford University Press, 2007), 41.

103. The dates of *Humble Words* come from Wang Qiongling 王瓊玲, *Yesou puyan zuozhe Xia Jingqu nianpu* 野叟曝言作者夏敬渠年譜 (Taipei: Xuesheng shuju, 2005), 348–51.

104. Xia Jingqu, *Yesou puyan* (Tianjin: Tianjin guji chubanshe, 2002), 5.171b, 174b. This detail about the titles Xuangu sees, however, is not available in the first edition published in 1881; rather, they first appeared in the 1882 edition. The debate concerning the authenticity of the 1882 edition can be found in Wang Qiongling, *Qingdai sida xiaoshuo* 清代四大小說 (Taipei: Xuesheng shuju, 1999), 95–109; Pan Jianguo 潘建國, *Gudai xiaoshuo wenxian congkao* 古代小說文獻叢考 (Beijing: Zhonghua shuju, 2006), 90–113, 123–130.
105. *Yesou puyan*, 1.36a–36b.
106. "男女之樂原生乎情，你憐我愛，自覺遍體俱春。. . . . 況且男女之樂，原只在未經交合以前，彼此情思俱濃，自有無窮樂趣。既經交合，便自闌殘。" Xia Jingqu, *Yesou puyan*, 2.44a–44b. For the discourse of norm and expediency in *Humble Words*, see Epstein, *Competing Discourses*, 238–48.
107. See chapter 2, section 2.
108. Martin Huang notes that emotion (*qing*) in this novel comprehends all kinds of physical contact except penetration (*Desire and Fictional Narrative*, 236), which he reads as a proof of the exclusion of desire (*yu*) from emotion. He goes on to show how *qing* is precariously close to *yu*, which makes it necessary to "contain *qing* within the proper limits of *li* [rite]." We should add that the "containment" functions here as a peculiar case that precisely puts this commonsense view of sexual love on trial.
109. Keith McMahon has called the novel a story of "chaste polygamy," in which a hero is entitled to many talented, unjealous women, with whom he delays consummation until being properly sanctioned by the sage mother. Such stories result from the compromising union between the moderate miser and the temperate shrew, which denies both monogamy (wished by the shrew) and unlimited sex for pleasure (wished by the miser). See McMahon, *Misers, Shrews, and Polygamists: Sexuality and Male-Female Relations in Eighteenth-Century Chinese Fiction* (Durham, NC: Duke University Press, 1995), 150–75. To this keen observation, we can add that by postponing and trivializing genital sex, the story of chaste polygamy indeed actualizes unlimited erotic pleasure for both the shrew and the miser.
110. What Freud left unexplained throughout his life, according to Ricoeur, is precisely what constitutes pleasure, and why pain, apparently contradicting what is pleasurable, can constitute pleasure. See Paul Ricoeur, *Freud and Philosophy: An Essay on Interpretation*, trans. Denis Savage (New Haven: Yale University Press, 1977), 321–22. To me, the crux here is that neither pleasure nor pain can be abstracted as principles but rather are constituted in a particular case.
111. Judith Butler, *Gender Trouble: Feminism and the Subversion of Identity*, 2nd ed. (1990; New York: Routledge, 1999).

112. Tim Dean, *Beyond Sexuality* (Chicago: University of Chicago Press, 2000), 61–93, 174–214. See also Cynthia Dyess and Tim Dean, "Gender: The Impossibility of Meaning," *Psychoanalytic Dialogues* 10, no. 5 (September 2000): 735–56. Note that although, unlike Wen Sucheng, Dean does not oppose desire to pleasure, he separates desire from the telos of genital sex and instead assigns it to the multitude of erogenous zones and objects *petit a*. In so doing, what Wen celebrates about pleasure in his critique of genital sex is transplanted onto desire in Dean's rereading of Lacanianism.
113. Jacques Lacan, "The Subversion of the Subject," 314–15.
114. Dean, *Beyond Sexuality*, 261–62.
115. "Correlation," however, is a tentative, unsatisfactory way to articulate space and time. Strictly speaking, theatricality is not correlative to ecstatic temporality; rather, as a historical mode of the spatiality of emotion, theatricality foregrounds the dehiscence inherent in the ecstatic unity of time through the prism of faceoff. See chapter 5, sections 1 and 4.
116. See *Xinbian Shitouji Zhiyanzhai pingyu jijiao* 新編石頭記脂硯齋評語輯校, comp. Chen Qinghao 陳慶浩 (Taipei: Lianjing chuban shiye gongsi, 1986), 135, 568.
117. Satō, "*Gōkyūden* jo," 171.
118. See John Forrester, "If p, then what? Thinking in Cases," *History of the Human Sciences* 9, no. 3 (August 1996): 1–25.
119. Immanuel Kant, *Anthropology from a Pragmatic Point of View*, trans. Robert B Louden (Cambridge: Cambridge University Press, 2006), 4–5.
120. See Chi-Ming Yang, *Performing China*, 148–83.

5. TIME-SPACE IS EMOTION

1. Shu-hsien Liu, "Time and Temporality: The Chinese Perspective," *Philosophy East and West* 24, no. 2 (April 1974): 146.
2. Li-chen Lin, "The Concepts of Time and Position in the *Book of Change* and Their Development," in *Time and Space in Chinese Culture*, ed. Chun-chieh Huang and Erik Zürcher (Leiden: E.J. Brill, 1995), 90.
3. Grier Hibben and Eric v. d. Luft, *Hegel's Shorter Logic: An Introduction and Commentary* (North Syracuse, NY: Gegensatz Press, 2013), 9, 19, 29, 188.
4. Christoph Harbsmeier, "Some Notions of Time and of History in China and in the West with a Digression on the Anthropology of Writing," in *Time and Space in Chinese Culture*, 52–56.
5. "久，彌異時也；宇，彌異地也。" A. C. Graham, *Later Mohist Logic, Ethics and Science* (Hong Kong: Chinese University Press, 2003), 293. See also note 161 below.

6. *Zhuangzi jishi*, 1:56, 4:1102. The translation is modified from Graham, *Chuang-Tzŭ*, 51, 283. Also see A. C. Graham, *Disputers of the Tao: Philosophical Argument in Ancient China* (La Salle, IL: Open Court, 1989), 78–79.
7. This is a paradox only because it challenges the linearity of time and space. Any proposed solution by citing calendars read in different time zones—or, as Joseph Needham suggests, in "different time scales" would only present a more complex system of linearity without engaging the paradox. See Joseph Needham, "Time and Knowledge in China and the West," in *The Voices of Time: A Cooperative Survey of Man's Views of Time as Expressed by the Sciences and by the Humanities*, ed. J. T. Fraser, 2nd ed. (Amherst: The University of Massachusetts Press, 1981), 94–95.
8. Martin Heidegger, "Building Dwelling Thinking," in *Poetry, Language, Thought*, trans. Albert Hofstadter (New York: Harper & Row, 1971), 154. (Hereafter this will be referred to as *PLT* followed by page numbers in parentheses.)
9. For Descartes, space and matter are one. "Empty" space is not a vacuum but the extension (length, breadth, depth) of substances. See René Descartes, *Principles of Philosophy*, trans. Valentine Rodger Miller and Reese P. Miller (Dordrecht: Kluwer, 1991), 46–47.
10. Gottfried Wilhelm Leibniz, *The Leibniz-Clarke Correspondence*, ed. H. G. Alexander (Manchester: Manchester University Press, 1956), 69–72; Immanuel Kant, *Critique of Pure Reason*, trans. Paul Guyer and Allen W. Wood (Cambridge: Cambridge University Press, 1998), 157–62.
11. The German original is from Martin Heidegger, "Bauen Wohnen Denken," *Vorträge und Aufsätze* (Pfullingen: Günther Neske, 1954), 157–58.
12. That is the stumbling block in Heidegger's 1925 lecture course, in which he tried to distinguish what he called "concrete intending"—for example, "I go down the hill and place myself before the bridge itself so that it is 'bodily present' to me"—from just thinking of it: "I can now envisage the Weidenhauser bridge. . . . *And yet it is not bodily given to me*." See Martin Heidegger, *History of the Concept of Time: Prolegomena*, trans. Theodore Kisiel (Bloomington: Indiana University Press, 1992), 41–43, italics mine.
13. Martin Heidegger, *Being and Time* (1927), trans. Joan Stambaugh, 62–83. (Hereafter this will be referred to as *BT* followed by page numbers in parentheses.)
14. Hubert L. Dreyfus, "Heidegger's Critique of the Husserl/Searle Account of Intentionality," in *Skillful Coping: Essays on the Phenomenology of Everyday Perception and Action*, ed. Mark Wrathall (Oxford: Oxford University Press, 2014), 76–91.
15. Martin Heidegger, *Sein und Zeit* (Tübingen: M. Niemeyer, 1953), 61–62. Both standard translations render *Aufenthalt* as "dwelling." For the sake of clarity, I

follow the translation in "Building Dwelling Thinking" in order to distinguish *Wohnen* (dwelling) from *Aufenthalt* (stay).

16. To follow Heidegger's distinction between *Dort* and *Da*, which will be explained later, here I translate *Dort* as "yonder" and save "there" for *Da*, as is done in *Being and Time*, trans. John Marcquarrie and Edward Robinson (New York: Harper & Row, 1962), 136, though occasionally I follow Stambaugh to use the more colloquial "over there" as an equivalent to "in the yonder."

17. Dis-tancing in this more fundamental sense is less about bringing things close than being the very condition of rendering things "close" or "far." Heidegger tends to mix up these two senses of *ent-fernen*, which he tries to sort out in the footnotes added to the 1953 edition of *Being and Time*. I follow the translation of *ent-fernen* as "dis-tancing" in Hubert L. Dreyfus, *Being-in-the-World: A Comment on Heidegger's* Being and Time, Division 1 (Cambridge, MA: The MIT Press, 1991), 130–32. And yet, we will see the sense of "bringing near" stay on in the late Heidegger when he shifts from human spatiality to the spatiality of things.

18. See Chan Kwok-kow, "Chen Shixiang lun Zhongguo wenxue: Tongwang 'shuqing chuantong lun' zhilu" 陳世驤論中國文學：通往"抒情傳統論"之路, *Hanxue yanjiu* 漢學研究 29, no. 2 (2011): 233–34; David Der-wei Wang, *The Lyrical in Epic Time*, 13.

19. Chan, "Chen Shih-hsiang," 234.

20. Dreyfus, *Being-in-the-World*, 164–66.

21. Jeff Malpas, *Heidegger and the Thinking of Place* (Cambridge, MA: MIT Press, 2012), 26–27.

22. Jean-Luc Marion, *In Excess: Studies of Saturated Phenomena*, trans. Robyn Horner and Vincent Berraud (New York: Fordham University Press, 2002).

23. Jean-Luc Marion, *The Idol and Distance: Five Studies*, trans. Thomas A. Carlson (New York: Fordham University Press, 2001), 198–253.

24. "Das Ding" was given as a lecture in 1950 and published a year later, before being included along with "Bauen Wohnen Denken" in *Vorträge und Aufsätze* (1954), 163–81. The translation is from *Poetry, Language, Thought*, 163–80.

25. Andrew J. Mitchell explains Heidegger's fourfold as "the minimal essential traits of any thing whatsoever: that they are ungrounded, mediated, meaningful, and open to us. These four aspects come together in what we have been calling the relational thing, whereby this relationality is understood as the interface of a finite thing with its beyond." See *The Fourfold: Reading the Late Heidegger* (Evanston, IL: Northwestern University, 2015), 259. In defining "thing" as "gathering-appropriating staying of the fourfold" (*PLT* 172), Heidegger is playing the obsolete meaning of "thing/*Ding*" in Old English and German as "assembly." In Chinese, the strong association with gathering can be found not in the older

term *wu* 物 but in its colloquial counterpart *dongxi* 東西, which literally means "East-West." According to the *Hanyu da cidian* 漢語大詞典, since things originate from different directions, things are therefore called "East-West." The usage of *dongxi* appeared as early as in a property law dated 848. See Li Shuyuan 李淑媛, *Zhengcai jingchan: Tang Song de jiachan yu* falü 爭財競產：唐宋的家產與法律 (Taipei: Wunan tushu gufen youxiangongsi, 2005), 83–84.

26. Martin Heidegger, "Time and Being" in *On Time and Being*, trans. Joan Stambaugh (New York: Harper Row, 1972), 1–24. (Hereafter this will be referred to as *T* followed by page numbers in parentheses.) See also Jacques Derrida, *Given Time: I. Counterfeit Money*, trans. Peggy Kamuf (Chicago: University of Chicago Press, 1994).

27. "The bridge gathers to itself in its own way earth and sky, divinities and mortals. Gathering or assembly, by an ancient word of our language, is called 'thing'" (*PLT* 151).

28. Martin Heidegger, "The Age of the World Picture," *Off the Beaten Track*, ed. Julian Young and Kenneth Haynes (Cambridge: Cambridge University Press, 2002), 69–70.

29. Martin Heidegger, "What Are Poets For?" in *Poetry, Language, Thought*, 125–27.

30. The meaning of dis-tancing here expands to cover both Da-sein's opening room for useful things to be near and far, and things' "nearing" each other when set apart.

31. Translations of these two terms have been chaotic. I find "situatedness" more comprehensible and proximate to *Befindlichkeit*—as compared to other candidates like "affectedness" and "affectivity" used by recent scholarship—while saving "mood" and "attunement" for *Stimmung*. In some contexts, I follow Heidegger in adding the adjective "moodlike" (*stimmungsmäßigen*) to modify "situatedness" so as to suggest the aspect of sensitivity rather than simply locality.

32. Martin Heidegger, *The Fundamental Concepts of Metaphysics: World, Finitude, Solitude* (1929), trans. William McNeill and Nicholas Walker (Bloomington: Indiana University Press, 1995), 66.

33. Heidegger, *Hölderlin's Hymns "Germania" and "The Rhine"* (Bloomington: Indiana University Press, 2014), 76–79.

34. Also see Dreyfus, *Being-in-the-World*, 173–74; Steven Galt Crowell, "Responsibility, Autonomy, Affectivity: A Heideggerian Approach," in *Heidegger, Authenticity and the Self: Themes from Division Two of Being and Time*, ed. Denis McManus (New York: Routledge, 2015), 220–23.

35. Heidegger, *The Fundamental Concepts of Metaphysics*, 68.

36. This question has been largely obscured for two reasons. First, by putting the discussion of "being-there" under the heading of "Being-in as Such," Heidegger

apparently assumes that being-there is just another expression for the spatiality of Da-sein per se ("being-in"). Second, in "Being-in as Such," the discussion has shifted from the issue of spatiality to "the existential constitution of the being" in terms of situatedness and understanding. The question of how mood (which emerges as the key to situatedness) is related to spatiality is not tackled.

37. "An attunement [i.e., mood] is in each case already there, so to speak, like an atmosphere in which we first immerse ourselves in each case and which then attunes us through and through" (*The Fundamental Concepts of Metaphysics*, 67). This embedding dimension seems to be most familiar in our everyday experience and to have been highlighted to define mood by other scholars. For instance, Chares Altieri writes, "Moods are modes of feeling where the sense of subjectivity becomes diffuse and sensation merges into something close to atmosphere, something that seems to pervade an entire scene or situation." See *The Particulars of Rapture: An Aesthetics of the Affects* (Ithaca: Cornell University Press, 2003), 2.

38. "Attunements [i.e., moods] are not placed into the subject or into objects; rather we, together with beings, are *trans-posed* into attunements" (*Hölderline's Hymns*, 75).

39. Heidegger, "The Age of the World Picture," 66. In his 1927 lecture course, Heidegger also contrasts "productive comportment toward beings" with "das anschauende Vorfinden," which is "a beholding perception, noein, or even theorein," "fixed as a proper access to a being in its being-in-itself." Hofstadter translates *Vorfinden* as to "find present" in order to convey the sense that this kind of perception renders things as objectively present—that is, in Heideggerian terms, present-at-hand (*vorhanden*). See *The Basic Problems of Phenomenology*, trans. Albert Hofstadter (Bloomington: Indiana University Press, 1982), 109–10.

40. Friedrich Schleiermacher (1768–1834) sees "feeling" as a mode of "immediate self-consciousness," which is prior to self-reflection. In feeling, "the separation between activity and object of activity is reduced to the minimum." But that only means that feeling signifies "the essence of the subject" as such, ironically hardening the subject-object separation that it is supposed to overcome. See David E. Klemm, "Schleiermacher on the Self: Immediate Self-Consciousness," in *Figuring the Self: Subject, Absolute, and Others in Classical German Philosophy*, ed. David E. Klemm and Günter Zöller (Albany: SUNY Press, 1997), 172, 174.

41. This final dimension of mood is elided from Heidegger right at the juncture where he should have acknowledged it: "We do not first have representations of the gods from somewhere—representations and a representing that we then furnish with affects and feelings. Rather, attunement [*Stimmung*], as transporting out and transporting into, first *opens up* that realm within which something can first be specifically set before us or represented." *Hölderline's Hymns*, 124,

emphasis original. The problem is conspicuous: "transporting out and into" does open up a realm but would never *set anything before us*; rather, what it would do is delivering us through the emotion-realm. The "setting before" must presuppose a different dimension of the realm than deliverance.

42. Heidegger mistakenly suggests that even "the purest *theōria*"—that is, the "theoretical looking at the world as objectively present"—"does not abandon all moods" but itself is enabled by letting what is objectively present "come toward us in a tranquil staying ... in *rhastōne and diagōgē*" (*BT* 130).

43. For Ricoeur's discussion of "discordance concordance" in the ecstatic unity of time, see chapter 4, section 4. By way of Heidegger's early discussion of mood and later reflection on the relationship between space and time, we can now clarify that discordant concordance is the dimensional incongruity of the emotion-realm.

44. To sum up, the early Heidegger grounds the spatiality of useful things (which lie around with varied handiness in a network of totality) on the spatiality of Da-sein per se (which stays yonder with things before coming back to its here, allowing them to be near or far); the late Heidegger reverses the orientation by grounding human spatiality on the thingness of things, which figure less as the totality of the world than as locations, each gathering and giving here and yonder (or past, present, and future) to one another in holding them apart. All these different levels of spatiality, however, should be ultimately grounded on the spatiality of mood.

45. Dreyfus, *Being-in-the-World*, 163.

46. Crowell, "Responsibility, Autonomy, Affectivity," 220.

47. Andreas Elpidorou, "Moods and Appraisals: How the Phenomenology and Science of Emotions Can Come Together," *Human Studies* 36 (2013): 565–91. For a critique of this kind of cognitive reading, see Katherine Withy, "Owned Emotions: Affective Excellence in Heidegger on Aristotle," in *Heidegger, Authenticity, and the Self*, 23–24.

48. Juliana Bruno, *Atlas of Emotion: Journey in Art, Architecture and Film* (New York: Verso, 2007), 2–12.

49. In this sense, affect is similar to mood, and it is no accident that some recent discussions try to reframe mood in terms of the taxonomy of affects. See, for instance, *Philosophy's Moods: The Affective Grounds of Thinking*, ed. Hagi Kenaan and Ilit Ferber (New York: Springer, 2011).

50. Kathleen Stewart, *Ordinary Affects* (Durham: Duke University Press, 2007), 2.

51. Kathleen Stewart, "Worlding Refrains," in *The Affect Theory Reader*, ed. Melissa Gregg and Gregory J. Seigworth (Durham: Duke University Press, 2010), 340.

52. Ruth Leys, "The Turn to Affect: A Critique," *Critical Inquiry* 37 (Spring 2011): 434–72.

53. Teresa Bernnan, *The Transmission of Affect* (Ithaca: Cornell University Press, 2004), 1, 76, 165.
54. Catherine Malabou, "Go Wonder: Subjectivity and Affects in Neurobiological Times," in Adrian Johnston and Catherine Malabou, *Self and Emotional Life: Philosophy, Psychoanalysis, and Neuroscience* (New York: Columbia University Press, 2013), 45–46, 54.
55. Anna Gibbs, "After Affect: Sympathy, Synchrony, and Mimetic Communication," in *The Affect Theory Reader*, 196.
56. Gibbs, "After Affect," 191, 193.
57. Henri Lefebvre, *The Production of Space* (Malden, MA: Blackwell Publishing, 1991), 73, 83, 85. (Hereafter this will be referred to as *PS* followed by page numbers in parentheses.)
58. Put differently, "the networks of paths and roads made up a space just as concrete as that of the body—of which they were in fact an extension" (*PS* 193). Foreshadowing affect theory, Lefebvre calls this affective marking "the intelligence of the body," preceding thoughts and intentionality (174).
59. Criticizing abstract representations in anthropology, Bourdieu similarly urges us to see "the body as geometer" at the level of daily practice. See *Outline of a Theory of Practice*, 119.
60. Quentin Meillassoux, *After Finitude: An Essay of the Necessity of Contingency* (London: Bloomsbury Academic, 2012), 5–11, 120–23.
61. As Graham Harman famously announces: "The true chasm in ontology lies not between humans and the world, but between *objects and relations*." See *Tool-Being: Heidegger and the Metaphysics of Objects* (Chicago: Open Court, 2002), 2.
62. Graham Harman, "On the Undermining of Objects: Grant, Bruno, and Radical Philosophy," in *The Speculative Turn: Continental Materialism and Realism*, ed. Levi Bryant, Nick Srnicek, and Graham Harman (Melbourne: re.press, 2011), 31, 35–37.
63. Levi R. Bryant, "The Ontic Principle: Outline of an Object-Oriented Ontology," in *The Speculative Turn*, 271, 273, 276.
64. Graham Harman, "Space, Time, Essence: An Object-Oriented Approach," in *Toward Speculative Realism: Essays and Lectures* (Winchester, UK: Zero, 2010), 162.
65. Łukasz Stanek, "Space as Concrete Abstraction: Hegel, Marx, and Modern Urbanism in Henri Lefebvre," in *Space, Difference, Everyday Life: Reading Henri Lefebvre*, ed. Kanishka Goonewardena, Stefan Kipfer, Richard Milgrom, and Christian Schmid (New York: Routledge, 2008), 62–79.
66. Lefebvre's stress on "life" can be understood in the light of his critique (dating back to 1967) of Foucault's cybernetic notion of control that dissolves the

humanist idea of subjectivity into just an effect of the total system of information exchange. See Céline Lafontaine, "The Cybernetic Matrix of 'French Theory,'" *Theory, Culture & Society* 24, no. 5 (January 2007): 37.

67. Michel Foucault, *The History of Sexuality: An Introduction*, trans. Robert Hurley (New York: Vintage, 1978), 42–43; *The Use of Pleasure*, 192–95, 215–25; Alan Bray, *Homosexuality in Renaissance England* (Chicago: University of Chicago, 1982), 13–32.

68. "One confronts both an immediacy and an objectivity of one's own. One places oneself at the center, designates oneself, measures oneself, and uses oneself as a measure. One is, in short, a 'subject'" (*PS* 182).

69. Thomas Laqueur, *Making Sex: Body and Gender from the Greeks to Freud* (Cambridge, MA: Harvard University Press, 1990), 82–83.

70. Charlotte Furth, *A Flourishing Yin: Gender in China's Medical History, 960–1665* (Berkeley: University of California Press, 1999), 25–48.

71. Mark Edward Lewis, *The Construction of Space in Early China*, 22–23.

72. Lewis, *The Construction of Space in Early China*, 20.

73. Lewis, *The Construction of Space in Early China*, 13.

74. Schematically speaking, there are two ways to talk about Chinese thought about the body, as Kuang-Ming Wu demonstrates: "On the one hand, we can start redefining the body according to classical Chinese thought, and proceed to describe how such a body, flowing perceptually, personally, interpersonally, and pervasively throughout the cosmos, also flows thinkingly." Taking this route, we see the dissipation of the body as an entity. On the other hand, Wu asserts, "I am my body. . . . My body *is* the system of all systems of perspectives; I am this system unfolding itself. . . . My body is this systematic experiential totality of constituting the world." I would argue that this leads back to the ultimate reification of the body as the vantage point of the world. See Kuang-Ming Wu, *On Chinese Body Thinking: A Cultural Hermeneutics* (New York: Brill, 1997), 17, 236–37.

75. Lewis, *The Construction of Space in Early China*, 2.

76. Lewis, *The Construction of Space in Early China*, 1.

77. To fill the void left by Heidegger's infamous evasion from the whole issue of corporeality (*BT* 52, 101), Maurice Merleau-Ponty stresses "the spatiality of one's own body," without which "there would be for me no such things as space." See *Phenomenology of Perception*, trans. Donald A. Landes (London: Routledge, 2012), 104. Other discussions try to highlight the late Heidegger's "felt body" contra the objectified body in bioscience. See David Michael Levin, *The Body's Recollection of Being: Phenomenological Psychology and the Deconstruction of Nihilism* (Boston: Routledge & Kegan Paul, 1985), 38–51. Yet, as affect theory demonstrates, even the felt body has been reified in

neurochemical terms. I would argue that the early Heideggerian suspension resists such reification by embedding the body back into "a totality of the interconnected places of the context of useful things at hand in the surrounding world" (*BT* 95, 101–2). This early stance should be redeemed for keeping at bay the regime of biopower that Heidegger and Nazism have often been said to share. What differentiates Heidegger from Nazism is not, as Agamben tries to say, that Heidegger renders life and world into an inseparable unity over which power can no longer hold. Rather, the impossibility of a seamless unity between life and world is reasserted, at least in the early Heidegger, by the secondariness of bio (body), whose centrality is suspended in the totality of the worldly context. What is being checked is not power but bio per se. See Giorgio Agamben, *Homo Sacer: Sovereign Power and Bare Life* (Stanford: Stanford University Press, 1998), 153.

78. Martin Puchner, *Stage Fright: Modernism, Anti-Theatricality & Drama* (Baltimore: The Johns Hopkins University Press, 2002), 6–22.
79. Tracy C. Davis, "Theatricality and Civil Society," in *Theatricality*, ed. Tracy C. Davis and Thomas Postlewait (Cambridge: Cambridge University Press, 2003), 132–35.
80. See Julie Stone Peters, *Theatre of the Book: 1480–1880* (Oxford: Oxford University Press, 2000).
81. Tracy C. Davis and Thomas Postlewait, introduction to *Theatricality*, 11. Davis and Postlewait themselves take issue with John Gassner's *Form and Idea in Modern Theatre* for putting even the realist Stanislavsky in the "theatricalist" camp (13).
82. Jacques Rancière, *The Emancipated Spectator*, 4–5, italics added.
83. "Whether you compose or act, think of the spectator no more than he did not exist. Imagine, on the theater's edge, a huge wall that separates you from the parquet; act as if the canvas did not rise." Denis Diderot, "Discours de la poésie dramatique," *Œuvres*, ed. Laurent Versini (Paris: R. Laffont, 1996), 4:1310.
84. Fried, *Absorption and Theatricality: Painting and Beholder in the Age of Diderot* (Chicago: University of Chicago Press, 1980), 103.
85. That is why Fried laments that the "Diderotian ideal" of absorption became increasingly disrupted by "the bare fact of the beholder's existence," to such an extent that any anti-theatrical device of absorption would soon be found selling out to the beholder's gaze. See Fried, *Absorption and Theatricality*, 157; and "An Introduction to My Art Criticism," in *Art and Objecthood: Essays and Reviews* (Chicago: University of Chicago Press, 1998), 49–50.
86. This is not because, as some critics assume, the modernist ideal of "artistic purity" denies the beholder as a matter of fact and is therefore "doomed to critique and to failure. . . . Absorption is, in the last analysis, a lie. In this dialectic

of absorption and theatricality, absorption may appear as the master theme but theatricality is the only real term." See Stephen W. Melville, *Philosophy Beside Itself: On Deconstruction and Modernism* (Minneapolis: University of Minnesota Press, 1986), 11. The beholder should never be presumed to be "real"; rather, the spectator historically comes into being through the fiction of absorption.

87. This study therefore does not regard "anti-theatricality" as a transhistorical aversion to theatrical performance, as suggested in Marvin Carlson, "The Resistance to Theatricality," *SubStance* 31, nos. 2 & 3 (2002): 238–49. Rather, it understands anti-theatricality as a constitutive drive for increasingly reifying the spectatorial position by apparent gestures of denial and exclusion.

88. Aram Vartanian, "Diderot and the Phenomenology of the Dream," *Diderot Studies* 8 (1966): 242.

89. Vartanian, "Diderot and the Phenomenology of the Dream," 250–51.

90. Fried, *Absorption and Theatricality*, 235 n. 81. See also Jennifer Vanderheyden, *The Function of the Dream and the Body in Diderot's Works* (Frankfurt: Peter Lang, 2004).

91. Jacques Derrida, "The Theater of Cruelty and the Closure of Representation," *Writing and Difference*, trans. Alan Bass (London: Routledge, 1978), 241, 243.

92. For such a cognitive reading of Diderot, see Lisa Zunshine, "Theory of Mind and Michael Fried's *Absorption and Theatricality*: Notes toward Cognitive Historicism," in *Toward a Cognitive Theory of Narrative Acts*, ed. Fredrick Luis Aldama (Austin: University of Texas Press, 2010), 179–203.

93. William Egginton, *How the World Became a Stage*, 33–66.

94. Paul Valéry, *Cahiers/Notebooks*, vol. 3, trans. Norma Rinsler, Paul Ryan, and Brian Stimpson (New York: Peter Lang, 2007), 481.

95. Egginton, *How the World Became a Stage*, 28.

96. Egginton, *How the World Became a Stage*, 4.

97. Egginton, *How the World Became a Stage*, 3.

98. David Marshall, *The Figure of Theatricality: Shaftesbury, Defoe, and Adam Smith and George Eliot* (New York: Columbia University Press, 1986), 180, 192.

99. David Marshall, *The Surprising Effects of Sympathy*, 129–30, italics original.

100. Liu Jiasi 劉家思, *Cao Yu xiju de juchangxing yanjiu* 曹禺戲劇的劇場性研究 (Beijing: Zhongguo shehui kexue chubanshe, 2010).

101. Lydia H. Liu, "The Question of Meaning-Value in the Political Economy of the Sign," in *Tokens of Exchange: The Problem of Translation in Global Circulations*, ed. Lydia H. Liu (Durham: Duke University Press, 1999), 14–47; Jean-Joseph Goux. *Symbolic Economies: After Marx and Freud*, trans. Jennifer Curtiss Gage (Ithaca: Cornell University Press, 1990).

102. Here I am responding to Louis Althusser's famous view on the relationship among dreams, ideology, and history: "(1) ideology is nothing in so far as it is

a pure dream"; "(2) ideology has no history, which emphatically does not mean that there is no history in it (on the contrary, for it is merely the pale, empty and inverted reflection of real history) but that it has no history of its own," since no social system can operate without ideology. See "Ideology and Ideological State Apparatuses: Notes towards an Investigation," in *Lenin and Philosophy and Other Essays*, trans. Ben Brewster (New York: Monthly Review Press, 2001), 108. An intervention from the Chinese dreamscape would instead assert that (1) dreams have no history of their own since any context grounding the historicity of a dream must be recontextualized as another dream, but (2) the dreamscape in general has a history bound up by its positioning vis-à-vis other historical regimes of spatiality of emotion.

103. Zou Diguang, "Guan yanxi shuo," in *Yuyi lou ji* 鬱儀樓集, 1604 ed., *juan* 42, 4a-5b, rpt., *Siku quanshu cunmu congshu* 四庫全書存目叢書 (Jinan: Qilu shushe, 1997), *Ji* 集, 158:762–63.

104. The term "dialectic" is invoked here not as a universal procedure of determinacy but should be ascribed to the historical dynamics pertinent to the interplay between the dreamscape and theatricality in the Western context, to which we will return below.

105. The motif of illusory dreams is no stranger to Western dramas, as exemplified in Calderón's *Life's a Dream* (1635), which proclaims "all human joy is, in the end, as ephemeral as a dream." But, precisely so, the play asserts that one focuses on "divine glory," through which the prince reforms himself and "rekindles [his] presence in [the king's] heart." Pedro Calderón de la Barca, *Life's a Dream*, trans. Michael Kidd (Boulder: University Press of Colorado, 2004), 146–47, 151–153. What makes *Life's a Dream* an early modern play is that the king is actually the spectator "with sympathy" to the prince's awakening engineered by the king as a play-within-a-play (131).

106. Egginton, *How the World Became a Stage*, 48–49.

107. Egginton, *How the World Became a Stage*, 73.

108. Derrida, "The Theater of Cruelty and the Closure of Representation," 249.

109. Lord Kames (Henry Home), *Elements of Criticism* (Printed for A. Miller, London; and A. Kincaid & J. Bell, Edinburgh, 1762), 1:115–16, 121–22.

110. Kames, *Elements of Criticism*, 1:108, 124.

111. Smith, *The Theory of Moral Sentiment*, 53.

112. Marshall, *The Figure of Theater*, 171.

113. The artificial differentiation between empathy and sympathy is irrelevant to this study. See prologue, section 3.

114. Heidegger, *History of the Concept of Time*, 243.

115. See note 99 above.

116. Marshall, *The Figure of Theater*, 173–77.

117. Cheng Shuda 程樹達, comp., *Lunyu jishi* 論語集釋 (Beijing: Zhonghua shuju, 1990), 4:1106; Jia Yi 賈誼, "Daoshu" 道術, in *Xinshu jiaozhu* 新書校注 (Beijing: Zhonghua shuju, 2000), 303; Cheng Hao, "Mingdao xiansheng yu yi" 明道先生語一, in Cheng Hao and Cheng Yi, *Er Cheng ji*, 1:124.
118. That is one of the ways Confucius defines benevolence (*ren* 仁). Cheng, *Lunyu jishi*, 2:428.
119. Justin Tiwald, "Dai Zhen on Sympathetic Concern," *Journal of Chinese Philosophy* 37, no. 1 (March 2010): 85. Despite his article's title, Tiwald's accurate observation that *shu* is based on what "all hearts would affirm in common" proves that *shu* is at odds with the modern notion of sympathy, according to which "we have no immediate experience of what other men feel" (Smith, *The Theory of Moral Sentiment*, 1). Another phrase, *tongqing* 同情, which nowadays is used to translate "sympathy," originally means "sharing common nature" in Classical Chinese, exactly what sympathy is not. See Eugenia Lean, *Public Passions: The Trial of Shi Jianqiao and the Rise of Popular Sympathy in Republican China* (Berkeley: University of California Press, 2007), 5.
120. In the previous section, we saw dis-tancing fall short of explaining why it is only in theatricality, not in other modes of spatiality, that distance becomes the defining problem. We need to go beyond dis-tancing to the more fundamental level underneath here and yonder—the situational "there" of the emotion-realm—in order to figure out why it is sympathy, rather than other structures of feeling, that spotlights the difficulty of feeling at a distance, from which is derived the whole problematic of identification. To put it in Chinese terms, we have to go beyond the discourse of *shu* in order to understand the peculiarity of the idiom *she shen chu di*.
121. "Zhongyong," in *Shisanjing zhushu: Liji zhushu* 十三經注疏：禮記注疏, ed. Li Xueqin 李學勤 (Beijing: Beijing daxue chubanshe, 1999), 2:1442–43.
122. Wei Shi 衛湜, comp., *Zhongyong jishuo* 中庸集說 (Guilin: Lijiang chubanshe, 2011), 219.
123. This is linked to my critique of Lefebvre: incorporation is not so much the bodily foundation grounding our experience of space as itself grounded on the dimension of embedment that belongs to the spatiality of emotion.
124. Zhu Xi, *Sishu zhangju jizhu*, 29. Guo Xiaodong 郭曉東 just takes this as one of the examples of how Zhu alludes to Lü to support his own interpretation. See Guo, "Lun Zhuzi zai dui *Zhongyong* de quanshi guocheng zhong shou Lü Yushu de yingxiang ji qi dui Lü shi zhi piping" 論朱子在對《中庸》的詮釋過程中受呂與叔的影響及其對呂氏之批評, in *Zhong Ri* Sishu *quanshi chuantong chutan* 中日《四書》詮釋傳統初探, ed. Huang Junjie 黃俊傑 (Taipei: Taiwan daxue chuban zhongxin, 2004), 2:302–3.

125. This bodily separation by skin took on political poignancy during the final years of the Ming dynasty, as demonstrated by Lu Xiangsheng 盧象昇, who described his predicament in handling a 1634 riot: "To those central and local senior officials, the pain and itch is outside their skin. Which of them ever puts himself in my place?" Lu Xiangsheng, the second letter of "Yu Shaosicheng Wu Cai'an shu" 與少司成吳蔡菴書, in Lu Xiangsheng, *Lu Zhongsugong shudu* 盧忠肅公書牘, in Congshu jicheng chubian 叢書集成初編 (Shanghai: Shangwu yinshuguan, 1935–36), 2970:10.

126. This aporia between the oneness and heterogeneity of time structures the entirety of Ricoeur's *Time and Narrative*, (1:16–22, 3:19, 21). A similar aporia concerning space is raised by Lefebvre, who explains it in terms of social contradictions (*PS* 292–300, 306, 352–54). The aporia of time and of space are not in an analogical relationship; rather, their nexus rests in the fundamental operation of "appropriation," which brings things near to one another in their mutual belonging while holding them apart. Applying this strongly spatial notion of appropriation to temporality, the late Heidegger puts forth the new notion of "time-space." This profound connection between the aporia of time and of space permits us to rework the meaning of imagination by reading Ricoeur and Heidegger together. Heidegger calls empathy "an 'as if,' " which "contains a fundamental mistake" (*The Fundamental Concepts of Metaphysics*, 202–3), not so much because fellow feeling can only be fictionalized "in thought" as because empathetic transportation has become so *real* that Da-sein would be compromised by losing its own position. Imagination, I would argue, is not just representation, because the transposition does actually displace Da-sein from itself and can be exploited as a critique of the centrality of Da-sein. More important, the "as if" does not really take place in the identification between self and other, since the self always already stays with the other, and therefore does not need to imagine into the other's position. Instead, we should follow Ricoeur's discussion of narrative poetics and place the "as if" at the level of dealing with the aporetic dissonance of time, or rather, of time-space. What is imaginative or poetic is not the self's identification with the other, but "the ecstatic unity of time" (see *Time and Narrative*, 1:64–73; also see chapter 4, section 4), or, as argued here, the supposed oneness among the incongruous dimensions of time-space.

127. This denial is usually made in the name of Brecht, who is said to seek an alternative to empathy in traditional Chinese theater. But he does not say that empathy does not exist in Chinese performance; rather, he recognizes that it exists in a more complex, mediated way. "To look at himself is for the performer an artful and artistic act of self-estrangement. Any empathy on the spectator's part

is thereby prevented from becoming total, that is, from being a complete self-surrender. An admirable distance from the events portrayed is achieved. This is not to say that the spectator experiences no empathy whatsoever. He feels his way into the actor as into an observer. In this manner an observing, watching attitude is cultivated." See Bertolt Brecht, "On Chinese Acting," trans. Eric Bentley, in *Brecht Sourcebook*, ed. Carol Martin (New York: Routledge, 1999), 13–20.

128. Smith, *The Theory of Moral Sentiments*, 157–58.
129. Eric Hayot, *The Hypothetical Mandarin: Sympathy, Modernity, and Chinese Pain* (Oxford: Oxford University Press, 2009).
130. Arthur H. Smith, *Chinese Characteristics*, 4th ed. (New York: Fleming H. Revell Company, 1894), 198, 94.
131. Lydia Liu, *Translingual Practice: Literature, National Culture, and Translated Modernity—China, 1900–1937* (Stanford: Stanford University Press, 1995), 45–76.
132. Lu Xun, "Nala zouhou zenyang" 娜拉走後怎樣, in *Lu Xun quanji* 魯迅全集 (Beijing: Renmin wenxue chubanshe, 1973), 1:150.
133. Lu Xun, "[Nahan] zixu" [吶喊] 自序, in *Lu Xun quanji*, 1:269–71.
134. Marston Anderson, *The Limits of Realism: Chinese Fiction in the Revolutionary Period* (Berkeley: University of California Press, 1990), 76–92.
135. Rey Chow, *Primitive Passions: Visuality, Sexuality, Ethnography, and Contemporary Chinese Cinema* (New York: Columbia University Press, 1995), 4–11.
136. Michael Berry, *A History of Pain: Trauma in Modern Chinese Literature and Film* (New York: Columbia University Press, 2008), 28–32.
137. David Der-Wei Wang, *The History That Is a Monster: History, Violence, and Fictional Writing in Twentieth-century China* (Berkeley: University of California Press, 2004), 17–25.
138. Haiyan Lee, "Sympathy, Hypocrisy and the Trauma of Chineseness," *Modern Chinese Literature and Culture* 16, no. 2 (Fall 2004): 92.
139. Lu Xun, "Zixu," 274; translation is taken from Lu Xun, *Selected Stories of Lu Xun*, tr. Yang Hsien-i and Gladys Yang (Beijing: Foreign Languages Press, 1972), 5, slightly modified.
140. Andrew Jones traces Lu Xun's trope to Victorian and late Qing fiction precedents sharing the common "scenes of a sleeping figure in a cell with an iron door serve as an antechamber to some sort of utopian realm, yet it remains unclear whether liberty is vouchsafed only to those who are captive to a dream." According to Jones, Lu Xun's parable "may well hinge on a dialectic of dreaming and waking. . . . The irony is that awakening is figured here as little more than a painfully lucid dream, a coming into consciousness of the inevitability of an ongoing nightmare." See *Developmental Fairy Tales: Evolutionary Thinking and*

Modern Chinese Culture (Cambridge, MA: Harvard University Press, 2011), 37–38. To this insight, I would add that what makes Lu Xun's iron house special is precisely the discontinuity of deliverance through dreams; the nightmarish scenario is too lucid to be a nightmare anymore. We will see the "dialectic of dreaming and waking" is actually a modern replacement of the traditional dreamscape, but Lu Xun turns out to reject this dialectic as well.

141. John Fitzgerald, *Awakening China: Politics, Culture, and Class in the Nationalist Revolution* (Stanford: Stanford University Press, 1996), 60, italics mine.
142. Fitzgerald, *Awakening China*, 43.
143. G. W. F. Hegel, *The Philosophy of History*, trans. J. Sibree (New York: Dover, 2015), 140–41; also cited in Fitzgerald, *Awakening China*, 43.
144. See prologue, section 1.
145. J. H. van den Berg, *The Changing Nature of Man: Introduction to a Historical Psychology*, trans. H. F. Croes (New York: Dell, 1961), 230–31.
146. Karatani Kōjin, *Origins of Modern Japanese Literature*, trans. Brett de Bary (Durham: Duke University Press, 1993), 17–41.
147. Tellingly, both schisms were put forth by the same ideologue, Cheng Fangwu 成仿吾, who famously pitched Yu Dafu's romantic "expression" against Lu Xun's realistic "depiction" but then converted from Romanticism to Marxism in a short time span. See Cheng, " 'Chenlun' de pinglun" 《沉淪》的評論 and "Cong wenxue geming dao geming wenxue" 從文學革命到革命文學 in *Cheng Fangwu wenji* 成仿吾文集 (Jinan: Shandong daxue chubanshe, 1985), 146–52, 241–47.
148. In the past, even the enlightened one had to re-enter the dream. In a thirteenth-century deliverance play by Ma Zhiyuan, the Daoist immortal Lü Dongbin sings: "Only if there is one jug to keep the ink traveler,/I'll enter the yellow millet dream *twice*." See Ma Zhiyuan, *Lü Dongbin sanzui Yueyang lou* 呂洞賓三醉岳陽樓, in *Quan Yuanqu*, 2:161. That is why around the same time Ma and others retold Lü Dongbin's origin story: instead of having Lü induce an unenlightened into a dream, as the original eighth-century tale tells us, the Yuan version of the same story delivers Lü himself into the dream in order to be awakened. See Paul R. Katz, *Images of the Immortal: The Cult of Lü Dongbin at the Palace of Eternal Joy* (Honolulu: University of Hawai'i Press, 1999), 183–84. It is as if, at the storytelling level, the enlightened one were forced back into the dream to renew his enlightenment. That cycle is terminated, however, within the walls of the iron house.
149. Cycles of deliverance are still portrayed in Lu Xun's stories but always end in a certain termination. In Theodore Huters's words, "Each utopian projection, however foreshortened, is immediately stymied by an abrupt encounter with a bitter reality that renders any prospect of implementing of change exceedingly

remote." See *Bringing the World Home: Appropriating the West in Late Qing and Early Republican China* (Honolulu: University of Hawai'i Press, 2005), 268. Deliverance is stalled but it is kept as a dutiful usher bringing us again and again to the same dead end.

150. Similarly, Hegel turns the Brahmin dream into something reminiscent of the European notions of real/ideal presence or the *naïveté* of the dream. "In the state of dreaming . . . this separation [between subject and object] is suspended. Spirit has ceased to exist for itself in contrast with alien existence, and thus the separation of the external and individual dissolves before its universality—its essence. The dreaming Indian is therefore all that we call finite and individual; and, at the same time—as infinitely universal and unlimited—a something intrinsically divine" (*The Philosophy of History*, 140–41). Nietzsche makes almost the same point but corrects one categorical mistake: the state of presence the Brahmin enters is not a dream but a deep sleep where "he sees no more dream images." See Friedrich Nietzsche, *On the Genealogy of Morality*, trans. Carol Diethe (Cambridge: Cambridge University Press, 1994), 104. A similar double misreading that confuses Vedanta's dreamless sleep with "a subjectless dream" and construes the Mahayana dream as a precognitive, nondualistic presence rather than a provisional, mediated truth can be detected in Thorsten Botz-Bornstein, "Dreams in Buddhism and Western Aesthetics: Some Thoughts on Play, Style and Space," *Asian Philosophy* 17, no. 1: 68–69, 71–73, 75–76. Bernard Faure argues that under the lingering influence of ancient shamanism, dreams in medieval Japanese Buddhism (as well as in Chinese Buddhism, he suggests) are "an 'arena of awakening' in which a truly real presence manifests itself." But at the same time, he notes, this dream culture recognizes that it is "in the last analysis as impossible to retrieve the original experience that left this trace, or even to affirm the existence of such experience, as to deny it." As long as dreams are recognized as traces, the "real presence" they supposedly conjure up always differs from and defers itself in the "deliverance" dimension of the dreamscape. See *Visions of Power: Imagining Medieval Japanese Buddhism* (Princeton: Princeton University Press, 1996), 142–43.

151. Lean, *Public Passions*, 11–12, 180–213.

152. Fitzgerald, *Awakening China*, 324–28.

153. "Enlightenment is caught up in the same internal conflict that it formerly experienced in connection with faith, and it divides itself into two parties. One party proves itself to be victorious by breaking up into two parties; for in so doing, it shows that it contains within itself the principle it is attacking, and thus has rid itself of the one-sidedness in which it previously appeared." G. W. F. Hegel, *Phenomenology of Spirt*, trans. A.V. Miller (Oxford: Oxford University Press, 1977), 350–51.

154. Theodor W. Adorno, *Negative Dialectics* (New York: Continuum, 1997), 143–61.
155. Adorno, "Subject and Object," *The Essential Frankfurt School Reader*, ed. Andrew Arato and Eike Gebhardt (New York: Continuum, 1982), 497–511.
156. Adorno, *Negative Dialectics*, 17–18. On the centrality of the suffering body to Adorno, see Kelly Fritsch, "On the Negative Possibility of Suffering: Adorno, Feminist Philosophy, and the Transfigured Crip to Come," *Disability Studies Quarterly* 33, no. 4 (2013), retrieved from http://dsq-sds.org/article/view/3869/3408. Reaching the same conclusion, Lefebvre turns the Hegelian dialectics upside down by establishing the body less as the negative nonidentical than the highest stage of sublation—i.e., the universal concrete. Abstraction, "the destroyer of nature and of the body," turns out to be "quite unable to neutralize the enemy within its gate. Far from it: it actually encourages that enemy, actually helps to revive it" (*PS* 354). And with this primacy of the body, it is not surprising that Lefebvre simply assumes the spontaneity of emotional expression just as Adorno does (300).
157. Except that Lu Xun is not alone. A contemporary Liu Dapeng from a declining northern village calls himself "the Man Awakened from Dreams." Liu takes the classic Daoist view that "all worldly achievement is merely an empty dream" but imbues this view "with Confucian moral values, for in his dream the immortal teaches him in words that was central to the moral vision of Confucianism." See Henrietta Harrison, *The Man Awakened from Dreams: One Man's Life in a North China Village, 1857–1942* (Stanford: Stanford University Press, 2005), 20. Occupying the opposite socio-ideological position to Lu Xun's, Liu surprisingly follows the same trajectory from the traditional dreamscape to an ultimate awakening to the final truth. Whether that final truth is called Confucianism or iconoclasm is of little importance, given both the modern intellectual and his conservative counterpart meet up at the end of the dreamscape once defined by deliverance.
158. One year after the preface, Lu Xun repeats the point in "Nala zouhou zenyang": "Nothing is more painful in life than waking from a dream and finding no way out." *Lu Xun quan ji*, 1:145.
159. Eileen J. Cheng, *Literary Remains: Death, Trauma, and Lu Xun's Refusal to Mourn* (Honolulu: University of Hawai'i Press, 2013), 26–28, emphasis added.
160. In other words, sympathy names the paradox central to theatricality and ultimately inverts the general structure of dis-tancing. Whereas, in dis-tancing, one initially stays with others in the yonder before coming back to the here, theatricality turns this trajectory into a confrontation between here and yonder and reifies the distance in between. One result is that I am not only initially in the yonder before coming to myself but *also initially at the same time in the here before staying with others*. But since I do not know even what to feel about

myself without feeling how others feel about me, the "I" that is initially in the here before staying with others does not feel at all.

161. Adam Smith envisages the greater misery a brave man would suffer "in the pillory" than "at the scaffold"—a misery "which is of all sentiments the most unsupportable"—namely, the shameful awareness that "there is no sympathy" in his spectators. See Smith, *The Theory of Moral Sentiments*, 71. For two reasons, the "cruelty" of China beats Smith's worst nightmare: even with the condemned dying at the scaffold, the Chinese spectators would not bless him with sympathy; worse still, the condemned himself feels indifferent to the entire situation.

162. Hayot, *The Hypothetical Mandarin*, 244–45.

Index

Abel, Lionel, 98
absorption, 212–213, 313–314*n*86
Adorno, Theodor W., 237, 321*n*156
affective atmosphere, 21–22
affective body: and anthropology, 207, 311*n*59, 312*n*68; classical Chinese approach to, 208, 312*n*74; and cognitive studies, 203–204; and distancing, 209–210; and mood, 310*n*49; and object-oriented ontology, 206–207, 311–312*nn*61,66; reification of, 205–206, 250*n*13, 312–313*n*77; and spatiality (space), 204–206, 207–208, 311*nn*58–59, 312*n*77; and winds, 208–209
Agamben, Giorgio, 313*n*77
Altenburger, Roland, 298*n*60
Althusser, Louis, 314–315*n*102
Altieri, Chares, 309*n*37
anachronism, 81, 132–133, 144–145, 152–153, 229–230
Anderson, Ben, 21–22

anthropology: and affective body, 207, 311*n*59, 312*n*68; and distancing, 185–186; and European readings of *Haoqiu zhuan*, 295*n*37; and order/disorder, 158–160, 184–185, 296–297*nn*42, 45; and *riken no ken*, 147–148, 291*n*5; and ritual drama, 107, 109, 147, 290*n*1; and spectatorship, 147–148, 152, 186, 291*n*2
Anthropology from a Pragmatic Point of View (Anthropologie in pragmatischer Hinsicht) (Kant), 158, 186
anti-theatricality, 212, 313*n*83, 314*n*87
anxiety, 60–61
ape tales, 273*n*114
appraisal (judgment), 2, 22, 59
Artaud, Antonin, 211, 213, 221
attribution, 2
audience, 92. *See also* spectatorship
avatar: and fictionality, 90; and spectatorship, 80–87, 272–274*nn*107–108,116–117

backstage, 135–136, *135*, 288*nn*121–122
Bakin, Kyokutei, 154, 177–178. *See also Daring Adventures of Chivalric Men*
balconies, 140–141, *140*, 143–144, 289*n*132, 290*n*138
beauty, 14, 247*n*41
Beheading the Drought Demon (Zhan Hanba), 104
Being and Time (Heidegger), 11, 194, 196–197
Bell, Catherine, 109, 147, 152
bestiality, 53–56, 261*n*5
Birch, Cyril, 39
The Black Whirlwind Plays the Judge (Heixuanfeng qiao zuoya) (Yang Xianzhi), 56, 74
The Black Whirlwind Plays the Teacher (Heixuanfeng qiao jiaoxue) (Gao Wenxiu), 56, 269*n*84
The Black Whirlwind's Double Exploits (Heixuanfeng shuang xian gong) (Gao Wenxiu), 56, 75–76
body: incommensurability of, 226–227, 317*n*125; and *she shen chu di*, 224–225, 316*n*123; and sympathy, 204, 230–231; and winds, 21. *See also* affective body; avatar
Book of Rites (Liji), 59, 61
Book of Songs (Shijing), 2, 24, 39. *See also* "The Great Preface"
Boulter, Jonathan, 273*n*108
Bourdieu, Pierre, 291*n*2, 311*n*59
Brecht, Bertolt, 211, 317–318*n*127
Brown, Steven T., 151
Buddhism: and deliverance play genre, 30–32; and dreamscape, 6, 7, 28, 320*n*150; and emotion-landscape mingling, 4, 245*n*17, 274*n*122; on emptiness, 70, 268*nn*68,72; and media/intermediation, 44–45;

on performance, 72; and shared dreams, 252*n*28; and Zeami, 149, 150. *See also* syncretism
"Building Dwelling Thinking" (Heidegger), 191–193, 195

Cai Shun Serves His Mother (Cai Shun feng mu), 282*n*75
Cai Yingjun, 2, 244*n*5
Calderón de la Barca, Pedro, *n*5*n*105
Carlson, Marvin, 314*n*87
Carlyle, Thomas, 210–211
Cartesian philosophy, 3, 46, 59, 194
case thinking, 153, 154; and collapse of universality, 175–176, 302*n*93; and dreamer-spectator, 176–177; and eroticism, 179–181, 183–184, 304*nn*108–110; and order/disorder, 185; and *she shen chu di*, 178–179; and theatricality, 177–179
Chan Buddhism, 4, 30, 70, 245*n*17, 268*nn*68,72
Chandler, James, 123
Cheng, Eileen, 239
Cheng Fangwu, 319*n*147
Cheng Hao, 62, 264*n*37, 265*n*50
Chen Tong, 41
Che Wenming, 131–132, 140–141, 287*n*114
Chinese Characteristics (Smith), 230–231, 238, 240
chivalry: and ambiguity, 298*nn*60–61; in *Daring Adventures of Chivalric Men*, 162–165, 171–172, 299*nn*65–66, 300–301*n*82; and European translations, 165–167, 299–300*nn*68,70; and martial arts fiction/film, 161; and norm/expediency, 162, 164–165, 299*nn*65–66; and temporal orientation, 171

cognitive studies, 3–4, 22, 203–204, 243*n*4
commodification, 47–49, 260*n*104
communication model of emotion, 22, 249*n*13
Complete Musical Notations to The Peony Pavilion (Mudan ting quanpu) (Ye Tang), 42
Confucianism: on norm/expediency, 169, 300*n*76, 302*n*92; and sympathy, 179, 223, 316*n*118. *See also* syncretism
Confucius, 2
Congregation of Immortals (Lü Dongbin huayue shenxian hui) (Zhu Youdun), 119–120, 121, *n*3*n*79
containment, 65, 179, 184, 298*n*61
Corrected Tunes from The Story of Soul's Return (Gezheng Huanhun ji cidiao) (Niu Shaoya), 42
correlationism, 206
correspondence (*gan ying*), 22, 88
cosmology, 21–25, 28–29, 88, 207–208, 250*n*12
"The Country Bumpkin Did Not Know Theater" ("Zhuangjia bu shi goulan") (Du Renjie), 92
A Course to Attain the Flower (Shikadō) (Zeami), 151

Damrosch, David, 295*n*35
Dances of the Tang Monk Fetching Sūtras from Western Heavens (Tang Seng xitian qu jing wu), 104
Daode jing (Laozi), 196
Daoism: and deliverance play genre, 30–32; and dreamscape, 6, 7, 28; on emptiness, 70, 71, 268*nn*70,73; and media/intermediation, 45; and syncretism, 266*n*57; and Zeami,

148–149. *See also* syncretism; Zhuangzi
Daring Adventures of Chivalric Men (Kaikan kyōki kyōkaku den) (Bakin): chivalry in, 162–165, 171*nn*, 299*nn*65–66*n*300–301*n*82; and *Haoqiu zhuan*, 160–161, 164; temporal orientation in, 171–172*nn*300–301*nn*82,83–84
Da-sein, 193, 194, 195, 196, 197, 199, 201, 317*n*126
Davis, John Francis, 165, 167, 299–300*n*70
Davis, Tracy C., 313*n*81
Dean, Tim, 182–183, 305*n*112
Debord, Guy, 109
deliverance, 25; and anxiety and annoyance, 60–61; and dreamscape as illusory, 220; and dreamscape-theatricality shift, 217, 218, 235–236, 319–320*nn*148–149; and enlightenment, 30; and metamorphosis, 282*n*72; and mirror, 79–80; and music, 60–62; and shared dreams, 74; and theatricality, 216–217. *See also* deliverance play genre; dreamscape
deliverance play genre, 30–32, 119–120, 283*n*79, 319*n*148
Derrida, Jacques, 213, 221
Descartes, René, 46, 191, 234, *n*6*n*9
desire: and eroticism, 181, 304*n*108; and nature-emotion relationship, 59, 60, 65; queer theory on, 182
Diderot, Denis, 212, 213, 219, 220, 231, 313*nn*83–84
distancing: and affective body, 209–210; and anthropology, 185–186; and faceoff, 212, 223, 227, 240–241; and *she shen chu di*, 225–226,

Index 325

distancing (*continued*)
321–322*n*160; and spatiality (space), 193, 194–195, 197, 200, 307*n*17, 308*n*30; and spectatorship, 83–85, 87, 89, 133, 186–187, 211–212, 287*n*118; and sympathy, 223, 316*n*120

Doctrine of the Mean (Zhongyong), 63, 90, 122–123, 224, 226

Dong Yue, 271*n*103. See also *A Supplement to The Journey to the West*

Dong Zhongshu, 302*n*92

doubling, 68; and avatar, 273–274*n*108; and nature-emotion relationship, 69–70, 71–72, 267*n*66, 269*n*78; and spectatorship, 58, 71–72, 73–74, 145, 269*nn*78,82

drama: and cult of *qing*, 19–20; monkey association with, 55, 261*n*8; and nature-emotion relationship, 55–56. See also ritual drama

dramatic form, 32–33, 254*n*52

dreamer-spectator: and case thinking, 176–177; and dreamscape as illusory, 220; and dreamscape-theatricality shift, 6–7, 36–39, 44, 46, 256*n*71; postdreamer, 38–39, 49, 134, 145; and theater architecture, 145–146

Dream of Handan (Handan meng ji) (Tang Xianzu), 30, 43–44

The Dream Recollection of Tao'an (Tao'an mengyi), 124

The Dream of the Red Chamber. See *Story of the Stone*

dreamscape, 25–33; and absence of spectator, 9–10; and absorption, 213; ambiguity of, 62; and anachronism, 81, 132–133, 144–145, 152–153; and annoyance, 61–62, 90, 188; and avatar, 81–82; defined, 6; and deliverance play genre, 30–32; and dramatic form, 32–33, 254*n*52; and enlightenment, 30; and faceoff, 221; Flaubert on, 248–249*n*52; and history, 217, 314–315*n*102; as illusory, 219–220, 315*n*105; and imposture, 74–76, 270*n*88; later resurrection of, 133; and media/intermediation, 44–45; and metamorphosis, 10, 27–28, 57–58, 112–113, 114, 116, 117, 263*n*21, 281*n*65, 282*n*72; and metatheatrical remarks, 96–97; and mirror, 79–80, 271*n*103, 272*n*104; and music, 62; and mystic vision, 28–30; and Noh theater, 177, 303*n*99; and passage stages, 136, 137, 289*n*130; and prognostication, 26; and "Real Presence," 214, 220–221; and shared dreams, 26, 33–35, 74, 75, 252*n*28, 255*nn*59–60; and *she shen chu di*, 232–233, 318–319*n*140; and Song-Yuan economic changes, 32–33, 254*n*54; and spectatorship, 7–9, 132–133; and sympathy, 215; and temporal orientation, 26–27; and travel, 25–26; and Zeami, 151, 152. See also deliverance; dreamscape-theatricality shift

dreamscape-theatricality shift, 6, 7–9; and awakening, 236–239, 320*nn*150,153,158; and deliverance, 217, 218, 235–236, 319–320*nn*148–149; as dialectic, 219, 236, 237–238, 315*n*104, 321*n*156; and discursive transparency, 216–219, 226; and dreamer-spectator, 6–7, 36–39, 44, 46, 256*n*71; and global history, 47; and readability, 43–44; and spectatorship, 73, 76, 78–79; and

split soul, 35–36, 37, 255n62. *See also* theatricality
Dream of the South Branch (Nanke meng ji) (Tang Xianzu), 30, 44, 273n113
Dudbridge, Glen, 266n56
Dunhuang Cave, 28–29, *29*
Du Renjie, 92

ecstatic temporality. *See* temporal orientation
"Effective Vision of Learning the Vocation of Fine Play in Performance" ("Yūgaku shūdō fūken") (Zeami), 150
Egan, Ronald, 61
Egginton, William, 46, 98, 116–117, 214, 220, 221, 276n17
Einfühlung (empathy), 13–17
Elvin, Mark, 33
embedment: and body, 316n123; defined, 21–22; and dreamscape-theatricality shift, 219; and emotion as field of cosmology, 23–25; vs. exogenous determinism, 22, 250n13; and shared dreams, 74. *See also* winds
emotion-landscape mingling (*qing jing₁ jiao rong*), 2–5, 244nn5–6; and Buddhism, 4, 245n17, 274n122; and *jing₂* (realm), 4–5, 245n17; and objectification, 234; and theatricality, 87–89; and topophilia, 244–245n13; Wang Fuzhi on, 87–89
emotion-realms (*qingjing₂*), 5, 188–189; aporia of, 227–228, 317n126; etymology, 246nn20–21; and historical ontology, 11–12; vs. mood, 202–203. *See also* dreamscape; mood; theatricality; winds

empathy, 13–18, 222, 247n41, 248n48
emptiness, 70–71, 268nn68–69, 72–73
entropy, 159. *See also* order/disorder
Erlang Shen, 55–56
Erlang Shen Locks up the Great Sage Equal to Heaven (Erlang Shen suo Qitian Dasheng), 73
eroticism: and case thinking, 179–181, 183–184, 304nn108–110; queer theory on, 182–183, 305n112
ethics, 12
excitement, 148, 291n8
exogenous determinism, 22, 250n13
external things (*waiwu*), 22, 250n13; and heart, 58, 62–64, 65, 265n50; and nature-emotion relationship, 59–60, 62, 265n50; neo-Confucianism on, 62, 264n37

faceoff: and distancing, 212, 223, 227, 240–241; and the front of the dream, 36–39, 50–52, 221; and mood, 200, 309–310n41; and objectification, 234; and spatial dimension, 199–200, 214, 309nn39–40; and spectatorship, 39–40, 46
faking. *See* fictionality
Fang Ying, 50
Faure, Bernard, 268n72, 320n150
Feng Junjie, 137
Feng Menglong, 23–24, 34–36, 37, 255nn59–60, 260n104
Feng Xiaoqing, 41
fictionality (faking, the unreal, playacting), 89–90, 114–116, 274n127, 280n59. *See also* imagination
film, 50–51, *51*, 52
Fitgerald, John, 236
Flaubert, Gustave, 15, 16, 248–249n52

Index 327

The Fortunate Union. See Haoqiu zhuan
Fortune, Robert, 290n138
Foucault, Michel: and affective body, 207, 311–312n66; and anthropology, 158, 160, 296n42; on ethics, 12; on historical ontology, 11, 247n30; on power, 12, 247n36
fourth wall, 9, 127, 286n109
Freud, Sigmund, 213, 304n110
Fried, Michael, 212, 213, 313n85

Gao Wenxiu, 56, 269–270n84
Gassner, John, 313n81
gathering, 195, 307–308nn25,27
geinoh, 303n99
ghosts, 24
Goethe, Johann Wolfgang von, 155–156, 157, 160, 295n35, 300n71
Golden Boy and Jade Girl from the Story of Mistress and Maid (Jintong yunü Jiao Hong ji) (Liu Dui), 95, 118–119, n3n77
Goldman, Adrea S., 290n135
Goldstein, Joshua, 131
Gong Pengcheng, 14
Gongyang Commentary to the Spring and Autumn Annals (Chunqiu Gongyang zhuan), 162, 300n76, 302n92
Goyama Kiwamu, 7
Graham, A. C., 59
"The Great Preface," 3, 21, 22, 61, 148, 193–194, 196, 251n18
Guan Hanqin, 31
Guanwu'an, 173
Guo Xiaodong, 316n124
Gu Yuanchang, 224

Hacking, Ian, 247n30
Hagiwara Hiromichi, 154

Hansen, Chad, 59, 263n26
Han Yu, 61
Haoqiu zhuan (The Fortunate Union or The Pleasing History), 154–155; ambiguity in, 161; and anthropology, 184–185; collapse of universality in, 175–176, 302n93; and *Daring Adventures of Chivalric Men*, 160–161, 164; European readings of, 154–157, 165–167, 184–185, 295–296nn35–37,39, 299–300nn68,70; Japanese readings of, 160–161, 162–163; nature-emotion relationship in, 184; norm/expediency in, 162, 164, 167–170, 300nn71–73; on sexual order, 160, 297n50; temporal orientation in, 175, 301n82
Hare, Tom, 292n15
Harman, Graham, 311n61
Harmony (*he*), 61, 264n34
Hayot, Eric, 230, 240
heart (mind) (*xin*): and multitude, 67–68, 267nn64–65; and nature-emotion relationship, 58, 62–64, 65, 66–67, 265n50; one-heartedness/single-mindedness, 58, 66, 70; and *she shen chu di*, 227; and spatiality (space), 196; spectators of one heart/one mind, 71–76, 134; and syncretism, 66–67, 267n62
Hegel, G. W. F., 234, 236, 237, 320nn150,153, 321n156
He Gong, 28
Heidegger, Martin: on Being-in as Such, 308–309n36; and Egginton, 214; on empathy, 222; and faceoff, 309n39; on givenness, 196–197, 198, 310n44; and historical ontology, 11–12; on intentionality, 192–193; on mood, 197–199, 201,

202, 308–310nn36–39,41–43; and reification of body, 312–313n77; on space as gathering, 195–196; on space as pervading, 191–192; on temporal orientation, 170–171; on time-space, 317n126
Heixuanfeng jieshi huanhun (Gao Wenxiu), 269–270n84
Hiromichi Hagiwara, 161, 164, 299n66, 301n83
historical ontology, 11–12, 247n30
History of Emotion (Qingshi) (Feng Menglong), 23–24, 35–36, 260n104
Home, Henry, 221
Hong, Jeehee, 9–10, 289n130
Huang, Martin, 304n108
Huineng, 268n68
Hui Shi, 191
Hu Ji, 95, 283n77
Humble Words of an Old Rustic (Yesou puyan) (Xia Jingqu), 179–180, 183–184
A Hundred Cases of Judge Bao (Bao Longtu pan baijia gong'an), 53–56, 57–58, 261nn6–7
Husserl, Edmund, 207
Huters, Theodore, 319–320n149
hybridization, 114–116, 281–282nn67,70
Hymes, Robert, 173

Idema, Wilt, 93, 95, 96, 118, 283n79
The Illusory Mirror of Fates in the World (Shiyuan huanjian) (Guanwu'an) 173–175
the imaginary: and the real, 182–183, 206, 221
imagination: and the Chinese, 156–157; and knowledge, 153; and spatiality (space), 98, 110, 205–206, 220; and

sympathy, 16–17, 40, 58, 90, 123–124, 151, 176, 183, 221–227, 274n127
imposture: and dreamscape, 74–76, 270n88; and nature-emotion relationship, 68–70, 72; and spectatorship, 73–74, 76–78, 86, 269n82, 270nn88,93; and winds, 79; in *zaju* plays, 75–76, 269–270nn82,84,88,93
The Injustice of Dou E (Gantian dongdi Dou E yuan), 46
"Inscription for the Temple of the Drama God, Master of the Pristine Fount, of Yihuang Prefecture" ("Yihuang xian xishen Qingyuanshi miao ji") (Tang Xianzu), 24–25, 54
intentionality, 192–194, 197, 306n12
interface. *See* faceoff
intermediation. *See* media/intermediation
Internet, 40–41
Isobe Akira, 270n93

Jennings, Theodore, 290n1
"Jiang Xingge's Reunion with the Pearl Shirt" ("Jiang Xingge chonghui zhenzhu shan") (Feng Menglong), 260n104
Ji Kang, 60–61, 264n34
$jing_1$ (landscape): and emotion-landscape mingling, 3
$jing_2$ (realm), 4–5, 245n17, 245–246n19
Ji Yun, 124–125
Johnson, David, 103–104
Jones, Andrew, 318n140
The Journey to the West (Xiyou ji) (1592 novel): doubling in, 58, 69–70, 71–72, 73–74, 145, 267n66; earlier versions of, 66, 266n56; emptiness in, 71; and *A Hundred Cases of*

The Journey to the West (Xiyou ji)
(1592 novel) (*continued*)
Judge Bao, 56; monkey trope in,
68–69, 73; multitude in, 67–68,
267nn64–65; oral provenance of,
270n92; and *The Peony Pavilion*,
262n13; and *she shen chu di*, 227;
spectatorship in, 57, 58, 76–78;
and syncretism, 58, 66, 67, 71,
266n57; and winds, 79. See also
*A Supplement to The Journey to
the West*

The Journey to the West (Xiyou ji)
(dramas), 57, 73–74, 76, 84, 262n18,
270n93, 273n114

The Journey to the West (Xiyou ji)
(other antecedents), 73

The Journey to the West (Xiyou ji) (*zaju*
play) (Yang Ne), 73–74, 84, 270n93,
273n114

Juelang Daosheng, 72
Jullien, François, 3

Kabuki theater, 177, 303n99
Kang Jinzhi, 270n88
Kant, Immanuel, 158, 186, 191, 207,
234
Karatani Kōji, 234–235
Keulemans, Paize, 258n86
Klevjer, Rune, 80–81
knowledge production, 153–154.
See also anthropology; case
thinking
Kong Guangsen, 302n92
Kong Yingda, 224
kyō/xia, 154

Lacan, Jacques, 182
landscape, 2, 234–235, 319n147
Lanzoni, Susan, 14, 16

Laozi, 196
Lean, Eugenia, 236
Lee, Haiyan, 179, 232
Lefebvre, Henri, 204–205, 206, 207,
213, 311–312nn58,66,68, 316n123,
317n126, 321n156
legal discourse, 173–175
Leibniz, Gottfriend Wilhelm, 191, 208,
234, 306n10
Lévi-Strauss, Claude, 147–148, 152, 159,
187, n1n5, n7n45
Lewis, Mark, 207–208
Leys, Ruth, 203–204
Liangshanpo Heixuanfeng fujing zaju
(Kang Jinzhi), 270n88
Liao Ben, 276n10
Life's a Dream (Calderón), n5n105
liminality, and dreamscape, 10
Lin Zhao'en, 66–67
Lipps, Theodor, 14, 15
"Listening to Reverend Ying Play the
Zither" ("Ting Ying Shi tan qin")
(Han Yu), 61
Liu Dapeng, 321n157
Liu Dui, 118–119
Liu Zongzhou, 64
Li, Wai-yee, 7
Li Yu, 16, 42, 124, 133, 279n47, 285n99.
See also *Sole Mates*
Li Zehou, 11
Llamas, Regina, 112, 113
Lü Dalin, 225, n6n124
Lü Dongbin, 235, n9n148
Luoism, 266n57
Luo Rafang, 20
Lu, Tina, 260n104
Lu Xiangsheng, 317n125
Lu Xun, 231–233, 234, 235, 238–
239, 318–319n140, 319n147,
321nn157–158

McMahon, Keith, 304n109
The Mad Drummer's "Thriceplayed Yuyang" (Kuanggu shi Yuyang sannong), 120–122, 145
Madhyamaka School of Buddhism, 28
Mahāprajñā-pāramitāhr-daya Sūtra, 67
Malabou, Catherine, 204
A Manual of Dream Interpretation (Jiemeng shu), 26
Mao Xianshu, 42
Marion, Jean-Luc, 194–195
Marshall, David, 17, 215, 221–222
martial arts (wuxia) fiction/film, 161, 298n57
Ma Zhiyuan, 319n148
Mazu Daoyi, 72
media/intermediation, 44–45, 258n90, 259n91; and theatricality, 10–11, 44, 45–46, 52, 92, 259n91
Mei Chun, 56–57
Mencius, 167, 168, 223
Merleau-Ponty, Maurice, 81, 312
metamorphosis, 110–117; and dreamscape, 10, 27–28, 57–58, 112–113, 114, 116, 117, 263n21, 281n65, 282n72; and hybridization, 114–116, 281–282nn67,70; and "Real Presence," 116–117; and role-type system, 113; and self-reflexive exposure, 111–112, 113–114, 280n61; and winds, 27, 252n33
metatheater. See play-within-a-play
Metzger, Thomas A., 266n53
Miller, Richard B., 248n48
Min Guangyu, 43
mirror, 79–80, 271n103, 272n104
"A Mirror to the Flower" ("Kakyō") (Zeami), 147–152, nnnn3,8, nnnn10,14–15

Mistress and Maid. See Golden Boy and Jade Girl from the Story of Mistress and Maid
Mitchell, Andrew J., 307n25
modernism, 210
Mohist Canons, 191
monkey impostor, 68–70, 72, 73–74, 76–78, 86, 269n82. See also imposture
monkey performance, 55, 261n8
monkey as trope of theatricality, 53–56, 57–58, 68–69
mood: and affective body, 310n49; vs. emotion-realms, 202–203; and faceoff, 200, 309–310n41; and inner-outer hierarchy, 243n3; and situatedness, 217; and spatiality (space), 1–2, 197–199, 200, 308–309nn31,36–38; and temporal orientation, 200–201; and weather, 1–2, 4, 244n12. See also emotion-realms
Mori, Mitsuya, 303n99
Mou Zongsan, 265n50
mugen, 151
music, 60–62
mystic vision (xuanlan), 28–30

Nakatani, Hajime, 259n98
nature-emotion relationship, 58, 59–73; and ambiguity, 59–60, 263n26; and anxiety, 60–61; and desire, 59, 60, 65; and doubling, 69–70, 71–72, 267n66, 269n78; and drama, 55–56; early notions, 59; and emptiness, 70–71, 268nn68–70,72–73; and external things, 59–60, 62, 265n50; in Haoqiu zhuan, 184; and harmony, 61, 264n34; and heart, 58, 62–64, 65, 66–67, 265n50; and A Hundred

nature-emotion relationship (*continued*)
Cases of Judge Bao, 54, 55–56;
and imposture, 68–70, 72; and
multitude, 67–68, 267nn64–65
Nazism, 313n77
Needham, Joseph, 306n7
neo-Confucianism: and dualism,
266n53; and emptiness, 70; on
exteriority, 58; on external things,
62, 264n37; on *qing,* 59; and *she shen chu di,* 224, 225; and syncretism,
268n70. *See also* Zhu Xi
neuroscience, 204
Nietzsche, Friedrich, 320n150
"Nine Ranks" ("Kyūi") (Zeami), 150
Niu Shaoya, 42
Noh theater, 148, 152, 291n5, 303n99.
See also Zeami
"no mind," 70, 150, 268n68
norm/expediency: and chivalry, 162,
164–165, 299nn65–66; and collapse
of universality, 175–176, 302n93;
Confucianism on, 169, 300n76,
302n92; in *Haoqiu zhuan,* 162, 164,
167–170, 300nn71–73; and legal
discourse, 173–175; and temporal
orientation, 169, 170–175, 302n92
Notebook for Transmitting the Ritual (Lijie chuanbu), 102–103, 104
nuoxi genre, 32, 254n52

object-oriented ontology, 206–207,
311–312nn61,66
"On Music" ("Yue lun") (Xunzi), 61
On Poetry (Shilun) (Zhu Guangqian), 14
order/disorder: and anthropology,
158–160, 184–185, 296–297nn42,45;
and case thinking, 185; and collapse
of universality, 175–176, 302n93; and
European readings of *Haoqiu zhuan,*
154–157, 295–296nn35–37,39. *See also* chivalry; norm/expediency
Other. *See* doubling
Owen, Stephen, 89

A Pair of Battling Quacks (Shuang dou yi), 118
Pang, Laikwan, 143
Pan Zhiheng, 20–21
passage stages, 136–138, *137, 138, 139,*
140–141, *140,* 289n130
patiency, 25
The Peach Blossom Fan (Taohua shan),
133
Pear Garden Basics (Liyuan yuan)
(Zhuang Zhaokui), 125
"The Pearl Shirt" ("Zhu shan") (Song
Maocheng), 260n104
A Peddler, Imitating Sounds in Storm and Rains (Fengyu xiangsheng huolangdan), 117–118, 121
The Peony Pavilion: A Youth Edition (Qingchun ban Mudan ting), 49–50, *50,* 52
The Peony Pavilion (Mudan ting) (Tang Xianzu): adaptations of, 26, 34–35, 255n59; criticisms of, 41–42; and cult of *qing,* 19, 20, 249n3; dreamer-spectator in, 37–39, 44, 145–146, 256n71; dreamscape in, 25–26, 29, 133; genealogy of emotion-realms in, 49; and *A Hundred Cases of Judge Bao,* 54; and inscrutability of *qing,* 20–21; and *The Journey to the West,* 262n13; and media/intermediation, 44, 52; misstagings of, 49–50, *50;* mystic vision in, 29; opera film version (1986), 50–51, *51,* 52; "Pursuing the Dream" scene, 38–39, 42, 44, 49–50, 255n67; readability

332   Index

of, 41, 42–43; self-image in, 40, 256–257*n*72; shared dreams in, 26, 37–38, 74; theatricality in, 40, 49; winds in, 23–24
Percy, Thomas, 155, 156–157, 165–167, 295*n*37, 296*n*40
performance theory, 182
Pigsy Gets Married (Bajie chengqin), 270*n*93
Plato, 98
playacting. *See* fictionality
A Playboy from a Noble House Opts for the Wrong Career (Huanmen zidi cuo lishen), 92–97, 94, 275*n*6; and anachronism, 145; antecedents to, 103, 104, 110, 275–276*n*10; and metamorphosis, 117; metatheatrical remarks in, 96–97; original version, 92, 93, 95–96; play-within-a-play in Bei Kun revision, 93, 94, 95, 275*n*8, 282*n*74; and ritual drama, 102–103, 104, 109–110, 278*n*38; and role-type system, 277*n*21; and *Sole Mates*, 102; title recitation in, 96; and *Wind and Moon in the Courtyard of Purple Clouds*, 95–96, 276*n*10
play-within-a-play: and anxiety about spectatorship, 97–98; and avatar, 83–85; in Bei Kun revision of *Wrong Career*, 93, 94, 95, 275*n*8, 282*n*74; in deliverance play genre, 119–120, 283*n*79; and dreamscape, 97; in *The Mad Drummer*, 120–122, 145; and metatheatrical remarks, 96–97; and print culture, 107, *108*, 279*n*49; and redemption, 100–101; and ritual drama, 103, 105–107, 110, 279*n*46; and role-type system, 99–100, 277*nn*21,23,26, 282*n*75; and self-consciousness, 278*n*34; vs.

self-reflexive exposure, 280*n*61; in *Sole Mates* opera version, 277*n*25; staging of, 102, 278*n*33; and theater architecture, 127, *128*, *129*, 286*n*103; and title recitations, 96, 276*n*12; and *yuanben*, 95, 103, 109, 118–120, 275*n*8, 282*n*75, 283*nn*77,79
playwright, 122–123
The Pleasing History. *See Haoqiu zhuan*
Porter, David, 295*n*37
postcognitive approaches, 243*n*4
Postlewait, Thomas, 313*n*81
power: and affective body, 313*n*77; Foucault on, 12, 247*n*36; of performance, 57, 263*n*20
Precious Vessel in a Time of Efflorescence (Shengping baofa), 76–78
print culture: and Kabuki theater, 303*n*99; and play-within-a-play, 107, *108*, 279*n*49; and theatricality, 43–44, 57, 78, 91, 210, 211, 258*nn*86,89, 260*n*106
The Production of Space (Lefebvre), 204–205
proscenium stage, 127, 130
Prous, Marcel, 256*n*71, 260*n*105
Psychology of Literature (Zhu Guangqian), 14, 15
Puchner, Martin, 210, 211
Puett, Michael, 263*n*26
The Purple Cloud Pavilion. *See Wind and Moon in the Courtyard of Purple Clouds*
Purple Hairpin (Zichai ji) (Tang Xianzu), 30

Qian Nanyang, 95, 275*n*6
Qian Peiming, 87

Qian Yi, 41
qing: cult of, 19–20, 249n3; inscrutability of, 20–21, 249n4. See also nature-emotion relationship
qing bu qing (emotional yet unemotional), 184
Qinhuai Zuihou, 101
Qu Yuan, 25, 29, 44

Rancière, Jacques, 211
Random Repository of Idle Sentiments (Xianqing ouji) (Li Yu), 124
rationality, 22, 251n18. See also cognitive studies
"Real Presence," 46, 47, 116–117, 214, 220–221
"Record of Music" ("Yueji"), 59
Records of the Grand Historian (Shiji) (Sima Qian), 163
Red Inkstone Commentary, 184
Ren Bantang, 261n8
representation, 191–192, 196, 199–200, 204–205, 207, 220–221
Rescriptor-in-Waiting Bao Thrice Investigates the Butterfly Dream (Bao daizhi san kan hudie meng) (Guan Hanqin), 31
"Rhapsodies of the South" (Qu Yuan), 25, 29, 44
Ricoeur, Paul, 170–171, 304n110, 317n126
riken no ken (Vision of a Distant View), 147–148, 149–150, 151, 152, 291nn3,5,8, 292n15
ritual drama: and anthropology, 107, 109, 147, 290n1; conjuring and sending off gods, 136, 288n124; and play-within-a-play, 103, 105–107, 110, 279n46; and *Wrong Career*, 102–103, 104, 109–110, 278n38; and

zaju plays, 104, 269n84. See also temple theaters
Rojas, Carlos, 256–257n72, 271n104
role-type system: and metamorphosis, 113; and play-within-a-play, 99–100, 277nn21,23,26, 282n75; and *she shen chu di*, 125–126, 285n100
The Romantic Dream (Fengliu meng) (Feng Menglong), 34–35, 255nn59–60
Rules of Opera (Qulü) (Wang Jide), 122

Sahlins, Marshall, 159–160
Schaberg, David, 251n18
Schechner, Richard, 105
Schleiermacher, Friedrich, 309n40
self-displacement, and theatricality, 6
self-negation, 14
self-reflexive exposure, 111–112, 113–114, 280n61
shared dreams: and dreamscape, 26, 33–35, 74, 75, 252n28, 255nn59–60; and storytelling, 112; and winds (*feng*), 270n91
Shen Fengying, 49–50, 50
Shen Jing, 26, 41–42
Shen Taimou, 142
she shen chu di (sympathy), 15–16; and acting, 124–126; and awakening, 238–239; and bodily incommensurability, 226–227, 317n125; and body, 224–225, 316n123; Brecht on, 317–318n127; and case thinking, 178–179; defined, 229; and distancing, 225–226, 321–322n160; and dreamscape, 232–233, 318–319n140; and empathy, 17–18; etymology, 224; and faceoff, 239; and fictionality, 90; and heart, 227; and objectification, 234–235;

and playwright, 123; popularity of term, 123; and spectatorship, 125–126, 229, 285nn98,100; and theater architecture, 143. *See also* imagination

Shi Junbao, 95–96

shu (fellow feeling), 223, 229, 316n119

Sieber, Patricia, 296n39

Sima Qian, 163

situatedness (*Befindlichkeit*), 197, 201, 217, 308n31

"sixth-eared macaque" (*liu'er mihou*). See monkey impostor

Slaying Generals at Five Passes (Wu guan zhan jiang), 104

Smith, Adam, 123, 215, 221, 222–223, 224, 230, 231, 232, 284–285n92, 322n161

Smith, Arthur Henderson, 230–231, 238, 240

sociocultural approaches, 22, 251n18

Sole Mates (Bimuyu) (Li Yu): and dreamscape, 145; opera version (2007), 277n25; and print culture, 107, *108*, 279n49; redemption in, 100–101; and ritual drama, 105–107, 279n46; role-type system in, 99–100, 277n26; self-consciousness in, 278n34; and *she shen chu di*, 125–126, 285n100; staging of play-within-a-play in, 102, 278n33; and theater architecture, 126–127, *128*, *129*, 286n103

Sommer, Matthew H., 261nn5–6

Song Maocheng, 260n104

spatiality (space): and affective body, 204–206, 207–208, 311nn58–59, 312n77; aporia of, 227–228, 317n126; and being-in-the-world, 193; classical Chinese approach to, 190–191, 207–208, 223, 312n74; Descartes on, 191, 306n9; and distancing, 193, 194–195, 197, 200, 307n17, 308n30; and dwelling, 191–192; and emotion-landscape mingling, 189; and faceoff, 199–200, 214, 309nn39–40; and gathering, 195–196, 307–308nn25,27; and givenness, 194–195, 196–197, 198, 200, 201–202, 310n44; and heart, 196; and ideal relations (Leibniz), 306n10; and intentionality, 192–194, 197, 306n12; Laozi on, 196; and mood, 1–2, 197–199, 200, 308–309nn31,36–38; as paradox, 191, 192, 306n7; and pervading, 191–192; and pure intuition (Kant), 191; and "Real Presence," 214; and situatedness, 197, 201, 308n31

spectatorship: and absence of spectator, 10, 130, 132; and anachronism, 132–133, 145, 152–153; and anthropology, 147–148, 152, 186, 291n2; anxiety about, 97–98; vs. audience, 92; and avatar, 80–87, 272–274nn107–108,116; and balconies, 141, 143–144; and distancing, 83–85, 87, 89, 133, 186–187, 211–212, 287n118; and doubling, 58, 71–72, 73–74, 145, 269nn78,82; and dreamscape, 7–9, 132–133; and dreamscape-theatricality shift, 73, 76, 78–79; and exclusion of spectator, 58, 216; and faceoff, 39–40, 46; and fictionality, 89–90; and *geinoh*, 303n99; and imposture, 73–74, 76–78, 86, 269n82, 270nn88,93; and Kabuki theater, 177; and misrecognition of theatricality, 47; and monkey trope, 57–58; participatory, 9, 131, 133–134,

spectatorship (*continued*)
210, 286*n*109; and playwright, 122–123; and print culture, 57; and proscenium stage, 127, 130; and *riken no ken*, 149, 151, 292*n*15; and *she shen chu di*, 125–126, 229, 285*nn*98,100; as subjective, 132, 287*n*114; and sympathy, 215–216; and syncretism, 72–73; and teahouse theaters, 130–131, 141–143, 286*n*109; and temple theaters, 131–132. *See also* dreamer-spectator; play-within-a-play; theatricality
specularity, 80, 256–257*n*72, 271*n*104. *See also* spectatorship
St. André, James, *n*1*n*7
Stanislavski, Konstantin, 313*n*81
Stewart, Kathleen, 203, 213
"Story of the Chaste" ("Jievi zhuang") (Tao Fu), 54, 261*n*2
Story of the Flowery Notepaper (*Huajian ji*), 155
The Story of Shared Dreams (*Tongmeng ji*) (Shen Jing), 26, 41
Story of the Stone, 133, 184, 260*n*106
The Story of the Western Wing (*Xixiang ji*) (Wang Shifu), 31–32, 41, 53, 57, 95
Struve, Lynn, 133
subject-object split. *See* Cartesian philosophy
sublime, 14, 247*n*41
Sun Xun, 266*n*57
A Supplement to The Journey to the West (*Xiyou bu*) (Dong Yue): avatar in, 80–87, 273–274*nn*116–117; distancing in, 83–85, 87; and dreamscape, 78–79; and emotion-landscape mingling, 88; faceoff in, 227; mirror in, 79–80, 271*n*103, 272*n*104; play-within-a-play in,

83–85; Qian Peiming's commentary on, 87
Su Shi, 256*n*69
Svensson, Martin, 251*n*18
sympathy: Adam Smith on, 123, 222–223, 224, 231, 232, 284–285*n*92, 322*n*161; and affective body, 204; and case thinking, 178–179; and distancing, 223, 316*n*120; and dreamscape, 215; and empathy, 16–17, 248*n*48; and fictionality, 274*n*127; misconstruction of, 221–222; neuroscience on, 204; and *shu*, 223, 229, 316*n*119; and spectatorship, 215–216; and theatricality, 6–7, 17–18; and *tongqing*, 316*n*119; and Western accounts of China, 230–232, 233, 238, 240, 322*n*161. *See also* imagination
syncretism, 58, 66–67, 72–73, 266*n*57, 267*n*62

Tanaka Issei, 33, 278*n*38
Tang Xianzu, 33, 258*n*84; *Dream of Handan*, 30, 43–44; *Dream of the South Branch*, 30, 44, 273*n*113; "Inscription for the Temple of the Drama God," 24–25, 54. *See also The Peony Pavilion*
Tan Ze, 41
Tao Fu, 54, 261*n*2
Tatlow, Antony, 148
teahouse theaters, 130–131, 141–143, 286*n*109, 289*n*134, 290*n*135
temple theaters, 131–132, 134, 135–136, 286–287*n*110, 288*nn*122,124. *See also* passage stages
temporal orientation, 65; aporia of, 227–228, 317*n*126; and dreamscape, 26–27; and eroticism, 183; and

mood, 200–201; and norm/
expediency, 169, 170–175, 302*n*92;
and theatricality, 305*n*115
theater architecture, 126–146; and
backstage, 135–136, *135*, 288*nn*121–
122; balconies, 140–141, *140*,
143–144, 289*n*132, 290*n*138; and
dreamer-spectator, 145–146; fourth
wall, 9, 127, 286*n*109; passage stages,
136–138, *137*, *138*, *139*, 140–141, *140*,
289*n*130; and play-within-a-play,
127, *128*, *129*, 286*n*103; proscenium
stage, 127, 130, 286*n*110; and ritual
drama, 132; roofless platforms, 134,
287–288*n*120; and *she shen chu di*,
143; and *Sole Mates*, 126–127, *128*,
129, 286*n*103; teahouse theaters,
130–131, 141–143, 286*n*109,
289*n*134, 290*n*135; temple theaters,
131–132, 134, 135–136, 286–287*n*110,
288*nn*122,124; and winds, 134–135
theatricality: and absorption, 212–213,
313–314*nn*313–4; and affective
body, 209–210; agony of distance
and identification, 89–90, 188;
and anachronism, 81, 132–133,
144–145, 152–153, 229–230; and
anthropology, 107, 109, 185–186;
and anti-theatricality, 212, 313*n*83,
314*n*87; and case thinking,
177–179; and commodification,
47–49, 260*n*104; defined, 6; and
deliverance, 216–217; and dreamer-
spectator, 176–177; and emotion-
landscape mingling, 87–89;
etymology, 210–211, 216; and faceoff,
39–40, 212; and historical ontology,
11; historical roots of, 8; and identity
crisis, 40–41; incommensurability
of, 154, 294*n*28; and interiorizing

effect, 49, 260*n*105; and media/
intermediation, 10–11, 44, 45–46,
52, 92, 259*n*91; misrecognition
of, 46–47, 152, 259*n*98; monkey
as trope of, 53–56, 57–58, 68–69;
and novel form, 56–57; and power
of performance, 57, 263*n*20; and
print culture, 43–44, 57, 78, 91,
210, 211, 258*nn*86,89, 260*n*106;
and self-image, 40, 256–257*n*72;
and storytelling, 112, 280*n*57; and
sympathy, 6–7, 17–18; and temporal
orientation, 229, 305*n*115; vs. theater,
276*n*17; and transformation, 110. *See
also* dreamscape-theatricality shift;
play-within-a-play; spectatorship
"The Thing" (Heidegger), 195
"Three Wives' Commentary" (Chen
Tong), 41
"Time and Being" (Heidegger), 195, 200
Titchener, Edward B., 14, 15, 16–17
Tiwald, Justin, 316*n*119
tongqing, 316*n*119
*Top Graduate Zhang Xie (Zhang
Xie Zhuangyuan)*: hybridization
in, 114–116, 281–282*nn*67,70;
insubstantiality of spectator in, 117;
and *The Mad Drummer*, 121; and
role-type system, 125, 126, 285*n*100;
self-reflexive exposure in, 111–112,
113–114; storytelling in, 112; and
theater architecture, 136
topophilia, 244–245*n*13
Tower of Myriad Mirrors, 227
trajectory of passion, 20–21
transformation (*hua*). *See*
metamorphosis
"Treatise of Music without Emotion"
("Sheng wu ai le lun") (Ji Kang),
60–61

Index 337

Treatise on Song Lyrics of the Human Realm (Wang Guowei), 3, 4, 245*n*14
Turner, Victor, 105, 107
The Twenty-eight Mansions Pay Homage to the Three Purities (Ershiba xiu chao Sanqing), 104, 105

the unreal. *See* fictionality
upaya, 28
urban life, 32–33, 254*n*54

Valéry, Paul, 214
Varsano, Paula, 272*n*104
Vartanian, Aram, 213
Versalius, 207
Virag, Curie, 59
Volpp, Sophie, 8, 133, 285*n*98

waicheng, 282*n*75
Wang Bi, 60, 264*n*37
Wang Chingling, 246*n*20
Wang Duanshu, 100–101, 126
Wang, Eugene, 28–29
Wang Fuzhi, 87–90, 274*n*122
Wang Guowei, 3, 4–5, 13–14, 202, 245*n*14, 247*n*41
Wang Ji, 251*n*24
Wang Jide, 122, 123
Wang Jinbang, 93
Wang Shifu, 31–32. *See also The Story of the Western Wing*
Wang Yangming, 64, 265*n*50, 268*n*70
Wang Yi, 25
Ward, James, 15, 16
Water Margin (Shuihu zhuan): drama antecedents to, 57, 262*n*18; imposture in, 73, 74–75, 269–270*n*84; and novel form, 56–57; oral provenance of, 270*n*92; shared dreams in, 112

weather, 1–2, 4, 244*n*12
Weber, Samuel, 98, 109
Wen Sucheng, 305*n*112
West, Stephen, 93, 95, 96, 117–118, 281*n*70
Whipping the Malady Ghost (Bianda Huanglao gui), 104
Wilkinson, James, 154, 165
Wind and Moon in the Courtyard of Purple Clouds (Fengyue Zhiyun ting) (Shi Junbao), 95–96, 110, 117, 276*n*10
winds *(feng)*, 21–25; and affective body, 208–209; and anxiety, 60–61, 90; and body, 21; and causality as secondary, 23; differentiation in, 251*n*24; and dreamscape-theatricality shift, 218; and emotion as field of cosmology, 23–25; and excitement, 148, 291*n*8, 292*n*10; and imposture, 79; and inscrutability of *qing*, 21; and media/intermediation, 44, 258*n*90; and metamorphosis, 27, 252*n*33; and patiency, 25; and shared dreams, 270*n*91; and theater architecture, 134–135; and voice, 287*n*119. *See also* embedment
Wrong Career. *See A Playboy from a Noble House Opts for the Wrong Career*
Wu, Kuang-Ming, 312*n*74
Wu Zhenshang, 273*n*113

Xia Jingqu, 179–180
xiangliang (immediate, intuitive comprehension), 274*n*122
Xiao Chi, 274*n*122
Xie Zhaozhe, 36–37, 43, 177–178
xing (poetic incitement), 2, 3
Xu Fuguan, 4–5

Xu Gang, 59
Xunxi, 59
Xunzi, 59, 61
Xu Wei, 120–122, 245–246n19

Yang, Chi-Ming, 295–296n39
Yang Ne, 73–74, 84, 270n93
Yang Xianzhi, 74
Ye Changhai, 249n4
Yeh Chia-ying, 14
Ye Tang, 42
yuanben, 95, 103, 109, 118–120, 275n8, 282n75, 283nn77,79
Yu, Anthony, 59
Yu Dafu, 235, 319n147
yūgen, 148-149, 151, 152, n2n14

zaju plays: doubling in, 73–74; imposture in, 56, 75–76, 269–270nn82,84,88,93; and play-within-a-play, 95–96, 110, 120–122, 276n12; and ritual drama, 104, 269n84; role-type system in, 282n75; and *Water Margin*, 57, 262n18; *yuanben* in, 95, 118–119, 283n77
Zang Maoxun, 41
Zeami, 147–152, 153, 291nn3,5,8, 292n10

Zeitlin, Judith, 133
Zen Buddhism, 149, 150
Zhang Dafu, 43, 258n84
Zhang Dai, 7, 8, 9, 124
Zhang Jiqing, 50–51, *51*
Zhang Zai, 62–63
Zhao Shanlin, 281n65
Zheng Xuan, 224
Zheng Yuyu, 250nn10,13
Zhongli of the Hand Leads Lan Caihe to Enlightenment (Han Zhongli dutuo Lan Caihe), 276n12
Zhongli Quan, 235, 253n45
Zhou Qi, 55
Zhuang Zhaokui, 125
Zhuangzi: and anxiety, 61; on dream interpretation, 26–27, 46; on emptiness, 71, 268n73; and external things, 60; and metamorphosis, 27–28, 29, 36, 113, 252n33, 263n21
Zhu Guangqian, 13–14, 15–16, 17
Zhu Quan, 55
Zhu Xi, 62–64, 90, 173, 225–226, 227, 255n62, 265n50, 316n124
Zhu Youdun, 119–120
Zibo Zhenke (Daguan), 30
Zou Diguang, 218

GPSR Authorized Representative: Easy Access System Europe, Mustamäe tee
50, 10621 Tallinn, Estonia, gpsr.requests@easproject.com